Also by John McCain and Mark Salter

FAITH OF MY FATHERS

WORTH THE FIGHTING FOR

WORTH
THE
FIGHTING
FOR

A MEMOIR

JOHN MCCAIN
with Mark Salter

RANDOM HOUSE / NEW YORK

All rights reserved under International and Pan-American Copyright Conventions.
Published in the United States by Random House, Inc., New York,
and simultaneously in Canada by Random House of Canada Limited, Toronto.

RANDOM HOUSE and colophon are registered trademarks of Random House, Inc.

A leatherbound, signed first edition of this book has been published by the Easton Press.

Library of Congress Cataloging-in-Publication Data

McCain, John
Worth the fighting for: A memoir / John McCain; with Mark Salter.
p. cm.
ISBN 0-375-50542-3
1. McCain, John, 1936– 2. Legislators—United States—Biography. 3. United States.
Congress. Senate—Biography. 4. United States—Politics and government—1981–1989.
5. United States—Politics and government—1989– I. Salter, Mark. II. Title.

E840.8.M467 A3 2002   328.73'092—dc21   2002021310

Random House website address: www.atrandom.com

Printed in the United States of America on acid-free paper

24689753

First Trade Edition

Book design by Casey Hampton

FOR CINDY AND DIANE

Fix your eyes on the greatness of Athens as you have it before you day by day, fall in love with her, and when you feel her great, remember that this greatness was won by men with courage, with knowledge of their duty, and with a sense of honor in action.

—THUCYDIDES, Funeral Oration of Pericles

CONTENTS

Being welcomed by President Nixon upon my release following five
and a half years as a POW during the Vietnam War, 1973.

UPI/Bettmann/News Photo

PROLOGUE

I was born into a tradition of military service. My forebears were not politicians, but they were leaders. And although they may have disdained the guile and artifice often associated with the practice of politics, they nonetheless recognized and admired national leadership when they saw it. If they measured it slightly less manful than martial valor, they still saw the honor in it. And they taught me to respect it, even if they expected me to keep a wary distance from it.

Political leadership is not so great a stretch for the military officer with a career change in mind. Those who manage it do so, I suppose, because they can't imagine a life without wanting a prominent place in the nation's affairs, a place of honor in a great nation's history. We are taught to think of the country as greater than ourselves, to love it not exclusively, but wholeheartedly. Even if we don't heed the lessons at first, war will usually convert us. And it becomes a love we cannot part with. Perhaps some of us come to believe that the country cannot part with us. That, of course, is a delusion, but it can be a beautiful delusion as long as it doesn't reverse the order of our allegiances.

I have now spent nearly as many years in elected office as I had spent in the navy. The years I have spent in public life have always seemed a natural extension of my former career. And I have brought to it the same idiosyncrasies that marked my career in uniform, chief among them my desire to be my own man, to serve, to the greatest extent possible, on my own terms. As it turns out, politics has been even more accommodating to someone with my eccentricities than was the navy. I suspect my personality might sometimes test the limits of that accommodation, as it has certainly tried the forbearance of my colleagues. But I have been granted a place, albeit a very small one, in American history, and I have been permitted, warts and all, to spend my entire adult life in the service of my country. Lucky me.

I'm sixty-four years old as we begin this book, which seems a bit old to be routinely described as a maverick. American popular culture admits few senior citizens to its ranks of celebrated nonconformists. We lack the glamorous carelessness of youth and risk becoming parodies of our younger selves. Witnessing the behavior can make people uncomfortable, like watching an aging, overweight Elvis mock the memory of the brash young man who had swaggered across cultural color lines.

I fear many things, but only few things more than appearing ridiculous. And my chest does not swell with pride when I encounter every reference to "Senator John McCain, the maverick Arizona Republican," even when it is meant as a compliment. I worry that the act might be getting a little tired for a man of my years. Better for old men to be known as collegial team players, who expect to find in the warmth of their associations a tonic for fears of approaching infirmity and extinction.

Beyond the question of appearances, I doubt my maverick reputation will give me much comfort when I have left the public arena. I learned in Vietnam how short a distance separates the individualist from the egotist and how neither can match the strength of a community united to serve a cause greater than self-interest. I have not forgotten the lesson, although some of my detractors might accuse me of lately avoiding its practical implications, and I have enough self-doubt to worry that they are occasionally right.

I am not, as some would have it, a loner. On the contrary, I am almost constantly surrounded by people, and I would not have it any other way. I find little peace in solitude. The restlessness that has always harassed me produces only uneasiness when I am alone. I need company, my family, my friends, my staff, to find a useful occupation for my energy.

Yet despite having a sociable nature, I often stray from certain conventions of the society in which I voluntarily sought membership. In too many instances, with more zeal than circumstances warrant, my expressions of independence reveal nothing more substantial than an instinctive resistance to institutional customs that strike me as empty gestures of submission.

I have an acute, much too acute, sensitivity to abuses of authority, which always questions, and often misinterprets (sometimes absurdly so), practical exercises of organizational leadership. Occasionally, when the Senate majority leader finds it useful to have the attention of all ninety-nine of his colleagues, he will summon us to the Senate chamber by ordering a roll call vote on a motion "to instruct the sergeant at arms to request the presence of absent senators." Sometimes, but very rarely, the instruction will be "to compel" our attendance. In either instance, fearing the exercise is an unwarranted infringement on my liberty, I vote against the motion. Of course, the leader's purpose has been served, since the vote, whether it be yea or nay, requires that I come to the chamber to cast it. Nor would I purposely begrudge the leader my presence whenever he requires it. It's just the idea of granting the sergeant at arms the authority to make me come that bothers me. I know it's a trivial matter, and my behavior might appear eccentric, but I find it hard to do otherwise.

In other, more important matters, I have also found it necessary from time to time to take a position or a course of action that puts me in conflict with my leaders and with the collected wisdom of my party they represent. I hope I have done so for better reason than because I've mistaken contrariness for self-respect.

I enjoy my work and am grateful for the honor of serving in the United States Senate. There are many people in Congress, and in the rest of government, who are smarter, wiser, and more capable than I am. To be in their company is a privilege and a first-rate education. Many who have served here have been an inspiration to me, and their example offers instruction in the obligations of public duty to anyone fortunate to serve in the same capacity. All the more reason to take better care to show my appreciation for this institution and the men and women who serve here.

But I am known more for my criticism than my admiration of the contemporary practice of political leadership. That is a failing I hope to correct in this book, which I intend to be an honest look at events from my career that balances criticism with tribute to the patriotism and conscientiousness of public servants whose example makes me all too aware of my own shortcomings. I do not want any criticism implied or expressed in this book to leave the reader with the impression that public service is anything less than an honorable profession, practiced more by the selfless than the self-serving. I have done that in the past, and what rebukes I have earned for it are more deserved than any praise I have received for my outspokenness.

A smart, young, conservative journalist who disapproves of me once wrote that at a weekly lunch of Republican senators, I show my disdain for my colleagues by always sitting at the same table with my back to most of my colleagues. I do sit at the same table every week with a few of my closer friends in the Republican caucus. But I never thought it displayed bad manners. I had not intended to offend anyone. I just enjoy sitting with my friends, and since many of my colleagues seat themselves in the same company every week, I don't find the practice to be out of the ordinary. Nevertheless, the complaint gives you an idea of the affection some of my colleagues have for me. The journalist doesn't attend our lunches. So one of my colleagues or one of the Senate leadership staff who does attend them must have portrayed my dining habits as an intentional discourtesy.

It is apparent that I'm not the most popular member of the Senate. Some detractors dismiss me as little more than a nuisance. More aggrieved critics consider me disloyal, unreliably partisan, and disrespectful of Senate traditions. I take no pride in their disapproval. But while I would like to have my colleagues' affection, I will settle for their respect. Even that, I must acknowledge, can be hard to gain when the animosity I occasionally incite among some obscures the purpose of whatever I had done that upset them.

Were I to catalog all my faults, they would run the length of this book. So I know I own a large share of the blame for the disaffection I am regarded with in some quarters. I'm not sure how much of it can be helped, though. We can all stand a little self-improvement from time to time, but it's hard to accomplish when you have reached my age. I have my reputation, and not enough years left in my career to improve it much. I'm an independent-minded, well-intentioned public servant to some. And to others, I'm a self-styled, self-righteous, maverick pain in the ass.

Life would be easier, if not as interesting, if everyone shared the more generous view of my public profile. No less than the next guy, I like to be liked, and I am genuinely grateful for the friendships I have formed in this business and for the measure of public approval I am lucky to possess. Perhaps I could be a more effective legislator if I showed greater deference to the customs of contemporary political culture, were I better at finessing my disagreements with my colleagues and with the leaders of my party, if I used a little more subtlety and a little less passion to pursue my goals. I can think of worse things to be than a well-liked member of the club. Yet I have never sought the distinction very vigorously.

In political parties, leaders more often than not work their way up a hierarchy, making more friends than enemies along the way and keeping their personalities firmly fastened to a corporate identity. Curiously, that is less often the case with those who have reached the pinnacle of the profession, the presidency. Maybe that was among the rationales I grasped when I decided to seek that office. Or maybe putting too much faith in the rationale contributed to my lack of success. I don't know. But God knows I wonder if I could have realized more of my own ambitions had I made less trouble for others and for myself.

This is a very competitive business. It is by nature adversarial. Enemies (professional, if not personal) come with the zip code. You don't have to accumulate them unnecessarily. Politicians with the longest and most successful careers are often those who have ruffled the fewest feathers. They zigzag toward their goals, twisting around obstacles, taking care and time to acquire as few opponents as possible and as much support as their success requires. I admire their patience and agility. I have too little of those attributes to work obliquely. God has given me heart enough for my ambitions, but too little forbearance to pursue them by routes other than a straight line.

Could I have gone further in this, my second career, had I tried harder to conform to established models for success? Would I have proved a better servant of my country? My mistakes, which I regret very much, have not discouraged my aspirations. Nor have the lessons they taught me, important lessons, worked a profound change on my personality. Some change, to be sure, and for the better, I hope. I would hate to think that I had never matured from the smart-ass Naval Academy plebe who thought personal honor was such a fragile thing that any slight or compromise threatened it. But I am not unrecognizable to those who knew me then, and I don't know if that should gratify or worry me.

At some point, my long-held aspiration to be a leader grew into something more grandiose. I wanted to lead my country. That was perhaps too great an ambition for a man so stuck in his ways. A quick adaptability to changing circumstances and public perceptions seems to be the common, critical faculty of successful candidates for the office, at least in recent times. I don't mean to imply that those who succeed where I had failed must surrender their principles to the pursuit or hide important truths about themselves. For it is hard to succeed if the public is convinced that you lack conviction or honesty. They just show a greater ability than I evidently have to meet the expectations, the frequently changing expectations, that other professionals, the press, and the public hold for winning candidates. They are masters of contemporary political conventions and, thus, are deemed fit to hold the office that for a time will determine what those conventions are.

That is not how my life has worked out. How I account for that will become, I suspect, one of my occupations when I, reluctantly, retire from public life. And although I seem to tolerate introspection better the older I am, there are still too many claims on my attention to permit more than the briefest excursions down the path of self-awareness. When I am no longer busy with politics, and with my own ambitions, I hope to have more time to examine what I have done and failed to do with my career, and why.

Now, and more so with every new year added to my total, I am a little more given to look back for clues to my life, but only in glimpses. I look ahead, as always, for the purpose of living. And when I do look back, I see people more than events, not all of them real, or, at least, not as real to others as they are to me. They are among the heroes of my fortunate past, who are as alive in my imagination today as they were when I imagined them observing the antics of the boy who foolishly thought himself man enough to emulate them.

Ernest Hemingway. *Corbis*

BEAUTIFUL FATALISM

I'm a little superstitious, not an unusual trait in a navy pilot but apparently eccentric in a politician. While my superstitions are, by the standards of the culture I was raised in, decidedly minor, they have attracted press interest and a little friendly kidding. That's a small price to pay for the peace of mind they provide me. They are, in truth, the habit of a lifetime, which began long before I entered the navy. In fact, I can't remember a time when I didn't indulge one or two superstitions, although I've concentrated harder on recognizing tokens of good luck than discovering omens of misfortune.

I can still vividly recall my excitement after finding two four-leaf clovers in the front yard of my parents' home in Arlington, Virginia. I was twelve years old and convinced that the discovery portended imminent good fortune. I raced into the house and headed straight for my father's study, where I grabbed the first book I could reach off his library shelves to press my prize in.

As I placed the clover between the pages, my eye was drawn to the text, and I began to read.

" 'What are you going to do with us?' one asked him.

" 'Shoot thee,' said Pablo.

" 'When?' the man asked in the same gray voice.

" 'Now,' said Pablo.

" 'Where?' asked the man.

" 'Here,' said Pablo. 'Here. Now. Here and now. Have you anything to say?'

" 'Nada,' said the civil. 'Nothing but it is an ugly thing.' "

I had opened *For Whom the Bell Tolls,* which from that day on would always be my favorite Hemingway book. The passage I had read was from the tenth chapter, a grim account of inhumanity in war. Pilar, a Republican guerrilla in the Spanish civil war, recounts how her man, Pablo, the leader of a small guerrilla band, after taking control of a small town, had organized the brutal murders of the local gentry. After shooting four policemen, Pablo ordered the town's "fascists" beaten to death one at a time in a gantlet and their bodies hurled over a cliff. After several were thus killed, their deaths depicted in simple, gripping dialogue, many of the peasants who had formed the gantlet, now drunk from wine and blood lust, stormed the building where the remainder were held, slaughtered them and the priest who had been hearing their last confessions.

The chapter, with its austere glare at the savagery that war can coax from even good-natured people, should disabuse the most immature reader of any romantic notions about the nature of organized bloodletting. But it cast an immediate spell on me, and after reading a few pages, I stopped, read the whole chapter from the beginning, and then turned to the first page of the book and read it through as quickly as I could. I have read it many times since, and it remains not only my favorite work by the author, but my favorite work of fiction.

Hemingway's hero, Robert Jordan, a college professor from Montana come to fight fascists in the Spanish civil war, is a rational man. Or rather, he is an idealist suffering from incipient disillusionment, fixed on his duty for the cause despite his doubt that his mission, the destruction of a bridge, is possible or necessary. So this rational man, a disbeliever in signs, begins the last three days of his life carrying explosives up a mountain trail led by an old man whose name, Anselmo, he has forgotten. He joins Pablo, a war-weary coward, and Pilar, who has kept her courage and who sees the omens that foreshadow Jordan's doom. And he finds Maria, the girl he falls in love with at first sight.

What a story I had found. Within those first pages, in characters portrayed in Hemingway's spare and elegant style, began a tale of heroism and sacrifice, of disappointment and redemption, that made my blood race as it gave flight to a boy's romantic notions of courage and love, of idealistic men and women ennobled by their selflessness and the misuse and betrayal they suffered for it. And it laid on so quickly such a heavy complement of obviously portentous signs that it made me feel not just equal to the task of divining their meaning, but superior to the hero, the man whom I recognized instantly as my ideal but who missed or ignored their secrets until the very moment of his death. With my superstitious nature, I saw it all coming, or at least that's how I remember it now, from the moment a bit of good luck had led me to this great story where portents of tragic heroism seemed to run through every page. I was the kind of boy who needed encouragement from such things, and Hemingway was my author.

For a long time, Robert Jordan was the man I admired above almost all others in life and fiction. He was brave, dedicated, capable, selfless, possessed in abundance that essence of courage that Hemingway described as grace under pressure, a man who would risk his life but never his honor. He was and remains to my mind a hero for the twentieth century, my century, the century when McCains went to war on ships and claimed our place in the great clashes among rival ideologies, fascism, communism, and self-determination, that made the age as memorable for its violence as for its progress. All three were at war in Spain in 1937 when the story begins and ends.

The Nationalists claimed for their cause anticommunism and the restoration of the monarchy and the Republicans the preservation of democracy. But fascists led the former, and communists, both the cynical and naïve varieties, sought control of the latter, and into that camp came idealistic freedom fighters from abroad like Robert Jordan. In the war that Hemingway remembered, they were dedicated to the cause, willing to sacrifice their lives for it, but vulnerable to disappointment at the hands of cynical politicians who controlled their fate and the weary realism of the people they had come to save. Their heroism was a beautiful fatalism.

They stayed loyal to a doomed cause. But their salvation was found in the ultimate discovery that they had not sacrificed vainly, that they had died for something else, something greater.

The Russian generals who had sent Jordan to blow up a bridge considered the mission nothing more than an interesting maneuver, unlikely to succeed given that its success would depend on Spanish peasants, the people in whose name Russian generals had come to save Spain. No worthy cause should be expected to survive such leaders, unsentimental, utilitarian soldiers accustomed to the rawest power politics in the service of a mock utopia.

Pablo, the guerrilla leader whose fervor had excited his followers to beat to death a small town's worth of dons in the scene that had drawn me into the book, had abandoned the cause with which he excused his cruelty. He had "gone bad," tired, no longer willing to fight, interested only in his own survival and protecting a few valuable horses he possessed. He was loathsome—even his horse was offended by his cowardice and selfishness—and estranged from his followers and from humanity, an "Island, intire of it selfe," in the poem that gave the book its title.

Jordan stood in relief beside these two archetypes, his idealism not defeated by their cynicism but coaxed toward another object, a more enduring cause. Coaxed by them and by his love for Maria. Maria, the daughter of two murdered Republicans, captured, tortured, and raped by fascists, leads him to his great discovery. His union with her, nurtured by Pilar, completed in the few days that remained to him, showed him that his cause wasn't a political philosophy, but a kinship with humanity, a kinship with Maria, with the poor souls he fought beside.

Distracted from his work by his sudden love for another, he worried that his sense of duty would suffer. Was the cause worth risking his love, worth sacrificing a new life with Maria? But rather than run toward a new, happier fate, he relinquished a part of his rationality, began to recognize signs and his destiny, fought for Maria, fought for people and not the ideology they falsely professed, the corrupted cause that cared so little for the lives it cost.

When an unexpected snowfall, the death of another band of guerrillas whose help he needed to destroy the bridge, and the anticipated failure to have the mission called off left him to contend with the insurmountable opposition of man and nature, Jordan persevered, saw to his mission, accepted his fate.

He blew up the bridge, at the cost of Anselmo's life and the lives of several others. Then Hemingway, the rascal, allows the reader a brief moment of hope with a quick feint toward a happy ending as the hero nearly escapes his fate and rides to a better life with his new love. Jordan, Maria, Pilar, Pablo, and the other survivors mount their horses, cross a road under fire, and race for safety, and I, still smug because I had penetrated the story's early mysteries, fell for it and cheered silently. So did Robert Jordan, I imagined. Although he was still in grave danger, and preoccupied with fear and the band's escape, I pictured him, as I was, allowing himself a moment's reverie about the bliss that might soon be his. And in that moment of joy, "he saw the bright flash from the heavy, squat, mud-colored truck," its shell exploding so close that it knocked his horse down on top of him.

Jordan's leg was crushed, as was my hope for a happy ending. But a much better ending graced the story's last pages and brought me safely through the temptation of a Hollywood reward to an inestimable prize, the understanding that health, good fortune, long years, domestic tranquillity, all the attributes of personal happiness, do not make a life well lived if we are afraid to risk it all for the love of something finer, something bigger than our own desires.

Jordan is unable to go on and orders his comrades to leave him and take Maria to safety. He remains behind to slow the progress of the cavalry that is chasing them. Resting against the trunk of a tree, with great difficulty he rolls himself into a prone position, grips a machine gun, and awaits his enemies. Fighting the temptation of suicide, pain, and approaching unconsciousness, he lingers for a while, noble and at peace.

"The world is a fine place and worth the fighting for and I hate very much to leave it," he thinks.

What a line, as perfect as a psalm. What a story I had found. How great it made me feel as I closed the book and charged on with my young life, aspiring to Jordan's courage and nobility and certain I would possess it someday.

I had not the wit, however, to articulate the truth it taught or the wisdom to really understand it. I just knew that I had read something special, something that showed me how and why to be brave, how a real hero lives and dies. I didn't aspire to or even imagine myself sacrificing my life for others. Surely there was a way to have my own Hollywood ending, to be ennobled by a sacrifice that didn't require my own death. And as months passed, I thought less about the book's great truth that no man is an island than about how a great man should style himself. A great man must always be his own man, I thought, remembering Jordan's lonely sacrifice but heedless of the book's warning not to carry individualism so far that it becomes egotism, and I looked for living examples to affirm my conviction.

WORTH THE FIGHTING FOR

With my father, Vice Admiral John S. McCain II, in front of a plaque commemorating the naming of McCain Field (a naval air station in Meridian, Mississippi, where I served as a flight instructor) for my grandfather John S. McCain. *Official U.S. Navy Photograph*

ONE

LAST SALUTE

We buried my father on a morning in the early spring of 1981. He had died of heart failure five days before, over the Atlantic, with my mother, his wife of forty-eight years, by his side.

He had been in poor health for most of the nine years that had passed since he had reluctantly retired from the navy. In his last few years, you could see life draining out of him. He had lost weight and become quite frail. He walked slowly, with his shoulders stooped, and was easily tired. He spent most of every day in his study, where he would read and nap on and off for hours. In his last year of active duty, as commander in chief of U.S. forces in the Pacific, he had suffered a seizure, which was initially believed to be a small stroke. For the remainder of his life, the seizures would recur more and more frequently, each one worse than the last, enfeebling him and destroying the great spirit that had enabled such a small man to live courageously a big, accomplished, adventurous life.

His doctors could never determine the cause of his convulsions. In his last years, they were as dramatic as grand mal seizures suffered by epileptics. He would bite through objects placed in his mouth to prevent him from swallowing his tongue. It seemed his brain would just quit functioning for longer and longer intervals. We would take him to the U.S. Naval Hospital in Bethesda, Maryland, where he would convalesce for a few weeks, while doctors searched futilely for a diagnosis.

I have always suspected that my father's long years of binge drinking had ruined his health. He had given up drinking years before, joined Alcoholics Anonymous, and although he would occasionally fall off the wagon, for the most part he maintained an admirable discipline in his sober years. But I suspect the damage had been done long ago, and with the onset of old age, the effects of his vice had shortened his life.

More damaging than drink, however, was the sadness he struggled to keep at bay since the day President Richard Nixon had presided over his change of command as a navy CINC, effectively ending more than forty years of active duty in the United States Navy. I've never known anyone who loved his profession more than my father had loved the navy. It was his whole life, from birth to death. He loved my mother, my sister, and my brother. But had you asked him to describe his family relationships, he would have answered, "I'm the son of an admiral and the father of a captain." He was so proud to be a sailor, considered himself so blessed to have remained always in the company of sailors, to have fought at sea, to have risen to the rank his father held, that any other life seemed dismal and insignificant to him.

Annually, all the CINCs are required to testify before the Armed Services Committees of the House and Senate. In his last testimony, aware that his career was near an end, he had complained that he didn't want to retire. But having reached the pinnacle of his career, having held the highest operational command in the navy, he knew his age and declining health had left him bereft of any hope that he would die in the uniform of his country. I am certain he would have preferred to leave this earth, as his father had, triumphantly, as his last war and command ended.

Even if his health had been better, even if his retirement had been occupied with important work and adventures, I doubt it would have alleviated his despair over leaving the navy. He kept the company of old sailors, which he cherished, but their society couldn't compensate him for the work he had lost, for his sense of purpose, for the ships that sailed at another's command, for the bluejackets who loved him, for the sea. He wasn't an invalid, but the seizures were debilitating, his spirits were poor, the quality of his life degraded. On good days, he would go downtown to the Army-Navy Club and swap stories with his old cronies. Most days, however, he remained in his study.

He did manage to travel fairly often. My parents loved to travel, especially my mother, and there were few countries they had not visited in the course of his long career. They tried to maintain their peripatetic lives to the extent my father's health would permit it. And it was on a return flight from Europe that he suffered the seizure that stopped his heart.

I received a call from my former wife, Carol, on a Sunday evening, March 22, 1981. Navy officials had contacted her after they had failed to locate me. They left it to her to inform me that my father had died, which she did with great kindness and tact. A crew member of the air force C-5 cargo plane had radioed a message that my father had suffered a heart attack on board and was presumed dead. The plane had landed at Bangor, Maine, to refuel, where a doctor confirmed my father's death and from there left for Andrews Air Force Base near Washington, D.C., where I would meet it. It was about a twenty-minute drive from my home to Andrews. I remember nothing of it. I cannot recall what I was thinking, or anything I said to my wife, Cindy, during the drive, or what she said to me.

The C-5 is a massive airplane, the largest plane ever built. It had three levels. On the top level, behind the cockpit and the seats for the rest of the crew, was a small passenger compartment with about twelve seats. You had to climb two ladders to reach it, and as I did so, I wondered how my father had managed the climb. My mother greeted us as we entered the compartment. She was very composed, very matter-of-fact, as she informed me, "John, your father is dead." My mother had dedicated her entire life to my father and his career. She loved him greatly. But she is a strong woman, indomitable. No loss, no matter how grievous, could undo her. Her face blank, she stared into my eyes for a long moment, as much, I suppose, to convey her own formidable resolve to maintain her dignity as to see if I could maintain mine. I looked past her toward a space behind the passenger seats, where he was lying, covered with a blue blanket, his brown shoes still on his feet, sticking out from under the blanket.

I remember little of the five days between that moment and the morning we buried him at Arlington National Cemetery, among the rows of white headstones that mark the many thousands of carefully tended graves on its sloping green acres, not far from where his father lay. My brother, Joe, had worked with the navy to make most of the funeral and burial arrangements. I was preparing to move across the country, and my mother was occupied with hundreds of sympathy calls and visits.

The funeral service was held in the Ft. Myers Chapel next to the cemetery. Mourners filled all its pews and stood along its walls and in the back. Nancy Reagan, just a few days after her husband, the president, had narrowly survived an assassination attempt, attended, as did Secretary of Defense Caspar Weinberger.

The navy, past and present, was represented by many of its most senior and honored officers, along with many eminent officers from the other services. The chief of naval operations, Admiral Tom Hayward, was there, as were his predecessors, Admirals Tom Moorer and George Anderson. Also among the mourners was Admiral Ike Kidd, a dear friend of my parents and the son of the famous Admiral Kidd (who had been killed at Pearl Harbor and received the Medal of Honor posthumously). He was overcome with grief, and one of my most poignant memories of the funeral is of Admiral Kidd sobbing loudly and struggling to regain his composure. The pallbearers included Admiral Arleigh Burke, whom my father had served under and revered; Admiral "Red" Ramage, a classmate, fellow submariner, and Medal of Honor recipient; General Eugene Tighe of the U.S. Air Force; Ellsworth Bunker, who had served as ambassador to South Vietnam when my father held the Pacific Command; Chief Roque Acuavera and Chief Ricardo San Victories, each of whom had served my father as chief steward for many years and who had loved him and been loved by him.

Joe and I were the only eulogists. Joe spoke first and gave a fine tribute, eloquently sketching his career and character. I spoke briefly and remember only joking that my father had probably greeted St. Peter with his lecture on "The Four Ocean Navy and the Soviet Threat." I closed my remarks with the Robert Louis Stevenson poem "Requiem," the beautiful homage to one man's free will that we had both loved.

> *Under the wide and starry sky,*
> *Dig the grave and let me lie.*
> *Glad did I live and gladly die,*
> *And I laid me down with a will.*

This be the verse you grave for me:
Here he lies where he longed to be;
Home is the sailor, home from the sea,
And the hunter home from the hill.

After the funeral service had ended, the mourners preceded my father's body to his burial site. It was a cool, overcast day; the trees were still bare and seemed so black against the gray sky and deep green field. We watched as a riderless horse slowly led the caisson and procession from chapel to grave. As they arrived, the Navy Band played a solemn march by Handel, the music that had accompanied Lord Nelson's funeral procession as it moved through the streets of London to his resting place at St. Paul's Cathedral. I kept my head erect and my eyes fixed straight ahead during the brief graveside service and as his casket was lowered into the earth.

After the service, my mother hosted a reception in her large Connecticut Avenue apartment. I was not distraught at the service or at the reception, but I was weary and had to force myself to be affable. At times I found it trying just to thank people for coming and for their expressions of sympathy. But my mother, my amazing mother, more than compensated for my reserve as she whirled around the apartment, seeming to take part in every conversation, as always, the center of attention.

My father's death and funeral occurred at a moment of great change for me and for the tradition that had brought honor to three generations of John McCains. I had arrived at my mother's apartment still wearing my dress blue uniform. I would never wear it again.

I left the reception after an hour or so and drove to an office in a nondescript building in Crystal City, Virginia, with the typically bureaucratic title Navy Personnel Support Activity Center. There I signed my discharge papers, applied for my retirement pay and health coverage, and turned in my identification card, ending nearly twenty-three years on active duty. For the first time in the twentieth century, and possibly forever, the name John McCain was missing from navy rosters. From there, I drove to the airport and boarded a plane with Cindy and her parents for Phoenix, Arizona, and a new life altogether.

Henry "Scoop" Jackson. *Corbis*

LIAISON

Several months before my father died, I informed him that I was leaving the navy. I am sure he had already gotten word of my decision from friends in the Pentagon. I had been summoned to see the CNO, Admiral Heyward, who told me that I was making a mistake and argued strongly, if not convincingly, that I should reconsider my decision. His attempt to dissuade me encouraged me to believe that I might have made admiral had I remained in the navy, a prospect that had been an open question in my mind.

Upon my return from Vietnam, I had worked hard with a physical therapist to rehabilitate the disabilities caused by my war injuries and had managed for a time to regain flying status. But in the years following that achievement, my condition had deteriorated to the point that neither I nor anyone else thought I would ever fly again. Some of my navy friends believed I could still earn my star; others doubted it. But even had I made rear admiral, the fact that I was permanently grounded would preclude my command of a carrier or battle group, making further promotion impossible. And so, when my current job was nearing an end, before a navy detailer could offer me a new assignment, I informed the Navy Bureau of Personnel that I would retire.

When I told my father of my intention, he did not remonstrate with me. He asked me to give the decision more thought but told me he would understand should I go through with it and offered that I had had an honorable career. I did not doubt his understanding or his pride in me. But I knew him well enough to know that he was disappointed. For when I left him that day, alone in his study, I took with me his hope that I might someday become the first son and grandson of four-star admirals to achieve the same distinction. That aspiration was well beyond my reach by the time I made my decision, but because he had been so determined to emulate his own father's illustrious career, the rank had been my father's consuming ambition and crowning achievement, and he must have grieved to know that it was not mine.

While I occasionally had reservations about my decision, most acutely on the day we buried my father, I did not anguish over it. I wasn't unhappy in the navy, but I doubted my future assignments would be as interesting and satisfying as my last eight years in the navy had been.

Since the day I entered the Naval Academy, I had had to contend with suggestions that my career had greatly benefited from my father's rank and influence. After the war, my status as a former prisoner of war was believed to have added yet another advantage to my father's patronage as a guarantor of professional advancement. I suppose that was true to an extent. Returning prisoners of war were afforded considerable discretion in choosing their future assignments, and I took full advantage of the opportunity. But once in a job, I worked as hard as I could to distinguish myself in it. And at the risk of immodesty, I can claim credit for my successes, if not my opportunities. Among its many other positive effects, Vietnam had made me a more serious officer, scaring off the last traces of my earlier indifference to the professionalism of an ambitious officer. And I came home determined to excel in my family's profession.

I think it's fair to say, however, that the navy had reservations about just how far I could excel in its ranks. I was emotionally healthy when I came home, but my physical fitness was another matter. I could not lift my arms above my head without great discomfort and could barely flex my right knee. Navy doctors made two surgical attempts to improve the condition, but their success was negligible. It was assumed that I would walk with a very pronounced, stiff-legged limp for the remainder of my life.

The military showed a great deal of deference to returned POWs and took care not to hasten our departure from service even if our fitness for active duty was questionable. We were also given considerable leeway in choosing our next duty station. I chose the National War College at Ft. McNair in Washington, D.C. It is prestigious duty, which was partly why I selected it. But more important, a year at the War College would allow me the opportunity to study why and how my country had fought in Vietnam, questions I had become more than a little curious about, while not imposing physical demands on me that I was not yet able to meet.

When I informed my detailer of my decision, he resisted, however. Although the navy intended to accommodate, within reason, our duty preferences, he felt I had taken this generosity a little too far. The Navy Promotions Board had just selected me for commander, but the promotion wouldn't go into effect for a while. I still wore a lieutenant commander's stripes, a fact that my detailer duly pointed out. Only commanders and captains, he explained, could attend the War College.

"But I've been selected for commander," I protested.

"I'm sorry, but you'll have to pick another job."

I did not, and I appealed his decision all the way to the secretary of the navy, my father's friend and now my Senate colleague, John Warner, who ordered the navy to grant my request and, by so doing, probably saved my career.

My good fortune increased when Diane Rauch, who would later marry my dear friend and revered commanding officer in Hanoi, Admiral Bill Lawrence, volunteered to be my physical therapist. She was generous, kind, but as fiercely determined as I was to rehabilitate my injured leg so that I would have a chance to fly again. The treatment wasn't pleasant, but it worked.

By the time my nine months of study at the War College ended, I had satisfied my curiosity about how America had entered and lost the Vietnam War. The experience did not cause me to conclude that the war was wrong, but it did help me understand how wrongly it had been fought and led. I was not an embittered veteran before I entered the War College, nor am I now. But I did resent how badly civilian leaders had mismanaged the war and how ineffectually our senior military commanders had resisted their mistakes. Most appalling to me was how Americans had let the least fortunate among us fight the war for them, while sons of privilege were afforded numerous opportunities to stay home. That was a political decision made not just by the president, Congress, and the services, but by the country as a whole, and I resented the hell out of it. No national endeavor requires as much unshakable resolve as war. Before we enter one, we ought to know that most Americans share the commitment and are prepared to make the personal sacrifices it entails. If only the poor and disadvantaged are expected to fight for us, then the country should belong to them and no one else. The rest of us should meekly live off their goodwill and charity, for they are the ones who have loved our country the most and are most deserving of her blessings.

I had gained more in that year than education and opinions. My knee had regained enough mobility for me to pass the physical examination and qualify, barely, for flight status.

Near the end of 1974, I became executive officer of VA 174, a replacement air group (RAG), which trained carrier pilots, at Cecil Field in Jacksonville, Florida. A few months later, I became the RAG's commanding officer (CO). Technically, I was not qualified for the command, and the assignment was controversial. The CO of a RAG had almost always previously commanded a fleet squadron. Fleet squadrons had twelve airplanes, sixteen pilots, and maybe around a hundred crew and support personnel. VA 174 had fifty airplanes and almost a thousand people. It was the biggest squadron in the navy. I was by then too senior in rank for a fleet squadron command, and I requested the duty assignment well aware that my audacity would provoke protests from a number of quarters that I was not qualified for the honor and too inexperienced to succeed. They were right on the first count but wrong on the second.

Among my doubters was my boss, the light attack wing commander, Captain Marv Reynolds. While Captain Reynolds believed I would fall on my face, he did not, I am grateful to say, try to ensure my failure.

At the time I assumed command, nearly twenty of the squadron's A-7 airplanes were in sufficient disrepair to be grounded. Some of them had not flown for three years. I went to see Captain Reynolds and told him that if he allowed me to move parts from one plane to another, before my tour was finished I would have every one of them in the air. He informed me, not unfairly, that I couldn't do it. No CO in his memory had ever gotten all the squadron's planes off the ground. But to his credit and my relief, he gave me permission to try.

I wouldn't have had a prayer of delivering on my boast if I hadn't had the honor of commanding the best pilots and maintenance crew in the United States Navy. Most of the best navy fliers were either test pilots or instructors in the RAGs, and I had more than my fair share of them. The quality of my maintenance crew was equal to the quality of my pilots. I commanded a large group of highly committed, hardworking, innovative, and lovely people. I'm indebted forever to all of them. My experience as the commanding officer of VA 174 was the most rewarding assignment of my naval career.

On the morning of my last day as commanding officer, shortly before my change of command ceremony, my friend Carl Smith kept my promise to Captain Reynolds and took off in the last of the squadron's grounded planes. The plane was barely ready for the test and flew with its landing gear down. Our squadron had also set a record for posting the longest flying hours without an accident. As a result of our hard work, VA 174 received its first ever Meritorious Unit Citation.

A short while after Carl had secured the squadron's reputation, I sat on a dais listening to Admiral Kidd commemorate my change of command by praising the McCains of the United States Navy and joining my name to the far more illustrious careers of my grandfather and father. My father was there, as were my mother and my wife and children. Friends from prison were also present. I have never cried easily, but I found it especially hard not to that day.

I had used my professional advantages well since I had come home from war and was building a decent reputation for myself in the navy. But I had not shown the same determination to rebuild my personal life. My marriage to Carol McCain was falling apart. Sound marriages can be hard to recover after great time and distance have separated a husband and wife. We are different people when we reunite. But my marriage's collapse was attributable to my own selfishness and immaturity more than it was to Vietnam, and I cannot escape blame by pointing a finger at the war. The blame was entirely mine.

———

My next job in the navy after leaving Jacksonville would be my last. I was assigned to the liaison office in the United States Senate, where I would serve as the navy's lobbyist in what is sometimes respectfully and sometimes ironically called the world's most exclusive club. My father had once served as chief of the Navy Department's Office of Legislative Affairs and, as always, had made the most of the job. Some months after I arrived in the Senate, I was promoted to captain. My promotion and my new duty brought me as close as I would ever get to matching the accomplishments of the old man's career. It would also mark my real entry into the world of politics and the beginning of my second career as a public servant.

Given my parents' many friendships with politicians, I was not overawed to find myself in the company of the hundred powerful souls to whom I would now report. Many of them knew and respected my father. Most of them knew about my service in Vietnam and showed me a respect that they might not have always accorded liaison officers, who were often viewed as temporary Senate staffers with a particular expertise in military matters. In some instances, we were expected to serve as caseworkers and gofers. But I enjoyed the job immensely and worked hard to cultivate relationships with senators, Republicans and Democrats, for the navy's benefit as well as my own.

I did a fair amount of public speaking when I returned from Vietnam, and sometimes after these occasions I would muse upon entering politics. Carol and I had also become friends with Governor and Mrs. Ronald Reagan and with several of their associates, especially Nancy Reynolds. Our friendship, and the encouragement of some people in their circle, also sparked a small interest in a political career. But I had never given it serious consideration until I came to work in the Senate and watched the senior members of that institution influence the shape and focus of the military more than most flag officers I had known.

My duties required me to attend hearings in the Senate Armed Services and Defense Appropriations Committees when my navy superiors testified and when the committees met to "mark up" the spending bills for the navy. There I would watch as prominent members of the committee worked with their staffs to quickly draft amendments on scraps of paper or hash out a compromise on a disputed matter that would profoundly affect the structure and operations of the navy. I was not naïve about the influence Congress had over my profession. Indeed, my father had imparted to me a healthy respect for and wariness of it. But I had no idea of the full extent of their authority until I personally witnessed it in practice.

I must admit that my personal regard for congressional leaders in general had declined during and after the Vietnam War. Like most professional officers, I had resented congressional opposition to the war and what we viewed as terribly misguided political interference in the war's conduct. Particularly offensive, we believed, was Congress's refusal to keep President Nixon's commitment of support to South Vietnam after American troops were withdrawn. I blamed Congress for willfully breaking America's word and gravely injuring our nation's reputation and standing in the world, a lack of faith I considered shameful.

Nevertheless, I quickly became intrigued by the enormous power over the nation's security exercised by senior members of the Armed Services Committee. I watched and admired Barry Goldwater, John Stennis, Henry Jackson, John Tower, Sam Nunn, and others wrestle with all manner of issues involved in America's defense with great skill, intelligence, and seriousness. They were statesmen, and although some of them had never served in uniform, I came to appreciate that most were patriots of the first order.

I was particularly fortunate to come to know many senators and their staffs quite well, even developing close friendships with more than a few of them. Senators Gary Hart of Colorado and Bill Cohen of Maine became then and remain my good friends. In 1988, Gary only nearly missed becoming the Democratic nominee for president. While he had been a critic of the war and held a political philosophy considerably to the left of mine, he was an independent-minded public servant and a thoughtful, serious legislator on many issues, including those that concerned America's defense and her role in the world, and I admired him. A man of many interests and talents, Bill Cohen also enjoyed a reputation for seriousness and political independence. I enjoy his company immensely. Gary and Bill were two of the younger members of the Senate, along with Joe Biden of Delaware, and close to my age. While as senators they were owed and received my deference, I considered them much closer to being my peers than I would have dared to consider the more venerable members of the institution.

Among the duties of a liaison officer is to act when requested as escorts on frequent trips overseas by congressional delegations—CODELs, in Capitol Hill parlance. The job was mainly to manage the logistics for the trips, which can become quite complicated, especially on large CODELs where Senate wives are included. The job entails a great many tasks from the mundane to the serious, from baggage handling to security. I enjoyed the duty and was, for various reasons, frequently requested to do it. Often I would escort delegations led by the most eminent and influential members of the Senate, many of whom I came to greatly respect and who by their example nurtured my growing interest in a political career. Two of them, I will remember forever.

The great Scoop Jackson of Washington was and remains for me the model of what an American statesman should be. He had no vices that I knew of or, for that matter, any hobbies or pursuits that would distract him for a moment from his duty. As with my father, his work was everything to him. By the time I met him, he had served in Congress, first in the House and then in the Senate, for thirty-seven years. He won his elections by landslides, yet he seemed to lack the outsize personality that is common to very successful politicians today. He wasn't charismatic in the style most politicians tried to ape since John Kennedy's election, urbane, witty, fashionable, comfortable with social mores of the times. He wasn't a gifted speaker. He couldn't tell a joke worth a damn. He wasn't ebullient or a backslapping, clubby man. He was a very agreeable, very pleasant man, but quietly so, and regarded by all but his family and intimates as dull and overly serious.

With few exceptions, his politics were conventionally liberal in economic and social policy debates. But on defense and foreign policy he was the Senate's—indeed, the country's—leading hawk. No member of the Senate was ever better prepared for debate than Scoop. Few members of

Congress have ever accumulated the record of accomplishment and influence Jackson claimed. Whatever he lacked stylistically, Scoop more than compensated for with hard work, intelligence, and a vision of America that was informed by his hardheaded, practical idealism. Most of all, Scoop had faith. He had faith in his country, faith in the rightness of her causes. He had faith that our founding ideals were universal, the principal strength of our foreign policy, and would in time overcome our enemy's resistance. Until the day he died, he never wavered in his faith. Not once.

Henry Martin Jackson was the son of Norwegian immigrants, the youngest of five children, and a self-made man, the kind of success story America prides herself in believing is possible for all her citizens. By 1940, when he won his first election to the House of Representatives at twenty-nine, he had put himself through college and law school and already been a successful politician from Everett, Washington, for several years.

Washington's second congressional district, which Jackson represented, professed a strong strain of isolationism, not uncommon before World War II and expected to reappear with the defeat of Germany and Japan. In his third term in Congress, he traveled to Germany at the end of the war. He visited Buchenwald eleven days after the concentration camp had been liberated. There he saw the measure of evil in human nature and the terrible power hate and intolerance wield when sanctioned by a political system. He left Buchenwald having gained a great moral clarity that rejected the isolationism of America's past as immoral and a hopelessly inadequate defense of American interests and values. He became an unyielding opponent to governments that gave legitimacy to the worst impulses of man. His conviction would stir his hostility to Joe McCarthy as readily as it did his hostility to an important wartime ally.

By the time he was first elected to the Senate in 1952, he was a model of the cold war liberal, an ardent supporter of the policy of containment, the strategic foundation of our contest with the Soviet Union, a policy that was, as hard as it is to imagine today, controversial at its inception and continually debated in American politics until the day its efficacy and Scoop's wisdom were proven with the collapse of the Soviet empire.

Jackson never lived to see that triumph for American policy, for our interests and values, and for humanity. But he never doubted it would come, as long as America remained as stubbornly resistant as he was, militarily, ideologically, and diplomatically, to the imperial ambitions of the Soviet Union, to its attempts to win an arms race by lulling the United States into carelessness, and to its dehumanizing ideology that viewed human rights as subordinate to the needs of the state. He was a champion for all people deprived of their liberty and an enemy to those who sought power for themselves by disregarding the humanity of others. Although many in his party and mine would fault him for being too stubborn in a world that required subtlety and cunning, he was a hero for our time, the last half of a violent century, and absolutely indispensable to our eventual success. Howard Baker, the Republican majority leader in the Senate, said of him that he "made sure we did not lose the cold war in the 1970s, so that Ronald Reagan could win it in the 1980s." That was a fitting and completely accurate judgment and an epitaph that Jackson would have been very proud of.

Bipartisan support for containment had been the rule until the Vietnam War claimed that consensus along with many other casualties. Harry Truman and his advisers had been the policy's first architects. By the time I got to know Jackson, hawks had become a minority within the Democratic Party, but those who survived proudly claimed their identity as Jackson Democrats. Jimmy Carter was president then. He was and remains a good and decent man. He was a Naval Academy graduate and a disciple of Admiral Hyman Rickover, the father of the nuclear navy. Yet I fear President Carter's innate goodness, despite the guidance of experienced, practical counselors such as his national security adviser, Zbigniew Brzezinski, bred in him a distrust of power politics and a naïveté about Soviet ambitions and the ruthlessness with which they would pursue them. But for Scoop's vigilance as he resisted the Carter administration's trusting, incautious idealism, the success of subsequent administrations in accelerating the Soviet empire's collapse would not have been possible.

He opposed the SALT II treaty, rang the alarm about Soviet imperial advances in the third world, and insisted that the defense of human rights remain central to American foreign policy. His opposition to Carter administration statecraft, verging on antagonism, was not, as some would claim, born of personal resentment over losing the presidential nomination to Carter, but simply the necessary extension of a battle he had waged for decades.

Relations between Jackson and Carter were never good, and no doubt some of the testiness in their personal relationship can be attributed to lingering hard feelings from their 1976 presidential rivalry. But Scoop Jackson's opposition to Carter administration policies was always principled and consistent with his well-established positions. He had long been the country's preeminent skeptic of the efficacy of arms control treaties, resisting, criticizing, and profoundly affecting the structure of the Limited Nuclear Test Ban Treaty in 1963, the Anti-Ballistic Missile Treaty in 1969, and the SALT I Treaty in 1972.

He clashed with President Nixon and the brilliant Henry Kissinger as they contended with the geopolitical consequences of our losing the war in Southeast Asia by pursuing détente with the Soviet Union. I believed the policy of détente as practiced by the Nixon administration, and the opening of our relationship with China, proved to be a well-considered, even ingenious, strategy for a perilous time in American history. If it had achieved no other success than exposing Soviet officials to the success of Western liberalism, an exposure that would convince a later generation of Soviet leaders that theirs was a failed ideology, it would have proven its worth. But had Richard Nixon and Henry Kissinger not had Scoop Jackson to contend with as he stubbornly insisted on investing their realism with a clear commitment to human rights, détente might have, as Jackson feared it would, unintentionally strengthened our adversary and sustained both its power and its noxious ideology beyond their natural life.

Most famously, he prevailed over Nixon administration objections in conditioning trade relations with the Soviets and other totalitarian regimes on the relaxation of their emigration policies. His success in that endeavor made him perhaps the most revered American hero to the thousands of Jews who escaped Soviet tyranny under the auspices of Jackson's legislation. His steadfast support for Israel made him a beloved figure to Jews.

He was not infallible. He voted with most of his party to cut off aid to South Vietnam after we had withdrawn our forces from the conflict, a vote I have never been able to understand, since he had supported the war.

I thought this the one inconsistent act of a famously consistent public life. To this day it puzzles me, and I kick myself for never asking him to explain it when I had opportunities to do so. Perhaps he thought that South Vietnam's surrender was inevitable and that our defense would be better served by using those resources elsewhere. But he was not the kind of man who cut and ran on an ally. I don't know, and it pains me to think that even for a moment Scoop Jackson would have bowed to political conventions he knew were wrong. So I assume he had reasons more principled than expedient for his action, even if I cannot grasp them. His integrity had earned that trust.

Jackson employed and was loved by the best staff in Congress, brilliant men and women, many of whom would go on to serve in important national security positions in the Reagan administration during the last battles of the cold war. For most of them, no matter what successes they would achieve after leaving his office, their service on Scoop's staff remains their proudest accomplishment. Jackson was famously accessible to all his staff and generous with advice both professional and personal to anyone who asked for it. He was kind and thoughtful to his employees, even the most junior, and enormously trusting of their abilities. He empowered them to play important roles in some of the greatest political debates of the day. And they repaid his kindness and his trust by remaining on his staff for more years than is common in the Senate, and with affection usually reserved for close family.

I thought him to be among the best people in the world to work for, and while I am not nearly the gentleman Scoop was, I have consciously tried to emulate his informality and his fairness to his staff. I have learned, as Scoop must have always known, that a loyal, well-treated staff is among the best, most gratifying, important accomplishments in a public career.

The late Dorothy "Dickie" Fosdick, daughter of the eminent pacifist theologian and pastor of the Riverside Church in New York, was his chief foreign policy adviser for almost three decades. I consider it a great stroke of luck that Dickie and I became good friends during my time in the navy's liaison office. Not only did I benefit from exposure to Dickie's intelligence and experience, but at her request I would serve as escort on several of Jackson's trips abroad, giving me the opportunity to observe at close quarters a great statesman at the height of influence.

It was, however, on a short domestic trip with Jackson to the christening of a new nuclear submarine in New London, Connecticut, that I first glimpsed the simple decency that bred such intense loyalty in the people who worked for him. Jackson had long been an ally of Admiral Rickover's, had helped save his career when the disagreeable, headstrong Rickover had been twice passed over for admiral by his superiors. As the undisputed czar of the nuclear navy, Rickover was accompanying Jackson to the christening. A famously prickly, idiosyncratic, rude, and self-absorbed man, Rickover was never pleasant to be around. He took notice of very few people beneath his rank and genius. Jackson was one of the privileged few. And although he held Rickover in high esteem as a visionary military leader, Jackson did not feel obliged to suffer the admiral's less than admirable personal qualities.

Rickover had been a contemporary of my father's, and to the extent that Rickover had navy friends, my father would have probably qualified for much of their association. He was such an old bastard, though, I doubt that exposure to his brilliance was reason enough to suffer a friendship with him. I never would have wanted it, a declaration that wouldn't have bothered Rickover in the least. He knew me because of my father, but on this trip, as in every other encounter I ever had with him, he ignored me or treated me as just another minor distraction from whatever important work was occupying his attention.

On most of the flight to New London, Rickover kept his nose buried in a sheaf of important papers. He did, however, possess a sense of loyalty to his most important congressional benefactor and would converse, even politely, when Scoop spoke to him. But he spoke little to anyone else except to issue orders to his aide. When Peggy Hieland, Scoop's longtime scheduler, approached him, Rickover couldn't be bothered to look up from the papers he was reading to acknowledge her until she asked him for his autograph. He jerked his head up and stared at her for a moment, then gave her a curt "No" before resuming his reading.

Scoop saw this, and with an impatience, informality, and slight sarcasm that only he would have had the nerve to use on Rickover, he said, "Aw, c'mon, Rick. What the hell's wrong with you? Give her your autograph." This, the old man proceeded to do, grumbling under his breath until the unpleasant task was finished. Only for Jackson, Rickover's aide later informed me, would his boss have ever relaxed his ironclad rule to never risk humanizing himself by the act of complying with a request for his autograph.

Two foreign trips I accompanied Jackson on stand out as among the most memorable of my three years in the liaison office, not the least because he was just such a pleasure to travel with. Escort duty on a CODEL is sought after, but not always a joy. I was fortunate to travel with some of the most senior members of the Senate, most of whom were personally decent and very admirable people. Often, especially on long CODELs, members traveled with their wives, and less often with their children. Sometimes, though thankfully not often, a senator's courtesy and fairness to staff are not virtues shared by his relations. I had on occasion run into trouble with some Senate wives who felt their husband's position entitled them to be imperious, short-tempered, and rather contemptuous of other people's convenience and work. That was never the case with Helen Jackson or with Scoop's son, Peter, and his daughter, Anna Marie.

Scoop had married late in life, but he had married well. Helen is a lovely person, and they raised two great kids. It was a pleasure to work for them. On trips when Peter and Anna Marie accompanied their parents, I took particular care to look after them. Not because Scoop demanded it or expected it, but because I enjoyed their company and because, like others who worked for him, I wanted to repay the man's decency by taking care with my responsibilities to him.

In June of 1979, I escorted a large CODEL led by Jackson on a ten-day trip to Israel, where, as I have already mentioned, Scoop is considered a hero. I had no idea just how great a hero until we landed at Tel Aviv. When we arrived we were transferred to a bus big enough to accommodate our large delegation, as well as the U.S. ambassador in Israel and several of his staff. About a hundred yards outside the airport, the bus was surrounded by a crowd of seven or eight hundred Israelis screaming for Jackson, waving signs that read GOD BLESS YOU, SCOOP, SENATOR JACKSON,

THANK YOU, and dozens of other tributes. They were ecstatic over Scoop's arrival. There were many other strong supporters of Israel on the trip, including Senator Jake Javits, but the crowd was there for Scoop. They mobbed us, slowing the bus's progress to a crawl. Scoop and Helen loved every minute of it, genuinely moved by the outpouring of affection. For a patriot like Scoop, their affection for him was nothing less than affection for America.

As the bus wound its way through the crowd, Scoop spotted Avital Sharansky, the wife of the imprisoned Soviet dissident Natan Sharansky. He instructed the driver to stop, and he and Helen got off to bring Mrs. Sharansky aboard. They spent the entire ride to the hotel, and a considerable time thereafter, in private, warm discussions with her, as if nothing on the trip would be as important as hearing her concerns.

My last trip with Jackson was the longest and most interesting event of my brief, minor association with him. For three weeks in August of 1979, I traveled extensively in China with the senator, his wife, and his children; Dickie Fosdick; Mr. and Mrs. Stan Golub, longtime friends and financial supporters of Jackson's campaigns; various other staff; and two Chinese government escorts.

If Scoop's principled opposition to the Soviet Union admitted one mistake, it might have been that his enthusiasm for a potential strategic partnership with the People's Republic of China overlooked Beijing's hostility to American political values. Surely Nixon's opening to China was a masterstroke in our strategic rivalry with the Soviets, one of the most timely and audacious diplomatic gambits of the century that contributed significantly to our cold war victory. Scoop had welcomed it—indeed, had been the Senate's leading advocate for improving Sino-American ties even before President Nixon and Henry Kissinger engineered it.

But Jackson's strategic attraction to China encouraged his unrealistic confidence that economic and social changes would soon profoundly change the political nature of the regime. I agree with the premise that over time, commercial and diplomatic ties to the West, and consequent exposure to Western political values, should encourage political liberalism in China, as it has the economic liberalism that is accelerating China's emergence as a great power. But time in China is measured in centuries, and the optimistic expectations for the pace and scope of political reform, expectations held not just by Jackson, but by many other statesmen, would be dashed by Beijing's brutal repression of liberty in Tiananmen Square in 1989 and in the disappointing years that have followed. Neither did Scoop or most others fully appreciate how, after the cold war ended, China's entry onto the world stage and its hostility toward American influence in Asia would become one of the most important strategic problems for the United States in the twenty-first century.

United by their shared distrust of the Soviet Union and the belief that U.S. and Chinese strategic interests were increasingly compatible, Jackson and China's top leaders, especially Deng Xiaoping, formed a close relationship that was exceptionally warm and open. Both Jackson and Deng were concerned that the Carter administration was taking too evenhanded an approach to our relations with the Chinese and the Soviets, particularly in the wake of China's recent military incursion into Vietnam. Much of their discussion dealt with how to politically tip the balance in China's favor. The trip was Jackson's third and most extensive visit to China, and the high regard he was held in by Deng and other Chinese officials was evident in the friendly familiarity that accented their discussions and in the extraordinary courtesies they extended to Scoop.

After several days of meetings with top officials, we were allowed to travel on Chinese military aircraft to provinces that few Westerners were ever privileged to visit. We traveled to Xi'an, the ancient Silk Road destination in Shaanxi province, where we admired the famous third-century B.C. terra-cotta warriors, an experience few Americans had shared at that time. We went to the farthest western provinces, staying in Chinese Communist Party guesthouses because there were no hotels.

There are two amusing incidents from that trip I still delight in recalling. Scoop, Helen, Dickie, and I had flown in a very small plane to a remote part of Xianjing province, in the far west of China, where we visited a nomadic community. The doctor accompanying the delegation, whose name I have forgotten, had stayed behind in the capital to visit a local hospital. We were brought into a yurt to meet with several of the village's leading citizens. Not long into the visit, our hosts served us bowls of a vile-smelling drink. I learned from our interpreter that the bowls contained fermented mare's milk. Grateful for the heads-up, I pretended to drink it without actually letting any of it pass my lips. Dickie, on the other hand, brave soul that she was, gulped it right down, exclaimed, "This is really good," and asked for another and then another. The stuff really did stink, and I remember thinking to myself, Holy shit, what is she doing? as Dickie knocked back one bowl after another.

At dinner that night after we returned to the capital, I asked the doctor what he had done that day, and he told me of his visit to the hospital.

"Learn anything interesting?" I asked.

"Why, yes, I did," he replied. "The doctors here have diagnosed a form of liver disease that's unknown in the rest of the world. It's very rare, even in China, but they've got quite a few cases of it up here."

"How do you get it?"

"From drinking fermented mare's milk."

I laughed until I cried. Dickie almost fainted.

One afternoon, we drove past a few acres of cornfields. Jackson thought it would be a fine idea if we were to have a little local corn with our meal that evening, and he asked me to see to it. I'm not a farmer, and I don't know a hell of a lot about agriculture. Evidently, neither did Scoop. I did know that there were two kinds of corn, one for human consumption and another for livestock. I suggested to the senator that perhaps the corn we had seen was feed corn. He dismissed my concern politely, with, "No, no, it looks like good corn to me, John. Let's have some." So I dutifully informed one of our Chinese escorts that Senator Jackson would like some of the locally grown corn and instructed him on how it should be prepared by boiling it. I recall he had a rather puzzled look on his face as he listened to me, but I assumed that he was just having a hard time understanding me. That night, as requested, we were fed the corn. One bite convinced us that while it might have been good corn for a cow or a pig, it was not fit for our consumption, and we left the rest of it untouched.

The delegation was not large, and I was included in most of the conversations with Jackson and the others. He had such a great breadth of knowledge and experience, and he enjoyed playing teacher to eager students, a station I was happy to occupy on the trip. He was, as I've said, a warm, informal man, and he didn't seem to mind my persistent questions, which mostly concerned, but weren't limited to, geopolitics. No matter how simple or simply phrased they were, Scoop answered all my questions thoughtfully and often at great length.

I asked a number of political questions as well, about his presidential campaigns, his assessment of the presidents he had known, his relationship with Carter. He answered those as carefully as he would have answered a question about the history of a particular piece of legislation he had authored. He and the Golubs often reminisced at length about his early campaigns and about politics during and just after World War II, and they kindly tolerated my occasional interruptions to ask questions. It was a fascinating trip for me, and I remember it often, fondly, when I travel abroad in my present capacity.

Scoop Jackson had once been his party's national chairman. Reportedly, he had been Jack Kennedy's first choice for vice president before the political necessity of shoring up support in the South obliged him to select Lyndon Johnson. He believed in an activist federal government and seldom strayed from liberal orthodoxy in his domestic policy views. He was a New Dealer all his public life. Presidents of both parties sought his counsel and support and had to contend with him when he found their policies lacking in strength and conviction. He was a towering figure in American politics. Yet in the end, he was a political maverick not because he had changed in temperament or conviction, but because he had not. His party had.

By 1972, when the Democratic Party had nominated George McGovern for president, a younger generation of Democrats was establishing a new identity for the party. It had become an antiwar party, and opposition to the Vietnam War was growing inexorably into a general suspicion of the military, of an assertive foreign policy, even of that sense of American exceptionalism that had been the transcendent faith of American leaders since our founding.

A lost war is a terrible calamity and, in this instance, all the more so for its last casualty, America's faith in herself. Thank God for Scoop Jackson, for his willingness to stand apart from the new conventions of his party. Without him, without his courage, I doubt we would have recovered from

Vietnam as quickly as we did, which would have left those who sacrificed there all the more haunted by the futility of the experience.

Political courage in practice is the resolve to do what's right whatever the personal consequences one must suffer. In a time of confusion and uncertainty, when the hard truths he had always served were unpopular in his party, Jackson held fast, a patriot with a patriot's courage, and suffered the disdain of elites who mistook fashion for wisdom. He was yesterday's man to the new establishment, unchanged in a changed world, an anachronism in a time when modernity had a twenty-four-hour shelf life. But he, not they, proved indispensable to the times, a man who made history by holding fast to his core conviction that right makes might, while others expected history to flatter them.

When he ran for president in 1972 and 1976, he failed miserably, despite his extraordinarily accomplished legislative career and his widely acclaimed reputation as a leading statesman of his time. His friends have told me that his lack of success as a presidential candidate caused him to think himself a failed politician. Would that more of us in public life fail so magnificently for such a good cause. Few presidents can claim to have served the Republic as ably, as faithfully, as Scoop Jackson did. What personal failures he suffered were nothing indelible. But his mark on humanity's progress, and on the civilization he considered a blessing to all mankind, was permanent.

Henry Jackson died of a burst aneurysm on September 1, 1983. He was seventy-one years old and had lived to see his convictions, his hardheaded idealism, embraced in the policies of the Reagan administration. His timing was perfect. He would be missed, but his country could now manage without him.

He had been, as Howard Baker eulogized, "a man who knew who he was and where he was going and where he wished to take the country." Should we ever expect more from a leader?

In a speech he gave to the Anti-Defamation League, Jackson offered a rare tribute to himself and to the companions he encouraged in his life's work.

"My friends, you and I fought for human rights before it became fashionable. I am confident that we will continue even after the fainthearted have tired of the struggle. Persistence has its rewards."

Yes, it surely does. In 1989, a Czech student stood before a million of his countrymen, while a hundred thousand Soviet troops still occupied his country, and read a manifesto that proclaimed a new day for Eastern Europe. But he began that new day with borrowed words when he read: "We hold these truths to be self-evident: that all men are created equal and endowed by their Creator with certain unalienable rights; among these are life, liberty, and the pursuit of happiness." Scoop Jackson knew that day would arrive. Persistence has its rewards.

—

Henry Jackson was, to me and many others, an ideal, a man whose example I revered but whom I knew only professionally. John Tower was my friend. That was unexpected when I began my work in the liaison office. Jackson was by far the more accessible person, friendlier and more open to people other than his peers, an independent thinker little tempted by the allure of Washington society and the self-importance prized by so many there. But he was beloved by many of his colleagues.

John Tower was loved by his family and intimates. Many of his colleagues did not care for him but had learned by experience to respect him. He was a very formal man, in dress and speech, and punctilious about the protocol and privileges of high office. I doubt Jackson cared much for such things, and I never gave a damn about them. But John Tower was my friend, as he was Scoop Jackson's, and I am the richer for it.

He had a quick mind and a sharp tongue. His colleagues appreciated the former and often suffered the latter. He disparaged one colleague by declaring that "he abused the right to be stupid." He was a curious, contradictory fellow, very short and a little stout, but vain in his appearance. He was quick to anger yet seemed most often very self-possessed. He appeared completely self-confident and gave the impression that his dignity was his most prized possession. But he indulged vices that hinted at feelings of insecurity. He affected the style and manners of a wealthy man, but he was born to a hard-up Methodist minister father and a sensitive, hardworking mother who wrote poetry, and he spent much of his youth on the family's East Texas farm he recalled as a "subsistence operation."

He was considered aloof and supercilious by some of his colleagues and the press. But to those who knew him well, he was genteel, a generous and caring man. He had strong convictions and was a tough partisan who raced to the guns when Republicans and Democrats were brawling. He counted loyalty among the higher virtues and spared none of it to his party. But he admired those who took their office and their politics seriously, no matter their party, and took pride in working with Democrats who shared his conviction that their highest loyalty was to the nation's defense. His critics claimed he never met a weapons system he didn't like and that he was too beholden to defense contractors. But he was the only senator of my acquaintance to have voted against a weapons system built in his own state.

He was proud, deservedly so, of his political successes. He won his Senate seat in a special election to replace the Senate's majority leader, Lyndon Johnson, who had just been sworn in as vice president. He was the first Republican to win statewide office in Texas, or in any state of the Confederacy, since Reconstruction. He was a skillful politician. But his proudest accomplishment, the distinction he cherished the most, was his World War II combat service in the Pacific as a seventeen-year-old enlisted man on a navy gunboat and his subsequent four decades as a petty officer in the reserves. I never saw him happier than when, shortly before I left the liaison job, the navy promoted him to chief.

He was for many years the most senior Republican on the Armed Services Committee, and after 1980, when Republicans took control of the Senate, he became the committee's chairman. He and Scoop Jackson had worked together for many years in support of a strong defense and in opposition to foreign and defense policies by both Republican and Democratic administrations that they believed lacked the strength of their convictions. They were a formidable pair, the nation's two leading hawks. No president would cross them without trepidation. When Ronald Reagan was elected president, plans that Tower and Jackson had labored on for years served as the blueprint for the Reagan defense buildup. And as chairman, Tower skillfully resisted attempts to scale down the ambitious increases in defense spending that would, sooner than anyone imagined, help hasten the Soviets into bankruptcy and persuade Mikhail Gorbachev of the futility of trying to keep up.

Tower knew my father well, and he knew of my grandfather. He respected my service in Vietnam. He was also, of course, a loyal navy man, and whenever he traveled abroad officially, he would request that I serve as his escort. I traveled quite a lot with him, perhaps on as many as twenty trips, all over the world. My first trip was to Munich, to an annual NATO conference Tower had helped organize for years. (After Tower retired from the Senate, Bill Cohen led subsequent delegations to the conference, and since 1996, when Cohen retired, I have had the job.) From that trip through the duration of my service in the liaison office, Tower never traveled with any other escort.

On a trip to the Middle East in 1979, Tower made a stop in Oman, where he was on close terms with the country's ruler, Sultan Qaboos. Every year the sultan would move his royal household to the middle of the Omani desert, where he apparently sought respite from the burdens of the crown. He invited Tower to join him there. We flew to Muscat, Oman's capital, and were escorted by the Omani foreign minister on the luxuriously appointed royal helicopter to the sultan's desert retreat. It was quite a memorable scene: dozens of emerald green tents rustling in the wind, strikingly attractive against the barren landscape; antiaircraft guns placed along the camp's perimeter; royal guards in robes and elaborate headdresses, scimitars at their sides, all standing at attention.

We were escorted to the largest of the tents and took our assigned places on the enormous Oriental rug that covered the floor, where the entire delegation, except me, sat cross-legged, awaiting the sultan's arrival. Because of my physical disabilities, I couldn't cross my legs. I might have tried to manage some other arrangement had I known at the time that one of the most unpardonable discourtesies in the Arab world is to show the soles of one's feet to another person. Somehow that small but inviolable rule of Arab culture had escaped my attention during pre-trip briefings. When the sultan arrived and seated himself, he paused for a moment as he noticed me, sitting right across from him, my legs sticking out in front of me, the soles of my feet pointing directly at him. He said nothing but was evidently distressed by something—as were the royal guards, who were growing visibly more nervous with every second I persisted in my gross insult to the royal person. Some of them were even gripping the handles of their swords.

Tower was a man of the world. He recognized my inadvertent rudeness at the first sign of disquiet among our hosts and quickly took the initiative to defuse the situation. "Your Royal Highness, Captain McCain is a decorated veteran of the Vietnam War who served his country honorably as a prisoner of war. He was gravely injured when his plane was shot down, and because of his injuries he cannot bend his legs. Please excuse the manner in which he has seated himself. It cannot be helped."

Lucky for me the sultan was a graduate of Sandhurst Military Academy and had served in the Royal Army. Out of respect for a fellow officer, and in deference to my combat service, he gallantly overlooked the offense and nodded toward his agitated bodyguards, who had heard Tower's explanation in translation, to relax. The crisis averted, the meeting and a lavish meal proceeded without further incident. Before we left, the sultan complimented my military service and graciously accepted my own apology as if it had been such a small and understandable breach that it had escaped his attention. Tower, however, never let me forget it and loved to remind me time and again how he had once saved my life in the Omani desert.

John Tower and I became close friends. His office was right around the corner from mine, and late in the afternoon, on almost every day that the Senate was in session, his secretary would call me to say, "The senator would like to see you." I would drop whatever I was doing and join him in his office for a drink. It was unusual for a liaison officer to be on such close personal terms with a member of the Senate, especially such an influential member. Friendships made in Washington are, in too many instances, reserved for one's professional and social peers, especially those who with their wealth or influence are in a position to help you advance your career. For all his reputation as a Washington grandee, Tower was not really that way. He loved good company, and that he thought me such is something I'm proud of.

I developed a few other close relationships with senators, but none quite like my friendship with Tower. One observer thought it had a familial quality. He was extremely generous to me, but we were not that intimate. Tower had three lovely daughters, whom I knew well, and he loved them dearly. His regard for me or for anyone else never approached his love for his girls.

He was not nearly as fortunate in marriage as he was in fatherhood. His first wife, Lou, a kind, loving person, remained a warm and caring friend to him for the rest of his life. His second marriage in 1977 to Lilla Burt Cummings was a disaster. She was a difficult woman, to say the least. "Loathsome" was an adjective commonly used to describe her. She was cruel to extremes to just about anyone she encountered, particularly to Tower's staff, to his family, and to him. I dreaded every occasion I was in her presence, especially when I was required to suffer her distemper for long periods on those occasions when she accompanied her husband on his travels. What possessed him to marry her is a mystery to me. They divorced ten years after they married. But Lilla, along with a few people whose enmity he had incurred and who possessed a rather accommodating view of Washington hypocrisy, would prove to be John Tower's undoing. But that is the subject of another chapter.

I have never had cause in my life to curse bad luck. What misfortune I have encountered has been insignificant in the balance of my life's experiences. My failures in my first marriage would have left me no cause to complain should I have proven as unlucky in my second marriage as John Tower had been. But I had better luck than John, whether I deserved it or not.

I met Cindy Hensley in Honolulu in the winter of 1979. I was escorting a Senate delegation to China that had stopped in Hawaii for briefings by the Pacific Command. I spotted her at a cocktail reception hosted by the CINC and immediately made my way over to her and introduced myself. She was lovely, intelligent, and charming, seventeen years my junior, but poised and confident. I monopolized her attention the entire time, taking care to prevent anyone else from intruding on our conversation. When it came time to leave the party, I persuaded her to join me for drinks at the Royal Hawaiian Hotel. By the evening's end, I was in love.

Cindy was vacationing in Hawaii with her parents, Jim and Smitty

Hensley. They lived in Arizona, where Jim owned one of the largest Budweiser distributorships in the country, and Cindy taught children with learning disabilities. Although they were a wealthy family, Cindy had no airs, and her loving, generous nature won her many admirers far more impressive than the anxious, older suitor with an uncertain future who couldn't get her out of his mind. No doubt she had inherited her good qualities from her parents, who were not born to wealth and were as down-to-earth and decent as any couple I have ever known. They were more welcoming of my attentions to their daughter than I had a right to expect. I doubt I could match their graciousness should I find one of my daughters attracted to someone who reminded me of me.

In the following months, I spent as much time with Cindy in Washington and Arizona as our jobs would allow. I was separated from Carol, but our divorce would not become final until February of 1980. Cindy and I were married the following May, and I have wondered over my good fortune ever since. She has compounded my blessings many times over, with the birth of our first daughter, Meghan, our two sons, Jack and Jimmy, and the adoption of our daughter Bridget. She has enriched my life beyond measure, making my successes and my defeats of much less consequence than my happiness at home.

We lived in a house in Alexandria, Virginia, during my last year in the navy. I had decided on a second career in politics, but before I met Cindy I had thought I would return to Florida, where I had lived on and off throughout my naval career and still had many friends, and pursue my political ambitions there. Cindy does not dislike Florida or Washington, but she cannot bear to be separated for any length of time from Arizona. Nor would she ever consider raising children anywhere else. I can't blame her, for Arizona is among the finest of Cindy's many gifts to me.

Once I had decided to enter politics, I sought advice from the three members of the Senate to whom I was closest, Gary Hart and Bill Cohen, who had served as groomsmen at my wedding, and John Tower. Gary and Bill patiently explained the difficulties entailed in what must have seemed to them a whimsical choice in second careers for someone who had no ex-

perience in running for office or, for that matter, any experience living in
the state I had decided I was suited to represent in Congress. Finding a
political base in a community usually takes years of work, building recognition and respect for your civic-mindedness, associating with a local political party and volunteering your time to its causes, and running for local
and state offices. I had neither the time nor the patience to follow a ten-
year plan for election to Congress. I was in my forties and in a hurry, ambitious for the kind of influence I had seen wielded by the country's most
accomplished politicians and worried that my chances were diminishing
by the day.

Gary and Bill knew how difficult a climb it would be for any novice,
all the more so for someone who didn't know a soul outside his family in
the place he would begin. Nevertheless, they gave me sound advice about
how I should proceed, how to build a public profile and organize grassroots support. Bill generously helped me raise money for a campaign and
even persuaded his political consultant to talk to me and consider taking
me on as a client. I had once persuaded Bill to take a seat on the Armed
Services Committee, and his work on that committee would eventually
lead him to the position of secretary of defense in the Clinton administration. He always credited me with helping him toward his most important government service, but my assistance to him was hardly comparable
to the invaluable help he gave me when my prospects for even minor political success were doubtful at best.

No one, however, was more generous to me than John Tower. He had
pretty much built the Republican Party in Texas and was a hugely important force in the rise of the Republican Party in the Southwest. He had a
rule that he would never make an endorsement in a competitive Republican primary. He broke that rule for me. He endorsed me over three
more experienced candidates. He flew all over the state of Texas with me,
raising money for my campaign. His professional fund-raiser, Brad
O'Leary, was dumbfounded that Tower would go to so much trouble for
a political beginner who might prove to be nothing more than a dilettante. He persuaded Paul Fannin, an old friend from the Senate, twice
elected Arizona governor and senator, to endorse me. John Tower was a

constant source of encouragement and counsel. Whatever I asked him for, he gave without hesitation. I was deeply in his debt then, and I remain so to this day. He died tragically, well before his time, in an airplane crash with his beloved daughter Marion. I would never have the chance to fully repay him for his many kindnesses to me or to tell him how much his friendship meant to me.

Billy Mitchell. *Corbis*

CRUSADER

My grandfather knew Billy Mitchell. They were contemporaries, my grandfather born five years later than the controversial army officer and most outspoken proponent of military aviation. The navy and army were smaller then, and prominent officers in both services were all acquainted with one another, had probably drunk a round together at the Army-Navy Club once or twice.

Slew McCain came late to the world of naval aviation, but once he was there, it became the most important work of his life, and it would have been hard for him not to know the man who had dominated aviation for twenty years. Every naval officer who served between the two world wars knew who Billy Mitchell was. And most of them hated him.

In 1906, the year my grandfather received his commission, Billy Mitchell's swift ascent up the ranks of the United States Army was well under way. At eighteen, he had left college to enlist in the First Wisconsin Volunteers for service in the Spanish-American War. His father was a United States senator from Wisconsin at the time and used his influence to procure for his son an officer's commission in the Army Signal Corps. Mitchell arrived in Cuba just after the fighting had ceased but soon saw combat in another theater of the war, the Philippines, where Filipinos, unhappy with the prospect of replacing one colonial master with another, were in open rebellion against the United States. His service there revealed his budding genius at organization, and he became a favorite of Brigadier General Adolphus Greely, chief of the Signal Corps and famed Arctic explorer.

Upon his return from the Philippines, in 1901, Mitchell was promoted to first lieutenant. A son of privilege and wealth, he rejected the opportunities doubtless open to him in commerce or politics for a career in the regular army, which had just begun its transformation from a garrison force in the American West to the instrument of world power it is today.

That year, Greely sent Lieutenant Mitchell to supervise the construction of a 1,700-mile telegraph line across Alaska. It was there Mitchell first showed the singular creativity and willfulness that would become the hallmarks of his extraordinary career and would in time spark his insubordination and ruin. The extreme hardships attending the construction of a trans-Alaska telegraph line made its accomplishment heroic. That Mitchell, with little apparent concern for the formalities of securing permission, exceeded the project's authorized $5,000 budget tenfold hardly detracts from the magnificence of the achievement. It did signal that the single-minded young officer did not possess a natural reverence for authority, especially authority that lacked his genius and zeal. But if his ample self-regard was apparent to his superiors at the time, it had not made the impression on them that it eventually would. In 1903, he was promoted to captain, the youngest man in the army to hold that rank.

Four years later, he was assigned to the prestigious Army School of the Line and Staff College at Ft. Leavenworth, Kansas, graduating with distinction in 1909. The year before he arrived at Leavenworth, he had published an article in the *Cavalry Journal,* in which he predicted that "conflicts, no doubt, will be carried out in the future in the air." At the time, he was referring mainly to dirigibles as a new instrument of warfare. The Wright brothers' success at Kitty Hawk had occurred only two years earlier. But his incipient interest in aviation would soon focus his attention on heavier-than-air flying machines, and airpower would become his grand passion, inspiring in him a crusader's zeal that paid little heed to the venerated traditions of the army and navy or the sensibilities and privileges of the senior officers who revered them.

In 1912, Mitchell was appointed to the army general staff. At thirty-two, he was the youngest officer ever to receive the honor. Assigned to the intelligence office to monitor events in war-torn Europe, he paid special attention to the growing role of airplanes in the conflict. The use of airplanes in Europe's armed forces, as both defensive and offensive weapons, had advanced well beyond their status as interesting gadgets of uncertain practical value in the United States. As the first bombs from aircraft were falling on the battlefields and seas of the Great War, the United States Army and Navy possessed only half a dozen planes. Mitchell was ordered to produce a report on the aviation needs of the military. He used the opportunity to issue his first warning that advances in aviation would eventually rob the United States of the security that distance and two oceans had long provided. It also marked the real start of his career as an outspoken champion of airpower in frequent appearances before congressional committees and in innumerable and often inflammatory reports and statements to the press that would become his preferred method for advancing his cause.

His zeal and impatience, and the unorthodox methods he used to express them, were by this time gaining the attention and concern of his superiors. His fitness reports of the period suggested Mitchell was better suited for service in the field than for staff work.

He was promoted to major at the end of his tour on the general staff, and in 1916 he was sent back to the Signal Corps as deputy chief of the aviation section. The army considered him too old and of too high a rank for flight training. So Mitchell hired at his own expense an instructor in Newport News, Virginia, to give him flying lessons. On his third solo flight, he crashed his plane on landing and later wrote that the experience "taught me more than anything that ever happened to me in the air." Despite the minor setback, he became a capable pilot and soon earned his wings as a military aviator.

By the end of 1916, America's entry into the war was a foregone conclusion. Mitchell was eager to get there first, despite suffering from a heart weakened by rheumatic fever that had led his concerned doctors to recommend his retirement from the army. He was sent to France as an observer in March 1917, one month before the United States entered the war that would make Billy Mitchell a hero and the most celebrated American airman of his time.

If you survive it, war can do wonders for a professional officer's career, accelerating promotions in rank that would take many years to achieve in peacetime. By May, Mitchell was a lieutenant colonel, and two months later, he was a full colonel. A year later, he was a brigadier general. Combat promotions are often reduced at war's end, but Mitchell kept his star for all but a few months of his remaining career.

Upon his arrival in France, Mitchell sought out and soon became a disciple of the commander of Great Britain's Royal Flying Corps, General Hugh "Boom" Trenchard. Trenchard was a headstrong visionary whose regard for the airplane as an offensive weapon with far-reaching uses equaled Mitchell's enthusiasm. He encouraged Mitchell to recognize the need for a unified command of military aviation. The prospect of an air force separate from the army and navy was unthinkable to the generals and admirals who ran the United States military, but Trenchard and Mitchell believed it necessary for aviation to be developed to its fullest potential. Their shared vision included both tactical and strategic uses of airplanes, seeing well ahead of the earthbound perspective of their superiors as they dreamed of ground attacks from the sky and long-range bombing runs on industrial centers well behind enemy lines. Their stunningly prophetic grasp of what war would become in the twentieth century seems obvious only in hindsight.

By the time the first doughboys disembarked from their troopships, Billy Mitchell had already claimed the distinction of being the first American in uniform to come under fire at the front and the first American to fly over enemy lines. His hyperactivity in the weeks before and after the American Expeditionary Force arrived in France, as he campaigned tirelessly for the creation of American air units, impressed and frequently exasperated French, British, and American commanders.

Mitchell was frustrated by the incredibly slow progress of American mobilization and by what he considered conflicting, uninformed interference with his work by the general staff. (It would take a year before the first American air unit was operational.) And when Mitchell was frustrated, he let people know. The higher their rank, the more he let them know. There were widespread reports of table-pounding outbursts from Mitchell in conference with General Pershing as he inveighed against the generals who impeded him and argued for the appointment of a single air commander in Europe. No doubt his tirades tried Pershing's patience. But Pershing, who was anything but a patient man, knew the value of his brash subordinate and soon gave Mitchell command of all American air units in combat.

In September 1918, he organized and led the largest air armada of the war, commanding thousands of Allied planes in mass bombing attacks during the Battle of St. Mihiel. The battle, waged in weather conditions that until then would have kept aircraft grounded, was a complete success. Mitchell's armada pounded German infantry and prevented enemy air attacks on American infantry; and by taking a considerable toll behind the front on German supply and communication lines, it proved the efficacy of Mitchell and Trenchard's comprehensive concept of airpower. It won Mitchell both the star he wore on his shoulders and his rising star as a daring hero and brilliant prophet of airpower's indispensability to America's success at arms. Ten days later, Mitchell's star and vision reached even greater heights as he commanded another huge and hugely successful bombing force during a massive offensive in the Argonne.

Mitchell came home from war heavily decorated and publicly acclaimed. He used his experiences, his new celebrity, and his natural talent for public relations to agitate relentlessly for the creation of an air force separate from army and navy command, funded generously to meet his sweeping ambitions and accorded the distinction of America's first line of defense. That such an exalted status would turn the entire American military upside down, bring an abrupt end to its nineteenth-century order, and break the hearts of admirals and generals who had prospered in it did not deter Mitchell, but roused him to ever-greater confrontation. He was, of course, right, and he never doubted it. Never. He held the military establishment arrayed against him in contempt for their refusal to submit to his genius, and he waged a war against them and the weapons they cherished.

The battleship, the superdreadnoughts that were the pride of modern navies, were his first target.

He was the deputy chief of the army air service, but no one mistook his superior for the army's first airman. In all matters involving aviation, Mitchell was supreme. Or so the public thought, and Congress, and Mitchell. He organized a mass flight to Alaska. He conceived and directed the army air service great transcontinental race of 1919, a round-trip air derby from New York and San Francisco. He ordered army pilots to fly around the perimeter of the United States. He badgered his pilots to set records for speed and altitude. He introduced the idea of aircraft large enough to carry troops, who could then be dropped by parachute behind enemy lines. He proposed long-range bombers that could cross the Atlantic with two huge, thousand-pound bombs in their payload. These and dozens of other radical innovations were dismissed by appalled generals and admirals as the flights of fancy of an increasingly unstable upstart.

Then, in 1920, *The New York Times* reported a Mitchell speech with the terrifying headline DECLARES AMERICA HELPLESS IN AIR WAR. With characteristic impetuousness, he pressed his theme in speeches, congressional testimony, interviews, and reports to his superiors. Battleships were vulnerable to attack by air, he argued to reporters, congressmen, and the War and Navy Departments, and obsolete as guarantors of our coastal defense. It seems a self-evident observation today. But in 1920, he might as well have accused the navy of treason for the outrage he provoked. Battleships conferred on a nation great power status, and the admirals who owned them loved them with a passion reserved for no other object, inanimate or human. Had Mitchell attacked their children, he could hardly have aroused greater animosity. But their hate for their intemperate opponent had yet to reach its full enormousness.

Mitchell challenged the navy to surrender several ships taken from the German navy at war's end as well as some of its own obsolete ships for use as targets for his bombers in a test he believed would establish once and for all the dominance of airpower in all future conflicts. The navy scorned the challenge. Secretary of the Navy Josephus Daniels responded by boasting that he would stand bareheaded on any ship Mitchell attempted to bomb. But neither he nor his admirals would agree to the challenge until pressure from the press, the public, and Congress forced their acquiescence.

On July 21, 1921, in the Chesapeake Bay, Mitchell would make them pay for their hidebound arrogance and earn their undying enmity.

In my second year at the Naval Academy, I was fortunate to study under the noted naval historian E. B. Potter, who had admired and written about my grandfather's service in World War II. It was in his lectures that I first heard discussed at length the story of Billy Mitchell's extraordinary career and his enormous contributions to the field I would devote most of my navy career to, military aviation. My interest sparked by Potter's regard for the man many old admirals still loathed twenty years after his death, I borrowed from the academy's library *General Billy Mitchell* by Roger Burlingame.

The book, which I now recognize is a rather uncritical examination of Mitchell's career, opened with an artistic (and, thus, all the more compelling to me) rendering of the day when Mitchell sank a battleship to settle an argument.

By the time the German dreadnought *Ostfriesland* sailed into view of anxious observers from the War and Navy Departments, as well as hundreds of assembled dignitaries from the Harding administration, Congress, the diplomatic corps, foreign militaries, and the press, Mitchell's bombers had already sent to the bottom a German destroyer and cruiser. But now, on July 20, the skeptics felt their confidence return as the massive battleship, twenty-seven thousand tons, triple hulls, heavily armored and unsinkable, offered a magnificent rebuke to the audacious "headline hunter" who flew just above their heads in his two-seater observation plane the *Osprey*, streaming a long blue pennant behind him.

His pilots dropped five 600-pound bombs on the *Ostfriesland* before inclement weather forced an end to the first day's assault. She had been hurt, but far from fatally, and overnight had righted herself after briefly listing to starboard. But the next morning, circling low above the target before his bombers arrived, Mitchell was as self-assured as ever and looked down at the *Ostfriesland* confident that before the day was over, no one would ever see her again.

In the months of preparation before the trial, Mitchell had assembled at Langley Field, Virginia, a large armada of planes commandeered from several air bases, planned his three wave attacks, supervised his overworked pilots in frequent trial runs, and ordered the manufacture of the two-thousand-pound bombs that few believed could be carried by any aircraft in existence.

The first bombs were dropped on and near the battleship around eight-thirty that morning. By twelve-thirty she was headed for the bottom. An old admiral who had witnessed the *Ostfriesland*'s end, and with it the old order of a great nation's seapower, was reported to have leaned against the railing of the observation ship, the *Henderson,* and wept. As Billy Mitchell flew above the roiling waters that had closed over the sinking *Ostfriesland,* he cried as well and then flew low over the *Henderson,* dipped his wings in salute, and laughed.

His pilots would sink more battleships in subsequent trials two years later. But that day, Billy Mitchell became the biggest hero in America. And while the guardians of the old order quibbled over the exact implications of his success, Mitchell matter-of-factly claimed, "No surface vessel can exist wherever air forces acting from land bases are able to attack them." The navy, however, had other ideas and began planning for the aircraft carriers that would replace battleships as the pride of the fleet, conquer the Pacific in the next great conflict, and carry my grandfather and me to war.

Mitchell used his success and celebrity to demand that money wasted on battleships now be given to him so that he could build the mightiest air force in the world. He staged mock bombing runs on eastern cities and a variety of other public relations stunts to press his point home. He continued to command headlines, dazzle congressmen with virtuoso performances before their committees, and harass the general staff with his grand ambitions.

To get him out of the headlines and their sight, his superiors sent him to Hawaii to inspect the air service there. Just married for the second time, Mitchell used the trip and an extended tour of the Far East as a honeymoon with his new bride. When he returned nine months later, he sent a report to the general staff that predicted a Japanese sneak attack at Pearl Harbor and Clark Field in the Philippines. The attack on Pearl would begin at approximately 7:30 in the morning, he prophesied. Clark would be hit at 10:40 the same morning. Seventeen years later, the Japanese would attack Pearl Harbor twenty-five minutes later than Mitchell had predicted and Clark Field a little less than two hours later than he had warned. His report was ignored.

Mitchell's campaign for huge sums of money to fund his airpower plans now tended to become personal attacks on admirals, generals, congressmen, executive officials, on anyone who stood in his way. By April 1925, his superiors had had enough. They refused to reappoint him as deputy chief of the air service, reduced him in rank to colonel, and sent him into exile at Ft. Sam Houston in San Antonio, Texas, with the hope that he would no longer disrupt their work and their lives. Mitchell had other plans.

On September 1, 1925, a navy seaplane was reported lost on a flight from San Francisco to Hawaii. Two days later, the navy dirigible *Shenandoah*, on a public relations tour of midwestern state fairs, was destroyed in a violent storm over Ohio, and the captain and thirteen of his crew were killed.

In an attempt to turn the stunned public's attention to the navy's advantage, the secretary of the navy released a statement asserting that the twin disasters proved that the United States had "nothing to fear from enemy aircraft that is not on this continent." Mitchell, unsurprisingly, took a different view.

Choosing loyalty to country, in Mr. Burlingame's opinion, over loyalty to his service, and fully aware of its consequences, he responded to the secretary's attempt at misdirection. In a lengthy written statement released to the press, he charged:

"These accidents are the direct result of the incompetency, criminal negligence, and almost treasonable administration of the national defense by the Navy and War Departments."

The statement continued at length and in the same inflammatory language, clearly surpassing his typically provocative methods of making his point. His accusations and the manner in which they were made constituted rank insubordination. Mitchell would have to be court-martialed for the act, and he knew it before he did it.

The arrest and court-martial of Brigadier General Billy Mitchell was the greatest public drama since the armistice; it consumed the entire nation's attention. Most of the press turned against him, and many former allies in Congress did likewise. The flag officers who had long opposed him found their fury over his accusations tempered by their pleasure in the knowledge that he had destroyed himself in the process. But the public, by and large, remained enthralled by him.

On October 28, 1925, twelve generals and one colonel, some of whom were friends of Mitchell's, convened in Washington to try their brother officer, the highest-ranking court ever convened for such a purpose. Supplying more dramatic moments than Shakespeare could have conceived, with the public's attention riveted on nothing else, the trial lasted seven weeks before the distinguished jury retired to deliberate. Thirty minutes later, they declared him guilty of eight counts of insubordination. Only Douglas MacArthur, a boyhood friend and neighbor, claimed to have voted for acquittal.

He was suspended from rank, command, and duty with no pay for five years. President Coolidge, sensitive to the raging public debate that the court-martial and sentence had ignited, changed the verdict to permit Mitchell half pay. Mitchell refused the offer and resigned his commission effective February 1, 1926.

The court-martial of Billy Mitchell completed his legend. The public understandably viewed it as the last glorious act in a thrilling passion play. Martyrdom, whatever its cost to the martyr, immortalizes the subject's reputation. In the remaining ten years of his life, Mitchell betrayed little bitterness over what his admirers viewed as a lynching. He did not act defeated or particularly upset by the circumstances that led to his sudden retirement from active duty. He seemed to take little notice of the attacks on his character occasioned by his insubordination. Attacks on his views did concern him, and he continued in retirement as he had for the previous twenty years, championing the cause that gave his life its most important meaning. In speeches, interviews, and books, he ceaselessly heralded the arrival of the age of aviation and constantly warned of America's vulnerability to a Japanese air attack. Pity he did not live to see the B-17s flying over Germany in World War II. And even though the carrier planes that played so great a role in the Pacific weren't a significant part of his vision, they also established the truth that airpower would dominate all future wars.

I too had thrilled at his rebellion and honored his martyrdom. I doubt Mitchell saw himself as such, but I was young when I read his story and had lately come under the full weight of military discipline. I had been called "Punk" in high school, and the Naval Academy had thus far failed to strip me of the attributes for which I had earned the sobriquet. But I had begun to worry that they would be my undoing and that I hadn't a good enough reason to justify my behavior or losing the privilege of service I feared would be its cost.

A rebel without a cause is just a punk. Whatever you're called—rebel, unorthodox, nonconformist, radical—it's all self-indulgence without a good cause to give your life meaning. I saw in Mitchell, in his willingness to throw himself on a bonfire of enmity for the sake of his cause, a glorious rebel who gave hope to the silliest of imitators, those of us for whom rebellion was a compulsion but who were looking to join their personality to a great purpose. Mitchell, I reasoned, had shown that a good cause could, if not excuse, at least compensate for a man's failings, no matter how many they numbered. And whatever pains his manner caused, they were fine, even admirable, if they served something greater than his vanity.

Poster from my first campaign for the
U.S. House of Representatives in 1982. *John McCain*

THREE

RUNNING

They call New Mexico the "Land of Enchantment," but Arizona surely merits such praise. Barry Goldwater lived on a mountain in a particularly beautiful part of Phoenix and had visited and photographed many times the most sublime natural features of Arizona's breathtaking landscape. Near the end of his life, he tried to describe to an interviewer his affection for the place he felt so privileged to call home. He began to identify some of the state's most beloved wonders but quickly became emotional. "Arizona is 113,400 square miles of heaven that God cut out," he proclaimed, and then, fighting back tears, he managed only to exclaim, "I love it so much."

Arizona is a prosperous, rapidly growing place with opportunities for anyone with initiative. But whatever brings us to Arizona, for most it is the thrill of living amid splendor beyond the reach of human beings to create that keeps us here.

All my life I had been rootless, part of a tradition that compensated me in other ways for the hometown it denied me. But without a connection to one place, one safe harbor where I could rest without care, I had lived my life on the move, never entirely at ease. And if most lives are episodic, mine has been a series of short stories. They shared a theme, but the landscape and characters passed too rapidly to form the attachments of common love that quicken your heart when age and infirmity have slowed your walk and deprived your restlessness of its familiar expressions.

My ambition brought me to Arizona. And my ambition keeps me away for more than half my time. But Arizona has given me a home, and in the more than twenty years that have passed since I moved here, it has worked its magic on me, enchanted me, made me feel a part of it. Cindy and I have a home in the northern part of the state, between Cottonwood and Sedona, which our family escapes to whenever we have the chance. It's on the bend of a creek, surrounded by hills, adorned with fruit orchards and roses, and shaded by tall cottonwoods and sycamores. I have never in my life loved one place more. And when my public life ends and my ambitions are at rest, I will be glad of its company as I realize the happiness of belonging to something smaller than a nation, smaller but no less a beautiful dream than were the aspirations of my peripatetic youth.

I came to Arizona impatient to start a political career. I was confident I would have to wait only a short while for my opportunity. The 1980 census would establish enough population growth in Arizona to require the addition of a new congressional district, and I was determined to represent it. Until then, I would work as an executive in my father-in-law's company. Jim Hensley was a kind, good man, who was deservedly proud of the successful business he had devoted years of hard work to build. He generously allowed me to handle most of Hensley Company's public relations, as well as a substantial part of its advertising. The upwardly mobile boss's son-in-law, who obviously lacks the experience and training typically required for the job he holds in a privately owned company, is a popularly derided stereotype. I certainly fit the bill, but I tried hard to justify Jim's generosity and confidence in me. He was a shrewd enough businessman, however, not to take too great a risk on someone whose tenure would be short and whose attention to business was distracted by his planning for another career. He made sure I worked with an assistant, John Vanderveer, who was experienced and talented, so that my brief employment at Hensley Company would be a happy experience for all concerned.

My plans hit their first snag when Arizona's legislature created the new district in the southern part of the state, much too far from Phoenix for me to risk further justifying the charge of carpetbagging I expected to face wherever I ran by suddenly relocating to Tucson. The other four districts were then represented by well-entrenched, very respected congressmen, including Morris Udall in the second district and John Rhodes, the Republican leader in the House of Representatives, in the first district.

So it appeared I was, for the time being, at least, out of luck. But I had learned long ago that luck changes quickly, and you have to be prepared to seize your opportunity when it does. I had already been talking to the political consultant Jay Smith, to whom Bill Cohen had introduced me. With his and others' help, I had been making the rounds of local political and media figures and become active in the local Republican Party. I had hurriedly begun studying up on local issues, raising my public profile in Phoenix by giving speeches on patriotism and public service to business and civic organizations, schools, and churches and writing the occasional op-ed on the same subject. I had been strongly advised not to seem too eager or opportunistic. But my natural impatience makes an affected nonchalance look a little too insincere even for politics, and I hurried along, plainly eager and opportunistic.

Then, in December of 1981, my luck changed. John Rhodes, a member of Congress for thirty years, declared his intention to retire. He had earlier announced that he would not seek reelection as minority leader in the wake of rumors that Congressman Bob Michel would challenge him for the office, and that announcement had sparked speculation that Rhodes might give up his seat. But a year had passed since he had declared his intention to relinquish the leadership without a subsequent declaration that he intended to retire from Congress, and most people had begun to assume he would run for another term.

Word leaked out about John Rhodes's decision a day or two before his announcement. By the time he made it official, Cindy had found and signed a contract on a house in the newly vacant congressional district. Not long after, I announced the formation of an exploratory committee to determine whether I should seek to represent the good people of the first district. Such devices are usually a fiction, intended to show a prospective candidate's sober humility as he thoughtfully weighs the public's interests above his own while managing to avoid some of the legal restrictions and enhanced scrutiny imposed on declared candidates. I was going to run, and no one and nothing was going to persuade me otherwise.

Thanks to my prisoner of war experience, I had, as they say in politics, a good first story to sell. And with my connections to national political figures, including the Reagans, the money I believed I could raise, much of which Cindy and I would lend the campaign, and an increasing number of new friends in my adopted hometown willing to get involved, I knew I had a pretty good shot at it.   .

The first district is overwhelmingly Republican, so the only real race was in the primary. Whoever won the primary was certain to be elected in November. In truth, I don't think I ever really doubted I would win. I worried a hell of a lot and strained constantly to think of ways to better my odds, but I can't say there was ever a moment I thought I would lose. I had three opponents, all longtime residents of the district, all with more experience in local politics than I had. But I believed I would have enough resources and local and national support to compensate for their advantages. And I knew I could outwork them.

Cindy, God bless her, was game and threw herself into the campaign with as much enthusiasm as I possessed. She had married a navy captain, not a politician. My retirement from the navy meant that she would not have to endure the nomadic lifestyle of a navy wife and could reside in the place she had grown up in and always loved. But a political career, while not carrying the risks of death or injury that are the constant concern of military families, imposes its own severe strains on a family. Neither she nor I really appreciated how demanding my new career would be and how seriously it would affect our home life. We didn't have children when I decided to run for office, but we were planning to start a family. Like the navy, politics would separate me by time and distance from those I love most, and my wife would bear the disproportionate share of the responsibility for raising our children.

She has raised our four children beautifully. They have never wanted for love or comfort. I was well into middle age when I began my second family, but time and experience have made me a little wiser. I can think of few sweeter blessings for a man of my years than to have young children at home. But my work has deprived me of their company too often. And when that work has had no greater purpose than satisfying my personal ambitions, it has not been worth the cost.

I have craved distinction in my life. I have wanted renown and influence for their own sake. That is, of course, the great temptation of public life. Few are immune to its appeal. The desire to be somebody has driven many a political career much further than the intention to do something. I have never been able to conquer it permanently, but I have tried—more now than when I first hurried along the streets of Maricopa County hustling votes.

I was in a hurry. The white tornado, my friends and supporters called me. I was also called a dark horse, presumptuous, inexperienced, too ambitious, too conservative, not conservative enough, a candidate whose only issue was himself, and a carpetbagger. But nobody was going to call me lazy. I knocked on thousands of doors in the furnace heat of a desert summer, hailing audiences assembled for other purposes, imposing on new acquaintances, courting the local press, begging for money, making a nuisance of myself to anyone who would give me a few minutes—all to make enough new friends and admirers that they would grant me the distinction of representing them in Congress.

The first district is a different place today from when I first ran for office. It was changing then, a magnet (as is most of the state) for people from other places attracted to its climate, beauty, and opportunities and who bring with them diverse political views. But in 1982, it was still a place of well-established political practices and players, especially in parts of the East Valley of Maricopa County that lay within the district's boundaries. The other Republican candidates were established names on the local political scene. Jim Mack was a respected state senator who represented Tempe. Donna Carlson West was a state representative from Mesa who was expected to win most of the women's vote there. Ray Russell was a well-known Republican activist in the East Valley and popular with the large, influential Mormon community there. I would have to concentrate on swing areas, places that attracted other new arrivals to the state—Scottsdale, the east side of Phoenix, parts of Tempe, and South Phoenix, which was predominantly Democratic.

Of all those places, Scottsdale was the most important, the swing district that very likely would decide my fate one way or another. I caught a big break when I went hat in hand to see Scottsdale's mayor, the late Herb Drinkwater.

Herb had moved to Arizona from upstate New York when he was seven years old and sick with asthma and a rheumatic heart. Ever after, he credited Arizona with saving his life. He wore a big Stetson and boots, liked to wander around town on horseback, and was more accessible to his constituents and the press than any politician I've ever known. Every politician has detractors and enemies. God knows I've never lacked them. But Herb had none that I knew of. In one poll, 96 percent of those surveyed approved of him. Mother Teresa might have had numbers like that, but only fictional politicians would ever dream of claiming them. Herb could only worry about what he had done to disappoint the other 4 percent. He was once reelected with 87 percent of the vote. When I called to congratulate him, he cut me off and asked, "John, why do you think that thirteen percent voted against me?" He sounded genuinely pained.

I gave Herb my pitch, begged him to consider endorsing me, and fully expected him to politely defer a commitment until sometime later, when I would read in the newspaper that he had endorsed one of my better-known opponents. Instead, the moment I finished my appeal, he looked at me, smiled, and said, "All right, I'll endorse you. You're a good man." Herb didn't anguish much about political decisions, and when someone asked him for help, he liked to give an answer right away, yes or no. I was stunned, stunned and elated. All the more so when Herb quickly convinced every member of the Scottsdale City Council to follow his lead and give the newcomer a real shot at being their congressman.

I can't think of a single Arizonan outside the confines of my own house who was more instrumental in my election to Congress. More than that, Herb remained my biggest supporter and one of my dearest friends for the rest of his life.

Shortly after I was elected to Congress, Herb let me know how he expected me to represent the people of the first district. I accompanied him to a Scottsdale hotel where a trade association was holding its national convention. I spoke first, and affecting a formal style that I thought appropriate to the office I had just attained, I gave brief, perfunctory, and none too memorable welcoming remarks. Content that I had satisfied my public responsibility to people who were, after all, not my constituents, I sat down to wait for Herb to finish his remarks so I could move on to my next appointment.

Herb looked at his audience and saw not tourists, but potential neighbors, and he began a conversation with them, a lengthy conversation. And the way he talked to them made every single one of them believe that Herb was absolutely delighted to meet them. He made them all feel that their visit had just made his day. He generously thanked them for coming and for having the good sense to choose "the finest city in America" as the site of their national convention. He went on at length, as Herb often did, about Scottsdale's many virtues. He promised them that Scottsdale would show them a great time and that they would all be treated with elaborate courtesy during their short stay; but in the unlikely event that they encountered any difficulty, Herb gave them his home telephone number and the assurance that he would handle the matter personally.

I left the convention with a much broader sense of my job.

I had occasion many years later to recall that early lesson Herb taught me. But I'm sorry to say that it was an occasion when I neglected to heed it. I took my children to an Arizona Coyotes hockey game one evening. It was a close game, and I was very much wrapped up in the action when one of my kids announced he needed to use the bathroom. As I hurried him along, anxious that I would miss a critical play, a constituent chose that moment to stop me and explain how wrong I was for supporting a certain piece of legislation that he believed posed a threat to the health of his profession. I reacted impatiently to his criticism and told him, unkindly, that I didn't appreciate his importuning me when I was obviously busy with my children, an abrupt response that he understandably found offensive.

Herb would have been disappointed in me. He would have handled the situation differently. He always gave his constituents whatever amount of his time they required, whenever they required it. One of Herb's constituents had once called him at two o'clock in the morning to ask for some information. Herb heard him out without complaint and told him he would get back to him with the answer within twenty-four hours. And he did, calling the guy back at two o'clock the next morning, waking his surprised constituent with the words "I knew you'd be up."

Had Herb been in my place at that hockey game, he would have listened patiently to his constituent's complaint and asked him politely to wait for a response until he returned from the rest room. Then, at the moment when it looked as if the Coyotes were going to score a goal, Herb would have dropped down into the seat next to the guy and begun to explain in great detail the finer points of the legislation in question. He was an ideal politician who put the rest of us to shame.

He died of cancer in December of 1997. He had beaten the disease once before, but the symptoms recurred while he was summering on an island in the St. Lawrence Seaway. It was an old family property he returned to every summer, the one other place on earth he loved as much as Scottsdale. When he told his loving wife, Jackie, that he thought his cancer had returned, she urged him to leave immediately for the Mayo Clinic in Scottsdale to seek treatment. He shook his head and said, "No. We'll stay here for one more summer."

When he came back in September, he fought the disease with his customary determination, sought and endured various experimental treatments, never complaining. Musing about the statistical probabilities of the disease, he observed, "A certain number of people have to get cancer. I got it, so maybe it means my wife and kids won't." To friends and neighbors, he was hopeful to the end but incredibly gracious and accepting of the likelihood that his luck would run out. When I went to see him for the last time a few weeks before his death, he was very frail, and it was clear to me that the end was near. But he managed to get out of bed and take me to see his next-door neighbors, whom I had not previously met. "You got to get to know these people, John. They can really help you."

His death hurt me as much as if he had been a close relative. I loved the guy. When I decided to run for president and had to worry that I might face a competitive primary in my own state, with too little money to spend on advertising in the place where I was best known, with an incumbent Republican governor who had endorsed my incredibly well-financed opponent, and with the *Arizona Republic,* the state's leading newspaper, intent on proving that I was intemperate, ungrateful, imperious, selfish, occasionally corrupt, indifferent to the people who had elected me, and probably a murderer, all I could think was, If Herb were alive, I'd beat 'em all in a walk.

I had made other important friends who were instrumental in my election. Darrow "Duke" Tully was the publisher of the *Republic* and its sister publication, the *Phoenix Gazette*. He too was larger than life, larger than reality, as it turned out. Cindy and I had become friends with a columnist at the *Republic,* Pat Murphy, and his wife, Betty. Murphy introduced me to Tully. He was one of the most powerful men in Arizona, whose favor Arizona politicians of both parties, of small and great stature, assiduously courted. An endorsement by the *Republic* would shine a spotlight on my dark horse candidacy and help allay voters' concerns about my political inexperience and brief tenure in the state.

Murphy had invited me to write an article on patriotism. Tully had read and liked it, and was, I suppose, predisposed to like me. We hit it off right away, making plans to go out to dinner with our wives the next week and almost instantly becoming fast friends. I needed his help, of course, and certainly that was motive enough to cultivate his friendship. But I liked him, too. A lot. He was an impressive man, confident, accomplished, gregarious. He was full of himself and headstrong, but in a way that made him seem lively and daring. He was also a combat ace, a decorated air force pilot in the Korean and Vietnam Wars, and our common experiences cemented our friendship. He loved to tell war stories, which a lot of veterans don't. But I didn't mind hearing them and shared a few of mine with him. He spoke with authority about his exploits, using the vernacular of the profession and the studied nonchalance that every flier affects when describing dangerous experiences he has survived. We try to talk like athletes when they recall famous moments from their careers that had thrilled their fans, dryly and to the point. The accomplishment speaks for itself, and telling it simply, without a lot of adjectives, seems to impress the listener, who has already imagined the terror and thrill of the thing. Once or twice, Duke seemed to exceed the normal reserve veterans show in such discussions. But I never doubted he had earned the acclaim he accepted with pleasure.

He ran the paper with an iron hand, and this endeared him little to the newsroom. Many of his reporters and editors thought him a bit of a bully. And when he fell, they seemed happy to help push.

The *Republic* endorsed me, and my prospects in the crowded primary got a whole lot brighter. I owe Duke for that. I think of him often, and not just of his unfortunate last days in Arizona. He was good company, and I miss him.

Several years after we first became acquainted, as I was preparing to run for the Senate, a local sheriff whom the *Republic* had recently given a hard time to revealed that Duke Tully had never served in Korea and Vietnam, had never been in the air force at all. He had made the whole thing up. I've known and heard of many people whose résumé padding eventually becomes an entirely invented life. Often they are very accomplished people who don't need to fabricate other accomplishments to enjoy the respect of their community. But self-respect is more demanding.

In some people's past, there are experiences that have made self-respect a more elusive attainment than it is for most of us. In Duke's past was a brother who had died while serving as a marine aviator in World War II, and a father whose grief over the loss led him to suicide. I guess, through no fault of his own, Duke must have felt that no matter what he achieved in his life, no matter the public acclaim he enjoyed, he could never hope to be worthy of that terrible measure of paternal affection that his fallen brother had claimed. I don't pretend to be a psychiatrist, but the diagnosis seems pretty obvious.

To say I was surprised by the discovery is an understatement. At first, I felt a slight resentment at having been deceived. Battlefield honors are hard earned, and veterans don't appreciate seeing people dine out on them for free. But I felt so sorry for the man that my resentment evaporated almost immediately. The story had first run, as I recall, in an alternative weekly, the kind of paper that lives for career-destroying scoops of a local big shot's bad behavior, even better when the big shot happens to be the biggest shot in the establishment press. When the management and editors of the *Republic* learned of it, they hurriedly met with Tully and decided that he would resign immediately. The next day the *Republic* headline read PUBLISHER TULLY QUITS; MADE UP WAR RECORD.

In an instant, Duke went from a man to be reckoned with to an object of almost universal ridicule, a fate more tragic than one I could endure. There was no escaping it, but I can't help feeling a little grieved at the aspect of human nature that takes such delight in the mistakes and misfortune of others whose prominence might have been publicly respected but privately resented. I thought the *Republic* was a little gleeful in its coverage of his downfall. The paper was obliged to report it, of course. But it seemed to go on for days, long after the story was known in all its details by anyone who read newspapers or watched television.

In one of its numerous takes on the subject, the *Republic* ran a story that puzzled over my inability to spot Duke's deception, given our close relationship. TULLY'S LIES RANG TRUE TO COMBAT FLIER McCAIN, ran the headline. Well, they also rang true to the reporters and editors of the *Republic*, people whose job it is to distinguish truth from falsehood. That story marked the first, but sadly not the last, episode in what can be fairly characterized as my antagonistic relationship with Arizona's leading newspaper.

One day I would give the *Republic* and just about every other newspaper in the country more than sufficient cause to shoot at me, and I would find myself in a four-alarm fire of a political crisis, in some ways the greatest crisis of my life. But that was a few years off from the day in 1981 when I spoke at a Navy League dinner in Phoenix, where a former naval aviator in World War II, who was one of the largest home builders in the state, listened attentively. When I finished my remarks, Charles Keating approached me, introduced himself, and said he had heard I was thinking of running for Congress. "I'll support you," he volunteered. And support me he did. Charlie Keating, his family, and his associates raised over $100,000 for my first campaign, and for each of the two that followed. That was a hell of a lot of money in those days, before political parties began to seriously exploit a loophole in campaign finance laws that allowed them to raise hundreds of thousands, even millions, of dollars from a single source.

To state the obvious, I valued his support. His role in my election was limited to the financial support he provided me. He was never involved in the planning and operation of my campaigns. But then, as today, the first question asked of a prospective candidate for Congress is, "Where are you going to get the money?" Supporters like Charlie were not easy to come by for a first-time candidate, and I made damn sure that he knew how much I appreciated his support. More important, I became friends with Charlie, his family, and many of the top executives and employees of his company, American Continental Corporation (ACC).

Charlie was a real go-getter. He had quite a reputation not only for his entrepreneurial genius, but also for his famously extravagant approach to business and life. When you visited his offices, you would have sworn the company was run by kids, very attractive kids at that, in their twenties and early thirties, there were so many of them swarming around the place. He could be an intimidating figure to his employees, but an extraordinarily generous one as well. He would pay for exotic vacations as rewards for hard work and fly secretaries off to Los Angeles, Chicago, or New York to deliver documents, putting them up for the weekend in the best hotels, with enough money to shop in the best stores and dine at the best restaurants. His employees received handsome salaries, large bonuses, and lavish expense accounts. At the drop of a hat, he would throw parties at his massive estate in Paradise Valley, using the best caterers and bands, parties that were talked about for weeks after.

His business empire was sprawling when I first met him and getting larger every day. Countless housing developments, shopping malls, and other commercial developments, elaborate and hugely expensive resort hotels, all bore the ACC logo. He was a risk taker and an eager proponent of the novel financial practices that gave the decade's business moguls their swashbuckling reputations. In 1984, he took control of a California savings and loan and made full use of the 1980s financial instrument of choice for raising huge sums of capital quickly—junk bonds. He was as close to the archetype of the high-flying eighties chief executive as anyone I had encountered, and he was a hell of a lot of fun to be around.

On several occasions, he invited Cindy and me to his beautiful vacation retreat at Cat Cay in the Bahamas, flying us there, with our infant daughter, Meghan, and her nanny, on his private jet. The place always seemed to have a huge, boisterous crowd in attendance; Charlie's children and grandchildren were always there, as were a number of other invited guests. He entertained us lavishly, as was his style. We would all crowd on his yacht, off for a day of swimming and snorkeling, and then return for another extravagant party with the best wine, food, and entertainment available. They were memorable experiences, and even though our trips there would almost lead to my ruin, I would be lying were I to deny just how much I enjoyed them and how eagerly I awaited invitations to Charlie Keating's Shangri-la.

Like Duke Tully, Keating had great respect for military people, which explained his unsolicited offer to support my political ambitions. In his case, however, the attraction was rooted in the shared experience of service. My opponents, two of them officeholders, were in a better position to help or hurt his business. I was a man of no influence in the state where Charlie was prospering. But, again, Charlie Keating was a risk taker, and I was, or so I thought at the time, very lucky to be the risk of the moment.

Lucky though I was in my success at attracting support from influential backers, I had one liability in that first campaign that was proving difficult to overcome. I had lived in Arizona for less than a year when I announced my candidacy. And although Arizona is a mecca for people intent on starting new lives, residents of such recent vintage as I were hardly ideal candidates for political office. My ambition was plainly obvious, and to some, it was presumptuous and arrogant. If not said, it was thought by many, that when I had decided to start a political career, I had looked around the country for a place where I thought the locals were gullible enough to take a chance on a novice. Worse, some critics contended that I had married Cindy because of her Arizona residency and her wealth and connections there. Neither charge is fair, and I am surprised at how angry I still become when some fool hints that such ruthlessness lay behind decisions to marry and relocate.

I married Cindy because I fell in love with her. I moved to Arizona because it was her home. I was intent on starting a political career when I moved there, but I had no idea where in Arizona or when I would begin it. I was lucky, very lucky. But as ambitious as I was then and later, I've never been a very calculating man. As a politician I am instinctive, often impulsive, and quick at recognizing and seizing opportunities. I don't torture myself over decisions. I make them as quickly as I can, quicker than the other fellow, if I can. Often my haste is a mistake, but I live with the consequences without complaint. Besides the obvious questions they raise about my character, those early allegations of coldly opportunistic personal decisions assume a strategic political genius I have never possessed.

Nevertheless, accusations of carpetbagging would have been hard to avoid even if I had lived in the district for several years instead of several months. I was well aware that many voters would be responsive to the charge, and were they to reject me, it would be because I had failed to offer them a reason to ignore it. For much of the campaign, I had failed to address that concern. Worse, I was letting the accusation get under my skin, more so with its every iteration. In truth, if you will pardon the vulgarity, I was becoming pissed off by the carpetbagger label, and my temper was getting the better of my judgment (as it often has). I felt that my family's service in the navy and my own, which had deprived me of the comforts of a hometown, entitled me to choose any place in the country to live, and no one had good cause to question my decision.

The carpetbagger question was raised in every one of the numerous joint appearances and debates I participated in. Jay Smith and my other senior campaign aides tried to help me craft a response that would finally put the matter to rest. Nothing worked. I usually responded with a brief, dryly delivered description of my itinerant childhood and my joy at finally having a home in the beautiful First Congressional District of Arizona, a formula I used to obscure the potent resentment I felt for the question's durability, a durability I ensured with the inadequacy of my answer. I needed one brief, dramatic response. Politics, like advertising, isn't communicated by elaborate gestures. You need a swift hard punch to break through the public's understandable skepticism of and indifference to a politician's self-serving claims of virtue. I didn't know I had one until I let loose my anger in a debate late in the campaign.

Over the years, my temper has become one of my most frequently discussed attributes. I have one, of course, and its exercise, usually when I am very tired, has caused me to make most of the more serious mistakes of my career. It is fair to say that my temper has now become legendary. But like most legends, it is exaggerated far beyond reality. I have used it for effect as often as I have lost it involuntarily. Also, I have in recent years managed to control it better than I ever could earlier in life. Whether the improvement is attributable to greater self-discipline or just the weariness that comes with age and experience I'll leave to others to judge. On this occasion, I was glad that I lacked a little self-control.

Hearing a questioner grill me for the thousandth time about my apparent opportunism, I snapped. "Listen, pal . . . I wish I could have had the luxury, like you, of growing up and living and spending my entire life in a nice place like the first district of Arizona, but I was doing other things. As a matter of fact, when I think about it now, the place I lived longest in my life was Hanoi."

Looking back, I think the race was effectively over right then. I had stunned the audience and finally put to rest the one nagging vulnerability that was still clouding my prospects. But I didn't know that then. I was just mad and had taken a swing. Nor was it the last time I vented my frustration in a debate. One of my opponents was on a fishing expedition into my personal life, and in a subsequent debate I wouldn't leave the stage until I had satisfied that matter as well.

He had called Carol McCain in an attempt to solicit, from what he assumed would be a bitter first wife, information about how I had ruined our marriage. Carol, an unwaveringly loyal friend, refused and called to inform me about the incident. I asked her to tell a local reporter about it, and she agreed. The *Phoenix Gazette* had already run the story, but I was still fuming about it during the debate. And I still had a hell of a head of steam from the indignation that the carpetbagger accusation had ignited, so why not put it to good use? When the debate ended, I walked over to the opponent who had attempted to mine some little nasty opposition research from my failed marriage and told him with as much steel as I'm capable of demonstrating, "If you ever try to hurt anyone in my family again, I will personally beat the shit out of you."

I went to the movies on primary day, beginning a superstition I have indulged ever since. When the results were in, I had won handily. It was my first and last truly competitive election in Arizona. Two months later, in the general election, the contest wasn't even close.

The day after I won the primary, I called John Tower first. I told him that I had won the primary, and the prospects for victory in the general election were virtually assured. I thanked him for all he had done for me. At the end of our conversation, he gave me one last piece of advice. "Always remember what my father told me, John, when I won election to the Senate. He said, 'Son, don't let your shirttail hit you in the ass. Keep running.'" I promised I would heed the advice, and it's a promise I've tried hard to keep in the twenty years that have followed.

Morris Udall. *Corbis*

FOUR

MO

In my haste and preoccupation, I have not always appreciated the ceremony and customs that ornament congressional careers. That was not the case, however, on an evening in early December in 1982, just weeks before I would be sworn in as a freshman member of the House of Representatives.

All Republicans who had won their first election to the House that year had been called to Washington in December for a week's orientation to the politics and practices of congressional service. The week concluded with a dinner given in our honor in Statuary Hall, the former House chamber in the Capitol. It was a lovely, memorable evening. Candlelight, strolling string musicians, inspiring tributes to the honor of service in the people's house, and Bob Michel, then the Republican leader in the House, offering a beautiful rendition of "God Bless America" in his rich baritone. I was, to say the least, moved. At the age of forty-six, I had returned to Washington, a city where I had lived as a boy, gone to school, ended my naval career. I had always felt outside it, a casual observer of the business that consumed the attention of most who lived there, but now I was to be a privileged resident, a member of Congress, with the opportunities to make a name for myself and a mark on history that I believed were the chief attractions of congressional office. That night I felt almost serene, a condition to which I am unaccustomed.

There were only twenty-four of us, newly elected House Republicans. In 1982, the first midterm election of Ronald Reagan's presidency, the country was in the midst of an economic recession. The Democrats had had a good election. Fifty-seven Democratic freshmen, more than twice our number, were sworn in that year. Twenty-five Republican incumbents had not been returned to office. Only one Democratic incumbent had lost reelection. Robert Shamansky, a first-term member from Ohio, had lost to my friend John Kasich.

We thought pretty highly of ourselves for having survived the country's clear preference for Democrats that year. And we were, or would prove to be, a fairly illustrious group of freshmen. Many of my fellow Republican freshmen were beginning very successful political careers. Kasich, Sherry Boehlert of New York, Nancy Johnson of Connecticut, George Gekas of Pennsylvania, and several others of our class would be reelected many times and rise to positions of considerable prominence in the House. Tom Ridge of Pennsylvania, Jock McKernan of Maine, and Don Sundquist of Tennessee would later be elected governors of their states. Connie Mack of Florida, Mike DeWine of Ohio, and I would eventually depart the House for the longer terms and, we thought, greater prestige of the Senate.

Our political attitudes were varied; our number included liberal, moderately conservative, and very conservative members. All of us, whether we thought the party's problems lay in either an insufficient or a too zealous regard for conservative principles, were determined to quickly show our independence and influence the direction of the administration and the party in Congress. But freshmen are seldom accorded by their seniors the influence they feel is their due, and most of us were subjected in our first years in Congress to a long lesson in patience and humility. Our leaders might have found our votes a little harder to control than in previous freshman classes, but that hardly moved them to take our pretensions too seriously. We were green, and politics in Washington is much too serious a business for experienced practitioners to entrust it to eager newcomers, no matter how bright and shining a group they think they are.

My career in Congress and in national politics began auspiciously. Every freshman class elects from its numbers a president, someone whom the class regards as possessing distinct leadership qualities. The honor is somewhat akin to being voted most likely to succeed. Although, in truth, almost every member feels the distinction best belongs to him or her, members choose to confer it on another either out of indifference or because they assume that it will take a while before their colleagues recognize their potential.

It is a delicate enterprise. The aspirant can't lobby his colleagues for the job, can't even announce his desire for it. It must be clear that he is qualified for the honor and would accept it with gratitude. But it falls to the candidate's friends to make his availability known to others in the class. The candidate must remain tactfully removed from the politics of it. It seems rather genteel, given how hard fought congressional leadership elections can often be. And, as is not uncommon in politics, the gentility can be a little fraudulent. I aspired to the office and was excited when Tom Ridge and John Kasich approached me to volunteer their help in securing it for me. The election would occur at the end of orientation week in December, and I probably met with Tom and John several times each day to discuss their progress. I was interested in every detail of the campaign and as involved in developing its tactics and arguments as were my two leading supporters.

Several other freshmen were also seeking the office, but thanks to Tom and John and a few others they recruited to help them whip the class on my behalf, we prevailed. I thought it was a pretty big deal and that my election as president marked me as the fastest up-and-comer in a notably up-and-coming class. Class presidents are often assumed to be future aspirants for senior party leadership positions, and considering how anonymous freshmen really are in the House of Representatives, class presidents are marginally less so. I might have garnered a little more attention in Washington than your average junior member, but my leadership career ended with that first success.

The House Republican Class of 1982 was sworn into office proud of our success in winning election in a Democratic year, and no one was prouder than its new president. But our organization and identity quickly dissipated as the new session of Congress got under way. Members of Congress will vote their interests, political philosophies, and districts, as they always have. Compared to those concerns, one's identification with colleagues who arrived in the same year is merely a coincidence of timing, and the differences among us, in personalities and interests, would be little affected by our shared early experiences, no matter how heady the moment had been.

The office of class president is an honor, but it carries with it no real responsibilities or influence. Like any other new member, I would have to gain stature and influence on my own without any particular institutional advantages. In any event, the discovery that the office of class president was little more than a title didn't disappoint me. I never intended to get on the leadership track in the House. I wasn't planning a particularly long career there. After his last and surprisingly close reelection in 1980, Barry Goldwater had announced that he would retire at the end of his term. Even before I had won that first election, I was determined to be his successor. And most of my time in the House was spent preparing for that event.

My chief preoccupation during my first days in office was landing the right committee assignment. Because of my previous career, the many military bases in Arizona, and the large number of active duty and retired military who reside there, most people assumed I would seek membership on the Armed Services Committee. And clearly my chief policy interests, those in which I had some knowledge and experience, were defense and foreign affairs. But I was all too aware that I lacked any experience in many matters of the greatest concern to my constituents—public land management, water rights, mining and timber concerns, and Native American issues, to name but a few areas where my deficiencies were evident. I would have to do something about that if my intentions to succeed the legendary Goldwater were ever to amount to anything more than laughable arrogance.

I lobbied very hard for a seat on the House Interior Committee, pleading my case repeatedly to Bob Michel; Dick Cheney, then the Republican whip in the House; Jerry Lewis of California, who was in charge of making committee assignments; and Manuel Lujan of New Mexico, the ranking Republican on the committee. Making a nuisance of myself is something that comes naturally to me, and in this instance I pestered the hell out of the leadership. They acquiesced and assigned me to the committee I was clearly desperate to get on. That was the single most fortuitous event of my career in the House of Representatives. As I hoped, my committee assignment helped me acquire an understanding of issues critical to my state, most of which fell under the committee's jurisdiction. I surely did not become the Arizona delegation's leading expert on local concerns, but I became competent enough to do my part in looking after them.

On issues affecting Native Americans, I did gain considerable knowledge and expertise. Moreover, I earned the trust of my constituents in Indian country, an accomplishment I am quite proud of. But the relationship I began during my service on the Interior Committee that I am most proud of, and most grateful for, was my friendship with the chairman of the committee, the extraordinarily decent Morris K. Udall, dean of the Arizona House delegation and the most widely respected man in Congress.

———

I loved Mo Udall. Absolutely loved him. He was a legend by the time I met him, a self-described "one-eyed Mormon Democrat from conservative Arizona," the scion of a politically prominent family of Arizona pioneers. He was a leader in the sixties and seventies of the Young Turks in the House who challenged the authority of conservative Democratic leaders and committee chairmen. An ardent environmentalist, early opponent of the Vietnam War, and committed liberal, he was also an old and very dear friend to Barry Goldwater. He was an effective partisan and an exceedingly accomplished legislator renowned for his practice of genuine bipartisanship in the pursuit of his goals. And he was stunningly candid to the press, to voters, and to himself, self-effacing and funny as hell, a man familiar with disappointment, defeat, and tragedy, who wanted very much to be president but couldn't.

For Mo, 1976 had been a spectacularly disastrous year. He had run for the Democratic presidential nomination, the first member of the House of Representatives in several generations to gamble on such a huge job promotion. Entering the contest late, and ridiculously short of funds, he lost twenty-two primaries, coming in second to Jimmy Carter in seven of them. Even though he lost those seven primaries by only a few percentage points, reporters, many of whom liked and admired him, thought he had run a pretty poor, although hugely entertaining, campaign and good-naturedly nicknamed him "Second Place Mo." It was the kind of humor Mo enjoyed and used on himself. It wasn't long before he was calling himself "ol' Second Place Mo." "Not everyone can come in first," he observed. "Even George Washington . . . married a widow." After the primaries that year, there was considerable chatter about Carter putting Mo on the ticket. In truth, Mo would have gladly accepted the honor, although as a realist and a pretty good judge of character, he assumed that the acrimony between the Udall and Carter camps that the campaign had bred made him an unlikely choice. When asked by the press if he wanted the vice presidential nomination, Mo, knowing it wasn't going to happen, responded, "I'm against vice in every form." In New York, the day before the Democratic convention opened there, Mo told a large, adoring crowd of his supporters, "The people have spoken—the bastards."

And so they had, although, as few failed presidential candidates before him had managed to do, Mo returned to Congress with a greater reputation and considerably more political influence than he had had when he began his campaign. He had built a loyal, national following, and he was determined to use his heightened stature to good public effect.

But 1976 had a few more surprises for him. He broke both his arms in a fall from a ladder, contracted viral pneumonia, suffered a burst appendix and peritonitis, and showed the first signs of the disease that eventually ended his career and his life. But he was not an easy man to keep down. He was accustomed to defeat and knew how to survive it. It took a long time for misfortune, and there was much worse to come, to destroy him.

When Mo came to Congress, conservative Democrats in safe, mostly southern districts, and older, urban liberals, impervious to the views and impatience of activist younger members, wielded most of the power. Their influence was the primary target of reformers who recognized Mo Udall as a leader. He managed to force some reform of the committee system in the mid-1960s and twice ran for leadership positions. He challenged Sam Rayburn's successor, the seventy-six-year-old John McCormack, for

Speaker in 1969, losing decisively, and Hale Boggs, the Democratic whip, for majority leader in 1971, coming closer but still losing by a substantial margin. When he returned to his office after the vote, he explained to his crestfallen aides the difference between a caucus and a cactus. "A cactus has all of its pricks on the outside."

Despite these defeats, and the enmity they incurred for Mo from some House barons, reformers were in ascendance in the House, and Mo was their increasingly respected leader. In the 1970s, especially after the Watergate scandal had excited the public's appetite for political reform, Mo and his fellow activists succeeded in transforming the House, changing many of the rules and practices that had preserved the power of the old guard, and imposing the first widespread reforms of the campaign finance system since the Truman administration, when direct contributions from labor unions had been outlawed. Among their successes, they had made committee chairmanships, which had always been awarded to the most senior Democrats on the committees, no longer a guaranteed privilege of seniority, but subject to a vote of the entire Democratic caucus by secret ballot. In 1977, the caucus elected Mo chairman of the House Interior Committee, and thus began fourteen of the most productive years of his public life. In a subsequent election to the chairmanship, he received the vote of every single House Democrat.

That was all I really knew of Mo Udall when I came to Congress in 1983, that he was chairman of the powerful (and all-important to the state of Arizona) House Interior Committee and the author of many landmark bills affecting Arizona and the nation. I was also aware that he came from a family whose prominence in my adopted state was well established before Arizona had become a state.

He was born in St. Johns, Arizona, a small town in northeastern Apache County settled by Mormons, high on a windy plateau scarred by drought and other extreme weather conditions, and many miles from a town of any size. In the 1880s, his grandfather David Udall had been instructed by the Mormon Church to lead a small group of Mormons to what was then just a way station between Ft. Apache and Sante Fe, New Mexico, and establish a community there, serving as its bishop. This he did with great courage and endurance, braving a long, dangerous sojourn, a harsh climate, barren land, the hostility of the few Mexican Americans and Indians residing there, and the anti-Mormon bigotry prevalent in the Arizona Territory.

In accord with his church's wishes, David Udall was a polygamist, eventually taking three wives and raising eighteen children. The aversion of non-Mormons to the practice, and the land disputes between the Mormons and earlier residents of the county, bred intense hostility to Udall and his followers. He was prosecuted for perjury in Prescott over his testimony in a land claim, but the harsh sentiments that engendered the suit were occasioned as much by Udall's polygamy as by his disputed testimony. He was arrested and charged in Prescott, Arizona, the territorial capital. A prominent Prescott merchant, Michael Goldwater, posted his bail, beginning a long friendship between the Udall and Goldwater families, a friendship that thrived when the grandsons of the two men, Barry and Mo, were their families' most prominent sons.

St. Johns thrived as well through the hard work and vision of Mo's grandfather and those early Mormon settlers, and the Udall family, like the Goldwaters, rose to prominence in the territory. By the end of the century, David Udall was elected to the territorial legislature, serving under Michael Goldwater, the body's president.

His son and Mo's father, Levi Udall, would reach greater prominence in his community and in Arizona politics. With a law degree from a correspondence school, Levi ran as a Democratic candidate for superior court judge and won. Sixteen years later, he was elected to the state supreme court and became a much admired pillar not just of the legal establishment, but of Arizona society in the mid–twentieth century. Mo's mother, Louise, was a much beloved figure in the state who developed, along with her husband, a special affinity and respect for Native Americans. Their two sons, Stewart and Mo, who would gain national prominence (Stewart was elected to Congress before Mo and left to become secretary of the interior in the Kennedy administration), attributed their successful careers and the good name they preserved solely to their parents' influence.

We had few experiences in common. Mo was a legend in Arizona by 1982, with deep roots in the state and the respect of almost every Arizonan, whether they shared his politics or not. If I was legendary for anything in Arizona, it was only for being an upstart. He was a practical but nonetheless devoted liberal. I was a Reagan conservative. He had tremendous influence in the Democratic majority that ran the House. I was the most junior member of the minority on his committee, a very small minority at that. Republicans had eleven fewer seats than the Democrats had on the Interior Committee.

Unlike the Senate, the House, with its 435 members, was too large for anyone to make much of a name for her- or himself quickly. There were so many of us that we never got to know most of our colleagues, much less form friendships with them. Also, the tight rules that run the place, far stricter than in the freewheeling, much smaller Senate, discouraged independent operators from flourishing. Moreover, freshman members are usually the most vulnerable incumbents and don't always survive their second election. In short, despite the euphoria I experienced upon my arrival in Congress, I was a nobody there and easy for a powerful chairman and national figure to ignore.

Mo had lost an eye in a childhood accident. The injury didn't stop him from enlisting in the army corps in World War II and learning to fly or from playing professional basketball for the Denver Nuggets. He had guts, desire, intelligence, and a capacity for hard work I've never seen the equal of. But all the intensity that these attributes normally engender in a personality was leavened by his humanity.

I flatter myself to think that our personalities had a few common qualities, but our temperaments were as distinct as our experiences. He was the gentlest of gentlemen, a partisan without harsh edges. Everyone loved him, and his staff, whom he treated with great courtesy and to whom he gave the greatest tribute, his trust, revered him. I was more of an emotional partisan, often thrilled by the sound of the guns and ready to jump into a brawl if my sense of fair play, rightly or wrongly, was offended, regardless of whether my staff thought it was a good idea or not. I made enemies as easily as I made friends. Mo had more important things on his mind. But those early days of our acquaintance occurred in an increasingly hostile partisan environment that made Mo's style seem anachronistic.

Politics was beginning to change in Washington then, returning to a state of more or less constant combat and permanent campaigns. In the

House, Republicans, especially younger Republicans, were increasingly frustrated with the lack of opportunities and perceived abuses of what then looked like a permanent Democratic majority. Those were the days when my party's Young Turks began their ascendance.

Newt Gingrich, Vin Weber, Dan Lungren, Bob Walker, and many others, with the counsel of more senior members such as Jack Kemp and Trent Lott, were fed up with the status quo and resolved to do something about it. They formed the Conservative Opportunity Society to change derisive stereotypes of conservatives as selfish, uncaring, and stern tribunes of corporate America and to wage relentless attacks on the Democratic leadership. Kemp was a kind of godfather to the group, but Jack was always a little too self-indulgent, lacked the discipline and tenacity, and, more positively, wasn't angry enough to make a good revolutionary. Newt was the man behind the movement. And he was very good at it.

They had asked me to join, and several of my freshman colleagues, including my good friend Connie Mack, had already done so, but I declined. I liked many of them, and often agreed with them, but I had reservations about some of the scorched earth tactics they were beginning to employ.

Also, I had decent relations with a number of Democrats. I liked Speaker Tip O'Neill a lot. He was a partisan, to be sure, but he was a good-natured fellow and an interesting man. He called me out of the blue very early in my first year in Congress, when he was in Phoenix for a fund-raiser, and offered me a ride to Washington in his airplane. On the long cross-country flight, he entertained me with his endless supply of anecdotes and insights about politics in Boston and Washington, about the Kennedys, Reagan, Ireland, and about more than a few of our colleagues, Democrat and Republican. Whenever I saw him on the floor, he would throw his arm around me, call me a name or tell me a joke, and laugh louder than anyone else. I enjoyed his company.

My relationships with Democrats, and my reservations about some of the more controversial tactics employed by fellow Republicans to right the injustices we suffered, did not prevent me, however, from rushing to join the fight when the opportunity presented itself. I am combative, there is little use in pretending otherwise, and never more so than when I am convinced that I am fighting for a good cause.

Democrats had grown arrogant in the long years of their majority and were often indifferent to Republican complaints of unfairness and, at other times, downright contemptuous of us. They ran roughshod over us, maintained terribly lopsided majorities on the committees, used the rules to keep us impotent, and made up new rules when the old ones weren't effective. The confidence that had become arrogance was beginning to become their political vulnerability. They were losing their sense of how the country viewed Washington, a development that their blindness to our concerns caused them to overlook. They were sowing the seeds of the revolution that would eventually lead to their downfall. Newt saw that, and he and others would make them pay.

Aggravating matters was the House Republicans' frustration with the Reagan administration. Not with the president himself, whom we all revered, but with some of his senior staff and cabinet officials, particularly the White House chief of staff, Jim Baker. Baker was an extremely capable chief of staff, very effective, and as smooth an operator as I've ever found in Washington. I respected and admired him. But it was apparent that the White House shared the general sense in town that House Republicans were irrelevant. Time is a precious commodity to an administration involved in as many fights as was Ronald Reagan's. Too precious, apparently, to waste much of it on people who were expected to vote as their leadership instructed, while the administration's senior officials worked more important precincts, courting boll weevil Democrats and tending to the needs of lordly Republican senators who were then in the majority on the other side of the Capitol. Rightly or wrongly, most Republicans viewed Baker as the leading architect of the administration's policy of benign neglect toward us, resented the hell out of it, and let their resentment fuel their aggressive tactics against the Democrats.

Things got increasingly worse, particularly in my second term. In 1984, a Republican, Rick McIntyre, won election, albeit narrowly, to Congress from the eighth district of Indiana. The outcome was disputed by the Democratic candidate, Frank McCloskey. On May 1, 1985, Democrats voted to seat McCloskey, an act that outraged even the most moderate, long-serving Republicans, those most accustomed to life in the minority and who had the most friends in the majority. The House seemed to explode; Newt and the other rebels were shouting charges of corruption, theft, and tyranny. But everyone got into the act. Even physical threats were exchanged that day. After the vote, the entire Republican membership stormed out of the chamber. I don't think partisan politics has ever really settled down since. We are living in the era of confrontation, bitterness, and far fewer cross-party friendships that began in earnest on that day.

The issues of the day were occasioning greater hostility as well. Policy differences were becoming personalized to an extent that hadn't been seen in some time. Reaganomics, the U.S. role in Central America, relationships with the Soviets, the nuclear freeze movement, defense spending increases, all were disputed between the parties with greater and greater vitriol. I joined in often enough and contributed my share to the era's excesses.

Not long after the vote on the disputed Indiana election, I found myself in a physical confrontation just off the House floor with Democrat Marty Russo of Illinois. Most Republicans believed that the Democrats were frequently short-counting Republicans when we requested roll call votes. As I was leaving the floor after one such incident, I encountered Jim Wright, then the majority leader, verbally abusing our leader, Bob Michel, a man with the mildest of temperaments. Michel had complained about the suspected short counting, and Wright had taken offense at the accusation. I jumped right into their argument, telling Wright to back off, only in words considerably stronger than that. Marty, who was close to Wright, heard me, rushed to me, and grabbed me by the throat, and we exchanged profanities as well as a few shoves, before I suggested that we take it outside to settle it. It was hardly seemly conduct for two adults, even less so for two members of Congress. Marty, to his credit, ignored my suggestion, and we both departed to our respective offices. He called soon after our disagreement and apologized for his action, and I apologized for mine. We have been on quite friendly terms ever since. But those kinds of confrontations were becoming increasingly common in those days as hard feelings grew harder. And while physical violence is still a rare event in Congress, and recent turmoil has never rivaled the violent exchanges in nineteenth-century Congresses, harsh partisanship remained the order of the day throughout the 1980s and 1990s, to the public's disgust. Congressional leaders don't often offer junior members of the other party rides on their airplane anymore, much less their friendship.

That was the temper of the time when Mo Udall offered his friendship to me. His committee also experienced the vitriol that was infecting the entire House. More than a few hard-charging partisans of both parties served on the committee, regularly exchanging insults with one another. But never Mo. Whenever things got testy in his committee's hearings, he could always be relied upon to make a joke and take a little of the sting out of somebody's tirade, occasionally mine, preventing an even more intemperate response from another member. Everyone on the committee liked and respected him. He was never arbitrary or abusive or autocratic, and I never heard a single Republican complain about the way he ran the committee. Republicans had their disagreements with some of the chairman's policy goals, but none of us could ever fault his fairness or his unfailing courtesy to everyone, even to those for whom courtesy could be an undeserved act of generosity.

A few years ago, one of Mo's former aides told me that on election night, Mo had told him to keep his eye on me, that I was going places. I've cherished that anecdote ever since. Maybe it partly explains why Mo bothered to reach out to me. But more likely it was just the way Mo was, decent, fair, and more interested in doing something than being someone.

Attending my first hearing as a newly minted, barely noticed member of the Interior Committee, I was surprised and pleased when the chairman asked to meet with me in his small office behind the hearing room after the hearing was adjourned. We had a pleasant, fairly lengthy conversation. We talked about a number of issues before the committee and about some of his legislative plans for the session. He advised me that Arizonans had always set aside their partisan differences to work on issues important to the state. He described how close he and Barry Goldwater had always been and offered that he hoped very much that he and I would become friends and work closely together for the benefit of the people we

served. I was bowled over and left our meeting convinced that a relationship with Mo would be the biggest break I was likely to receive at the start
of my career and, as I came more fully to understand over many years, one
of the biggest breaks of my life.

The House Interior Committee had for many years a Subcommittee
for Indian Affairs. By the time I joined the committee, it had been abolished. The last chairman of the subcommittee had apparently taken his
responsibilities too seriously, treating Native Americans with dignity and
concern and seeking to redress some of the many injustices that America,
to our shame, has accorded them. A majority of his non–Native American
constituents, however, thought he had showed their Native American
neighbors a little too much attention, attention they wrongly claimed had
come at their expense, and they voted him out of office. Members of Congress pay very close attention to one another's elections, scrutinizing the
returns and the decisive issues of the campaign for lessons on how better
to protect their own seats. In this instance, the lesson they took from their
former colleague's misfortune was to avoid, at all costs, getting mixed up
with Indian country. No one on the committee would agree to serve on
the subcommittee, much less chair it. So they abolished it.

This didn't sit well with Mo. He was not a man to shirk his responsibilities, especially his responsibilities to a people whom his parents had
taught him to admire. The committee he chaired had jurisdiction over the
government's Bureau of Indian Affairs, and he intended to discharge his
responsibilities faithfully. The next time Mo and I met for a private conversation, he asked me to form with him an ad hoc subcommittee for Native Americans. It would consist of two members, Mo for the Democrats
and me for the Republicans. He and I both went to Manny Lujan, the senior committee Republican, to ask him to appoint me to this informal
position. Manny was always very good to me. He agreed to the idea immediately, pleased, I suspect, that one of his subordinates was willing to
relieve other Republicans of the responsibility.

Mo and I held hearings on all manner of issues related to Indians, just
the two of us, trying diligently, if not always effectively, to address the
long, sorry catalog of problems and wrongs that afflicted them and made
so much of life on the reservations squalid and miserable. "Never lie to

them," Mo taught me. "They've been lied to enough." I have never regretted my involvement and remain to this day as grateful to Mo for his invitation to help him as I am for any other of his many acts of kindness to me.

In early spring of my first year in Congress, Mo invited me to accompany him to Casa Grande, Arizona, where he was going to hold a press conference to talk about issues before the committee affecting the state. The differences in our public profiles in Arizona was vast, his stature so infinitely greater than mine. He could turn out a crowd a hell of a lot bigger than any group willing to waste a Saturday listening to me. Mo spoke first and, as always, very knowledgeably. As he addressed each issue, he would preface his comments with, "Congressman McCain and I are working on . . ." Of course, we weren't. Not me, anyway, not yet. I barely understood the difference between the U.S. Forest Service and the Bureau of Land Management and couldn't tell a copper mine from a cotton farm. At the end of his virtuoso performance, he paused and said he was more interested in my thoughts on the issues. I gulped discreetly and managed to spend a few minutes faking some competence on the issues without completely embarrassing myself.

My nervousness notwithstanding, I knew that Mo's affected confidence in me was an act of kindness and offered in trust that I would eventually learn enough about the issues to warrant his faith. He was deliberately sharing his prestige with me to help me build greater credibility with my constituents, an uncommonly generous thing to do on behalf of a member of the opposite party. But Mo never saw me as an opponent or a threat or even as an uninformed, inexperienced, somewhat presumptuous politician. He had no reason to doubt my character, thought I worked hard and had potential, and might someday be able to help him accomplish important things for Arizona and the country. So he put his trust in me, and I wanted very much to convince him that he had not made a mistake.

After the press conference, he asked if rather than have our staffs drive us back to Phoenix, he and I could ride together. I drove and Mo talked. He talked about his early days in the House, about Arizona, about Barry, about stories of territorial politics that the Goldwater and Udall families had figured so prominently in, about his presidential campaign, and about the man who had beaten him. All of it was fascinating, and all of it was very useful to me as I struggled to understand my new profession and my new state. We parted that day friends, and friends we remained for the rest of his life.

He loved Arizona, always as romanced by its grandeur as he was as a boy growing up on a high, stark, and magnificent plateau. He wanted to preserve as much of its wilderness as he could, given the demands of its industries and the strains that Arizona's astonishingly fast growth imposed on its fragile, inspiring beauty. He was a genuine and genuinely effective environmentalist, if not as fashionably radical as some would have preferred him to be. He searched for ways to reconcile Arizona's and America's material needs with the emotional sustenance we derive from our proximity to nature's treasures.

Several years before I came to Congress, Mo had led the effort to preserve immense tracts of federally owned Alaskan wilderness, claiming over a hundred million acres for new national parks and forests and permanent wilderness areas. He had triumphed over the intense opposition of energy and mining interests, local developers, and Alaska's congressional delegation and had persuaded his conservationist allies to settle for legislation that protected less land than they had initially wanted. It had been a long and often bitter struggle, earning Mo, at least for a time, the enmity of a good many Alaskans who objected to an Arizonan's interference in decisions affecting the quality of their lives. As always, Mo took it all in good humor, knowing that the heat of the battle would eventually subside and appreciation for the accomplishment would correspondingly increase. Years later, on a return trip to Alaska, he joked: "Times have changed when I come up here. . . . When people wave at me they use all five fingers."

He had led a similarly contentious, if less ambitious, fight in 1964 to save a million acres of Arizona land from development. Now he had a plan to take another 2.5 million acres of Arizona land, at the time managed by the Forest Service and the Bureau of Land Management, and place it in permanent wilderness status, safe from encroachment by the busy hands of man. He was Congress's leading conservationist, and as he looked for allies, I should have seemed an unpromising prospect. My party's general hostility to federal interference in questions of intense local concern, my pro-growth, free enterprise views and the local political and financial support they earned me, and my own uncertain future in Arizona politics all argued for a very studied, cautious response when Mo asked me to join his effort. But I jumped at the chance. Though I had known him for barely a year, I trusted him completely and saw more opportunity than risk in being identified with his singular stewardship of Arizona's public lands.

I cosponsored two bills with Mo. The first, enacted in 1984, added 1 million acres to the wilderness area established in his 1964 legislation. The second, enacted four years after my election to the Senate, set aside 1.4 million acres of Arizona desert wilderness. The Arizona congressional delegation split over the bills, with several Republicans opposing it, supported by the state's development forces. But Barry Goldwater had agreed to sponsor the legislation in the Senate, which made my support of the 1984 bill a lot easier and a lot less significant.

Mo had come to see Barry and ask for his help, which Goldwater gave without hesitation. The trust between the two of them, based on a lifetime of friendship, was complete and unaffected by their political and ideological differences. I took notice of that in those early lessons of my political career and took to heart its priorities of friendship and patriotism, although its impact on my behavior was seldom as obvious as was my frequent partisan belligerence.

My contribution to the successful passage of both bills was a fraction of Mo's, but I consider them to be among my proudest achievements as a legislator. The second of them, the Arizona Desert Wilderness Act, which passed in 1990, was to be the last major legislative triumph of Mo's long, successful career.

During a meeting in his office to discuss the 1990 act, I saw Mo reach for his glasses on the coffee table in front of him, lose his balance, and fall forward, striking his head on the table. His Parkinson's disease was very advanced by then, and it was evident that it would soon force an end to the life of public service he had loved so well. When we first became friends, the disease's effect on him was barely noticeable. But by the time we began work on the second wilderness bill, his tremors and the tremendous difficulties he had when walking and speaking were almost all you did notice about Mo. By then he had to wear a microphone around his neck when chairing a committee hearing so his voice could be heard by the colleagues who were seated closest to him. His last election had been a mistake. His public life was over, even if he wouldn't accept it and surely didn't deserve it.

His deterioration had accelerated relentlessly since the day in August 1988 when he had awakened at home to find his wife, Ella, dead by her own hand. She had been his second wife. Mo's first marriage had ended in divorce many years before, although the six extraordinary children it produced would distinguish the union far more than its failure. One of those children, Mark, is now a member of Congress from Colorado. He has his father's looks and his wit. I can't look at him without being reminded of Mo, an experience I relish.

Mo's marriage to Ella lasted twenty years before depression claimed her. She had been by his side at all the great moments of his career, his defeats and his victories. I didn't know what to say to him when she died. The circumstances of her death and its effect on him were so awful, and my own experience with grief so less terrible than his, I was incapable of finding adequate words of comfort. When I first saw him after the tragedy, I mumbled a few banal condolences. He responded with a quiet, "Thank you." No other words on the subject ever passed between us.

Mo's closest friends undertook the task of bringing him back to life, none more effectively than Norma Gilbert, a former staffer on the House Interior Committee. She and Mo were married a year after Ella's death. And although his health deteriorated rapidly in the nine years of their marriage, Norma was a loyal, loving, and I'm sure comforting presence in those last years of his life.

A fall at home in 1991 forced an official end to a career that had become impossible to maintain. He broke four ribs and his shoulder in the fall. He was admitted to the Veterans Hospital in Washington, where he remained for the next seven years. He resigned from Congress on May 4, 1991, ending his thirty-year congressional career. His administrative assistant signed the resignation letter for him. After his injuries had healed,

Norma would bring him home for frequent visits. Within a year, even these brief paroles from the hospital were too much for him.

When I first began visiting him in the hospital, a short drive from my office and no inconvenience to me, Mo was always seated in a wheelchair. In those days, we could converse after a fashion. I would talk about the political stories of the day and things that were going on in Arizona, and Mo would sort of grunt his acknowledgment and amusement. Too soon, even rudimentary communication was beyond him, and I found him more and more often in bed when I arrived, no matter the hour of the day. Often enough, though, he would awaken for the visits, and I was convinced he recognized and understood me. Eventually his eyes opened only occasionally, and I just imagined that he recognized his visitor. He died in his sleep of heart failure on December 12, 1998.

When he gave the nominating speech for Mo at the 1976 Democratic convention, Archibald Cox offered the best summary of a good man's public career:

> By the count of the votes, he did come in second, but he succeeded in the larger aim, for he proved that a public figure, even in a long and heated political contest, can exemplify the best of the American spirit, that honor need not yield to ambition.

What motivates us when our ambitions begin to lose their allure as our defeats or infirmity make a mockery of them? Do we miss the futility that others see and pursue them as desperately as we did when our futures were measured in decades? Public life is hard to relinquish, and I know Mo did not let go of it willingly. I like to think that honor was the unyielding desire that drove him on. And what is honor? So often we mistake it for privilege and honorific. It's a more transcendent attainment than that. I think it's the act of making the people we love and are proud of, proud of us. Mo was proud of his parents, proud of his children, proud of the people he worked with and for and who trusted in his leadership, proud of his country, and he wanted them to be proud of him.

I'm proud of Mo, and I will always want him to be proud of me.

With Nancy and Ronald Reagan at Governor Reagan's prayer breakfast,
Sacramento, California, 1973.

FIVE

IN OPPOSITION

I came to a Congress in the middle of the "Reagan Revolution." No one had a more pronounced influence on my political convictions than Ronald Reagan. I embraced all of the core Reagan convictions: faith in the individual; skepticism of government; free trade and vigorous capitalism; anticommunism; a strong defense; robust internationalism that championed our values abroad; and most important, his eloquently stated belief in America's national greatness, his trust in our historical exceptionalism, the shining city on the hill he invoked so often, in which I heard the echoes of my great political hero Teddy Roosevelt.

I could also claim the privilege of a personal relationship with the Reagans. Or at least I once could. We had been social friends in those first years after my homecoming. I had been invited to the Reagans' home, dined with them, spent New Year holidays with them at the Annenbergs'. I enjoyed their favor, and I delighted in it.

My divorce from Carol, whom the Reagans loved, caused a change in our relationship. Nancy, for whom Carol now worked in the White House, was particularly upset with me and treated me on the few occasions we encountered each other after I came to Congress with a cool correctness that made her displeasure clear. As a very junior member of Congress, I saw the president infrequently, but when I did he continued to treat me with his typical courtesy and good humor.

The president always held a dinner for the freshmen at the start of every new Congress. I was seated at the president's table, and he could not have been nicer to me. Ronald Reagan was always an entertaining host, regaling his guests with Hollywood stories and anecdotes from his days as a sportscaster. In 1987, attending my second freshmen dinner at the White House as a newly elected senator, I was again seated at the president's table and entertained with the very same stories and jokes I had heard four years earlier, as happy to hear them repeated as he was to retell them. More than once, I was informed by mutual friends that the president was keeping an eye on me and looking for opportunities to give my career a boost. I was very flattered by the thought that the old man had a special regard for me, and this strengthened my already deep sense of loyalty to him. Nevertheless, we weren't social friends any longer. There were no more holidays at the Annenbergs' for me.

I had, of course, deserved the change in our relationship, and I knew it. And my personal and political admiration for the president and Nancy never diminished. On the contrary, I thought the Reagan presidency was the best thing that had happened to America in a long time, and I thought them both wonderful people. From her kindness and my good luck, Nancy and I recovered our friendship long ago and remain friends to this day. She asked me to speak at the president's last public appearance before Alzheimer's disease, its effects already evident in his hesitant demeanor, forced his seclusion.

What disagreements I had as a freshman congressman with the Reagan administration were always directed at the president's subordinates, never at him, and even those differences I was careful to express mildly. I never relished disagreeing publicly with the man whom my fellow POWs and I had admired long before we came home, and whose public virtues and political prospects we had often discussed in tap code and whispered conversations. To break faith with him, even when that faith contended with older, greater allegiances, was no small matter for me. And when such a moment arrived in the eighth month of my first year in Congress, I felt genuine despair.

On September 28, 1983, I asked for recognition on the House floor to speak in opposition to granting the president authority to keep U.S.

Marines deployed in Lebanon for eighteen months as part of a multinational peacekeeping force in that benighted country. It was the first controversial and unexpected act of my political career, and I've not had a harder time with an important decision since.

Lebanon was not Vietnam. The dimensions of our involvement there never approximated those of our involvement in Vietnam. Indeed, we never intended to wage war in Lebanon. We were there just to keep peace, somehow. But the purposes and planning of our intervention there were, if anything, as confused and dangerously impractical as the most glaring misjudgments of the best and the brightest during the Vietnam War. And the factional strife that tortured the country was, if anything, more complex and varied than had been experienced in the war between North and South Vietnam. There was no peace to keep in Lebanon, and the sixteen hundred marines we sent there were a fraction of the force that would have been required to make one. We never intended to wage war in Lebanon. And we never expected anyone there to wage war against us.

In the 1980s, Lebanon was a sick country on the verge of extinction. Civil war that resumed in 1975, ending a long period of religious tolerance and a flourishing economy protected by a power-sharing agreement between Lebanese Christians and Sunni Muslims, had fractured Lebanon into almost as many pieces as there were ethnic groups there. Maronite Christians, led by President Amin Gemayel, who had succeeded his assassinated brother, Bashir, pretended to rule the country as the legitimate government of Lebanon. In truth, they were but one faction in the civil war, no longer claiming a majority of the Lebanese population, diminished in legitimacy as Muslim birthrates soared and theirs declined and lacking the power to govern more than half of the capital, Beirut.

Entering Lebanon in the turmoil of civil war, Syrian forces were now occupying much of eastern Lebanon and had artillery in the Chouf Mountains overlooking Beirut. Palestinian refugees flooding into Lebanon after the Arab-Israeli wars and their expulsion from Jordan in 1971 had established a "state within a state," the principal base of operations for the Palestinian Liberation Organization (PLO), from which they waged a terrorist war and shelled settlements in the north of Israel. In June of 1982, Israel invaded Lebanon, advancing all the way to Beirut, intent on destroying the PLO, defeating Syrian forces, and recovering the sovereignty of the Gemayel government. The first two aims were possible. The third was not.

No Arab or Islamic states would rush to the Palestinians' defense, except rhetorically. Nor would any Muslim in Lebanon make much of an effort. They would fight the Israelis, but not for the Palestinians' sake. Within a month of the invasion, their Sunni allies in Lebanon asked Yassir Arafat to take his state within a state somewhere else. And in a temporary cease-fire in August 1982 brokered by the United States, Arafat did just that, departing Beirut with twelve thousand of his commandos, fleeing yet another refuge, ever further from his impossible ambition to claim Israel from the Israelis.

The largest single religious community in Lebanon, the Shiite Muslims, hated the Palestinians and were glad to be rid of them. They did not, however, intend to tolerate an Israeli occupation as a substitute for a Palestinian one. Muslim Druze in the Chouf Mountains were intent on destroying their Maronite enemies. Syrians, and their ruthless and cunning president, Hafez Assad, despised Arafat and would not fight for him. They would fight the Israelis, however, for their own pleasure. And although they were no match for them in conventional military encounters, they were not going to abandon their stake in Lebanon because their air force had been nearly destroyed by Israel, and some Syrian forces had been compelled to leave Beirut with the Palestinians, particularly when they could depend on the Soviet Union to quickly rearm them. They stayed to fight with their proxies, the Shiites in the Bekaa Valley and the Druze militia in the Chouf.

They also sent an agent to Beirut with a suitcase of explosives to blow up Lebanon's newly elected president and Israel's ally, Bashir Gemayel. The Iranians soon joined the party as well, dispatching hundreds of Revolutionary Guards to the Bekáa to infect Lebanese Shiites there with the same fanatical revolutionary zeal that had toppled the shah three years earlier.

Even these basic distinctions, Christian, Shiite, Sunni, Druze, Syrian, Palestinian, and Iranian, did not constitute the whole bloody mess that confronted Israel and the Americans and Europeans who came to keep the peace after the PLO fled. In Lebanon, there were factions within factions. Christian sects hated other Christian sects, Muslim sects hated other Muslim sects, Palestinian factions hated other Palestinian factions. And the violent atrocities that kind of intense and varied hate engenders had no bloodier theater in the world than Lebanon. Simply put, as a nation-state, Lebanon in the 1980s was implausible.

As part of the cease-fire agreement that allowed for the evacuation of Palestinian forces and their leaders, the United States had sent a small contingent of marines to safeguard remaining Palestinian refugee camps. They left two weeks later on September 10, 1982, following which the Syrians assassinated Bashir Gemayel, Israel occupied Muslim West Beirut, and the Phalangists, the Maronite sect to which the Gemayels belonged, massacred hundreds of Palestinian refugees in Sabra and Shatila.

So we came back, late that September, as part of a multinational peace-keeping force with French, British, and Italian forces. The Europeans were stationed in the heart of West Beirut. Sixteen hundred U.S. marines joined elements of the Lebanese army in and around the Beirut airport.

Things went well enough for a while. It appeared initially that Lebanese of all persuasions welcomed a respite from their many-sided, bloodthirsty civil war and the Arab-Israeli conflict that had erupted within it. It didn't last long.

The Reagan administration assessment of the mess that was Lebanon confused symptoms with causes. It saw that Lebanon had a weak central government and army. Until that was remedied, the country couldn't be unified or pacified. In reality, the situation was exactly the reverse. Lebanon was a country with only the briefest, most tenuous experience as a nation. Where there was disunity on the scale of Lebanon's, where ethnic identity politics was the only politics, there could be no strong, central government recognized as legitimate by all the governed. That was particularly so when the central government America decided to strengthen and protect would be dominated by a sect of Christians ruling over a Muslim majority. And emboldened by their new superpower patrons, their rule would not prove to be enlightened.

Peacekeeping was the expressed purpose of our presence in the Beirut cauldron. But we mistakenly decided that peacekeeping meant strengthening the Gemayel government. And, thus, the marines' duties came to include training and equipping the Lebanese army, while the United States employed its diplomacy to strengthen the Lebanese government. Its Druze and Shiite enemies had a very different interpretation of peace, and they had no intention of suffering American presumptions about how they should be governed. They allied themselves with the Syrians and resumed their civil war against the Phalangists and their new benefactor. Early in 1983, the nearly universal warm welcome that had greeted the marines became something quite different. Suddenly they were the target of Lebanese stone throwers and worse. In March, we suffered our first casualties. Five marines were injured in a grenade attack. The next month, a suicide bomber drove a truck packed with explosives into the American embassy, killing sixty-three people.

In May of 1983, the United States pressured Gemayel to sign an accord with Israel that called for the simultaneous withdrawal from Lebanon of Israeli and Syrian forces, while promising ample security concessions to Israel around its northern border. It was well-intentioned diplomacy on our part but doomed to failure. The Syrians had no intention of leaving, and their new Druze and Shiite allies were not disposed to do without their ally while the Phalangists still counted a superpower as theirs.

By September, the Israeli army, which had been stationed between Muslim forces in West Beirut and American marine positions at the airport, withdrew from Beirut and from their positions in the Chouf to positions along the Alawi River to the south. The Syrians didn't go anywhere. The Druze, Syrians, Shiites, Sunnis, and Palestinians seized the opportunity afforded by the Israeli withdrawal to launch new offensives against the Lebanese army. The Lebanese army was happy to oblige them but soon encountered greater difficulty than it had anticipated in the battle with the Druze and their allies to control the Chouf.

Our marines, suffering under restrictive rules of engagement—they could not fire unless fired upon; they were not even allowed to keep a round chambered in their weapons—were still hunkered down at the airport and clustered together, making them easy targets for more than stones and grenades. They were undermanned, underarmed, and encircled by hostile forces. American warships patrolled offshore, but they provided insufficient defense for the kind of warfare practiced in Lebanon.

On September 19, Druze, Syrian, and Palestinian forces fought the Lebanese army for control of a strategic ridge overlooking Christian East Beirut. For some foolish reason, the United States engaged in the battle. American naval forces were ordered to open up their guns on the Druze, Syrian, and Palestinian positions. We would now be seen by all the parties at war in Lebanon as a belligerent, another faction in a land so accustomed to factional fighting that it could always accommodate one more. To show the locals that we would not be so easily swallowed up by the conflict and to add more muscle to our diplomatic attempts to impose a cease-fire, the administration dispatched the battleship *New Jersey* to join our little armada off Beirut. The presence of the huge warship, with the immense firepower of its sixteen-inch guns, was intended as an impressive display of American power and resolve. But it was not impressive enough to change permanently the nature of the conflict we had foolishly entered. A cease-fire was agreed to, but it proved as temporary as our resolve.

The Reagan administration had long contended that the marines' mission in Lebanon was a peaceful one and thus did not require congressional authorization under the provisions of the War Powers Resolution. For that matter, the administration and most Republican members of Congress, including me, didn't accept the constitutionality of the War Powers Resolution. But things had changed. Our naval bombardment had made it rather plain that we were now engaged in Lebanese hostilities. Four marines had also been killed in a shelling of their positions that didn't appear to be indiscriminate. The constitutionality of the War Powers Resolution aside, the administration now had political need for support from Congress for their attempt to bring order to Lebanon by strengthening the Gemayel government.

By the time Congress roused itself to debate and vote on a resolution authorizing the marine deployment, the administration appeared to have rounded up enough support to carry the argument. My opposition to the authorization would not affect the final outcome, and I knew it. The administration had secured the support of both the Democratic and the Republican leadership, and while sizable minorities in both parties would oppose the resolution, everyone knew that it would pass by a comfortable margin. That knowledge made my decision easier. I would risk less opprobrium for my opposition. The president and his people were far too busy to worry much about the reservations of a little-known freshman congressman. What mattered most to them was getting the Democrats to acquiesce and not make a partisan issue of the president's Lebanon policy. Once they had Speaker O'Neill's support, they could afford to be gracious to a few dissenting voices in their own party.

No one pressured, threatened, or, for that matter, made much of an effort to elicit my support. So I can hardly claim my dissenting vote was a singular act of political courage. It came at little cost to my political ambitions. It actually benefited my career a little. It caught the attention of the Washington press corps, who tend to notice acts of political independence from unexpected quarters, and it distinguished me from other newcomers to national politics. My press secretary, Torie Clark, began receiving interview requests from national print and broadcast media. Because of my POW experience, I had always enjoyed a little more celebrity than is usually accorded freshmen, but not so much that my views were solicited or even taken very seriously by the national media. Now I was debating Lebanon on programs like the *MacNeil/Lehrer NewsHour* and in the pages of *The New York Times* and *The Washington Post*. I was gratified by the attention and eager for more.

As events turned out, my opposition to the president would prove to be well-founded. But by then I could take little solace in the soundness of my judgment. Whatever confidence it gave me was offset by a nagging sense of something close to shame that my opposition had had little greater effect than to profit me personally by raising my national profile.

My dissenting vote was unexpected. A freshman Republican, particularly one who had been a professional military officer, was expected to support the commander in chief in all national security matters. And I did not then, nor would I now, object lightly to any president's call to arms, especially from a president to whom I felt personally loyal. My disdain of congressional interference in the conduct of the war in Vietnam made all the stronger my natural antipathy to the notion of 535 self-styled secretaries of defense second-guessing and hamstringing the president's authority in national security matters. I would have much preferred giving the president my support, had I thought his policy had a chance in hell of being successful.

The description *quagmire* is an overused cliché since it became a synonym for the Vietnam War. It is routinely, and often ridiculously, applied to most conflicts where the application of American military force is considered. And no sooner is one conflict unquagmired by force of American arms than the term is again hastily invoked to warn against entry into another. I am always reluctant to use it. The professionalism and power of our military, stronger by a magnitude of ten than the armed forces of any other nation on earth, is something only a fool would underestimate. When it is brought to bear in great and terrible measure, it is a thing to strike terror into the hearts of anyone who opposes it. But we were not bringing it to bear in Lebanon in great and terrible measure, no matter how imposing were the guns of the mighty *New Jersey*. Thus, Lebanon was indeed a quagmire for the sixteen hundred confused, unprotected marines, hostages to the interminable hatreds of people whose patriotism would not extend from their own tribes to a nation-state that had been cobbled together by foreigners. There was no peace to keep in Lebanon, and to make one would require a force ten times larger than the one we had sent there. It didn't require much wisdom or experience to know that we were making a serious mistake. It was obvious, and grasping it was certainly not much of an insight. I knew we would fail, and I knew our failure would claim both our marines and our reputation as casualties.

Still, I tried for several weeks to suppress my fears about the approaching calamity that seemed so plainly evident. We had committed the prestige and power of the United States to a worthy, if misunderstood, task, and to withdraw before we had accomplished it would be more than an embarrassment. It would sow doubts in the minds of our friends and enemies that America had the stomach for world leadership. It would encourage all the usual delinquents in the Middle East tinderbox to start playing with matches. And, of course, it would consign Lebanon to the ash heap of history.

But I could not stop thinking that all those things were going to happen anyway, and more quickly if our policy failed than they would if we reconsidered it now. But I argued back and forth in my mind for many days, unsure what I should do. What difference would it make if I voted with the president? My opposition wouldn't persuade a majority to do likewise. And would I really want it to? Would I want to be the author of such a rebuke? Would I want to help rob the president of his authority as commander in chief? Wouldn't such an accomplishment do more long-term damage to American world leadership than the failure of our Lebanon intervention would do?

A few days before the vote was scheduled, I called an old friend, General Tom Carpenter, and asked him to come see me. Tom was a West Point graduate and a corps commander there. He had served three tours in Vietnam and had rapidly ascended to the rank of major general. He had been a classmate of mine at the National War College, where he was recognized as an outstanding student. He had studied the Vietnam War and understood what had happened there and why better than anyone I knew. He was a genuine soldier-scholar, and I admired him very much.

We talked it over for a long time. We agreed that Lebanon was not Vietnam, but that we were not likely to achieve our ends there with the means we were prepared to employ. Tom cogently compared our policy objectives to the force we had committed to their accomplishment and to the commitment of our adversaries, and found the imbalance to be badly to our disadvantage. He also judged as weak the American public's commitment to a conflict that few Americans could begin to comprehend, and believed it would not survive the inevitable setbacks we would experience. In the end, he reasoned, faced with a choice between escalating our military engagement or cutting our losses and running, the administration, one year out from an election, would cut and run. "There's no point to it, John," he concluded. "No viability at all. We're not going to keep the peace there. Not with this force, and we shouldn't take any more casualties to figure that out. You should vote against it." And so I did.

On the spot, Tom and I wrote the statement I would give on the House floor three days later, explaining my opposition. I put it in a desk drawer and left to find Bob Michel to tell him what I had decided. I gave him all my reasons for opposing the resolution in a tone that suggested they were more of an apology than an explanation. He listened patiently and seemed curious about, but not upset with, my decision. He had the votes, and one less wouldn't matter.

"You know, you make a good argument, John. I hope you're wrong."

"So do I."

The next day, I called the White House Legislative Affairs Office and told a friend there that I was going to vote against them. He made a brief attempt to talk me out of it, defining the vote as a loyalty test. But he didn't waste much time arguing, and he was too good a friend to threaten me. He didn't bother to have the president call and ask me to reconsider. They had the votes.

On September 28, the acting House Speaker recognized me to make a brief statement. I read word for word from the text Tom and I had drafted.

Mr. Speaker, it is with great reluctance that I rise in opposition to this resolution. I am well known for my respect for the President of the United States and for supporting his policies. I do not believe the President should be restricted in fulfilling his constitutionally mandated responsibility of conducting our nation's foreign policy. However, when called on to make a judgment, as I am by this legislation, I have a responsibility to my constituents to carefully evaluate the alternatives, using whatever resources are at my command.

I have agonized over this issue, not only because of my personal experiences, but more importantly because of my training in military doctrine, strategy, and tactics. . . . I have listened carefully to the explanations offered for our involvement in Lebanon. I do not find them convincing.

The fundamental question is "What is the United States' interest in Lebanon?" It is said we are there to keep the peace. I ask, what peace? It is said we are there to aid the government. I ask, what government? It is said we are there to stabilize the region. I ask, how can the U.S. presence stabilize the region?

Since 1975 we have seen a de facto partition of Lebanon. I see little possibility of this changing any time soon. I ask you, will the

Lebanese Army ever be strong enough to drive out the Syrians, let alone the PLO? If the answer to this question is no, as I believe it is, then we had better be prepared to accept a lengthy and deeper involvement in the area.

I ask my colleagues, what incentive is there for the Syrians to engage in constructive peace talks? What do they gain from a peaceful Lebanon? Do you really think naval forces off the Lebanese coast are going to intimidate the Syrians so much that they engage in meaningful negotiations? For this to occur, the Syrians must believe we will use the full military power at our disposal. Are we prepared to use this power? I do not think so, nor do I believe the Syrians think so.

The longer we stay in Lebanon, the harder it will be for us to leave. We will be trapped by the case we make for having our troops there in the first place.

What can we expect if we withdraw from Lebanon? The same as will happen if we stay. I acknowledge that the level of fighting will increase if we leave. I regretfully acknowledge that many innocent civilians will be hurt. But I firmly believe this will happen in any event.

What about our allies and worldwide prestige? We should consult with our allies and withdraw with them in concert if possible, unilaterally if necessary. I also recognize that our prestige may suffer in the short term, but I am more concerned with our long-term national interests. I believe the circumstances of our original involvement have changed, and I know four American families who share this view.

I am not calling for an immediate withdrawal of our forces. What I desire is as rapid a withdrawal as possible.

I do not foresee obtainable objectives in Lebanon. I believe the longer we stay, the more difficult it will be to leave, and I am prepared to accept the consequences of our withdrawal. I will vote in opposition to this resolution.

Later that evening, the House adopted the resolution, 260 to 170. The Senate followed suit the next day. The president had a free hand in

Lebanon, at least for the next year and a half, confident that with aggressive diplomacy, a battleship, and a few brave marines, he could bring order to a country that had plunged into anarchy.

For the next three weeks, marine positions came under increasing mortar and sniper fire, adding two more American names to the list of those killed in action. In retaliation, our warships lobbed shells toward the Chouf Mountains. No attempts were made to move the marines to more secure positions. They held their low ground at the airport, sitting ducks for even the most incompetent marksman.

At 6:20 Sunday morning, October 23, 1983, a Mercedes-Benz truck, variously reported as black, gray, yellow, tan, and red, loaded with a ton of TNT bore down on the front door of the Marines' Battalion Landing Team headquarters in Beirut, where four hundred marines were sleeping. Behind the wheel was a smiling zealot, mostly likely a member of the Hezbollah, the Party of God, the terrorist organization trained and supported by Iran, taught to blaspheme the Koran by mullahs who believed in offering human sacrifices to the greater glory of Allah.

A few minutes later, two miles to the south, another suicide bomber drove his truck into the barracks of a company of sleeping French paratroopers. The death toll would eventually rise to 241 marines and 58 French soldiers. Snipers from one or another of the various Muslim militias harassed the marines as they dug the bodies of their fallen comrades out of the rubble and evacuated their wounded to the USS *Iwo Jima*.

On November 4, the Reagans traveled to Camp Lejeune in North Carolina to attend a memorial service for the fallen. During the service a child cried out, "Where is my daddy?" As taps played, the First Lady wept and the president looked stricken. After the service, they offered their personal condolences to the families of the dead, embracing many of them and whispering, "God bless you," the president's normally sunny countenance grimacing in sorrow. He described the day as his "most difficult moment," and I have no doubt that it was. His administration had made a terrible mistake, and as the president walked among the families who were so sadly burdened with the immediate consequences of that mistake, he seemed for the first time to show his age. But he was the president, and presidents cannot let grief or regret incapacitate them. A few minutes after he left the mourners, he called for Americans to show courage and determination. "We must not and will not be intimidated by anyone, anywhere." Quoting John Stuart Mill, he said, "War is an ugly thing, but not the ugliest of things. The ugliest is that man who thinks nothing is worth fighting and dying for, and lets men braver and better than himself protect him."

About a week later, the House voted on a resolution to cut off money for the marine deployment in Lebanon and, thus, force their withdrawal. The president had promised retaliation and urged the country to remain resolute and not surrender to the enemies of peace. The American people, outraged by the worst attack on American forces since the Vietnam War, sided with the president. As did I. I voted against the resolution, which ultimately failed, because a withdrawal after the attack would instruct our enemies throughout the Middle East that they could win a conflict with the United States on the cheap—cheaply to them, anyway. I could not bring myself to help give the bastards who had committed the atrocity the satisfaction of a full American retreat. It was a futile gesture.

Six weeks after the attack, we launched ineffectual air strikes against Syrian positions, losing two planes and a pilot to a Syrian surface-to-air missile (SAM). More weeks and months passed. We fired missiles and shells in the general direction of our enemies. They sniped and fired mortars at us. Twenty more marines died in the bargain.

On February 7, the president ordered the "redeployment" of the marines to naval ships offshore. No one bothered to shoot at them as they retreated. The British and Italian peacekeepers had already left. By April, the French had joined the allied retreat.

We left behind a disintegrating Gemayel government, a defeated Lebanese army, Syrian, Palestinian, and Israeli forces. We also left behind a growing contingent of Iranian Revolutionary Guards bent on gaining new recruits to their political-religious doctrine of terror from a seemingly endless pool of willing converts. Lebanese factional fighting continued apace, further damaging our reputation as a force to be reckoned with in the Middle East. In the months ahead, many Americans who bravely chose to stay in Lebanon, embassy personnel, a CIA station chief, members of UN peacekeeping forces, academics, journalists, relief workers, and clerics, were kidnapped, and some were murdered, by men who somehow find harming innocent people valorous. We left Lebanon to the Lebanese and anyone else crazy enough to want a piece of it. Those responsible for the killing of our marines escaped punishment. And to this day we are living with the ramifications of our defeat.

Marlon Brando. *Alfred Eisenstaedt/TimePix*

VIVA ZAPATA!

Emiliano Zapata surely had failings. His manner—humorless, unyielding, and violent—needed a good cause to make it tolerable. He
was small, dark, and quiet, with a long drooping mustache; a mestizo, part
Indian and part Spanish; intelligent, courageous, and a hell of a fighter. At
age thirty, in 1910, he started an insurrection in southern Mexico, while
Pancho Villa rebelled in the north, that within a year brought an end to
the corrupt, thirty-five-year dictatorship of President Porfirio Díaz. But
tragic Mexico, where for so many years bad men were deposed for their
tyranny only to be replaced by other bad men, gave him cause to keep
fighting for another eight years.

His legend exalts him as the purest Mexican revolutionary who ever
took up arms for his oppressed people. He fought to restore lands stolen
by rich landowners to the campesinos who revered him. He fought for
them and for nothing else. Although the revolution he led was bloody and
he could be quite cruel to his enemies, he did not enrich himself or seek
to rule Mexico by conquest. He had, a biographer wrote, "the rare plain
qualities of unambitious courage and dogged, abiding integrity." He
wanted to give back to his people the land they had farmed, no small endeavor, but a simple, selfless ambition for a man who might have been
master of a big country. It was not his triumph, but his integrity, and the
price he paid for it, that gave his legend its grandeur.

I live in Arizona, a state with a large Mexican American population and proud of a culture broadly influenced by our southern neighbor. Zapata remains as much a folk hero in many Arizona neighborhoods as he is in the southern Mexican state of Chiapas, where in 1994 an impoverished people took up arms in insurrection and called themselves Zapatistas.

But I did not come to admire Zapata out of respect for Arizona's diverse culture. Zapata did not figure in my family culture. I wasn't instructed in his example by my parents or by my teachers or by any influential people in my life. The closest personal connection I could establish with Zapata is a highly tenuous one. My great-uncle Wild Bill McCain rode into Mexico with General Pershing to fight Pancho Villa, Zapata's ally in the north. Neither did a bit of good luck lead me to a biography or article about him. I don't think I had ever heard his name mentioned until the day in 1952 when I took a bus into Washington, D.C., with a couple of high school friends to see Marlon Brando, in dark makeup, long mustache, and big sombrero, ride a white horse in *Viva Zapata!*

I went to see the movie twice more over the next two weeks, and I have watched it many times since. It is my favorite movie, and I doubt I'll ever see a better one. Directed by Elia Kazan, with a screenplay by John Steinbeck, it is the least remembered of three Kazan and Brando collaborations, the other two being the classics *On the Waterfront* and *A Streetcar Named Desire.* That's too bad, for I've always thought it was the best of the three. And while it takes liberties with the subject's life and times, it does so with far less abandon than is typical of Hollywood. Zapata was big enough and good enough not to sensationalize.

It is a dark, occasionally melancholy movie, all the more so for its black-and-white cinematography and Brando's performance as a somber, pensive, and at times explosive Zapata. There are moments of triumph for Zapata and his followers, when the music swells and campesinos celebrate, that offer the thrilling exultation of an injustice corrected that Hollywood can excel at producing. But for the most part, the movie is filled with a foreboding of recurring misfortune. And while it celebrates the heroism of one man with courage, independence, and an ardor for doing justice, its central theme is the futility—a glorious futility, to be sure, but a futility nonetheless—of expecting one person to save us all from iniquity. All human beings are flawed and by ourselves not strong enough, or brave enough, or honest enough, to vanquish inhumanity. One man on a white horse cannot make history. He can make a difference. He can do justice. He can help force the moment when enduring change occurs, when history swings on its hinge toward a better world. But alone he cannot make a lasting, just civilization, any more than a dictator can oppress forever a people determined to have their liberty.

In the movie's crucial scene, following the discovery that his own brother had exploited the revolution for personal gain, Zapata tells his people not to depend on a strong man to save them. "There are no leaders but yourselves. A strong people is the only lasting strength." That was the lesson that Robert Jordan had learned by the end of his life. Selfish ambition, and the power politics it can incite, will always threaten to corrupt the just man's dreams when ideologies clash on battlefields. But we prevail even in defeat if we fight not for abstract notions of freedom and justice, for intellectual disputes turned violent, but for a kinship of those ideals, for the people we love and who make history with us.

But as I missed the great lesson of Hemingway's masterpiece, so too my teenage intellect overlooked the central contention of *Viva Zapata!* I loved so much the idea of one man on a white horse, fighting for justice, of course, but fighting because he had the courage to, fighting to prove himself better than his enemies, fighting because that was the essential truth of his life: He was a man who fought.

Zapata's sermon that a people must trust themselves to keep the freedom that another has fought to win for them was not my favorite scene in the movie. I was moved by it, and I might have sensed its significance. But there are two scenes I remember so vividly that almost fifty years after first hearing it, I can still closely paraphrase their dialogue. The first scene begins the movie.

A delegation of campesinos, all dressed in white and clutching their sombreros in front of them, waits nervously to meet their president.

They've come to tell Díaz that wealthy landowners had stolen their land. Díaz calls them his children and dismisses them with platitudes and empty promises. Only one of the campesinos has the courage to challenge Díaz's condescension. "My President, we make our tortillas out of corn, not patience," he tells the indignant dictator.

"You!" Díaz shouts.

The campesino points at his own chest as Díaz repeats his shouted command.

"What is your name?" he thunders.

"Zapata. Emiliano Zapata."

Díaz glares at him, picks up a pen, and, to the accompaniment of a swelling, ominous-sounding score, circles the hero's name on a list an aide has handed him.

Zapata leaves to begin the revolution that will drive Díaz from office.

Later in the movie, after General Zapata has been left in de facto control of the country (a fiction), another delegation of aggrieved campesinos arrives to complain to the new man in charge. And thus begins my second favorite scene.

Zapata greets them warmly, calling them by name.

They complain that his brother has stolen their land and their wives. Zapata promises to look into the matter, but one man refuses to be so easily dismissed. Like the Zapata of old, he demands action now; this provokes the general's temper, and he furiously demands the man's name.

"Hernandez."

Zapata begins to circle the name on the sheet of paper before him. Stops. The music rises. He recognizes what he has become and furiously scribbles out the circled name. His aide, a grim man and assumed communist ("I am a friend to logic and nothing else," he cries), pleads with him not to resume his rebellion. "You won't live long," he warns.

"I won't live long anyway," Zapata replies as he leaves with the delegation to begin the fight again.

Those two scenes made the movie for me. And the experience enlivened my dreams of fighting for justice as fearlessly as Zapata had. But even more important to me was my hope that by doing so I would provoke the right sort of enemy. I wanted to be a good man, of course, and fight in a good cause. But what was the point of being good if it didn't gain the attention of the bad? To do that, I reasoned, the good man has to know how to be a little bad sometimes, as long as his misbehavior is for the right cause. I wanted to have my name circled, too.

Me, as U.S. Navy liaison to the U.S. Senate,
with John Glenn and Barry Goldwater, 1978.

SIX

FOLLOWING BARRY

I liked Bruce Babbitt, as did most Arizonans. He was a popular governor—young, smart, enthusiastic, politically moderate, and scion of a well-established Arizona family. His appeal was widespread enough to overcome the conservative state's reluctance to elect Democrats. The late Burton Barr, the Republican majority leader in the Arizona House of Representatives when Babbitt was governor, loved him. Burt and I were good friends, and he would often bring Bruce and me together. He saw to it that we stayed on cordial terms even while we were perceived to be rivals.

I assumed, as did every political pundit in Arizona and Washington, that Bruce would be the Democratic candidate for Barry Goldwater's Senate seat in 1986. I knew he would be tough to beat. But I intended to try, and I seldom let a day pass during my time in the House without preparing myself for that challenge. I worked hard to make a name in Arizona, and if I was not as well known or as well liked as the governor, I had come a long way from my beginnings as an alleged carpetbagger. I also had the state's Republicans leaning in my favor, as well as an experienced campaign team, a proven track record as a successful fund-raiser, and at least as much ambition as my probable opponent. Prominent national reporters were already handicapping the contest. Ours was expected to be one of the marquee races in the country in 1986.

It never happened. Bruce's real ambitions extended beyond the Senate. He had his eye on the 1988 Democratic nomination for president. He knew he would be a dark horse in the presidential primaries, and a successful Senate race might have made him less so. But a losing race would cost him any chance at all of being president. He might have been a narrow favorite against me, but he was far from a certain winner. So on March 18, 1985, he announced that he would not be a candidate for senator. I announced my candidacy the next day.

I did not necessarily have a clear path to my party's nomination. Bob Stump, a five-term congressman from Arizona's third district, thought he had a better claim to succeed his friend Barry Goldwater. Bob and I weren't adversaries, but we weren't the best of friends, either. I'm sure he thought me undeserving of the nomination because my ties to Arizona and my political experience were shallow compared to his. He had the unofficial but active support of Barry Goldwater's chief aide, Judy Eisenhower, who for reasons unknown to me didn't care for me one bit. More worrisome to me were suspicions that her dislike of me was shared by Barry himself. Nevertheless, I had already managed to position myself as the favorite, both in the public's mind and in the view of the political cognoscenti, and I was attracting the kind of support from both the local and national political establishment that favors front-runners. Two months after Bruce Babbitt declared his intentions, Stump announced that he would run for reelection to the House in 1986.

Thus, before the Democrats had any idea whom they would find to oppose me, I became the heavy favorite to succeed a political legend, Arizona's favorite son, a conservative icon, and an authentic maverick who had, more than any single person, broken the Democratic Party's hold on Arizona politics and then the East Coast establishment's hold on the Republican Party. Barry Goldwater was irascible and principled, fiercely independent and deeply patriotic. He was his own man always and his country's loyal servant. He appealed to every principle and instinct in my nature. And I really don't think he liked me much.

I don't know why that was. We both had military backgrounds. Barry served in World War II as an army air corps pilot and had continued to serve for years in the air force reserves, rising to the rank of brigadier general. He revered military service. He knew and liked my father. He told me once that my father was a great man. He liked my mother, and she considered herself a huge Goldwater fan. He respected my war record. We got along well when I had been the navy's liaison officer to the Senate.

As a politician, I was gaining a reputation for candor and outspokenness, qualities Barry was famous for. I always showed him great deference. Every several months, I would ask for an appointment to see him. In those meetings I observed all the proprieties governing our relationship, making clear I understood the differences in our stature. I would ask for his counsel on issues affecting Arizona as well as on defense and foreign policy questions of the day. We never disagreed or quarreled. I wanted to succeed him, so of course there was an element of self-interest in my courtesy to him. But that was a small part of it. I admired him to the point of reverence, and I wanted him to like me.

Maybe he too thought I was too junior, too little accomplished, and too new to Arizona, the place he believed formed the essence of his character, to presume to succeed him. He and his friend Harry Rosenzweig had pretty much built the Arizona Republican Party from scratch. From its territorial days, the Democratic Party had dominated Arizona politics, exemplified by the lifelong reign of Carl Hayden, United States senator from Arizona for forty-two years. Barry and Harry, who served for many years as party chairman, had ended all that. They offered Arizonans a kind of Republicanism that reflected their character, freedom loving, enterprising, confident, bold, self-reliant, and patriotic. It was a self-image shared by most westerners, even those whose pedigrees were as short as mine and whose mass migration to the West had challenged East Coast domination of American politics and culture. Barry wasn't just steeped in this tradition, he was the tradition. He defined both the style and the political substance of western conservatism.

Maybe Barry just saw me as an eager beaver, getting his name in the papers and his face on television, a guy who had barely spent five years in Arizona, while he had toiled for decades to remake national politics into the image of Arizona. And he thinks he can be the standard-bearer for all of that, I imagine him thinking. What kind of bullshit is that?

Six years after my first election to the Senate, several of the surviving founders of the Arizona Republican Party, including Paul Fannin, former governor and senator, and Harry Rosenzweig, spoke at a fund-raising dinner for the party and for my reelection campaign, billed as a "Salute to Barry." Harry spoke off-the-cuff, reminiscing about the early days of Barry's and the party's rise to prominence. They were just anecdotes, colorful and entertaining, but a little disjointed, one abruptly beginning after another had abruptly ended. They had been through a lot together, made their share of history, and, as is often the case with old men, lived much of their retirement in a reverie of their past. They communicated in a sort of shorthand, full of obscure or forgotten references to people and events, assuming that their audience knew enough of their history to catch on. Whether they did or not was probably not the point. That night Harry was speaking just to his friend Barry. The rest of us were eavesdropping.

At the end of one story, Harry started on another and then stopped, looked at his old friend, and asked, "Have I said enough, Barry?"

Barry nodded. "Yeah, you've said enough." And Harry gathered up his notes and sat down. Who was I to intrude on the history they made? It was so personal to them.

Whatever he thought of me, he was never outwardly hostile, just a little reserved and occasionally a little short in our conversations. I don't know that his opinion of me was as slight as I imagined it to be. He was usually cordial, just never as affectionate as I would have liked. He kept his distance. But as far as I know, he never tried to prevent me from succeeding him. He might have preferred Bob Stump, but he didn't promise to endorse him.

Nor did he dissuade anyone from supporting me. In 1985, I went to see Harry Rosenzweig and asked for his endorsement, which he promised on the spot. He wouldn't have done so if Barry had quietly put out the word that I was not his choice. As far as I could tell, Barry applied his live-and-let-live philosophy to the contest that would determine his successor.

Judy Eisenhower, however, made her opposition to my ambition quite plain. She had worked for Barry for a long time, as had her husband, Earl Eisenhower, President Eisenhower's nephew, whom Barry had placed on the Senate Intelligence Committee staff. I know Judy influenced Barry, but I never knew to what extent. I also knew she disliked me from the start, but I never knew why. She had caused me some grief in my first campaign for the House. During the campaign, the army had announced that it had selected a Mesa defense contractor to build the new Apache helicopter. The decision was a boon for the local economy, and I wanted to steal a little of the public joy over the decision. As a public relations executive for a beer company, I couldn't exactly claim that I had been instrumental in the decision. But I did claim that as the Senate's navy liaison I had supported building the new state-of-the-art gunship, a bit of a stretch since the army didn't really care what a sailor thought of its weapons programs. More truthfully, I argued that my military experience made me the best-qualified candidate to protect the contract.

Shortly before primary day, Barry released a statement accusing me of claiming credit for something I had nothing to do with. Judy Eisenhower made sure my opponents had a copy of the release before it was given to the press. That was the kind of last-minute surprise a candidate in a close election dreads. I immediately called John Tower, who was traveling in Europe with Barry, explained the situation to him, and asked him to intervene with Barry on my behalf. It was the middle of the night in London, where I had reached him, but John graciously offered to wake up Barry and find out just how big a problem I had with the old man. True to his word, he walked down the hall to Barry's room, woke him up, and asked him why he had criticized me publicly. Stirred from his slumber, Barry thought for a second before dismissing the inquiry with, "Oh, that, it was just something Judy wanted to do. Tell him not to worry about it," and then he went back to sleep.

I did worry about it, though. Republican voters paid attention to Barry Goldwater's likes and dislikes. But Tower, who helpfully put out a press release the next day asserting that I had advised him to support the Apache project when the issue had been before the Armed Services Committee, told me not to worry, that the controversy wouldn't have an impact on my race or on my relationship with Goldwater. He was right.

The day after I won the primary, Barry called to congratulate me and said he was pleased and that he looked forward to working with me. He never mentioned the Apache matter, nor did I.

Still, as I worked hard to stay in Barry's good graces during my four years in the House, Judy's dislike for me was always plainly evident. Whenever I came to his office for a courtesy call, Judy always greeted me with, if not a scowl, then something that didn't exactly approximate a smile, either. Some senators tend to look down on colleagues from the other legislative body, viewing the Senate as a much more select society than the 435-member House. Barry wasn't like that, but the Senate's institutional sense of superiority has been known to affect a few senior Senate staff members, who consider their own stature to be just a notch below that of their bosses and, as such, themselves to be grander than most of the tiresome, minor figures who toiled anonymously, and to little effect, in the lower body. Judy Eisenhower possessed such self-assurance. She thought Bob Stump was a more deserving aspirant and tried in small ways to help his candidacy. But without Barry's active involvement, her opposition, while noteworthy, was not insurmountable. And when Stump decided to leave the nomination to me, I kept a respectful distance from Judy, and she kindly tolerated my existence.

Far from being the marquee race everyone looked forward to when Bruce Babbitt was the presumptive Democratic candidate, my first race for the Senate was pretty close to a foregone conclusion. I led in the polls from start to finish. My eventual opponent, Richard Kimball, had won statewide election as a public utilities regulator. He was a tall, good-looking guy who shared his name with the hero of a popular 1960s television drama, *The Fugitive.* He was a nice man and a well-intentioned public servant. But for all his fine qualities, he was not the first-tier candidate the Democrats had hoped to field. Arizona, even more so then than now, was a decidedly Republican-leaning state.

The Democrats had elected one of their own to the Senate, Dennis DeConcini, so the task wasn't impossible. But there were few Democrats around who were politically moderate, savvy, and well known enough to overcome the electorate's attraction to the strong strain of libertarian conservatism that Barry Goldwater practiced so faithfully. Babbitt was the only potential candidate who seemed to possess crossover appeal to Republican-leaning independents and to moderate and liberal Republicans. With his practiced political skills, personal appeal, and high name recognition, Bruce was the future of the Democratic Party in Arizona. But he was checking out to pursue a bigger prize, and he left a vacuum in the Democratic leadership.

Thanks in large part to Mo Udall, I had gained stature in every county in the state and had begun to exhibit my own appeal outside my party. I had been preparing for a contest with Bruce for several years. I was revved up for the great race, as intrigued by the national attention to an expected cliff-hanger as I was by the powers of the office I sought. As boastful as this seems, a part of me was disappointed when Bruce dropped out. Of course, had I a say in the matter, I would have encouraged Bruce not to run. I'm not that much of a sportsman that I would exchange a front-runner's advantages for the thrill of political combat. But in the many years that have passed since I worried about it, I often wondered who would have won and imagined how exciting it would have been had the answer been me.

I stayed revved up, working just as hard as I had in my first campaign, even though the race was unlikely to be close. I started with greater name recognition, broader support, more money, better organization, and a more energized base. Kimball had only three hopes for an upset: I might screw up monumentally on my own; an unforeseen scandal involving me could suddenly and publicly erupt; or he could try to clobber me in tele-vised debates. None of those things happened, as events turned out. But, at times, I appeared to be doing my part to make it a close race.

I'm a wise-ass. And that flaw has gotten me into more trouble in my life than I deserved to get out of. But the habit is irremediable, apparently. Or, to put it less charitably, I occasionally prove to be a ridiculously poor student of experience. I like to laugh, and I like to make people laugh. Solemnity isn't my natural condition, and I'm glad it isn't. But occasion-ally my sense of humor is ill considered or ill timed, and that can be a problem. More than once, I've made some crack that was better left unut-tered, attempted unsuccessfully to wink and nod my way through any repercussions, gotten slapped for it by the press, and then sworn to myself that I would forevermore resist the allure of sophomoric humor. In-evitably I fail, making my own shortcomings at self-improvement funnier than my jokes.

During the summer of the campaign, I gave an address to students at the University of Arizona in Tucson. Near the end of my remarks, I made my usual appeal to young people, who are less inclined to exercise their franchise than are other demographics, to get out and vote, even if they intend to vote for my opponent. Typically, I exhort them to emulate the example of senior citizens, who are the most reliable voters in our society.

Arizona's climate and recreational opportunities have long been a magnet for retirees, and we have a great many quality retirement communities promising a relaxed life in the sun, with limitless access to golf courses and excellent geriatric health care. One of the better-known brand names in the retirement resort business is Leisure World. Everyone in Arizona seemed to have a relative in one of the Leisure World communities. And it struck me as I addressed my youthful audience that a little colorful wordplay with the name of the place some of their grandparents called home might be a good way to humor them into voting that November, preferably for me. I think I was about fifteen years older than Kimball, and I suppose I thought I could blur that distinction by employing a little youthful irreverence. An easy enough task for me, since irreverence is the one attribute of my youth that has not been worn away by the accumulation of years.

So I seized the moment and told my listeners of the civic-mindedness so common among the residents of "Seizure World," where "ninety-seven percent of the people who live there come out to vote while the other three percent are in intensive care." Ha, ha. Everybody laughed, including me, except, I assume, the young Democrat who was dutifully recording my remarks so that he or she could share them with the Kimball campaign.

Predictably, a minor storm erupted as Democrats assailed my gross insult to Arizona's wonderfully public-spirited senior citizens who deserve so much better from the men and women they elect to office. It passed without doing serious damage to my campaign. But it would have passed a hell of a lot faster if I had listened to my advisers and apologized immediately and fully for my discourtesy. Instead I insisted on responding to every accusation of insensitivity by launching into a litany of my steadfast support for any and all interests of concern to the elderly, without actually getting around to saying "I'm sorry."

My opponent gamely tried to exploit the increased press attention to my capacity for self-injury that my blunder had encouraged by piling on accusations that, besides being a shockingly remorseless seniors basher, I was also an unthinking conservative reactionary, a special pleader for fat-cat defense contractors, and a cowardly debate ducker to boot. I am, at times, a little slow to admit mistakes, but I eventually come around. But before I do, I can get angry, more at myself than at others, although others sometimes bear the brunt of it until I accept my own responsibility. On this occasion, I let myself get a little mad at Richard Kimball, whose charges of misconduct were pretty standard and predictable campaign fare for an underdog that wouldn't normally have bothered me were I not suffering a self-inflicted wound. Consequently, Kimball began to cut into my lead, although never enough to bring it below double digits.

I eventually apologized and moved on, but not before agreeing to give Kimball his debates and a couple of clubs to swing at me when we met. He made a game of it, but I successfully dodged most of his swings during our first debate in mid-October. Kimball went on at considerable length about my many failings. We mixed it up a few times, often about foreign and defense policy. Curiously, he thought Arizonans, many of whom were employed by defense companies, would take exception to my support for increased defense spending. He never really drew blood, so when he used his closing statement to continue his attacks, I was able to ignore them, adopting a conventionally senatorial tone to wax on about the privilege of service.

I think Kimball had thought that first debate was his last chance to really change the dynamics of the race, and it probably was. His campaign seemed demoralized after he failed to land any serious blows, and the subsequent debates were, by and large, nonevents. I ticked up in the polls again, and for the remainder of the campaign, I managed to keep in check my natural ability to agitate an otherwise tranquil situation into something of a commotion.

Election day, November 4, 1986, was not a happy occasion for Republicans nationally. Elections in the sixth year of a presidency are usually a dangerous time for members of the president's party in Congress. That was certainly the case this time. Senate Republicans got clobbered, losing seven incumbents, four open seats, and control of the Senate. I was one of only two Republican challengers for an open Senate seat to prevail.

I was a little dispirited by the knowledge that after four frustrating years as backbencher in the House minority, I would still be a junior member and still in the minority party. Also, there is something in my character that always acts as a brake on my emotions in moments of triumph and achievement. I'm never quite as thrilled as I had anticipated I would be when I have fulfilled some great desire. Even when I was released from prison, a slight feeling of anticlimax mitigated my joy. My mind seems to race ahead of the experience in anticipation of new challenges. I don't mean to suggest that I wasn't pleased to have reached, in just a little over five years, what I believed was the summit of my political ambitions. I was a United States senator-elect, successor to the great Goldwater, with the privileges and prospects possessed by those great and influential men whom I had admired and studied while making sure their bags weren't lost and their hotel rooms were ready, and I was very proud of the accomplishment. Still, even in the midst of my private revelry, I felt an emotional need to envision some future goal, something that I could fix my gaze on and concentrate my energy to attaining.

Barry Goldwater had ended all of his Senate campaigns as well as his campaign for the presidency with a rally at the Yavapai County Courthouse in Prescott, Arizona, the old territorial capital, where long ago his grandfather had posted bail for Mo Udall's grandfather. I asked him to accompany me there for one last rally on the night before the election. It was a beautiful fall evening, cool and clear, and the courthouse square was filled to capacity with cheering supporters. The local high school band played near the statue of Bucky O'Neil, the legendary Arizona Rough Rider who had fought in the Battle of San Juan Heights with Teddy Roosevelt. I knew I would win the election the next day, and I was moved more that night by the poignancy of Barry's last hurrah than by the excitement of my own imminent success. There were a lot of speakers, all of whom recalled memories of Barry's distinguished career and the experiences they had shared with him. Election eve rallies are supposed to be a call to arms, to encourage the faithful to make an extra effort to get out the vote the next day. This was, appropriately, a tribute to the life and times of an American original, a man who rose to greatness without losing his authentic identity, who would forever own a chapter in American political history, who knew where he stood and why, and whose beliefs and example rang as true to his countrymen as they did to him. In the emotions of that moment, the next day's election was largely forgotten, and I, like everyone else there, was just happy to witness a great man's curtain call.

In the years that followed my election, I managed to forge a closer relationship with Barry. I touched base with him often when I was home from Washington, frequently bringing Cindy with me. Barry seemed to enjoy Cindy's company more than mine. We would go see him at his house on a mountain overlooking Paradise Valley, where we would make small talk for a while, but eventually we'd get to discussing politics and the personalities that shaped the profession in Arizona and in Washington. In his last years, he spent more time during my occasional visits reminiscing about the old days. He was a hell of a storyteller, and I was always content to be his audience.

His wife of fifty years, Peggy Goldwater, died in 1985. Seven years later, Barry was remarried to his nurse and good friend, Susan Wechsler. Cindy and I became good friends with Susan, too, and our visits to their home became more frequent. Eventually his pleasure in seeing me began to become almost as evident as his pleasure in seeing my wife, which delighted me no end.

Barry never lost his enthusiasm for shaking things up, and even when his life was nearing its end, he still managed to make news and get people riled up, particularly people whose conservatism had a more religious cast than Barry's libertarianism. In 1987, he called on Arizona's controversial Republican governor, Ev Mecham, a hero to many conservative activists in the state, to resign. I called for Mecham's resignation as well, for which I earned the lasting enmity of some of his supporters. But my statement hardly raised the ruckus that Barry's did. He also became increasingly outspoken in his defense of abortion and gay rights, and in 1992, he stunned Republicans by formally endorsing the Democrat in an Arizona congressional race over the party's candidate who was identified with the religious Right. The breach of party loyalty really inflamed the anger of social conservatives, the more intemperate of whom seemed to forget Barry's unsurpassed contributions to the conservative movement as they gave full vent to their outrage over his apostasy. None of the protests bothered Barry, however. As always, he seemed to enjoy the commotion.

He had never been much of a fan of the television evangelists who were spearheading the advances religious conservatives were then making in Republican Party politics. He didn't like to be told what to think, and he didn't like people who thought he needed to be. It gave him great pleasure to let political "preachers" know he didn't give a damn for their sermons or for what they thought of him. He once suggested that Americans "boot" a nationally prominent televangelist "right in the ass."

One of his grandchildren was gay, and Barry, who loved the boy, never felt the least bit bothered by the fact. The question of gays serving in the military became one of the earliest controversies in Bill Clinton's presidency. Barry decided the debate could use a little dose of his live-and-let-live philosophy, and he came out swinging on behalf of the change in military policy. His statements on the subject were direct, cantankerous, and funny as ever.

This latest defection from conservative orthodoxy, however, was a bridge too far for a number of the state's more outspoken social conservatives, who promptly branded him sinner, traitor, and, worse, a liberal. They demanded that the state party rename the Barry Goldwater Republican Party headquarters in Phoenix. I and most other Republican leaders spoke against the change, suggesting that but for Barry, Democrats might still be running the state. The protesters eventually exhausted themselves in their fit of righteous indignation, but I don't think they ever forgave Barry. And I don't think Barry ever gave a damn, either.

I think he appreciated my support during the controversy, and we became better friends, although the years left to enjoy that relationship were few. He had been troubled by health problems long before he retired from the Senate. Those problems multiplied during the 1990s, and they were taking a toll on the once vigorous and proudly self-reliant westerner. He suffered a stroke in 1996 and a year later was diagnosed with early Alzheimer's disease. After that, every time I paid him a visit, he seemed to have grown considerably frailer since the last time I saw him. The end came in 1998.

One Thursday morning in May, Susan Goldwater called me and suggested that Cindy and I come over that day to see Barry, because he hadn't much time left. When we arrived, we found Barry curled up in a hospital bed in his living room, looking out a picture window at the valley he loved. Susan was lying next to him on top of the covers. It was a moving scene to witness, and my throat thickened before I could speak. We could see at once that he was very near death.

Susan alerted him to our presence, and he turned his head, smiled, and greeted me with, "Hi, buddy." He kept looking at us for a moment as we returned his greeting and asked how he was doing. He didn't answer but turned to Susan and asked if he was still in the hospital.

"No, Barry. You're home."

"Oh, wonderful, home."

We stayed only a little while, not wanting to intrude on his last reminiscences. I shook his hand to leave, and he smiled. When Cindy reached to do the same, he grabbed her hand and held it very firmly. He said nothing, but he didn't seem to want to let go of her.

Finally, with some difficulty, Cindy withdrew her hand, and we told him good-bye and God bless.

In the hallway as we were leaving, Susan remarked, "You know, Barry always loved a beautiful woman." We laughed and nodded, and I thought to myself, If we don't have a sudden rush of enlightenment when we die, then there are surely worse things to fill our last thoughts on earth than the memory of a pretty woman's face. Cheered by the thought, I drove home smiling.

Barry Goldwater died a little after sunrise the next morning.

With John Tower, after the Senate rejected his nomination
as secretary of defense. *Corbis*

SEVEN

JOHN TOWER'S HONOR

On January 6, 1987, fifty-one years old, my wife and children surrounding me, I was sworn into office as a member of the United States Senate by the vice president of the United States, George Bush. A few months later, I moved into my new offices in the Russell Senate Office Building, just down the hall from the small room where I had worked as the navy's liaison, a pleasing reminder of how far I had come in so few years. I was in no less of a hurry for distinction in that elite institution than I had been to enter politics five years before. I knew I would find it easier to raise my profile in the nation's capital as one of a select hundred; that my opinions, if no wiser than in years past, would receive more attention; that my ambitions, whatever they were, would experience greater scrutiny.

I arrived in the Senate with a reputation as a reliable conservative partisan given to irregular fits of outspokenness and independence. I was received warmly and treated well by the Senate Republican leadership. Bob Dole, the Republican leader, was exceptionally considerate to me, giving me responsibilities that were not always accorded to junior members.

The Reagan administration's Central American policy was still the subject of intense partisan disagreement in Congress and claimed as much of our attention as it did the interest of the press. I had become very active in the House in support of President Reagan's policies and intended to remain so in the Senate. The Senate's Democratic and Republican leaders had established a Central American Negotiations Observer Group, ostensibly to encourage greater bipartisan cooperation in efforts to resolve the multiple conflicts that were tormenting the region. Dole made me the group's Republican co-chair, a minor but still unexpected honor for such a junior member. Dole often sought out my views on most major foreign policy and national security issues. Most important, he saw to it that I won a seat on the Senate Armed Services Committee, the committee that had excited my interest in politics, and where I had developed friendships. I became a member of the Commerce Committee and the Committee on Indian Affairs as well. While the work of those committees attracted my interest, it was the Armed Services Committee that held the greatest allure for me. I was very grateful to Bob for helping me reach what had been the summit of my political ambitions just five short years after I had first set my sights on it.

My Senate career has had its ups and downs over the years. But for most of those first two years, everything seemed to exceed my expectations. I was generally regarded as an up-and-comer, someone to keep your eye on. And if I showed a little independence from time to time, opposing the administration on a few civil rights or environmental or foreign policy issues, I was still considered a loyal Reagan Republican with a promising future.

I even ran for a leadership post, chairman of the Republican Senatorial Campaign Committee, a position of considerable responsibility since the occupant was charged with recruiting, financing, and helping manage the campaigns of Republican Senate candidates. I lost the election, decisively, but not by an embarrassing margin, to Don Nickles of Oklahoma, who rose from that auspicious beginning to occupy the second-highest position on the leadership ladder as the assistant Republican leader.

I don't like to lose at anything, so I can't say I was indifferent to my first political defeat. Nevertheless, the loss wasn't a major setback. It didn't disrupt relationships with my Senate colleagues or my belief that things were generally working out just fine for me in my first Senate years. By the summer of 1988, I was on the shortlist of possible running mates for Vice President George Bush. Whether it was the vice president's shortlist is an open question. A number of political reporters kept speculating that I was in the mix right up until the decision was announced during the party's national convention in New Orleans. I had clearly made the press's shortlist. However, since neither the candidate nor anyone associated with his campaign ever contacted me about possibly joining the ticket, I never really believed that my name was prominent on George Bush's list. But in politics, the next best thing to being the vice presidential nominee is to be considered by the Washington cognoscenti as "vice presidential material." And in that capacity, I was asked by the vice president's good friend and convention manager, Fred Malek, to deliver a prime-time speech to the convention on the evening of Ronald Reagan's valedictory address to the Republican Party.

I was nervous as hell, but thrilled by the opportunity. Speaking in prime time at the party's convention is a national political introduction, and I didn't want to blow it. I worked hard on the speech and did a fairly credible job. However, it strains credulity to imagine that any American who viewed the convention proceedings that evening would remember anything that happened except for Ronald Reagan's stirring good-bye and moving evocation of his "shining city on a hill."

Of course, not content to bask in the good graces of the Bush campaign, and the minor celebrity it afforded me for a few days in New Orleans, I typically blundered into a little controversy. Shortly after Senator Dan Quayle's selection as George Bush's running mate was announced, the press jumped with abandon into the controversy about whether the lucky winner of the vice presidential sweepstakes had evaded the draft during the Vietnam War by seeking special treatment to gain admission into the Indiana National Guard. When a reporter asked me if I thought the choice of Quayle would be problematic for the ticket, I replied by saying something like "Well, only if he did get special favors to help him evade the draft." In my defense, the story had just broken minutes before I was asked to comment on its implications, and my response seemed to me to be the rather obvious one. I didn't know if he had received favorable treatment to get out of Vietnam, but if he had, it seemed pretty likely that it would be a little hard for the ticket to stay on-message. That was not, however, the response the Bush campaign wanted to hear. They preferred, understandably, to have the selection defended without qualification. And the press frenzy that erupted over the controversy did have a pretty loud "guilty until proven innocent" tone to it. I can certainly understand why the Bush campaign felt that now was not the best time for any Republican, especially one who had just been favored with a prime-time speaking opportunity, to act as a political analyst for the media instead of just cheerleading for the party's standard-bearer's choice.

Things quickly calmed down, however, for me if not for Dan, and I don't think my small indiscretion caused any irreparable harm to the ticket or my relationship with them. I was elated when George Bush overcame his opponent's sizable lead to be elected the forty-first president of the United States. We weren't close friends, but I liked and respected President Bush. He is a good man, a public servant who always acted in what he believed were the country's best interests. He was always considerate and gracious and never succumbed to the pomposity that is an occupational hazard of a job commonly described as the most important in the world. He genuinely hoped that his presidency would usher in an era of greater civility and bipartisanship in national politics. His personal decency and evident discomfort with some of the more callow attributes and artifice of modern politics made him vulnerable to attack by political opponents. But he was a much stronger personality than his detractors gave him credit for being, possessing a fortitude that was a credit to him and the country.

He had served with distinction on an aircraft carrier in the Pacific in World War II, the youngest naval aviator in the war. He had been shot down, which gave us something in common. There was another event, of greater relevance to me, in the new president's biography. He had served under the command of my grandfather, a fact he frequently mentioned to me. His evident pride in the distinction made me proud to serve under his leadership. And though we would part company on the occasional issue as I grew more confident in my own political judgment, I always trusted that the country was in good hands when he was our commander in chief, a trust that proved well placed during his leadership in the Persian Gulf War.

When he was defeated for reelection four years later, I thought the voters had made a serious mistake and that the country would be the poorer for it. I watched him, as did all Americans, glow with paternal pride as his eldest son took the oath of office eight years after his own defeat. Although that event came partially at the expense of my ambitions, I could not help but be pleased if his son's success took a little of the sting out of the memory of his own disappointment when the country he had served well and long had treated him less generously than he had treated her.

The inauguration of the Bush administration would occasion the first major political fight of my career. And although today I am noticed more for my disagreements with my party's leaders, that initial battle was a strictly partisan affair. And in many ways its outcome has had more influence on my opinion of partisan politics and the institution I had been so intent on joining than any other experience since.

I believe John Tower had prepared all of his public life for the honor George Bush accorded him by nominating him to be secretary of defense. He craved the identity of a statesman and worked diligently to deserve the distinction. Few senators understood the large strategic premises of national defense and the most intricate details of defense policy as well as John Tower understood them. Few knew the caliber of the men and women, officer and enlisted, who fight for us and the quality of the weapons we give them to fight with as well as John Tower did. Few senators had as extensive contacts with the leading international statesmen as John Tower did. He traveled abroad frequently and knew personally every major foreign leader of his time. He was thoroughly familiar with the force structure, the deficiencies and strengths of the militaries of both allies and enemies. At the time, Mikhail Gorbachev's political and economic reforms were unexpectedly and powerfully affecting the political aspirations of people throughout the Soviet empire. In less than a year, the empire and the Soviet Union itself would collapse. No one knew then how quickly this great historical transformation would occur, but you could sense change coming, and you knew it would profoundly affect the defense structure of the United States. John Tower wanted to be there when it happened and lend his experience and wisdom to the many systemic changes in security alliances, military readiness, arms procurement decisions, and arms control treaties that the end of the cold war would necessitate. Few were better suited for the task. He was a superb selection for the office of secretary of defense.

As chairman of the Armed Services Committee, he could be imperious, hard-nosed, and disinclined to substitute the judgment of his colleagues for his own better-informed opinions. He was not a beloved member of the club, but he was an effective leader whom few dared to cross or dispute unless they were prepared to confront an adversary whose determination to prevail in debate was formidable and not hampered by a delicate sensitivity to the needs of his opponents' egos. He and Scoop Jackson had provided most of the legislative muscle behind Ronald Reagan's unbending determination to repair the nation's defenses from the low state of readiness they had deteriorated to in the years following our withdrawal from Vietnam. They shared Reagan's conviction that no other responsibility of his administration was more urgent, and they were admirably single-minded in their efforts to ensure that he discharged it without delay or qualification.

After retiring from the Senate in 1984, Tower tried his hand at defense consulting and lobbying, a common and usually lucrative second career for former members of Congress. But wealth was a poor substitute for the power he had wielded, for the influence he had once had over the public affairs of a great nation. He liked fine things, good food, expensive suits, first-class travel. But he enjoyed statecraft considerably more than he enjoyed his luxuries.

In the four years that elapsed between his retirement and George Bush's election, he accepted with pleasure three offers to continue in public service. Shortly after the Iran-Contra debacle erupted on the front pages of every newspaper in the country, President Reagan asked him to head a review board, along with former secretary of state Edmund Muskie and former national security adviser Brent Scowcroft. They were charged with investigating and analyzing the events that had led to the fiasco and recommending precautions that would prevent something like it from staining the reputation of another administration. He also served, with ambassadorial rank, as a member of the American delegation in Geneva, Switzerland, negotiating the first Strategic Arms Reduction

Treaty (START) with the Soviets. Last, he agreed to serve as the head of the President's Foreign Intelligence Advisory Board, an organization established to provide the president with independent intelligence analyses that were unaffected by the bureaucratic intrigues and institutional mindsets that often color the reporting of intelligence agencies. In all three capacities, he served with distinction.

But for all these distinguished occupations, I think he was really just waiting for the opportunity, should the Republican Party's hold on the White House extend beyond Ronald Reagan's incumbency, to become the nation's first minister of defense policy. He had endorsed Vice President George Bush in the primary, and after his candidate had won, I think he had every expectation that he would be on the president-elect's very short list of possible defense secretaries.

During the presidential transition, there was some speculation in the press, fed by leaks from inside the Bush operation, that Bush might turn to a successful corporate manager to run the Department of Defense, with the hope that a bottom-line-focused businessman might finally get a handle on the department's sluggish bureaucracy and chronically wasteful procurement system. Toward that end, CEO types are usually considered for the deputy defense secretary position and, less frequently, for the number one job (Robert McNamara being a notable exception that proves the rule and the reasons underlying it). But George Bush was an experienced hand in national security policy, and he prized strategic vision as the most important attribute of a statesman. And although he took his time in naming a defense secretary (the announcement wasn't made until six weeks after the election) and lots of CEO-versus-politician speculation filled the void, Tower's name always figured prominently as the probable front-runner for the job. When it became official on December 16, 1988, no one was surprised. John Tower stood contentedly within reach of the summit of his ambitions. I couldn't have been happier for him, or for myself, for that matter. It's no small thing for a junior member of the Senate Armed Services Committee to have the secretary of defense as a close friend and mentor. I could look forward to a rapid increase in stature in national security debates if Washington believed I had the trust and the ear of the defense secretary. But there was more than self-interest behind my enthusiasm for John's nomination. John Tower was my friend, and I was delighted in his success and the happiness it gave him.

I owed him a lot, and I take my debts seriously, particularly debts I incur to friends as loyal as John Tower was to me. But I had no idea that the time was at hand when I would begin to repay him for his many kindnesses to me. His confirmation was expected to be a simple formality, and like everyone else in town, I assumed his confirmation hearings would be perfunctory, notable only for the lack of aggressive questioning from committee members, who usually spare their former colleagues such discourtesy.

In hindsight, I might have sensed trouble coming, given my familiarity with John's personal life and the excessively disagreeable nature of his ex-wife Lilla. I should have been all the more alert when several weeks before his nomination was announced, the *Atlanta Journal-Constitution* ran a story with the headline TOWER: TOO HOT FOR BUSH TO HANDLE? that reported the details of a divorce settlement dispute during which Lilla's lawyers accused Tower of marital misconduct and demanded depositions from three women they alleged were the objects of his misconduct. A few days later, NBC ran a rehash of the allegations on the evening news. Other stories calculating the odds of a Tower nomination had also included vague references to reports of womanizing and excessive drinking. But since senators are not exactly unaccustomed to hearing such rumors about their colleagues, or about themselves, for that matter, and since the rumors didn't seem to have unduly concerned George Bush or the people vetting John's nomination, I didn't expect them to be too much of a problem. Embarrassing? Surely. But disqualifying? Not unless Washington was unexpectedly seized by one of its periodic fits of puritanism. And that, I felt sure, was not a likely scenario. There were too many hearty drinkers around the place who might not always have been the most exemplary of devoted spouses to begrudge John his vices, even if they were as exceptional as some wilder imaginations thought they might be, which, as is usually the case in scandal-loving Washington, they were not.

I had seen John Tower drink. I had seen him inebriated on occasion, but never incapacitated, never falling-down drunk. I was familiar enough with the behavior of alcoholics to recognize the symptoms in others. John

Tower wasn't an alcoholic. He wasn't a binge drinker. He didn't hide his liquor and drink secretly. I never saw him indulge in more than a glass at a meal during daytime hours or sip a small amount of champagne after he boarded a plane.

He worked hard and liked to relax at the end of the day with a glass or two or even three of Johnnie Walker Black. When I traveled with him as his navy escort, it was usually my job to make sure his hotel room had an adequate, but not unusually ample, stock of his preferred beverage. We traveled to a lot of dry Middle Eastern countries together where drinking spirits of any kind is a crime. Saudi Arabian prohibition, for instance, is particularly severe in its punishment of alcohol consumption, although I have seen more than a few Saudi officials take a rather more tolerant view of the transgression at private receptions hosted by visiting foreigners. As long as their guests indulged their Western habit discreetly and, of course, had the good grace to politely ignore those Saudi officials who, out of the public eye, might like to sample a beverage or two, the criminal sanctions that punished such behavior were avoided.

Nevertheless, it can be hard to find a drink in the country. Getting caught violating the local custom, without the benefit of a drinking companion who claimed membership privileges in the royal House of Saud, could land a fellow in a particularly unpleasant Saudi jail. So whenever we traveled there, I had to smuggle in a dozen or so single-serving bottles of Johnnie Walker obtained on the flight over. These I would deliver to Tower's room after I checked us in, so that he and his traveling party could wind down in his accustomed way at the end of a long day. These were hardly occasions of riotous drinking that Tower's detractors assumed he chronically engaged in. Just a drink or two, a little conversation, and then all parties were off to get some sleep before beginning another long day. Traveling and socializing with John Tower was interesting and fun, but never an occasion for embarrassment or concern over his drinking. Whatever he drank, he could hold; he seldom relaxed the rather formal comportment he prided himself on. Even when he felt high-spirited, his behavior hardly exceeded the bounds of good manners.

In fact, Tower seemed to rely on me to provide a little rough humor when the occasion called for it. I drink very little, but I am not inclined to

observe situational formalities as scrupulously as Tower did. I could usually be counted on during our many foreign travels together to liven
things up somewhat with an impetuous reaction to circumstances I felt
could be improved by a little informal entertainment.

On one such occasion, having arrived at night in Riyadh, Saudi Ara-
bia, tired and impatient to get to bed, I stood in line at a hotel desk waiting to check us in when two Frenchmen decided to shorten their own wait
by cutting in front of me. When I protested, they turned, sneered at me,
and aimed a few French expletives in my direction. Not wanting to cause
an incident that would embarrass the senator, I refrained from pressing
the matter further beyond offering my rude acquaintances a couple of expletives of my own. Adding insult to injury, I was forced to share an elevator ride with the two as I went to Tower's room with several little bottles
of Johnnie Walker Black in my briefcase. We disembarked on the same
floor, and I made a mental note of the room they entered in case the
knowledge should be of later use.

After little more than an hour, Tower's quiet cocktail party ended. I
said good night to John and the other members of his delegation and left
for my own room, charged, as was my duty, with finding a discreet loca-
tion to dispose of the empty Johnnie Walker bottles. As I passed the
Frenchmen's room, I noticed they had set two room service trays with a
full cargo of plates and glasses outside their door, providing a place to deposit my empties as well as an opportunity to exact a little vengeance.

My first thought upon awakening the next morning was how much
trouble I had managed to cause with my retaliatory prank. I assumed that
a few confusing minutes after being awakened by humorless Saudi police,
my two antagonists had probably persuasively pleaded their innocence
and avoided arrest. But I wouldn't have been terribly bothered if they had
not been so fortunate. The thought of their predicament kept me amused
for the rest of the day. Tower exploded in laughter when I told him the
story over breakfast, and he forever after delighted in recounting it, with a
little embellishment, over a few drinks with friends.

Wild behavior, or just notably inappropriate conduct, was something I
saw Tower enjoy only vicariously, sober or not. By the time of his nomination for secretary of defense, he no longer indulged his fondness even

for Johnnie Walker. He had given it up years before and restricted his alcohol consumption to a few glasses of wine with dinner. His divorce from Lilla, as messy and bitter as it was, had also relieved him of the burden of great unhappiness. She had fought with his daughters, mistreated his staff and friends, embarrassed him constantly, and generally made his life miserable. Freed from the marriage, he was a visibly happier man, more easygoing and amiable. He had had, as he was eventually and embarrassingly forced to admit, extramarital affairs during his first marriage. But he claimed never to have strayed during his marriage to Lilla, and I believed him. I had never seen him chase women, force his unwanted attentions on anyone, or, for that matter, behave at all improperly to a woman. I certainly didn't recognize the portrait of an unregenerate satyr that the press, reacting to the slander they were leaked, painted of John Tower. By 1988, he was in a committed relationship with Dorothy Heyser, a fine lady of mature years, and he seemed to me more serene and at ease than I had ever known him to be during his marriage to Lilla.

But his serenity was short-lived, as his peace of mind and reputation were soon ruined in a brutal confirmation process, a spectacular if unanticipated sacrifice of one man's name and fortune for the sake of other people's ambitions. At the hands of his former colleagues, Tower was made to endure a ritualistic and peculiarly Washington persecution that Bill Cohen, near the apex of our mutual friend's disgrace, compared without exaggeration to the seventeenth-century witch trial dramatized in Arthur Miller's play *The Crucible*.

Sam Nunn, the senior senator from Georgia, had become chairman of the Senate Armed Services Committee in 1986, succeeding Barry Goldwater, who had succeeded John Tower two years earlier. He was respected on both sides of the aisle for his intelligence, seriousness, proficiency in the theories and details of defense policy, and particularly for what most observers, including me, believed was his thoughtful, nonpartisan approach to conducting the committee's business. He was the grandnephew of Carl Vinson, a durable chairman of the House Armed Services Committee and frequent guest at my parents' table, and he succeeded to the Senate one of its most respected members, Richard Russell, a legendary chairman of the Senate Armed Services Committee, illustrious and very

powerful forebears of estimable public-spiritedness who were thought to
be the prototypes for Nunn's own reign as chairman. He was the last person anyone expected to wield power cruelly for personal or partisan advantage.

Sam Nunn is a straitlaced fellow, and his sensibilities might very well
have been offended by rumors of John Tower's licentious and dissolute
lifestyle. Everyone suspected that Lilla was spreading malicious gossip
about her ex-husband, and Nunn, who probably wasn't familiar with just
how toxic Lilla's spite could be, might have genuinely believed some of the
slurs to be true.

Some people close to Tower believed Nunn's attitude toward his former colleague was influenced more by self-interest than personal rectitude. When he had been chairman, Tower could be quite autocratic at
times and dismissive of more junior members when their views were not
in accord with his own. Apparently, he had not always treated Nunn tactfully and was often indifferent to the younger man's opinions. More than
once, Nunn had been lashed by Tower's sharp tongue and resented it.
Some of Tower's friends who had observed their earlier relationship
thought that Nunn's assumption of the role of Tower's chief antagonist
was nothing more complicated than revenge for those past slights. Others
thought that Nunn viewed Tower merely as a formidable rival for dominance over national defense policy—a rival who, if past practice was any
guide, might not always remember the formal courtesies that cabinet secretaries are expected to pay congressional committee chairmen who authorize their department's budgets.

I don't know which is the true explanation for the way Sam Nunn
treated John Tower, offended virtue, wounded pride, or contesting egos.
Whatever it was, I didn't see it coming, and to this day I cannot understand it.

Nunn's first comments on Tower's nomination were approving, similar
to the normal expressions of support and friendship that most of Tower's
former peers volunteered when his nomination was announced. Whether
those tributes were genuine or affected, as a majority proved to be, didn't
really matter at the time they were offered. What mattered was that they
indicated Tower would enjoy the usual favoritism granted former col-

leagues whose new occupation was subject to the Senate's advice and consent. Nothing in Nunn's initial reaction or any other senator's betrayed the slightest hint of the ordeal that was to come.

Nor did the Federal Bureau of Investigation report on Tower's background, completed just before the White House announced his nomination, raise an alarm that his confirmation might be endangered. The FBI had interviewed seventy-nine people during the course of their initial investigation, only one of whom had accused Tower of having a drinking problem, and even that accusation was offered only on condition that the accuser's identity not be disclosed. Nor did the investigators find credible evidence to support allegations of the nominee's habitual philandering.

After reviewing the report, President Bush instructed the Bureau to brief the chairman and ranking Republican member of the committee, Senators Nunn and John Warner, on its contents. Nunn didn't share the president's satisfaction that the report had put to rest concerns about the nominee's character. Washington was beginning to buzz with gossip about Tower's personal life, malicious and unproven though most of it was. Nunn might have thought there was more substance to the rumors than the FBI had found, or that given enough time, the rumors might multiply and pose a more serious challenge to the nomination. I don't know what his original motives were for insisting on another, more exhaustive investigation before the committee scheduled its first confirmation hearing. But the Bush administration complied and promptly ordered a second investigation. To avoid charges of partisan mischief making, Nunn was careful to secure Warner's agreement that further inquiries were warranted.

John Warner is a good man who has neither the zeal nor the stomach for political brawling. I'm sure he intended his close cooperation with the committee chairman to reflect the committee's reputation for civility and bipartisan cooperation. John's good nature and respect for committee traditions were characteristics of his generally trusting personality. But politics is a business where a naturally suspicious nature can be a tactical advantage and where John's admirable virtues can be seen as weaknesses by less benevolent characters. Unbeknownst to all of us, Tower was about to find himself in a knife fight. He would need defenders on the committee with an aptitude for street fighting, and he would have to look for that type of support from someone other than the committee's senior Republican.

That reality should have been clear to all of us when, in a break from committee tradition, Sam Nunn instructed that access to the FBI background reports would no longer be restricted to the chairman and ranking Republican. FBI reports are mostly a compilation of raw data about a nominee's past, often including many false and unsubstantiated charges of wrongdoing and suggestions of disqualifying character flaws. For that reason, it is exceedingly rare for members other than the committee's top Democrat and Republican to review their contents. In Tower's case, not only were all committee members to be made privy to the report's details, but some senior committee staff were to be granted the privilege as well. This included Nunn's senior staffer on the committee, Arnold Punaro. Tower's supporters eventually suspected Punaro of being the source for many leaks to the press of salacious and inflammatory accusations uncovered by investigating agents, although, in fairness, our suspicions were never proven and probably focused on Punaro by default. We doubted that Senator Nunn himself would retail unproven allegations to reporters. That all of these charges turned out to be baseless was of little value ultimately to Tower's confirmation. He would be tried and convicted in the press before the Senate roused itself to finish the job.

The leaks began almost immediately after Nunn and Warner received the first FBI report. Clearly, more than Lilla's whispering campaign was behind the flourishing public attention to the nominee's rumored character flaws. And as the media's sensationalism intensified, the number of unsolicited reports of immoral or unethical behavior in Tower's past sent to the FBI and the committee increased correspondingly, launching what one senior committee Republican, Malcom Wallop, would aptly term a "trial by transom."

Added to the multiplying reports of lewd and drunken behavior were allegations that Tower had misappropriated campaign funds and as a defense consultant had used classified information shared with him in his capacity as an arms control negotiator. Still, as investigators plowed through the ever-growing thicket of charges and suspicions of misconduct, they managed to knock down most of them and were unable to substantiate the remainder. But, as everyone in public life who has been falsely charged with misdeeds and been deprived of the accused's right to the presumption of innocence has been heard to lament, you cannot prove a negative.

Nunn dismissed as incomplete the second FBI report, delivered to the committee on December 23 and containing even more sensational, though discredited or unsubstantiated, accusations than the first. It's possible that he found the accusations more credible than had the FBI. Keeping the investigation open would also provide more time to search for information to substantiate them. But three FBI investigations of a nominee's background was far from standard procedure and beginning to look like little more than a fishing expedition. Equipped with this lengthy catalog of Tower's alleged personal misconduct, unsupported by established facts, with more accusations flying over the transom every day, and with the press corps beginning to suspect that it might soon be treated to a genuine bloodletting, Nunn convened the first confirmation hearing on January 25, to hear the testimony of the nominee himself.

Most of the hearing, which lasted for two days, was uneventful. The chairman opened the hearing with praise for the "well-qualified" nominee and assurances of a smooth confirmation. Committee members by and large avoided asking questions of an indelicate nature. Most of the Democrats on the committee were concerned with conflict of interest questions and whether or not Tower would exercise greater restraint over defense spending than had his predecessors. Tower handled their concerns skillfully and with tact. Most members seemed satisfied with his answers and little inclined to up the ante with more titillating inquiries, giving hope to Tower's friends that he would be shown the same courtesies granted other former senators. This disappointed those reporters who had hoped to cover a first-class spectacle, as well as the more lethally partisan Democrats in town, who savored the prospect of taking down a new Republican president's nominee.

After two days of successful testimony, Tower was excused, with the committee's thanks and best wishes, and the hearings were adjourned for the weekend. As members began to collect their papers and leave, Nunn informed them that confirmation hearings would reconvene the following Tuesday to hear the testimony of, among others, Paul Weyrich.

Weyrich was a social conservative activist of no national prominence, but known within Washington as an often intemperate and pompous defender of the faith within the increasingly influential Christian evangelical wing of the Republican Party. He had never been known to participate in national security debates. No one even knew if he actually had any views on the subject. So his appearance on the witness list raised a few suspicions about the purpose of his testimony. To my knowledge, he had no friends among committee Republicans and certainly none among the Democrats. Even Republicans with New Right credentials, who traveled in the same circle of activists as Weyrich, didn't consider his views on national defense, whatever they might be, particularly noteworthy.

I knew him slightly at the time, and although I didn't have any strong feelings about him, I can't say that I cared much for him. Weyrich possesses the attributes of a Dickensian villain. Corpulent and dyspeptic, his mouth set in a perpetual sneer as if life in general were an unpleasant experience, he is the embodiment of the caricature often used to unfairly malign all religious conservatives. He is the joyless preacher who for the sake of God and country sorrowfully consents to participate in the profane business of politics, and whose sour disposition is a natural reaction to the distasteful duty of consorting with the morally inferior beings who populate the profession. His moral certitude left little room for the basic rules of behavior that secular politicians, sinners though we surely are, feel obliged to respect. Facts are mere inconveniences to him if they don't serve his purposes. And what is truth if it is not subordinate to God's truth as revealed to a select few apostles of Weyrich's stature?

Like a thankfully small minority of religious conservative leaders who give politically active people of faith an undeserved reputation for intolerance and a meager capacity for charity, Weyrich was a selective observer of the Ten Commandments. They have no equal when it comes to honoring the Sabbath and refraining from taking the Lord's name in vain. And only God shares the measure of their disdain for sinners who violate the Seventh Commandment's prohibition on committing adultery. But they are often considerably less conscientious about honoring the Ninth Commandment (Thou shall not bear false witness against thy neighbor), since that commandment sometimes proves to be an impediment to enforcing the other nine. Thus, if necessary, its mandate can be temporarily suspended by those whom God has anointed as His political consultants on earth.

To Weyrich's crowd, it was only a sinner's guilt that explains my hostile reaction to the perfect specimen of Christian manhood who wished to draw the committee's attention to his personal knowledge of the nominee's dangerously libertine nature. But I like to think I know a pompous, self-serving son of a bitch when I see one, a facility that God, who loves His sinners as well as His saints, has seen fit to bless me with.

Typically, on those occasions when the committee must hear testimony of a prurient nature, a generally uncomfortable experience for all concerned, it does so behind closed doors. For unexplained reasons, Weyrich was permitted to answer in public session a question posed by the chairman soliciting the witness's firsthand knowledge of any "defects in the nominee's personal behavior." As it turned out, Mr. Weyrich did indeed claim such knowledge, which he proceeded to unburden himself of with the evident displeasure but steely resolve of a pious man obliged to discharge a distasteful public duty.

To paraphrase Thomas Jefferson, Weyrich fairly trembled for his country as he considered God was just and not likely to let pass unnoticed the presence of a boozy reprobate in the highest councils of our government. I don't know why not. God has seemed to suffer more than a few such scoundrels lowering the moral standards of public office since the very first days of the Republic's founding, and still He continues to bless our country with His bounty. Nevertheless, Weyrich felt that Tower, if confirmed, would soon prove to be a "national embarrassment" who would likely bring ruin to the rest of us.

Weyrich, as he frequently reminded the committee, was a family man. As such, only when forced by public and religious duty to frequent the habitat of drinkers who carried on their revels in mixed company was he likely to come into contact with low characters such as John Tower.

"I do not frequent social activities of Washington," he assured committee members, who no doubt were relieved that the witness's cloistered

lifestyle reduced the odds that they might encounter him in less than advantageous circumstances. "In fact, I avoid them because I find that is
good for family life. And so, if I encounter somebody, then my presumption has to be that probably there has to be a problem, because, first of all,
I do not seek such information on anybody, and, second, I do not go to
enough activities that I would be inclined to encounter somebody who
was occasionally having a problem."

Exactly what compromising behavior had he accidentally witnessed
the nominee engaged in? Weyrich could barely bring himself to utter it.
Well, "over the course of many years, I have encountered the nominee in
a condition—a lack of sobriety," he gasped, "as well as with women to
whom he was not married." As reporters began scratching furiously in
their notepads, the witness probably expected committee members to
clutch at their palpitating hearts in mortal distress for our own salvation,
lest we be fatally corrupted by mere exposure to such shocking revelations.
But instead we reacted, not inappropriately, by immediately becoming involved in a procedural dispute.

Weyrich's damning disclosures had apparently shocked Chairman
Nunn into remembering that such tawdry discussions were better conducted in closed session, and he quickly moved that the committee retire
behind locked doors, where we would endure any further shocks to our
sensibilities in private.

Committee Republicans complained that it was unsporting to allow
the witness's allegations to hang in public air, while a cross-examination
that might prove his memory to be faulty or qualified or invented would
be conducted beyond the observation of the press corps and, thus, subject
to selective interpretation by individual senators, some of whom, I was beginning to suspect, had less than honorable intentions. The chairman was
unmoved by our protests and after a brief debate took the committee into
closed session, leaving amused reporters with only their active imaginations to conjure up the ribald discussions of bawdy behavior we would be
entertaining ourselves with until we leaked it to them later.

I will leave it to Senator Nunn to explain why he had allowed Weyrich
to testify in the first place if he hadn't known the man was going to regur-
gitate some sensational incident from Tower's scarlet past. Weyrich was

hardly an authority on the throw weight of nuclear missiles or on any other defense question, for that matter. I smelled a rat, as did Tower's other supporters. What none of us knew was just how many rats would soon be swarming around John Tower's troubled nomination.

True to form, Weyrich proceeded to make an ass of himself behind closed doors, sputtering his charges somewhat incoherently while his little-amused audience asked him to elaborate. Pressed, he offered that he had seen Tower "coming on" to a woman at the Monocle, a popular drinking and dining establishment a short walk from Senate office buildings. "What do you mean by 'coming on'?" I asked him.

"He was holding her hand."

"You mean holding someone's hand is immoral behavior?"

Weyrich stared at me as if the answer to my question were self-evident. I had apparently led a less sheltered life than the witness had and had traveled in circles where the standards of evidence for moral turpitude were considerably stricter than hand-holding. Weyrich was also repeatedly asked to provide the committee with details of Tower's behavior that indicated his state of inebriation. This, too, was beyond Weyrich's ability to credibly explain. He offered nothing in closed session, absolutely nothing, that convinced any of us that the conduct witnessed by Weyrich, if in fact he hadn't made the whole thing up, was sufficient to trouble even the most prudish senator's conscience. It was, in short, a crock, and I suspected intentional slander offered for reasons other than the good citizenship Weyrich claimed as his purpose.

John Tower was pro-choice, which endeared him little to social conservatives. When he had been chairman of the National Republican Senatorial Campaign Committee, he had refused to heed the demands of Weyrich and others to limit the committee's support to only those candidates who held pro-life views. Moreover, reports that the more egotistical social conservatives like Weyrich felt that the Bush administration was paying insufficient deference to them were widespread. Some of us suspected that an attack on a Bush nominee who was regarded as insufficiently conservative by their lights would be a good way for social conservatives to intimidate the president and force him to give them the respect they felt, for reasons unfathomable to me, they deserved. That such a controversy would probably help a little with their fund-raising only made the tactic more attractive.

Honesty obliges me to admit that I have had my share of trouble with social conservatives generally over the subject of political fund-raising, which I will detail in a later chapter, and with Paul Weyrich specifically. Twelve years after the Tower confirmation battle, when I ran for president, Weyrich, who preferred almost any other candidate to me, felt disposed to criticize the breakup of my first marriage, as well as traffic in allegations that I had committed treason while a prisoner of war in Vietnam.

When senators trooped back into public session, it was clear that the committee had not found the witness's credibility to be something they would personally vouch for. Tower was called back into the witness chair and asked by Nunn if he had a problem with alcohol. Tower replied, "I have none, Senator. I am a man of some discipline." This response might have struck some as arrogant, but the committee lacked any credible evidence to suggest he was lying.

One might have thought that Weyrich's gambit had failed, given the committee's evident disregard of it. But, alas, such a reasonable conclusion would prove to be nothing more than wishful thinking. The frenzied Washington speculation about just how big a lecher and drunkard John Tower was had officially commenced. His enemies—who were beginning to come into view—and the press prepared for theatrical and bloody political combat, a spectacle that could end only when Tower's body lay lifeless on the sands of the coliseum.

But this sad conclusion to the affair did not seem inevitable to Tower as he concluded his additional testimony in the late morning of February 1, satisfied that Weyrich's unconvincing performance and his own boast of self-discipline had satisfied the chairman's concerns about "defects in [his] personal behavior." Tower and most Republicans on the committee expected the vote on his nomination to occur the following day, barring any new developments. As Tower and Sherrie Marshall, a White House lawyer who was serving as his counsel, made ready to leave the hearing room, Arnold Punaro hustled over to them with a couple of new developments in hand. The committee had completed a favorable report on his nomination, Punaro pleasantly informed Tower, assuring him that the committee would vote, presumably the next morning, to approve his nomination. Punaro then handed a note to Marshall that described two new allegations of misconduct the committee had just received, allegations that would have to be put to rest before a vote on the nomination could be rescheduled.

A woman had telephoned the committee to report that an intoxicated Tower had twice driven his car into a gully near his apartment building. Moreover, the caller claimed she had been a television talk show host and in that capacity had received unsolicited phone calls from women who had alleged that while serving on Tower's staff, he had sexually harassed them. Tower knew these latest charges were false and that no new investigation would prove otherwise. But he also knew that there would be another investigation and that the committee vote would be delayed. There was nothing he could do about it. Chagrined and discouraged, he left the hearing to keep a lunch date with Dorothy Heyser at the Jefferson Hotel, after which he would begin working with his aides to refute the new accusations of misconduct.

Tower was already seated at a table in the hotel's dining room when Dorothy arrived. Knowing that the day's events had clearly depressed him, she thought she could lift his spirits by making fun of her friend's by now much publicized and much exaggerated racy reputation. While patting his leg, she asked Tower if he'd enjoy having his knee fondled.

A distorted account of Dorothy's playful attempt at gaiety was reported in a *Washington Post* gossip column the next morning. Washingtonians, including the less than amused chairman of the Senate Armed Services Committee, woke up to read in their morning paper that the president's nominee for secretary of defense had "lunged" at his girlfriend in a public place and declared, "I'm going to fondle you." That such "fondling" was done in jest and not in the throes of reckless passion hardly excused the indiscretion in the eyes of the serious men who now sat in judgment of John Tower. To Sam Nunn, and those senators who shared his misgivings about Tower, the incident, at best, could only be interpreted as the nominee's open ridicule of the very serious allegations about his fitness for high office that the committee was bound by solemn duty to examine.

That same day, the chairman announced that a vote on the Tower nomination had been postponed pending completion of a fourth FBI investigation of two new charges of personal misconduct.

The conflagration that ensued was, as many had hoped, spectacular. The FBI would find no evidence to substantiate either the drunken off-road driving allegation or the sexual harassment charge. Tower's aides and administration officials worked quickly to establish that there was no police report, insurance claim, or bill for repairs to back up the alleged driving mishaps. When the FBI investigated the sexual harassment charges, the woman could not provide the names of Tower's accusers or the dates and time they called her or any tapes or notes of the calls. The accusations, like those that preceded it, were false. It couldn't have mattered less.

The steady stream of allegations that had plagued the nomination from the start, some anonymous, others on-the-record, turned into a torrent. In phone calls to the chairman and ranking Republican, and almost certainly to reporters, Lilla was expanding her long list of grievances against her former husband. The first editorials calling for the withdrawal of the troubled nomination appeared. Leaks of raw data contained in the various FBI reports, detailing every wild rumor and spurious charge about Tower's character flaws, increased exponentially, often seeming to appear in print before they had been brought to most committee members' attention.

A report surfaced of Tower drunk and disorderly on a flight to Paris, so drunk apparently that he had been unable to disembark the airplane unaided. I had shared many overseas flights with Tower. I had never seen him drunk on any of them. On the contrary, he had a habit of eating and drinking very lightly while traveling, spending most of the time reading and sleeping so that he would be prepared upon arriving at his destination for a full day of meetings. I knew the allegations weren't credible, a conclusion shared by the investigating agents. The flight attendant who reported Tower's airborne revels, who hadn't actually worked in the first-class cabin where Tower had been seated, couldn't recall the flight number, the date, any other members of the crew, or any passengers who might be able to corroborate her story. When the FBI finally located the one plane manifest where the names of both Tower and his accuser were recorded, they interviewed a flight attendant who had worked in the first-class cabin, and she reported a sober and perfectly well-behaved Tower, who exited the plane without assistance or any visible difficulty. Three other flight attendants confirmed her account, while his accuser failed a lie detector test.

A traveling businessman informed the committee that on three separate occasions he had seen Tower drunk at the Jefferson Hotel. He helpfully provided the committee with the dates of those occasions. As it turned out, Tower was in Pakistan, Texas, and Seattle on the three evenings in question. Another businessman said he saw Tower falling-down drunk at a party in Germany, naming five other people as witnesses. Two of the witnesses said they hadn't seen Tower drunk. The other three said they hadn't attended the party, and one of them said he had never even met John Tower.

Tower was reported to have kept a Russian ballerina living in Houston as his mistress, with whom, on one riotous evening at a Houston country club, he danced on top of a piano. No Russian ballerina living in Houston or anywhere else in Texas Tower visited was ever found. Nor were there any witnesses to a loaded Tower dancing at a country club. Nor could the piano in question be located. The country club where the incident was alleged to have taken place didn't have one.

These represent but a small sample of the wild accusations and outright slander that the committee was daily entertaining and leaking to keep the media fire stoked. Had Tower's enemies all along sought a pretense with which to threaten his nomination, they could have never dreamed they would possess such an abundant, if untrue, supply.

Senate battle lines were beginning to form, as Nunn started to work on fellow Democrats to refrain at least from declaring their support for Tower and preferably to help Nunn organize opposition to him. To this day, I don't know if Sam Nunn had intended all along to undermine Tower's nomination or if the flood of rumors and calumnies surprised him with a motive and opportunity to do so. I don't even know what his motives were. I never asked him point-blank whether he had hidden reasons for opposing Tower. His public explanations that the allegations of misconduct were too serious and too numerous to dismiss always ignored the fact that they were either unproven or provably false. And I guess I assumed he was using the allegations to prosecute Tower for personal or political reasons he preferred not to disclose. As I said, I liked and respected him. There would be times after Tower's fate was decided that I would disagree with his position on an issue. And there would be other times when I would agree with him and find many qualities about Nunn to admire. But in all fairness, and without lingering bitterness, I must say that I found his treatment of John Tower, and the way he worked his will during the confirmation battle, whatever his motives were and whenever he decided to take that road, to be inexcusable.

He preferred to work through others. I suspected his staff, either on his order or because of his indifference, of leaking damning information to the press. When the time came to publicly suggest that Tower might not be confirmed, he used other senators, whenever possible, to deliver the message. He always tried to maintain the appearance of bipartisanship by persuading John Warner to acquiesce in his calls for further investigations and his decisions to delay the committee's vote. Few other Democratic senators welcomed the responsibility to kill the Tower nomination that Nunn was forcing upon them. The sins Tower was accused of were hardly Washington novelties. That they were allegedly committed so indiscreetly was worrisome, but even then they would not normally muster a majority to vote against the nomination. Add to that the disturbing fact that most of the allegations had a tendency to prove unconvincing, the call for a public hanging of the nominee struck most senators, of both parties, as excessively severe punishment.

Nevertheless, Nunn was beginning to transform the surprisingly unsettled and much too colorful confirmation process into a pitched battle between Democrats and Republicans. Once Tower's nomination was considered within the question of whether the Democratic congressional majority would prevail over the Republican administration and congressional minority, the Democratic leadership would become engaged, and most if not all Democrats would fall, albeit reluctantly, into line. At that point, there would be no saving John Tower.

To make sure it became a question of party loyalty, Nunn would need some committee Democrats to begin making a fight of it before most Democrats knew they would eventually be expected to join in. In most instances, Democrats on the committee weren't comfortable making a case for opposing Tower on the basis of the nominee's alleged and, as they knew, exaggerated behavioral defects. He was, whether they liked him or not, a member of their club and certainly not the first of his kind to be accused of exhibiting a few personal foibles. They preferred to make what case they could against Tower on the grounds of an apparent conflict of interest arising from the perceived close nexus between Tower the consultant to defense contractors and Tower the arms control negotiator. Or they relied on allegations of financial impropriety or on the argument that Tower was too uncritical a proponent of excessive Pentagon spending to base their concerns about the nominee's suitability.

Slowly and, for most of them, with evident timidity, they began to voice those concerns. Many of these senators had respected reputations for their serious and not overly partisan approach to their work. They were good legislators. Many of them were my friends. Some of them remain so. All of them, however, could not see their way clear to refusing their chairman's appeal to support his decision that John Tower's nomination must be defeated. In some instances it is understandable, but not excusable. Newly elected Democratic members on the committee, as was my friend Joe Lieberman, would have been hard-pressed to take the very difficult step of refusing to defer to their powerful chairman's judgment. I understand that, and I appreciate the difficult circumstances they found themselves in, in which all committee Democrats found themselves. But I cannot accept it as a mitigating factor in what, after all, was a conscious (if coerced) decision to do wrong to a man and, by my lights, to the public trust they held.

There were, of course, a few of the chairman's acolytes who appeared more than willing to serve as character assassins in the Tower fight. Some had never liked Tower. A few even hated him. For some, politics was simply a transactional business. They considered every vote, every issue, every fight, in terms of how it would benefit them personally in the short and the long term. In this instance, would it profit them more to support Nunn or Tower? For most Democrats, that was an easy choice. Maybe they weren't the bravest or the most intelligent members of the Senate.

Maybe they lacked enough self-knowledge to see that they might open themselves to charges of hypocrisy. I don't know, and I don't care. They disgraced themselves, just as much as Paul Weyrich had disgraced himself. There is little that can be said in their defense.

In the campaign to destroy John Tower, J. James Exon of Nebraska, the second-ranking committee Democrat, was Sam Nunn's earliest and most eager lieutenant. It first became clear that Nunn had decided to defeat Tower's nomination the moment Exon roused himself from his usual indolence to ruminate aloud about the nominee's character flaws. No allegation of personal misconduct was too dubious or too inflammatory to give Exon pause before speculating about the terrible concerns they raised. Of all the indignities Tower was forced to suffer that winter, to be judged and found wanting by someone of Jim Exon's caliber surely had to be among the most distressing. But such was the misfortune of a nominee who had always acted in accordance with the culture's established rules but who suddenly found those rules had been changed without his knowledge.

Alert to signs that a scandal concerning a colleague was beginning to taint their reputations, a few Republicans were starting to express concerns about the nomination. Most, however, especially those on the committee, were getting angry at what was beginning to look like a well-orchestrated campaign to destroy with slander and innuendo the reputation of an eminently well-qualified nominee.

Tower had many able defenders on the committee. Bill Cohen, Malcom Wallop, and Pete Wilson were exceptionally skillful and pointed in their defense of Tower's good name and qualifications for the job. I was probably less adroit and considerably less tactful in my efforts to support my friend and mentor than were my more senior and experienced colleagues. They had been around long enough to know when cool reason and calm persuasion were sufficient to prevent an injustice and when it became necessary to start breaking arms. I thought that in light of the damnable tactics that were being used to destroy John Tower, the sooner we started inflicting casualties on the other side, the better.

Nunn had begun telling Democrats that he intended to oppose the nomination. And I began to harass a few of the Democrats on the committee, cajoling, pleading, and demanding that they treat my friend with the respect and fairness he deserved. In the weeks ahead, my advocacy for Tower would become sharper and angrier.

On February 7, White House lawyers briefed Republican senators on the results of the FBI's latest investigation, assuring them that there was no evidence to substantiate the allegations of drunk driving and sexual harassment. At the invitation of the White House, he and Warner went to see President Bush. Apparently, the president, although courteous as always, didn't intend their discussion to be a one-sided affair, where he would listen attentively to the senator from Georgia as he detailed his grave concerns about the suitability of the president's nominee. Nunn raised his concerns, of course, although he didn't go so far as to declare his opposition to Tower. The president, more forthrightly, informed both senators that he had no intention whatsoever of withdrawing Tower's nomination. As he bade good-bye to his guests, the president might have believed that his firm assurance that John Tower remained his choice for secretary of defense would make it harder for Nunn to cross the line into open opposition. He only had to wait until the next day to find out how mistaken he was.

The New York Times ran a story quoting Nunn's designated stalking-horse, Jim Exon, that if FBI investigators were merely unable to substantiate the charges against Tower, that would not be sufficient to prevent both Exon and Sam Nunn from voting against his nomination. As of that moment, they both intended to oppose Tower, and only if the FBI came up with something "to ease their doubts about reports of Mr. Tower's drinking and his behavior with women" would they be inclined to change their negative disposition toward the nominee. Dispensing with all rules of evidence and the most basic standards of fairness, it now seemed that, as far as the chairman of the committee and his accomplice were concerned, accusations alone, whether they were exaggerated, unproven, unfounded, or entirely fictional, were enough to deny John Tower his life's ambition.

This was a grave turn of events for Tower, a clear signal that the vote on his nomination had become a political fight to the finish between the president and Senate Democrats. When Nunn and the Democratic leadership began to impress fellow Democrats with their resolve to defeat

Tower, few would be able to resist their entreaties. Had the vote been held within the next day or two, prior to the ten-day Senate recess that began on February 11, enough Democratic votes could still have been found to confirm him. But with every passing day that Tower was denied a vote, Democrats prepared to break with their party would become increasingly scarce.

Nunn had taken the position that the latest FBI investigation had failed to put to rest doubts about Tower's character. The report, which was delivered to the committee on the same day as publication of the *New York Times* story revealing Nunn's probable opposition, should have made it clear to any fair-minded Democrat that even if its contents failed to allay the chairman's concerns, it surely didn't vindicate Nunn's view that Tower's confirmation would recklessly endanger the security of the Republic. Nor, for that matter, would it justify postponing a committee vote until after the recess. But, alas, yet another allegation surfaced that would give Nunn the time he needed to work his will within the Democratic caucus.

The president's chief legal counsel, C. Boyden Gray, informed the Senate that the White House had just received a report alleging that Tower had accepted an illegal campaign contribution from a defense contractor implicated in a recent defense procurement scandal. Although the FBI had just delivered what had been intended as its last report on Tower, the Bureau would now resume its investigation to look into this latest accusation of wrongdoing. Thus, regrettably, the White House itself requested that the committee's vote be delayed until the matter could be resolved. This was a mistake by the White House, made on the advice of Boyden Gray.

I don't know Gray well. But I've never been much impressed with either his political sense or his legal skills. He had always struck me as a dilettante, an Ivy League patrician who plays politics with alternately a pretended enthusiasm or a gentlemanly disdain for the crudeness of a business in which one was obliged to consort with those of less aristocratic breeding. He wasn't a politician or a very able government leader. And he certainly wasn't a wartime consigliere for a new president in danger of having his authority badly damaged in a losing confirmation fight for one of his most important cabinet posts. But he was a close friend of the president's, and his attitude toward the nominee was likely to be misinterpreted by Tower's and the president's enemies as reflecting the real extent to which the president was prepared to fight for his nominee. In this, just as in his poor counsel to delay the committee vote, he would prove to be a liability to the president, to Tower, and to Tower's friends.

Gray had made light of Tower's personality in an earlier conversation with Nunn, suggesting that a man of Tower's short physical stature might be suffering from a Napoleonic complex. According to Tower, whom I believe, Gray consistently displayed a lack of enthusiasm for Tower and an excessive deference to Nunn even after it became clear to all but Gray that Nunn intended to deny the president his choice as defense secretary.

In hindsight, I think Tower's sorry fate was pretty much sealed at this point. But we were in the thick of the battle, and those of us who counted ourselves as his friends and supporters, confident that the latest allegation against him would be shot down, felt Tower still had a good chance to be confirmed. The last FBI report was completed and delivered to the White House on February 20, the day the Senate returned from its recess. Unsurprisingly, it knocked down the charge of receiving illegal campaign contributions, as previous reports had knocked down so many others. But in the ten days that had elapsed, more damage had been done. The details of the latest allegation were leaked, and the press, in its habitual desire to fill the void during a slow news period, recycled a good number of the earlier unproven allegations. Of course, the steady stream of lies and distortions received over the transom continued uninterrupted during the recess. Lilla was rumored to be still prosecuting her endless catalog of grievances against her former husband. The shortest trip in Washington was the distance traveled by details from the FBI reports in committee files—no matter how salacious, absurd, or provably false—to the front pages of the nation's newspapers.

President Bush, a man of greater integrity than were many of his Senate antagonists, declared that the latest and final investigation had "gunned down" all the "rumor and innuendo" plaguing his embattled friend and called on the Senate Armed Services Committee to do the right thing by the nominee and the country and quickly vote to confirm John Tower as his secretary of defense. Sam Nunn swiftly responded by saying that while the president was entitled to his opinion, the chairman of the Armed Services Committee did not share it. The next day, the president left for a trip to Asia. The day after that, February 23, the committee rejected the nomination of John Tower, eleven to nine, on a strictly party line vote.

In the days before that vote, I had been virtually beside myself as I frantically sought to convince one or two Democrats to vote for confirmation. In one instance, both Tower and I had solicited a firm pledge from a committee Democrat to break with Nunn and vote for confirmation. At least, we thought it was firm. When the committee clerk calling the roll reached Richard Shelby from Alabama, the senator responded with, "Nay." I thought I would erupt right there in full view of the press and public by denouncing Shelby's bad faith. But I managed to exercise a little self-restraint and waited until after the vote, when only a few senators would be present as witnesses, to bring my nose to within an inch of his as I screamed out my intense displeasure over his deceit and my general frustration with the injustice that was being done to my friend. Shelby was by no means the worst offender in Tower's witch trial or the biggest hypocrite during the whole miserable ordeal. I was madder than hell when I accosted him, though, and the incident is one of the occasions when my temper lived up to its much exaggerated legend. There were other memorable occasions during John Tower's ruin when I would reveal a less than senatorial demeanor. I exchanged harsh words with many of my colleagues, including Nunn, who because I had respected him so much disappointed me the most. But Jim Exon probably caught the worst of it. More than once I dispensed with all institutional decorum to offer Exon my most candid opinion of his character.

"I know what I know," he once offered in response to my argument that he didn't have a good reason to oppose Tower.

"What you know is a lie," I replied, "and you're a goddamn liar."

Committee Republicans, meeting before the vote, were surprised to discover that John Warner had still not grasped the personal and political reasons behind the campaign to destroy Tower and apparently remained in thrall to the chairman's professions of impartiality and due diligence.

He opened the meeting by asking, "Tell me why I should vote for this man." His Republican colleagues were all convinced that that question had been settled some time ago and that we were now in the thick of a battle to right a wrong. To us, this hardly seemed a propitious time for the committee's ranking Republican to persist in his earlier well-intentioned inclination to keep an open mind about the controversies surrounding the Tower nomination.

No sooner had Warner finished his question than I shouted back at him, "Tell me why you shouldn't vote for him."

Warner might have expected such a response from me. But it was Strom Thurmond, then eighty-five years old, who impressed upon Warner the extent to which Tower's confirmation had now become a matter of intense interest for all committee Republicans. Thurmond had been in the Senate longer than any other member. Were he to relinquish his senior position on the Judiciary Committee, he could claim Warner's office as the ranking Republican on Armed Services. Warner was obliged to pay careful attention to Thurmond's views lest he find himself moving one seat farther away from the chairman's. So when Strom stabbed John in the chest with his finger and told him in no uncertain terms that he must vote to confirm John Tower's nomination, the old man's clarity of purpose had the welcome effect of curing Warner's ambivalence.

In his explanation for his vote to reject Tower's nomination, Sam Nunn admitted that there was no evidence to support accusations that Tower had sexually harassed members of his staff or had endangered national security by indulging in romantic attachments to foreign nationals. However, other reports of questionable behavior, which Nunn refrained from describing, and evidence of the nominee's history of excessive drinking, would have disqualified John Tower from holding command of a bomber squadron or a submarine armed with nuclear missiles. And in the view of the chairman of the Armed Services Committee, the nominee for secretary of defense should be held to no less strict a standard. Tower's supporters on the committee observed that evidence of a disqualifying drinking problem was far from conclusive, but fair standards of evidence didn't seem to concern the chairman by then.

Usually, when the committee of jurisdiction votes to reject a nomination, that is the end of the matter. Nominees are expected to announce immediately after their humiliation that out of concern that the president and the country not suffer the absence of a vitally important high official indefinitely, and to spare themselves the indignity of almost certain rejection by the full Senate, they have asked the president to withdraw their nomination. In this instance, however, the president and his nominee, as well as Tower's Senate supporters, intended that this unusual confirmation fight would remain unusual to the end. We would slug it out on the floor of the Senate, knowing that the odds were heavily against confirmation and that the little partisan restraint that had governed the proceedings to date would disappear altogether.

Nunn was not pleased by this decision and tried to persuade the administration and Tower that further resistance was as unwise as it was futile. He threatened to reopen committee hearings, to entertain more testimony from witnesses who might allege all manner of unsavory behavior on the part of the nominee. He also ordered that the FBI reports, with all their wild and sensational calumnies against the nominee's character, would be placed in the Senate's secure briefing room, where all senators would be encouraged to review their contents (and, it was unspoken but anticipated, then leak them to reporters). But President Bush, to his great credit, remained firm. Tower, and those of us who fought for him, too inured to the excesses of Tower's enemies to be intimidated by the threat of more, were equally determined to see the thing through to its inglorious end.

Debate on the Senate floor would formally begin on March 2, but it really began immediately after the committee rejected the nomination. Many of us went to the floor right away to denounce the committee's vote and to decry the tactics employed to achieve it. Bob Dole, in his typically understated style, suggested that there "could be some hypocrisy here." Few of us were as restrained as the Republican leader. The debate raged for six days, setting a modern record for its bitterness, certainly for the vitriol senators directed at one another and for the ill-treatment accorded a former colleague. Republican charges of character assassination, dishonesty, and malicious partisanship were countered with ominous Democratic warnings of a blindly drunk defense secretary, with other worrisome shortcomings, staggering around the Defense Department with his trembling hand all too near the nuclear button. Democrats who could not quite bring themselves to contribute to the doomsday speculation were content to voice concern about apparent conflicts of interest, suggesting that the nominee appeared to be entirely in the pocket of defense contractors. Columnists and editorial writers on both sides of the issue joined the fray in earnest, many of them imitating the sarcasm and acerbity that characterized the Senate debate.

Tower, in the vain hope that there was something he could do to save his nomination, appeared on one of the Sunday political talk shows to pledge that were he confirmed he would refrain from taking a drop of alcohol for the length of his tenure as defense secretary. Unencumbered by even an affected sense of fair play, Jim Exon exposed what an impossible predicament Tower was in by suggesting Tower's pledge "might be interpreted as meaning he wants the job too badly." Three days later, in an appearance at the National Press Club, Tower was pressed into curtly admitting past marital infidelity. I felt embarrassed for my friend. Whatever his faults, he was a better man than his enemies, and I would have much preferred that he tell them all to go to hell rather than submit to the humiliation of public confessions and promises that he would be a good boy.

Ostensibly to aid senators who chose to review the FBI files, Nunn instructed his staff to prepare a summary of the allegations. To no one's surprise, it was a conspicuously slanted document, identifying many of the most damning accusations of misconduct with cursory (if any) mention of information rebutting them. After fuming about it for a few minutes, and roaring my contempt for its authors, I demanded that Republicans be allowed to prepare our own summary, which Nunn agreed to without argument.

Regrettably, the anger that seized me as I began to review the document caused me to overlook an allegation that Nunn's staff had included in the summary that had never been seriously considered by committee staff or members. A retired air force sergeant had contacted the FBI to report that when he had been stationed at Bergstrom Air Force Base in Austin, Texas, he had witnessed a staggering drunk John Tower on two separate visits to the base fondle a secretary and an enlisted woman. For reasons that would become clear later, neither the FBI nor committee staff considered the witness to be credible, and his report was relegated to the file reserved for information received from suspected cranks. Nevertheless, it managed to make its way into the Democratic summary, and on the morning of March 2, the first day of full Senate debate on the Tower nomination, onto the front page of *The Washington Post*. The story carried the distinguished byline of Bob Woodward.

As it turned out, the source had been stationed at Bergstrom from February 1976 to March 1977; John Tower's one and only visit to Bergstrom, as confirmed by the base commander and two other officers at the base whom Bill Cohen and I contacted, had occurred in 1975, six months before his accuser had reported for duty there. The accusation was entirely bogus.

The debate ran on, as bitter and personal on the last day as it was on the first. Friendships between some Democrats and Republicans were injured for a long time—some forever. Three Democrats spoke up for Tower: Chris Dodd of Connecticut, Howell Heflin of Alabama, and Lloyd Bentsen, Tower's fellow Texan. Dodd was particularly eloquent and steadfast in his defense. His father had served with Tower. He had been accused of financial impropriety and subjected to censure by the Senate. Tower had voted against the censure, an act that appropriately earned him the gratitude of Thomas Dodd's son. "Of course I won't forget how John Tower voted," Chris admitted. "What kind of son would I be if I did? I won't vote for John Tower because of the vote he cast twenty-two years ago regarding my father's censure. But I certainly won't vote against him because there's a herd mentality." Chris not only spoke up for Tower and voted for his confirmation, but he played an active behind-the-scenes role in organizing his defense. Chris and I have had our differences over the years about various issues, particularly over U.S. policy in Central America. But he was my friend from that day on and will remain so. I'm no more able to forget his fairness to my friend than he was able to forget Tower's fairness to his father.

By March 9, the day the Senate voted fifty-three to forty-seven to reject John Tower's nomination to be secretary of defense, both Tower and

I had grown weary of the fight. But neither of us yielded an inch until the battle was decided. I continued to browbeat, chastise, and try to shame members into supporting Tower. On that last day of debate, many Tower supporters did themselves and John Tower great credit with their eloquent and deeply felt closing statements on his behalf. Bill Cohen's speech was exceptionally moving and evidence of Bill's great decency and strength of character.

My speech was less memorable, and brief. I was exhausted and close to becoming undone by my emotions, barely managing to utter at the end of my remarks, "God bless you, John Tower. You're a damn fine sailor."

After the vote, I left immediately for the Pentagon to meet with Tower in the small, nondescript office he had used there while his nomination was pending. He was obviously hurt, but stoic and quiet. I was less reserved, swearing vengeance against the men who had done this to him. I know he was hurt by the discovery that many of his colleagues disliked him so intensely or at least felt so little friendship for him that they would join in the destruction of his reputation. He wrote it off to his unwillingness to suffer fools gladly or let sensitivity to his colleagues' egos inhibit what he believed was an honest defense of the security interests of the United States. He acted as if the discovery of his poor standing in the affections of some of his former colleagues weren't a surprise or a particular concern to him. But he wouldn't have been human if it hadn't hurt him a little and raised some self-doubts about whether he might have still achieved his purposes by paying more elaborate courtesy to the views and vanity of others.

I knew he was hurt, although he would never tell me as much. He believed he had an honorable career, and it pained him to think that others thought it less so. John Tower was not an emotionally demonstrative man, and only my intuition informed me that, like all human beings, he had his share of regrets about the choices he had made in life. As a rule, he wasn't the hugging kind. But when I went to leave, he embraced me, with tears in his eyes. The act instantly provoked my own emotions, which I had expressed until then only with anger and industry. I said good-bye to him and left hurriedly so he would not see my tears.

We were tough guys, he and I, or so we liked to think of ourselves. The emotions we felt at the moment of his defeat did not mean we would not recover from the anguish it had caused us. But John never had a chance to completely recover from the experience. Almost immediately he began working on a book about his life in politics and its sad conclusion. Published in 1991, it was an honest, fair, well-written, and entirely accurate account of the injustice that had been done to him. He was proud of it, as he should have been. But many reviewers, a number of whom were political reporters, dismissed it as a poison-pen letter to his enemies, the work of a bitter man who was incapable of just moving on.

On April 5, 1991, on their way to a party to celebrate his book's publication, John Tower and his beloved middle daughter, Marion, died in a plane crash near Brunswick, Georgia. I was traveling in Asia when I received word that my friend and political mentor had died. All of his obituaries, of course, focused on his rejected confirmation for secretary of defense. Pity. There had been a hell of a lot more to his life than that. Most of the obituary writers chose the adjective "embittered" to describe his state of mind at the end of his life. "Outraged" would have been a better word. John Tower was strong enough not to let that experience, as awful, unkind, and wrongful as it was, permanently destroy his love of life. But outraged he was, and outraged he should have been. Why should politics, of all professions, denigrate the virtue of outrage as a response to injustice? John Tower was intent on defending his honor. And honor is a thing worth earning and fighting for. Had his enemies known the value of personal honor, they would have spared him their attacks on his.

I raced home from Asia to attend his funeral in Dallas. Three weeks later, I spoke at a memorial service for him at Arlington National Cemetery. As I sat among the other senators attending the service, most of whom had supported him and some of whom had not, I reflected on how much Tower's defeat had changed my feelings about the institution that I had longed to be part of. It no longer held an unalloyed attraction for me. For all my experiences with politics and politicians before my election to the Senate, I had arrived there with more than a little awe for the eminence of the place and the people who inhabited it. Now I would never feel quite the same about it. John Tower's experiences taught me that partisanship could be worse than disagreeable. It could be dishonorable. And politics could offer just as serious a challenge to one's honor as those I had found in war—a lesson that was reaffirmed many times over in the months after John Tower and I had hastily parted company so as not to seem unmanful in the hour of his disgrace. For no sooner had John Tower seen his reputation destroyed than I found myself in a desperate fight to save my own.

Defending myself before the Senate Ethics Committee against
accusations of impropriety. *Associated Press*

EIGHT

KEATING FIVE

S hortly before the outbreak of the Seven Years' War, Admiral John Byng was ordered to sail a small fleet to Minorca in the western Mediterranean to relieve a British naval base that was being harassed by a French fleet. Evidently not much of a fighter, Byng contented himself with a spiritless engagement with the enemy before quitting the scene altogether and abandoning the naval base to French dominion. The British public and government were outraged by Byng's timidity. The prime minister, Lord Newcastle, seeking to assuage British anger, promised that Byng "shall be tried immediately, and hanged directly." Which he was, except he was spared the indignity of hanging from a ship's yardarm. Instead, he was promptly executed by firing squad. Voltaire referred to the incident in *Candide,* observing that the British felt compelled from time to time to shoot an admiral "in order to encourage the others."

The events I set in motion a little over two months after being sworn in as a United States senator, and their near consummation in the public execution of my political career and reputation, have served, I suppose, as encouragement to other members of Congress. Surely, those events forever after cautioned me. Learning from my unhappy experience, I have refrained from ever intervening in the regulatory decisions of the federal government if such intervention could be construed, rightly or wrongly, as done solely or primarily for the benefit of a major financial supporter of my campaigns. But more than that, I have tried as hard as I possibly can to merit a reputation as an honest servant of the public interest.

Nearly a decade after the ordeal, my career and reputation painstakingly recovered from the ruins they once seemed consigned to as a member of the unfortunate association known as the Keating Five, I needed to raise a great deal of money to finance my campaign for president. Faced as I was with an infinitely better-funded opponent, I had to appeal for support from many quarters, including from Washington lobbyists who represented concerns with interests before the Senate committees on which I served.

Government relations work is not a dishonorable calling. As with any profession, it claims as members men and women of good character as well as a few with less sterling qualities. Having worked in Washington for so long, I can claim with gratitude a good number of lobbyists as friends and supporters, many of whom supported my presidential campaign.

Nevertheless, as a leading advocate for the reform of campaign finance laws, whose central message as a presidential candidate was a promise to restrain the excessive influence of special interests in Washington, I expected my opponent and the press to scrutinize the source of every dollar contributed to my campaign and to treat any support from what might be termed the "usual suspects" in Washington as a chink in my reformer's armor.

That was certainly the case when, in February 2000, I held a fundraiser at the Willard Hotel in Washington attended by quite a few lobbyists. Accusations of hypocrisy by the Bush campaign, echoed by more than a few reporters, persuaded my campaign staff and me that I should remain on the campaign trail to avoid attending the event myself, a reaction I consider in hindsight to have been a little cowardly. But the good folks who did attend the event treated my politically motivated discourtesy with good humor and tried as they added to my campaign coffers to support as well my contention that I never let campaign contributions outweigh the public good in the discharge of my public duties. Outside the Willard, as my guests walked through the press gantlet and past a few Bush supporters shouting abuse and denouncing "McCain the phony," they sported large red, white, and blue buttons proclaiming, "McCain voted against my bill."

The buttons were intended to emphasize, of course, that I was not the kind of politician who could be bought, even if I had my hand out to people whom voters tend to perceive as prospective buyers. Politicians are expected to claim such respect, whether they deserve it or not, but I would very much like to think that I have never been a man whose favor could be bought. From my earliest youth, I would have considered such a reputation to be the most shameful ignominy imaginable. Yet that is exactly how millions of Americans viewed me for a time, a time that I will forever consider one of the worst experiences of my life.

The story started to attract widespread public attention within weeks of John Tower's ruin. But it began two years earlier, in the spring of 1987, when I made the worst mistake of my life by attending two meetings, the first with the chairman of the Federal Home Loan Bank Board, the government agency charged with regulating the practices of the nation's savings and loans, and a week later with four bank examiners based in San Francisco who were at that time investigating the investment and lending practices of Lincoln Savings and Loan of Irvine, California, owned by my good friend and generous supporter Charles Keating.

Charlie had come to Phoenix in 1978 to start a residential home construction company, the American Continental Corporation. By the time I met him three years later, he was well on his way to becoming the largest land developer in Arizona, with two thousand employees on his payroll and a reputation as one of the most commercially and socially prominent businessmen in my state. The early eighties were boom years in Arizona, and Charlie, aggressive, sharp, hardworking, was poised to make one of the bigger fortunes in a time of considerable affluence. He was also colorful, great fun, and generous. As I recounted in an earlier chapter, we became friends almost from the moment we met, and he, his family, and his associates became early and generous donors to my first campaign for the House, for my reelection campaign two years later, and to my first campaign for the Senate. He was quite obviously an important supporter of my ambitions. But more, I genuinely liked him and enjoyed being around him, especially on those occasions when Cindy and I and our oldest child, Meghan, were invited to his family's vacation home in the Bahamas. I was never concerned that the time I spent enjoying Charlie's company would raise public doubts about my judgment. He was a successful, prominent Arizona businessman, widely admired in the state, and I didn't believe his support and friendship were based in anything other than political and personal affinity. He was also a self-starter, a man of great confidence and daring who saw life as a huge adventure. People like that appeal to me. Attracted to their boldness and vivacity, and to the achievements of their enterprise, I have sometimes forgotten that wisdom and a strong sense of public responsibility are much more admirable qualities. That was, ironically, among the most important lessons I learned from my association with Charles Keating.

In 1984, American Continental acquired for $51 million an underperforming California thrift, Lincoln, that had only that year shown a profit of a few million dollars after running losses for several preceding years. The savings and loan business was thriving then, along with the boom in home construction in the Southwest. But they were also branching out into much more speculative and risky investments than home mortgages. The industry had been deregulated during the Carter administration, increasing the limit on federally insured deposits from $40,000 to $100,000 and raising the ceiling on interest payments they could make. And in 1982, Congress passed legislation that allowed savings and loans to make unsecured business loans and invest directly in huge commercial real estate ventures. These were heady days of overnight fortunes made in land development deals and brokered deposits. Many thrifts were joining in the fun, but Lincoln had not been one of them until Charlie acquired it.

The year Lincoln became a wholly owned subsidiary of American Continental, 48 percent of its $1.1 billion in assets were home loans. Twenty-four percent were considered risk assets. It had no brokered deposits. Lincoln's conservative management had maintained the slow-growth policies based on home mortgage lending traditionally associated with the thrift industry.

In seeking approval for the acquisition, ACC promised to keep Lincoln's current management and concentrate on mortgage lending and the slow, safe growth policies that had produced a modest profit for the thrift in 1984. However, immediately upon acquiring Lincoln, Charlie fired the existing management and threw the thrift headlong into the accelerated-growth policies that would propel many savings and loans into astonishing, if brief, profitability before sinking the entire industry into a crisis that saw scores of thrifts fail, sticking American taxpayers with a more than $500 billion bill to refund the vanished but federally insured savings of millions of depositors.

Lincoln instantly became the engine of ACC growth, diving eagerly into nontraditional direct investments in risky land development projects and underwriting sizable commercial and construction loans, many of them to ACC. By the end of Lincoln's first full year as a subsidiary of American Continental, Charlie and his associates had more than doubled the thrift's assets, but home loans had fallen to 15 percent, while brokered deposits now accounted for 37 percent and risk assets an alarming 54 percent. That said, by the end of 1985, Lincoln reported income of an impressive $80 million, up from $3 million the year before.

The first signs of the approaching savings and loan catastrophe had already become apparent in 1984, and the Federal Home Loan Bank Board began feeling pressure to rein in the high-flying industry. The board's chairman, Ed Gray, a Reagan administration appointee whose association with the president dated back to Reagan's California gubernatorial administration, was rightly concerned that absent some corrective action, the bank board would shoulder much of the blame should the thrifts' accelerated growth, and the direct investments and questionable loan underwriting practices that fueled it, end in massive thrift failures and the bankruptcy of the deposit insurance fund.

So the bank board proposed a new regulation restricting direct investments to 10 percent of a savings and loan's assets, scheduled to go into effect on January 31, 1985. This new rule, as prudent as it would eventually be seen, was contested by virtually the entire industry. But no thrift opposed it more vigorously, and with more disastrous consequences, than Lincoln Savings and Loan. Charlie embarked on a crusade, supremely confident in the superiority of his business acumen over what he saw as the excessive caution of government regulators. He hired distinguished economists, among them the future chairman of the Federal Reserve Board, Alan Greenspan, to provide informed arguments in opposition to the new rule. Along with state and national savings and loan associations, he energetically lobbied Congress and administration officials (many of whom he counted as friends and beneficiaries of his political largesse) to prevent the promulgation of the rule. When these efforts failed, he just as energetically sought political help in securing an exemption from the rule for Lincoln. I was among those whose assistance he sought in his battle against the regulation he derided for its pernicious effects on his bottom line.

While serving my second term in the House of Representatives, I had heard frequently from Charlie on the matter, and from the ACC general counsel, Bob Kielty, and Charlie's lobbyist in Washington, Jim Grogan. My office had also been contacted on numerous occasions by thrift associations and other industry representatives. Although I think Charlie despaired that I would ever grasp the fundamentals of his industry, and the threat posed to it by the direct investment rule, I and my staff thought the complaints were sound enough to warrant our assistance. I sent or cosigned as many as five letters to Ed Gray and White House officials, and in January 1985, I cosponsored a House resolution calling for the promulgation of the regulation to be postponed. All such efforts came to naught, however. The rule was promulgated on schedule, and Lincoln's application for exemption was rejected.

Near the end of 1985, the San Francisco district office of the Federal Home Loan Bank informed Lincoln's management that the rapidly growing thrift was in violation of bank board regulations. Three months later, the San Francisco bank began the first of several examinations of Lincoln, the high-risk projects it had directly invested in, and what the bank believed were questionable land valuations behind much of Lincoln's commercial loan underwriting. Examiners were also alarmed by the tripling of junk bonds Lincoln held in the two years since ACC acquired it and asked Lincoln to provide them with monthly reports on the holdings.

Thwarted by what he considered a senseless and injurious government regulation authored by bureaucrats who cared little for the profits he was making, Charlie was not likely to acquiesce quietly in further government meddling in his affairs. He rejected their request for monthly junk bond reports, calling it "arbitrary and unreasonable." This prompted the examiners to meet with Lincoln officials, including Charlie, in what both sides characterized as a very contentious, unproductive exchange. A few days after the meeting, Lincoln's attorneys informed the bank that their examination of Lincoln was imposing an "extraordinary burden on officer and employee time," and henceforth all requests for information would have to be made through Lincoln's legal counsel in New York. This, no doubt, annoyed the examiners.

A month later, more than halfway through their examination of Lincoln, the San Francisco regulators alerted the board in Washington to their growing concerns about Lincoln's practices. They took particular exception to the $600 million in Lincoln's direct investments above the 10 percent limit, as well as what they considered inflated land appraisals and other questionable underwriting practices Lincoln used in making at least fifty-two separate loans, joint ventures falsely classified as loans to skirt the 10 percent rule, and a concentration of loans to one borrower, American Continental.

Whatever irritation Lincoln's tactics caused was insignificant compared to the towering rage the examiners had stoked in Charlie Keating. From the moment of that first meeting's unfortunate conclusion, Charlie considered his relations with the Federal Home Loan Bank Board to be little short of war, and Ed Gray, his chief nemesis. In a letter to me, he called Gray "a madman" who was creating a "police state." Thereafter, Charlie would constantly accuse the bank board chairman of pursuing a vendetta against him. And Charlie being Charlie, he intended to defend himself vigorously.

Among his many strategies to get federal regulators off his back was an aggressive lobbying campaign to fill the bank board's two vacancies with individuals who were more sympathetic to the thrift industry's new ways of doing business. The board had three seats; thus, if two of those seats were occupied by industry-approved members, Gray's interference in the industry could be controlled until Charlie and other influential thrift executives managed to engineer Gray's removal from the board. Lee Henkel, a former associate of Charlie's, was Lincoln's top candidate for one of the board's vacancies, and Charlie set about securing him the position with all the influence he could muster, which was considerable.

Charlie had good relations with many senior administration officials and with even more members of Congress. He and his associates worked their Rolodexes assiduously, contacting every politician with whom they had built relationships, primarily on the strength of campaign contributions.

I was among the politicians who were asked to help secure Henkel's nomination, and in 1986, I called my friend Will Ball, a White House lobbyist, to inquire into the status of the appointment. I did not argue for Henkel's appointment. I don't like to push nominations of people about whose record or character I know little, if anything. Nevertheless, even seemingly benign inquiries by members of Congress into the status of a nomination can be interpreted not unreasonably by administration officials to be an indication of support.

As it turned out, I had met Lee Henkel once before, though I had forgotten the occasion by the time Charlie asked me to support his nomination to the bank board. He had been among Charlie's guests at his vacation home in the Bahamas two years before, one of the occasions when Cindy and I had been there. We arrived at Cat Cay at the same time, having flown together on an ACC corporate jet.

In November 1986, the bank's first examination of Lincoln was completed. Among the numerous worrisome findings noted above were $135 million in losses, and examiners began a series of meetings with Lincoln's executives, none of them very satisfactorily concluded, to discuss these problems.

Lee Henkel received his nomination to the bank board on October 7, 1986. Charlie happily and publicly claimed credit for the appointment. Two months later, attending his first board meeting, Henkel proposed a grandfather clause to an even tougher new direct investment rule. The clause would have primarily benefited one institution, Lincoln, but Henkel denied that he was acting at Lincoln's behest or that he even knew that Lincoln would be favorably affected by his proposal. He admitted only to having been contacted by a national savings and loan association. The new rule was eventually adopted without Henkel's proposed grandfather clause. Lincoln's attorneys filed a lawsuit to have the new regulation overturned. And a little more than a month later, Henkel resigned from the bank board.

The day after the meeting, the board, at the urging of the San Francisco examiners, approved an investigation into suspected "file stuffing" and backdating of documents at Lincoln. The examiners believed the thrift's executives were trying to make it appear as if their underwriting of certain loans had been far more careful than it really had been. Early in the new year, the bank board informed the Securities and Exchange Commission (SEC) that Lincoln might have violated SEC regulations.

We now arrive at the point in this narrative that chronicles my nearly inextricable and disastrous involvement in what came to be known as one of the greatest financial calamities in American history, the collapse of the savings and loan industry. Because of the increase in the limit of federally insured deposits, few thrift customers were ruined by the scandalous, near total destruction of financial institutions that once had been regarded by middle- and low-income investors as reliably sound, if modestly profitable, guardians of their wealth. However, the cost to the federal government for covering insured deposits lost by the failed thrifts, if apportioned to every American citizen, would eventually approach $2,000 for every man, woman, and child.

Quite a disaster, and as in all public calamities of such immense dimensions, there was a long list of culprits who could be fairly blamed for it. Reckless savings and loan operators deserved most of the blame, corrupt ones even more.

Government, of course, congressional and executive branch officials, deserved a good-size share. Government had not just sanctioned many of the thrifts' reckless practices, in the usually economically advantageous cause of deregulation; it abetted their even greater excesses by failing to practice the scrupulous oversight necessary to restrain people from acting on the often irresistible urge to make huge amounts of money in the short term with little regard for their long-term consequences. For, as the saying goes, in the long term we're all dead.

The press, too, shoulders a little of the responsibility for not reporting on the approaching calamity as early and as fully as it should have and calling to account those responsible for it. But then, with so many culprits involved, it's hard to get a handle on the problem in a way that is interesting and understandable to readers. I helped the press locate easily identifiable villains to use as shorthand for the whole sorry mess and give the public a target for their justifiable wrath.

I became one of the Keating Five, an association of senators who had benefited from Charlie Keating's generosity and not only were available to listen to his complaints about the "bastards" he said were out to get him, but tried in varying degrees to help him out of the jam. And when his high-flying savings and loan became the biggest of all the thrifts to collapse, we were available to the public to take more of the blame for it than anyone save Charlie himself.

Until I got myself stuck in the scandal, most of the political damage had been inflicted on Democrats. That was part of my misfortune. Of course, Republican members had been every bit as negligent as their Democratic colleagues. But the first political casualties claimed by the mounting scandal were Democrats, and very prominent Democrats at that.

In 1989, Jim Wright, the Democratic Speaker of the House, and Tony Coelho, the Democratic whip (the number three House leadership position), both of whom had been the subjects of an ethics investigation, were obliged to resign their seats in Congress, partly because of their relationships and actions on behalf of certain disreputable savings and loan operators. Fernand St. Germain, a Democratic congressman from Rhode Island, had been deposed as chairman of the House Banking Committee and defeated for reelection in 1988, for even more questionable associations and for his key role in securing passage of the legislation that sanctioned thrifts' recklessly fast growth policies at the expense of their future solvency. A couple of House Republicans failed to win reelection in 1990 as a result of their role in the savings and loan mess. President Bush's son Neil had served on the board of a failed Colorado thrift, an association the Democrats tried hard to use to divert public outrage toward the Republican administration. But Republican casualties were obscured by the national prominence of Democrats tarred by the scandal. As equally culpable as both parties were, Democrats unhappily suffered most of the blame.

Of the five United States senators whose participation in two meetings with federal savings and loan regulators earned them the censorious appellation the Keating Five, only one was a Republican. Me. And given the dimensions of the crisis with which we were now associated, and the feared political fallout, my continued misfortune as a Republican object of public scorn for the political cupidity that had helped engender the enormous financial catastrophe would become a political priority for the Democratic Party.

On March 6, 1987, Senator Don Riegle, a senior member and future chairman of the Senate Banking Committee, met with Ed Gray to discuss several issues, among them the board's problems with Lincoln Savings and Loan. A week earlier, at Keating's request, Riegle had met with Lincoln's auditor, Jack Atchison, the managing partner of the Phoenix office of the accounting firm Arthur Young. Atchison gave Riegle a long letter documenting what he and Lincoln's owner felt were serious abuses on the part of the San Francisco bank examiners and asserting that Lincoln's practices and financial health were sound. In his meeting with Gray, Riegle suggested he meet with a group of senators who had concerns about the bank's examination of Lincoln. Reportedly, Gray responded that a meeting was unlikely to change anything, but Riegle persisted in recommending it and informed Gray that he would soon hear from the interested senators. Unfortunately for Riegle, these events occurred within weeks of his receipt of $76,000 in donations to his 1988 reelection campaign from Charlie Keating, members of his family, and his business associates.

On March 17, Atchison sent my Arizona colleague Senator Dennis DeConcini and me letters with detailed complaints about the Lincoln examination nearly identical to the letter he had handed Riegle. Neither my staff nor I would remember seeing the letter addressed to me, but on March 19 we did receive a faxed copy of the letter to Senator Riegle, sent to my legislative assistant for banking issues, Gwendolyn van Paasschen, by Charlie's lobbyist, Jim Grogan.

Both Dennis and I and our staffs had heard frequently from Charlie and Jim Grogan about Charlie's problems with the bank board. I had even discussed some of those concerns with Riegle, whose views Charlie or one of his associates (I cannot recall which) had suggested I solicit. Those brief discussions occurred on the Senate floor and just outside Riegle's office. Later on, when discussions between members of the Keating Five became a matter of intense public interest, an aide to Senator Riegle would assert that I had asked Riegle to join Dennis and me in a meeting with Gray. That assertion was untrue and intended, I suspect, to obscure Riegle's own role in arranging the meeting. But I did discuss with Riegle Lincoln's problems, something that, like the meeting with Gray, I wish I had not done. Over the course of subsequent events, Senator Riegle went to great lengths not just to underplay, but to disguise the extent of his involvement in the Keating affair. But the central role he played in arranging the meeting, his assertions to the contrary notwithstanding, became clear in public testimony during Senate Ethics Committee hearings and in Lincoln's legal filings in federal bankruptcy proceedings, which disclosed that Charlie had asked Riegle to arrange the meeting with Gray.

Charlie was never shy about asking for help, and he made it clear that he wanted our help now, as his relations with Ed Gray had become increasingly bitter and the bank board's examination threatened to become a very serious problem for Lincoln and for him. At Keating's suggestion, Dennis sought out Don Riegle's advice, and Riegle advised him that a meeting between a group of like-minded senators and Gray to discuss Lincoln's problems was the best immediate course of action.

In the late afternoon of March 19, Dennis and I met in my temporary quarters in the Hart Senate Office Building at his request to discuss Lincoln's problems. Dennis and I did not have much of a relationship, as I was new to the Senate and a member of the other party. Of course, Arizona's congressional delegation worked closely together in a bipartisan fashion on issues of specific importance to the state. As a member of the House, I had found Dennis and his staff easy to work with on such matters. And our relations were cordial and largely trouble free at the time of our meeting to discuss Lincoln. Our relationship would become a little strained in 1988, when, as Arizona's senior elected Republican member of Congress, I campaigned for Dennis's opponent. And Dennis's vote in opposition to John Tower's nomination, and his speech on the Senate floor to explain it, had angered me. But whatever the difficulties in our relationship, they were nothing compared to the open and very bitter hostility between us that would result from our efforts to extract ourselves from the scandal we were about to enter.

Dennis's banking aide, Laurie Sedlmayr, and my aide, Gwendolyn, joined us in my office that afternoon. My recollection of the meeting has, of course, dimmed over the passage of fifteen years. Indeed, I have forgotten many details of my entire experience as one of the Keating Five. They are unpleasant memories, to say the least, and I have willfully tried to banish them from my memory. But quite an extensive public record exists, replete with hundreds of hours of sworn testimony before the Senate Ethics Committee and barrels of ink used in an untold number of press accounts in virtually every newspaper and magazine in the country. That's not to say I didn't learn important lessons from the experience. I surely did. And I've never forgotten a single one of them.

Dennis and I discussed the possibility that without some regulatory relief, Lincoln might go into receivership, and its effect on American Continental and its two thousand Arizona employees could prove fatal. Dennis suggested that he and I go to see Chairman Gray together in his office at the Federal Home Loan Bank Board, and if that didn't work, that we fly to San Francisco when we were next back in Arizona and meet with Lincoln's examiners directly. I remember rejecting the latter suggestion and saying I would think about visiting Gray in his office. But Gwendolyn recalls that I was simply noncommittal to both ideas. After a little less than half an hour, our meeting concluded. Once Dennis and Laurie had left, Gwendolyn immediately voiced her concerns about the suggested meetings, both with Gray and with the San Francisco regulators, particularly the latter. She was new to my office, as was my chief aide, Chris Koch, who had taken that day off. My election to the Senate had necessitated and provided a larger budget for hiring staff than I had had in the House. Gwendolyn and Chris had previously worked for Senator Slade Gorton of Washington, who had been defeated for reelection the year I had been elected. Both had sterling reputations as talented public servants, and I was fortunate to secure their employment on my staff. They would both prove time and again the merits of their professional and personal reputations that had encouraged me to hire them. In fact, but for their wise and forceful counsel, I doubt very much that I would have survived this experience.

Gwendolyn was quite explicit in identifying the potential political controversy, not to mention the considerable ethical questions the meetings would raise, and she strongly urged that I not allow myself to be "coaxed into" doing something I would almost surely regret. Not that I didn't have my own concerns about intervening in Charlie's problems with the federal government, even in a limited way. I normally have pretty good political instincts, and by now they were clearly alerting me that I might be heading into troubled waters on behalf of a friend and benefactor.

In 1986, just a few days before my election to the Senate, one of the wire services had run a story about half a dozen congressmen who had received substantial donations from Charlie Keating and had joined efforts to delay the promulgation of the direct investment rule. I was the first name mentioned in the story, and its appearance caused my campaign aides and me more than a little anxiety. So I knew well before my conversation with Dennis that Charlie's situation was fraught with press controversy and that any political help he received could potentially afflict the source with unwanted headlines.

My concerns and the alarm raised by Gwendolyn, who had seen the 1986 wire story about my relationship with Charlie as well as press stories about Charlie's controversial management of Lincoln, were sufficiently troubling that I never seriously considered the idea of meeting with the regulators in San Francisco or going to Ed Gray's office. If I did not reject it out of hand when Dennis suggested it, I suspect it was only in the expectation that he would drop it without my immediate consent. Among my failings as a public servant is an occasional urge when I'm confronted by conflicting interests to delay decisions in the anticipation that their necessity will be overtaken by events if I procrastinate a little. I think I have largely corrected the weakness over the years, thanks in large part to my memory of the trouble caused me by my failure to make early and decisive judgments about Charlie Keating's requests, as well as my memory of the trouble spared me by those occasions when I did act decisively to refuse him.

Nevertheless, after my conversation with Gwendolyn, one of my aides called Dennis's office and made it clear that I would not be going to San Francisco or to Gray's office. I should point out that Dennis eventually forcefully denied that he ever suggested going with me to San Francisco. But both Gwendolyn and I are confident in our recollection that he had.

My instincts failed me, however, a short time later, when Dennis proposed that we meet in his office with Gray along with Senator Alan Cranston, who represented California, the state where Lincoln and its branches were located, and Senator John Glenn, from Ohio, Keating's home state and where American Continental was chartered. Riegle was also expected to attend, but as it turned out, the senator from Michigan passed on the opportunity. I agreed to the meeting and informed Chris and Gwendolyn of my decision after the fact. Jim Grogan had also called my office to ask if I would be available to meet with Keating, which I agreed to do on the afternoon of March 24.

To prepare for the meeting with Charlie, and to make certain we had sufficient cause to meet with Ed Gray, Chris Koch wisely instructed Gwendolyn to call Jack Atchison and go over the points he raised in his letter to Don Riegle. She reported back to Chris and me that Atchison stood by his belief in the soundness of Charlie's complaints that he was being unfairly harassed by the bank board, that the examination of Lincoln was unusually long and intrusive, and that the auditor's argument seemed on its face to be compelling.

In the late morning of March 24, Charlie Keating and Jim Grogan met with Dennis and his banking aide, Laurie Sedlmayr, to discuss the forthcoming meeting with Ed Gray. Keating went over the points he wanted senators to make with Gray, going so far as to suggest a quid pro quo he hoped would entice the bank board into a new, less intrusive relationship with Lincoln. He proposed that the bank board grant Lincoln an exemption from the direct investment limit, and in exchange Lincoln would agree to devote more of its assets to home mortgage lending. He also informed Dennis of the lawsuit he had filed challenging the rule and promised to withdraw it should the bank board change its attitude toward him.

At some point in their discussion, Dennis told Charlie that I was apprehensive about becoming too involved in the matter, to which Charlie responded, characteristically, "Ah, McCain's a wimp," and words to the effect that he would straighten me out when he met with me later that day.

I do not like to have my courage questioned. I have a tendency to overreact to any suggestion that my cautiousness when deciding whether or not I will become involved in a matter betrays cowardice rather than concern for the propriety of my actions. And however well-founded that concern, it will probably seem slightly less important to me at the time than a strong defense of my courage, which I will usually express in words and manner little changed from the reactions to such provocations I had as a schoolboy. This is, I admit, an immature and unprofessional reaction to slights, which are, of course, an experience common to politicians. But in this instance, however, I am glad that I had never quite succeeded in controlling my bad habit.

Shortly after Keating had left Dennis's office, Laurie Sedlmayr called Gwendolyn and told her that her boss had defended me when Charlie had called me a wimp. As he would later recall, Chris Koch was somewhat concerned about how I would react to the news that a major Arizona employer and important supporter of my campaigns considered me a coward, because "John has a little bit of an Irish temper." But he also saw an advantage in apprising me of the insult, hoping that the anger he was sure the disclosure would provoke might encourage greater reluctance on my part to do Charlie any favors. Although as new to my office as Gwendolyn was, Chris had serious concerns about becoming involved too closely in regulatory matters concerning Charlie's interests, based on what he knew of the thrift industry's problems generally and Lincoln's situation specifically, and what he saw as Charlie's confrontational operating style.

Chris is a smart man, and I would have been well advised to pay even greater heed to his counsel. He was right about the effect Charlie's insult would have on my temper and on my attitude toward Charlie's subsequent requests for assistance. I was, even before learning of the wimp remark, sufficiently concerned about the situation to establish certain parameters in my own mind governing just how far I would go with the bank board. I had decided that I would limit my questions to Gray to just two inquiries about the length of the examination, which had already become one of the longest, if not the longest, examination in bank board history, and about the accuracy of the land valuations the bank used to determine the soundness of Lincoln's underwriting. Beyond that I would not go. As for any future requests from Charlie, there wouldn't be any after our meeting on March 24. Our friendship would effectively end that day.

Charlie and Jim Grogan arrived in my office around two o'clock, several minutes before I returned from a weekly caucus lunch. Gwendolyn went to meet them in our front office and introduced herself. Charlie told her he was glad I had hired new staff to work on financial issues because I had never really understood his business, and maybe she could help enlighten me. He also, according to Gwendolyn, grumbled a little about my lack of sympathy for his predicament. He was, at that time, unaware that I had learned about his wimp remark and had no idea just how unsympathetic he would find me a few moments later when Chris and I returned to the office to keep my appointment with him.

As Chris, Gwendolyn, and I recall, my first words to him were, "Charlie, I am not a coward, and I didn't spend five and a half years in a Vietnamese prison so that you could question my courage or my integrity." It went downhill from there. It was an angry exchange on both our parts, and for a while it appeared to me that all it would produce were hard feelings. I guess I wanted an apology from him and kept returning to the insult until I got some satisfaction. Charlie didn't defend the remark, but he didn't apologize, either. And he clearly indicated that he wasn't about to stand being talked to in the manner in which I was then addressing him. Charlie was not going to accept being dressed down by me or anyone else.

At moments, tempers cooled, and in these intervals Charlie attempted to focus my attention on what he wanted us to discuss with Gray. To which I would respond, "It wouldn't work, Charlie. It wouldn't do you or me any good. Gray will just cause us both trouble. I can't negotiate for you. I can ask questions and try to see that you're being fairly treated. But I can't negotiate for you." I did say that I would inquire about the length of the examination and about the appraisal issue, but Charlie, as if he hadn't been listening, kept referring to his proposed talking points, stressing the importance of getting Gray to agree to some regulatory forbearance for Lincoln. I would repeat my unwillingness to negotiate for him and my intention to stick to more limited inquiries. Our tempers would spike again and we would repeat the drill, to no one's satisfaction.

At some point in our exchange, Grogan signaled Chris to leave the room with him. Outside my office, he asked Chris why this was going so badly. Chris observed that you couldn't expect it to be going much better after Charlie had called me a wimp, and Grogan nodded that he understood.

Near the end, frustrated and angry, Charlie dismissed me with, "Ah, John, don't go to the meeting. You're a United States senator. Do whatever you want."

"No, I'm going to the meeting, Charlie. You're an important employer in Arizona, and I can ask fair questions for you; I just can't negotiate for you. It wouldn't do either of us any good."

"Do what you want, John."

At that, our meeting was at an end, lasting a little less than half an hour. I told him I was going to the meeting to ask my two questions, and he said he didn't care. He and Grogan left, and we never met again. I never had another conversation with him.

A day or two later, Chris, Gwendolyn, and I discussed my participation in the Gray meeting. Neither Chris nor Gwendolyn thought I needed to go given the acrimony of my exchange with the man whose interests were to be the subject of our discussion. I said I was going to keep my promise, that I was going in spite of Charlie and not because of him, that American Continental still employed more than two thousand Arizonans, and that I had some responsibility to help protect their jobs. To their credit, they argued that I shouldn't. I countered with what at the time seemed to me a circumstance that allayed any fears about the impropriety of the meeting or the appearance thereof. Dennis had told me that other senators would be attending, and for some reason I thought there would be safety in numbers.

Moreover, I told them Dennis and I had agreed to limit our discussion with Gray to the subjects I had mentioned to Keating and to avoid saying anything that could be construed as negotiating on Lincoln's behalf. These assurances somewhat mollified their concerns.

On April 1, the day before the scheduled meeting with Gray, Gwendolyn met with Laurie Sedlmayr to confirm what I had told her was an agreement between Dennis and me to limit the topics of our discussion with Gray. Laurie said that was her understanding as well.

When she returned to our offices, Gwendolyn immediately began to draft her own memo to prepare me for the meeting, reminding me that Dennis and I had agreed that beyond inquiring into the length and status of the examination, I would raise only the appraisal issue, and that the direct investment limit "is one of the issues you were requested to bring up at the meeting, but we have all agreed you should not. Dennis DeConcini will not, either."

The April 2 meeting with Gray turned out to be something of a dud. Nobody's questions were answered, regardless of how limited they were in scope. Gray had no answers, pleading that he just wasn't familiar enough with the case to render any informed opinions. He had come to play rope-a-dope, and he was probably smart to do so. Listening to him, I found it hard to imagine why Keating would suspect the chairman had a vendetta against him, since Gray would hardly admit to cursory knowledge about his bank's examination of Lincoln. At times, I almost thought Gray would respond to one of our questions with, "Lincoln who?"

After Senators DeConcini, Glenn, Cranston, and I shook hands with Gray, and we settled into our seats, Dennis began the discussion by observing that we were here to "discuss our friend at Lincoln." An unfortunate choice of words, which Gray would remember and repeat publicly many times. After Dennis spoke, I asked the first question, both to assure myself of the meeting's propriety and to put Gray at ease. I began by observing that American Continental was a major employer in my state and that all our states had a stake in Lincoln's solvency, and then I asked the chairman if he thought there was anything improper in meeting with him. He replied that it was "not improper to ask questions." And that was how we proceeded. As I recall, most of our questions were about why the examination was taking so long, to which Gray consistently replied that he "really had no idea," or words to that effect. It made follow-up questions difficult to ask, since we had little to premise them on. In truth, we all were a little irritated with Gray's inability or unwillingness to respond to any questions, no matter how proper and noncontroversial. At one point, John Glenn expressed his annoyance with Gray's unresponsiveness and told him something to the effect that if Lincoln had done something wrong, then charge them; if not, they should finish their investigation and leave them alone.

Eventually, our attention waned as we all settled into a common boredom with this unproductive routine. We stopped paying attention to one another's questions and roused ourselves from other thoughts and distractions only to take another stab at getting one of our own questions answered. I don't remember asking anything about the bank's appraisals, since I couldn't establish what, if anything, the examiners were still looking at.

Later, Ed Gray would angrily relate to aides, the press, and eventually to the Senate Ethics Committee that he had felt threatened by the meeting and had attended only because legislation to recapitalize the federal insurance fund was still pending and he was worried that his failure to subject himself to our inquiry would have risked losing our support for the bill. I don't remember it that way. Although unresponsive, Gray seemed fairly genial, if a little nervous, and he had concurred that there was nothing wrong with asking him questions. He did, however, after the fact, allege that Dennis offered what amounted to a quid pro quo on Lincoln's behalf, relaying Keating's offer to increase the amount of home mortgages the thrift made in exchange for the bank board's forbearance in enforcing the direct investment limit to Lincoln. I do not remember Dennis making that proposal. Nor did Senators Cranston and Glenn. Dennis vociferously denies that he did. It is possible that having lost interest in the discussion, Glenn, Cranston, and I might have missed an attempt by Dennis to negotiate for Charlie. But I'm not at all certain that he did. I can't call Gray a liar, but I think I would have remembered if Dennis had exceeded that substantially our informal agreement to limit the scope of our questioning.

Near the end of the meeting, Gray advised us that the regulators who were actually conducting the examination of Lincoln were in a better position to answer our questions and suggested we consider talking to them directly. I immediately asked him if he thought such a meeting would be proper, and he allowed that it would. Dennis then asked him to help arrange the meeting, and Gray agreed to do so. With that, the meeting broke up, and we all went back to our offices, wondering, I suspect, why we had bothered to show up in the first place.

When I got back to my office, I briefly recounted the substance of the meeting to Chris. In short, there had been no substance, I told him. Gray claimed he knew none of the specifics of the Lincoln examination and told us to talk to the examiners themselves. I came out of the meeting much more relaxed than I had been going into it. I was still a little troubled by the idea of meeting with the examiners, having two weeks earlier rejected such a meeting when Dennis suggested it. But since the chairman of the bank board didn't seem to have a problem with the idea, maybe a discussion with the regulators wouldn't be as problematic as I had earlier thought.

Why didn't I fully grasp the unusual appearance of such a meeting and anticipate at least some of the consequences that might ensue from its public disclosure? Bringing four obscure federal regulators, none of whom had probably ever been asked to meet with a United States senator before, across country to discuss with five senators the regulatory problems of a single, recklessly operated savings and loan, whose rash and controversial owner happened to be a major contributor to each of our campaigns, is not exactly a routine encounter for regulators or senators.

The fact that Ed Gray suggested the meeting explains a little of my improvidence. I wouldn't have agreed to the meeting had he not assured us of its propriety. But I failed to appreciate the situation that Gray and his subordinates felt themselves in, called to account for their actions by five prominent senators, who had it within our power to make their work and their lives quite difficult. Gray, who had been instructed not to bring an aide to the meeting, had merely sought to placate us, avoid remaining the object of our scrutiny, and prevent his agency from suffering congressional retribution for its part in the collapse of Charlie Keating's empire.

That I had resolved to restrict my questions to what I believed were uncontroversial and defensible subjects also calmed some of my misgivings. And, as naïve as it sounds, the fact that my friendship with Charlie

Keating had ended in our last acrimonious encounter encouraged my false sense of security. It was wishful thinking, really, that our recent estrangement would, in the court of public opinion, count for more than our six-year friendship and the $112,000 Charlie had raised for my campaigns.

These were the rationalizations I used to overcome my concerns, my political instincts, and the reservations of a young, conscientious staffer and my equally conscientious chief aide. I thought the circumstances allowed me room to split the difference between indifference to Keating's problems and crossing the line into self-interested, special pleading for a valued supporter. This was my mistake, and its consequences would be more severe than I had ever anticipated.

Working with Gray's office, Dennis and his staff arranged the follow-up meeting with the San Francisco regulators on April 9. What transpired then would render moot the dispute between Dennis and Gray over whether or not a quid pro quo had been offered on Lincoln's behalf in the April 2 meeting. It was clearly offered in the April 9 meeting. Not only do all participants remember it being suggested by Dennis, but one of the examiners, William Black, took such copious notes of the meeting that they served as a virtually verbatim transcript of the discussion. It was so accurate that most of us thought he had surreptitiously taped the meeting. But Black claims that on Gray's advice, he took extremely detailed notes.

The same senators attended the meeting who had participated in the fruitless discussions with Gray, although Cranston, who was managing legislation on the Senate floor that day, was there only very briefly. In addition, Senator Riegle joined us this time. But, being the cautious man that he was (had I known how cautious, I might have been more concerned about attending the meeting myself), he had apparently asked Dennis for a letter from Dennis and me asking him to attend for the purpose of lending his Senate Banking Committee expertise to the discussion. Dennis obliged him, sending him a letter, dated April 9, requesting his attendance on both his and my behalf. I did not sign the letter. Nor did Dennis ask my permission to be included in the invitation. Nor did he share the letter with me or with my staff. I never saw it until February 1990, when a special counsel hired by the Senate Ethics Committee to investigate the meetings showed me a copy of it.

The meeting began at six o'clock in the evening. Interrupted twice for Senate votes, it lasted over two hours. The regulators attending were four senior officials at the San Francisco bank: Jim Cirona, the bank's president; Mike Patriarca, the bank's director of agency functions; Richard Sanchez, the supervisory agent for Lincoln; and the aforementioned Mr. Black, prodigious note taker and the bank's general counsel.

Cirona started the discussion by introducing his colleagues, amid an atmosphere of general unease on the regulators' part and a little small talk from Dennis and me to ease the tension. Each senator, with the exception of Cranston, who merely stuck his head in the door to explain why he was necessarily absent, would qualify our various questions with declarations of neutrality in the bank's dispute with Lincoln and successive recitations that we had serious constituent interests at stake that went well beyond our relationship with Keating. Most of the points we raised were a variation on the theme "If they're guilty of serious wrongdoing, charge them; but if the thrift's problems are less egregious, then why is this examination dragging on so long?"

But Dennis did, at the very outset, relay what Lincoln was prepared to do for an exemption from the direct investment limit. He thanked the regulators for coming, then immediately informed them that "Lincoln is willing to take substantial actions to deal with what we understand to be your concerns." Elaborating on "substantial actions," Dennis listed Charlie's offers to increase the percentage of Lincoln's assets dedicated to home mortgages and limit Lincoln's high-risk bond holdings and investments. But in exchange, Dennis noted, Lincoln required some forbearance from the enforcement of the bank board regulation lest the thrift's profitability decline so dramatically that it was forced into conservatorship. He suggested that the bank board grant Lincoln forbearance while its lawsuit against the regulation was pending.

He also took issue with the examiners' appraisal values, calling them "grossly unfair" and suggesting that they reach some compromise with Lincoln on the disputed appraisals. In fairness to Dennis and to Lincoln, the bank board's appraisals of property in Arizona, where the real estate market was booming, did seem to be substantially lower than the market would warrant.

I had not come to the meeting to negotiate for Keating, and I thought it was generally understood that we would not suggest any quid pro quos to the bank board, as Charlie had asked us to do. Nevertheless, I didn't emphatically or even directly disassociate myself from Dennis's offer. Neither did Senators Glenn and Riegle, and thus, we would find ourselves accused of silently acquiescing to it. I did jump in immediately after Dennis had finished to assure the regulators that I didn't "want any part of our conversation to be improper. We asked Chairman Gray about that, and he said it wasn't improper to discuss Lincoln." I then immediately turned to the issue of their appraisals, observing that "land values are skyrocketing [in Arizona], and that has to be taken into account." Glenn and Riegle spoke after me, both questioning the length of the examination but offering assurances that they were not taking sides.

Cirona was the first of the regulators to speak. He accepted responsibility for the length of the examination, and then, I assume in response to my observation about the propriety of the meeting that Gray had attested to, he said rather forcefully, "This meeting is very unusual, to discuss a particular company." At that point, I should have stood up, thanked them for their courtesy, and assured them that they weren't obliged to answer our questions any further. Instead, I listened as Dennis responded, "It's very unusual for us to have a company that could be put out of business by its regulators." A brief exchange on the appraisal issue followed before we had to suspend the discussion for ten minutes or so while we went to cast a vote. I shouldn't have come back. Gray's assurance had been trumped by Cirona's exclamation that our discussion was "very unusual," and that nagging sense that I was headed into trouble returned in strength.

But I did come back, and I listened as the regulators described in increasing detail the problems they had identified. They betrayed no timidity in disputing Atchison's corroboration of Lincoln's sound business practices, going so far as to imply that the auditor had prostituted himself on behalf of his client. They disagreed strongly with the argument that Keating had turned an insolvent thrift into a profitable one. And as time went on, they got clearer and clearer in their suggestion that Lincoln was on the verge of bankruptcy and closer and closer to accusing the thrift's management of criminal wrongdoing.

John Glenn asked the question that elicited the answer that profoundly affected both the tone and the substance of the meeting. "Have you done anything about these violations of law?"

Mr. Patriarca responded as emphatically as he could.

"We're sending a criminal referral to the Department of Justice. Not maybe, we're sending one. . . . I can't tell you strongly enough how serious this is."

After this, we adjourned briefly for another vote. This time I really shouldn't have come back. I had all the information about Lincoln Savings and Loan that I would ever need. I guess I returned, as did the others, to ensure that any impression the regulators had that we were attempting to defend Lincoln's practices was surely no longer the case now that we had been informed in no uncertain terms of the gravity of the situation. In the half hour or so that remained of the meeting, we all were circumspect in our remarks to our guests and, at times, downright deferential as we listened to their long litany of Lincoln's abuses and their failed attempts to get the thrift's management to change their ways. No one really took serious issue with anything the regulators said after Patriarca dropped his bombshell of a disclosure. Near the end, Dennis asked what we could tell Lincoln, and Black answered, "Nothing with regard to the criminal referral. . . . Justice would skin us alive." Riegle, with an aspect of weary resignation, asked if there was anything that could be done to salvage the institution. The response was not encouraging, and the meeting concluded with Patriarca's observation that Lincoln had bet "it all on sixteen black in roulette," and that eventually would destroy the thrift.

Out we scurried, back to our offices and, for my part, as far away from Lincoln's problems as I could possibly get. Riegle, too, abandoned all interest in the thrift's concerns, and John Glenn, but for one additional contact with Keating when he arranged a meeting between Charlie and Speaker Wright, stayed well clear of the mess. Dennis and Alan Cranston were not quite so careful. When, the following year, Charlie was shopping for buyers to unload his troubled thrift, they both contacted state and federal regulators to urge them to permit the sale. Cranston also contacted Gray's successor as chairman of the bank board, Danny Wall, to urge the bank to speed up what was then its second examination of Lincoln.

When I got back from the meeting, Chris followed me into my office and asked how it went. I raised my eyebrows and said Charlie's problems were a lot worse than we thought or he knows, and I mentioned the criminal referral to him. "We're done with Lincoln," I told him. Or so I thought.

A few weeks after the April 9 meeting, Lincoln's regulators recommended that Lincoln be seized and placed in conservatorship for operating "in an unsafe and unsound" manner. Three weeks later, the bank board voted two to one to take the San Francisco bank off the Lincoln case, and the new bank board chairman ordered an independent review of the Lincoln examination.

In April 1988, American Continental informed the SEC that it intended to sell $300 million in subordinated debt through its Lincoln branches, and the commission allowed the sale. Eventually, ACC unloaded through Lincoln $250 million worth of its debt. More than half of the twenty-three thousand buyers were over sixty years old. Many of them would later claim they had been led to believe that they were buying federally insured certificates of deposit. They learned that they were holding much riskier investments a year later when American Continental declared bankruptcy and the next day Lincoln was seized by the Federal Savings and Loan Insurance Corporation (FSLIC). Twenty-three thousand Lincoln bondholders then discovered that the portion, and in many cases virtually all, of their retirement savings invested in Lincoln's junk bonds was absolutely worthless.

Two years elapsed between the regulators' dire warnings to us of Lincoln's imminent collapse and legal jeopardy and the thrift's seizure by the federal government. In the interim, the Federal Home Loan Bank Board conducted two more examinations of Lincoln, assigning the responsibility to several regional banks, but not the San Francisco bank. Both examinations came to the same conclusions as the first.

On April 17, 1989, the bank board sent criminal referrals to U.S. attorneys in Phoenix, New York, and Los Angeles. Lincoln's collapse and the government's obligation to cover all of its insured deposits would cost taxpayers $3.4 billion.

I have risked deluging the reader with numbing details and regulatory arcana involved in the Lincoln story, which many may not understand any better than I do. I have done so to convey, I hope, a sense of the dimensions of the problem, the extent of the federal government's oversight, and the unusual and outrageous length of time it took to bring an end to Lincoln Savings and Loan's excesses. What outrage there was at the time of ACC's bankruptcy and the terrible consequences it imposed on its bondholders, and it was very considerable outrage indeed, was focused in the main on us.

We were a small, easily identifiable group, consigned in the public conscience to that popular category of typically self-interested, probably corrupt politicians who would wreck the country for the sake of our personal ambitions. Our meetings had not caused the delay in Lincoln's seizure. Even the regulators we met with testified that once they had informed us of their intended criminal referral, we had pretty much adopted a "do what you must" attitude. But in the absence of any other prominent culprits, in a story that is complicated and difficult to tell, we became the public's villains by default. Whatever the intentions of each senator who discussed Lincoln's situation with federal regulators, and however we conducted ourselves during the discussions, to a press and public eager to assign blame for the Lincoln debacle, the meetings themselves appeared to be an attempt by money-driven politicians to dissuade regulators from diligently discharging their responsibility. And that appearance of impropriety became the basis for a public indictment of responsibility for Lincoln's collapse, if not the whole savings and loan disaster.

The first story broke on September 27, 1987, five months after the meetings occurred, when a thrift industry weekly, the *National Thrift News,* ran a front-page story reporting the details of the April 9 meeting replete with exact quotes from our discussion. FIVE SENATORS MET WITH DISTRICT BANK ON DISPUTED APPRAISALS AT LINCOLN, ran the headline of the story that characterized the meeting as "an unprecedented display of senatorial effort on behalf of thrift institution." The story was based on an interview with a confidential source, most likely one of the San Francisco examiners.

Washington is a newspaper-reading town, but even here the *National Thrift News* has a small readership, and the story failed to make much of a splash. The *Los Angeles Times* picked it up the next day, which was alarming. It certainly caught my office's attention. We were not called by the reporters for comment, or at least we had no record of such a request, but we quickly prepared to explain the reasons for my attendance and my conduct in the meetings to any reporters who were writing follow-up pieces. The calls never came. Not for a long while, anyway.

The next story appeared in the *Detroit News,* five months later. In February 1988, sensing bigger trouble, Don Riegle decided to return the campaign contributions he had received from Keating and associates, which gave the paper a hook for repeating the story that had run in the *Thrift News.* United Press International picked it up the next day, and the Associated Press ran with it a week later, including the first quote from my office on the subject, declaring my intention not to return Charlie's contributions to my campaign. A few days later, the *Los Angeles Times* published a long story about Charlie Keating and his operations that again included a description of our meetings. The Detroit paper's report caught the attention of my hometown paper, the *Arizona Republic.* Its first coverage of the Keating Five controversy, which included both Arizona senators, amounted to two wire stories buried in the paper's back pages. It would later make up for its initial lack of enthusiasm.

Mike Binstein, a talented investigative reporter working with columnist Jack Anderson, who would become the most informed reporter covering Charlie Keating, his war with federal regulators, and his influence with friends in high places, wrote the first story to appear in the paper everybody reads in Washington, *The Washington Post.* The *Thrift News* continued periodically to report and update the story, as did the *Los Angeles Times.* But despite the diligence of these newspapers, press attention to our meetings was far from constant and certainly nothing like the frenzy it would later become.

My staff and I were certainly on notice that we had a potentially significant public relations problem on our hands. But for eighteen months, press attention to what had yet to be labeled the Keating Five scandal was spotty. It wasn't until ACC declared bankruptcy in April 1989 and Lincoln was seized that the press began to suggest a connection between our meetings with Lincoln's regulators and the indefensible delay in bringing the thrift under control. Charlie continued to evade sanctions for his management of Lincoln for two years after the San Francisco district bank had decided to refer the case to the Justice Department. So, too, did the Keating Five manage to avoid being called to account for our involvement in the story.

The press's initial inconsistent attention to my role in the Keating affair didn't breed complacency in my office, but it didn't ring four alarms, either. A few weeks after I left John Tower's office the day the Senate rejected his nomination, those alarms rang, all four of them, loudly. In February 1989, my campaign consultant, Jay Smith, received a letter from ACC's tax accountant, David Stevens, informing him that the IRS had refused to accept as tax deductions the expenses American Continental had incurred flying Cindy and me, our daughter, and her baby-sitter to the Bahamas on ACC corporate aircraft, as well as several trips to other destinations. He attached an itemized list of the trips. Mr. Stevens's letter also politely inquired whether the senator intended to reimburse the company's costs.

I always assumed we had, and I was very sorry to discover otherwise. We had reimbursed for some of the trips, but not for most of them. It was an oversight on our part that would have rather serious consequences for me and for Cindy, who, as our household's bill payer, assumed more of the blame than she deserved and suffered far more emotionally from guilt than the mistake warranted. It was an innocent mistake, but it was going to be hard to explain.

After Chris Koch went to considerable lengths to determine from Stevens what the correct payment should be, I had Cindy write two checks to provide, as I explained in a letter Chris drafted, "full payment for all travel that Cindy, my family, and I took on American Continental aircraft during 1984 and 1985. . . . Please let my Senate office know immediately if you ever encounter any other question in this regard." Stevens had found no record of unreimbursed trips in the latter two years. Five months later, Stevens sent a letter of apology to Chris, noting that two of the trips we had reimbursed had been paid for at the time they had occurred. He wanted to know if we would like a refund, which, given that Lincoln was then in bankruptcy and the claims on its assets were many, might be hard to do. I told Chris to forget about it.

I also remembered Cindy and I had flown as far as Miami on ACC aircraft on our vacations with Charlie in the Bahamas but had had to take chartered aircraft from Miami into Cat Cay. Stevens had billed us only for corporate plane rides, and I couldn't remember if ACC or I had paid for the charter tickets. I still don't know. But I had Chris figure out the cost of those flights and send checks to cover them.

Last, I sent letters to both the House and Senate Ethics Committees, informing them of the mistake and the actions I took to correct it. The Senate Ethics Committee responded that the matter was beyond its jurisdiction, since the trips in question had occurred before my election to the body. The House committee said it lacked jurisdiction because I was no longer a member of that body, but that they didn't require that I amend my financial disclosures for the relevant years because I had now fully reimbursed American Continental.

The rulings of the Ethics Committees did little to quiet my anxiety over the late payments. By the time I became aware of the problem, Lincoln's ruin and the story of the Keating Five, although the term had not yet been coined, were fast becoming the object of intense press interest and biting editorials. Most of the largest metropolitan dailies, the *Los Angeles Times* still leading the pack, had published or were working on reports of Lincoln's long road to conservatorship and the role five senators played in the story. The news departments of the television networks had also begun to cover the story, and I was spending more and more time defending myself in interviews. A few weeks after ACC declared bankruptcy and Lincoln was seized, Charlie, with his usual impolitic audacity, helped along the press's storyline that in exchange for campaign donations, powerful senators had helped a crooked businessman evade justice. He was asked by a reporter if he thought his financial support to the five of us had encouraged our intervention in his regulatory problems. "I want to say in the most forceful way I can," he replied, "I certainly hope so."

On June 13, *The Wall Street Journal* published a scathing assault on our characters, calling us "Senatorial Shills." I began to dread that a wildly growing public scandal was threatening to leave my reputation in ruins, as John Tower's reputation had been ruined. I was determined to expend every possible effort to extract myself from the mess before the press and public reached a verdict of guilty, and before the kind of destructive political partisanship that had done in John Tower focused its attention on the single Republican involved in the controversy, and carried out the sentence.

Throughout that summer, I struggled to contain the damage, talking frequently to the press, stressing that I had, at the cost of my relationship with Charlie, limited my involvement to a narrow inquiry into the status and methods of the examination. I repeatedly emphasized that I had refused to negotiate on behalf of my former friend, and, once informed that Lincoln's abuses were serious enough to warrant a criminal referral, I had distanced myself entirely from the matter.

For a while, my efforts seemed to pay off. Reports acknowledged the difference in degree between the role I played and that of some of my colleagues. That understandably disturbed Dennis, who, by appearing to negotiate a deal on Charlie's behalf and by subsequently calling regulators to urge them to allow Lincoln's sale, had exposed himself to greater criticism. Unavoidably, our relationship, which had never been close, began to deteriorate from mutual suspicion to open antagonism. By the summer's end, Dennis was working as hard to keep me mired in the scandal as I was working to extricate myself from it. In September, the *Arizona Republic* published the false allegation from Don Riegle's chief Banking Committee aide that I had asked his boss to attend the meeting. Dennis was quoted in the story saying it didn't matter if McCain was "distancing himself or not. . . . He's in it like I am."

As consuming as it was, I didn't spend every waking moment defending myself to the press or plotting ways to evade further entanglement in the scandal. I tried to focus on other tasks, to keep up the schedule of a busy legislator, and to suppress my fears that my Senate career was in danger of ending almost as soon as it had begun. I authored legislation to repeal an unpopular income-based surtax imposed on Medicare recipients to help cover the costs of a huge new social entitlement created during the Reagan administration to provide catastrophic health insurance to the elderly. Since both the Democratic and Republican leadership in Congress opposed repealing the tax, as did the Bush administration, it was a difficult undertaking. But I had the support of Americans affected by the tax, and there was strong press interest in my efforts.

What strategy I had for dealing with press inquiries about the Keating controversy was, until the fall of 1989, inconsistent at best. I alternated between acting on my natural impulse to respond to every question and worrying that my availability to the press was helping to keep the story alive. Worse, I was beginning to let myself get angry at the constant drumbeat in the press for more information about our relationships with Charlie Keating and whether we were at least partly responsible for helping Lincoln continue its reckless practices and their inevitably disastrous consequences.

No doubt adding to my aggravation was my knowledge that I had a greater political liability, the late reimbursements for my flights on ACC aircraft, that was now in the public domain, which I knew I should disclose to reporters before they uncovered it on their own. By October, I decided to release the information to the press myself. My office informed two *Arizona Republic* investigative reporters, Andy Hall and Jerry Kammer, of my mistake. At the time, they were already working on another story suggesting that my ties to Charlie were closer than previously understood.

My father-in-law's company, of which my wife was a partner, had made a minority investment in a shopping center development called Fountain Square, whose principal investor was Charlie Keating. The investment shouldn't have been too hard to uncover since I had duly reported it in my financial disclosure reports, as required by law. The law requires that I identify both Cindy's assets and mine annually. Thus, the reports contained detailed information about Hensley Company's many and various holdings, information that I had little knowledge of (or interest in, for that matter). I knew vaguely of the shopping center investment and that Charlie was the lead investor. But I never anticipated that it would provoke greater skepticism of my relationship with Charlie Keating and my involvement in his regulatory problems.

On October 6, 1989, just after winning the biggest legislative battle of my brief Senate career, the first repeal of a social entitlement program, catastrophic health insurance, in history, I picked up a message that the

Republic's two investigative reporters, Hall and Kammer, had called to discuss among other things the Bahamas flights. When I returned the call, they surprised me with questions about the Fountain Square investment. I reacted poorly, to say the least. I lost my temper, and then some. And for years after, my temper would remain the subject of frequent editorial criticism in the paper.

On this occasion, I concede that my self-control was woefully weak. The reporters kept asking me to admit that the investment posed a conflict of interest. I simply couldn't understand how anyone would ever believe that a relative's investment, which I barely recalled, would cause me to violate the ethics of my office or do anything that would bring shame upon the name of my forebears, who had lived their whole lives without ever once lying, cheating, or stealing and who had urged my allegiance to the same standard. But Hall and Kammer didn't want to take my word for it, nor were they obliged to, and their persistence in questioning me on the matter provoked me to rage. I told them the accusation was unfair and if printed would be incredibly damaging. When they wouldn't accept my protestations that Cindy and I had a prenuptial agreement that kept her wealth under her control, that the investment had nothing to do with my attendance at the meetings, and that there wasn't any reason anyone should think otherwise, I called them idiots and worse. I shouted at them, cursed them, and eventually slammed the phone down on them. It was ridiculously immature behavior, which, although I have been irritable with reporters on occasion, I never repeated, having learned my lesson from the aftermath of that distressing exchange.

I don't know how Hall and Kammer would have reported the story had I been more civil and understanding or just more of a professional during the interview. But they no doubt used my outbursts to spice up their report, even adding a few unfair shots at my expense to recompense them for the abuse they had taken from me. During the interview, they had asked me if the scandal's effect on me was worse than my experiences in prison. I replied, accurately, that at least the Vietnamese hadn't questioned my ethics.

When the story ran two days later, under the headline KIN'S DEAL, TRIPS REVEAL CLOSE McCAIN-KEATING TIE, in which I "angrily denied" that the investment "influenced [my] actions in behalf of Keating," they reported that in addition to the Fountain Square investment, "the Republic has *found* [italics added]" that I had failed to reimburse for the flights until years after they occurred. They made no mention of the fact that "the Republic ha[d] found" out about the flights from me. Neither did they mention the fact that they had asked me to compare the scandal to my prison experience. They noted only that "McCain said the controversy has been worse than the nearly six years he spent as a prisoner of war in North Vietnam." I had not said it was worse. I had said only that the Vietnamese had left my ethics unquestioned. The impression left by Hall and Kammer's exaggeration was reinforced in a sarcastic editorial two days later, AND NOW McCAIN, that criticized my temper along with my ethics and accused me of "coyly tugging at [my] war record." *Republic* columnists, writing later, had even less charitable things to say.

I was in a hell of a mess. And I decided right then that not talking to reporters or sharply denying even the appearance of a problem wasn't going to do me any good. I would henceforth accept every single request for an interview from any source, prominent or obscure, and answer every question as completely and straightforwardly as I could. I was confident that the facts were on my side, and only if the facts were disseminated broadly in the media would they spare me from a terrible fate. And they wouldn't be disseminated broadly unless I talked to the press constantly, ad infinitum, until their appetite for information from me was completely satisfied. It is a public relations strategy that I have followed to this day, and while it has gotten me in trouble from time to time, it has on the whole served both my interest and that of the public well.

I began a few days later, in Phoenix, where I held an exhaustive press conference with any and all reporters interested in talking to me about the subject. As it turned out, quite a few were interested. Three days earlier, the government watchdog group Common Cause formally filed a complaint with the Justice Department and the Senate Ethics Committee, urging an investigation of the legality of Charlie Keating's campaign contributions to the Keating Five. It was, as far as I can determine, Common Cause that first labeled us the Keating Five, but the term was quickly picked up by virtually everyone who had something to say about the controversy, complicating my efforts to ensure that the actions of each of us were judged individually. We were now a two-word shorthand for the entire savings and loan debacle and the rotten way American political campaigns are financed.

The press conference lasted nearly two hours. In my opening statement, I admitted to paying insufficient attention to the appearance of my actions, to the late reimbursements to ACC, and to various other errors of judgment. But I steadfastly maintained that I had not abused my office "to aid any individual improperly." That was the truth, and I laid out the facts of the case to support it. The questions were various, some hostile, others not, but eventually all questions that could be conceived to explore the depth of my involvement were asked and honestly answered. It was the first step toward my political recovery. There was still a long, difficult, depressing road ahead of me before I could begin to imagine that I might someday be known as something other than a member of the Keating Five. But my candor with the press immediately began to help. The next day, the *Republic* editorialized that I had forthrightly accepted responsibility for my actions, had offered credible explanations for my involvement, and "ought to be out of the woods." I wasn't, but I appreciated the sentiment. The editorial even noted that the previous criticism that I had tried to exploit my war record to the paper's investigative reporters had been wrong and that the reporters had solicited the response. The *Republic's* editorial page editor at the time, Bill Cheshire, was a friend of mine, and throughout the tough days ahead he defended me, but always in reaction to evidence that I was, as I insisted, innocent of genuine impropriety.

The Keating Five story, however, was not going to go away just because I had survived a long press conference. The same day the *Republic* reported my press conference, the paper also ran a story about Laurie Sedlmayr's memo to Dennis outlining the deal Keating wanted us to help him arrange with Gray. Dennis blamed me for leaking the memo, and our relationship, already foundering, was nearing a complete break. I knew how serious was the trouble we were in. And I knew that not only Dennis, but the Democratic Party as a whole, couldn't afford to have the one Republican implicated in the scandal spared an equal measure of blame.

For should I be judged less culpable than others, the Democrats feared that their party would appear to the public to be the worst offender in the government's grossly negligent oversight of the failed savings and loan industry.

I was equally determined to clear my name, as quickly as I could, by using the true facts of my involvement and letting others use whatever tactics they chose to defend themselves. I was not going to acquiesce in my reputation's destruction simply because the facts helped others less than they helped me. My approach led to furious exchanges of mutual re-criminations between Dennis and me. We accused each other of leaking to the press, of bad faith, and of orchestrating third-party attacks on each other. It wasn't pretty, and I regret the acrimony and the injuries it caused. But I did not then, and I would not now, defend my name any less vigorously.

The House Banking Committee hearings were predictably awful. The committee's chairman, Henry B. Gonzalez, called dozens of witnesses, the impoverished Lincoln bondholders, Ed Gray, the San Francisco reg-ulators, and some Keating associates (Charlie and his former outside au-ditor, Jack Atchison, exercised their Fifth Amendment right to avoid testifying). Gonzalez also hinted that he might call the five of us, but pro-tocol between the houses of Congress prevented that spectacle. Neverthe-less, the public sensation provoked by the hearings and the ever-widening press criticism (it seemed at times that hardly a day passed without an ed-itorial in *The New York Times* urging an investigation of the Keating Five) convinced the members of the Senate Ethics Committee that they would have to open at least a preliminary inquiry into our actions. They an-nounced their intention on November 17, 1989, along with the commit-tee's appointment of respected Washington attorney Bob Bennett as a special outside counsel charged with conducting the investigation.

The committee membership is divided equally between the parties, three on each side. While I didn't have particularly close relationships with the Democrats on the committee—Chairman Howell Heflin of Al-abama, David Pryor of Arkansas, and Terry Sanford of North Carolina—I didn't have bad relations with them, either. And I was very friendly with two of the Republicans, Vice Chairman Warren Rudman of New Hampshire and Trent Lott of Mississippi. Jesse Helms of North Carolina, the third Republican, wasn't a close friend of mine, but we got along well enough. I had total confidence in Warren, whose reputation as one of the fairest, most honest men in Washington was well earned. And I knew that should Democrats on the panel treat my case unfairly, Trent would fight hard to stop them. I knew Helms to be a fair man in matters affecting both senators' and the Senate's reputations.

From the moment the committee announced its inquiry, I wanted to appear before Bennett and the members as quickly as I could to answer all their questions and hopefully speed things along. I hired John Dowd, a well-known and highly respected Washington attorney, to represent me, and without his experienced and wise counsel, his courtroom skills, and his generous friendship, I don't think I would have survived the experience.

All five senators were instructed to prepare written reports with the committee explaining our actions. I filed a ninety-six-page comprehensive account of the circumstances leading to my participation in the meetings and my actions during and after the meeting. In what now seems a comical, but at the time just a bizarre, incident, a Senate page mistakenly delivered Don Riegle's report to my office. My office contacted a Riegle aide, who promptly arrived to take possession of the document. Shortly after he did, Riegle burst into my mailroom and began ordering my staff to help him locate his missing testimony, not paying any attention to my staff's attempts to explain that the document had already been returned. The young page, who for some reason was still on the scene, caught the brunt of the frazzled senator's ire, receiving a tongue-lashing she was unlikely ever to forget. Eventually, Riegle was persuaded that the document was no longer in my office and departed, no doubt still nursing the suspicion that I had somehow engineered the mishap in order to get an advance peek at his prepared defense.

In March, I gave my sworn deposition to the committee, as did Chris and Gwendolyn. Over the next couple of months, the committee took depositions from all the subjects of their investigation and from every principal witness involved in the case. As summer approached, we still had no word from the committee when their investigation would be concluded. We were all under tremendous assault in the press (a small newspaper in

Maine had recently run an editorial that especially grieved me, calling us "five ethical morons who owe the United States their resignations"), which I was trying gamely to contain by keeping up an exhaustive regimen of television, radio, and press interviews.

I was at this point, it is fair to say, obsessed with the inquiry and bringing the whole controversy to an end. I was tired, anxious, and increasingly fearful that I would never be able to restore my reputation. I talked of little else to family, friends, staff, and colleagues, all of whom began to worry about my emotional stability. I kept it together in public, kept my temper in check, and as self-interested as this sounds, I was relieved when Iraq's invasion of Kuwait in August of that year gave reporters some other reason to talk to me and something else to report. But I was fast reaching the point when I didn't think I could stand one more moment of the public infamy that had become my fate. My popularity in Arizona was in free fall, dropping in one poll nearly twenty-five points by September from my standing two years earlier. Numbers like that usually indicate a nearly mortal wound, and I expected a rough, and quite possibly unsuccessful reelection campaign in 1992. To the extent I was known nationally anymore, it was as one of the crooked senators who had bankrupted the thrift industry.

In June, I asked John Dowd to request a meeting with the full committee to answer any additional questions in the hope that we could finally resolve the matter. The committee rejected my request, saying it was obliged to await the report of its special counsel before discussing anything with the five of us. But when would that report be finished? I anguished, day after day and through many a sleepless night.

As it turned out, ten months after it was begun, Bennett delivered his report to committee members in September 1990, one week before a California court issued an indictment against Charlie Keating, requiring him to post a $5 million bond before he could be released from jail.

A month after the report was filed, the committee met with all five of us to ask additional questions and to share with us some of Bennett's conclusions. I learned, to my great relief, that Bennett was convinced Glenn and I had not attended the meetings to reward Keating's campaign donations, that we hadn't negotiated with Charlie, and that we took no further action on his behalf. Thus, he recommended that the committee drop its investigation of our conduct. We were to be free men again, with an opportunity to restore our damaged public reputations. I was elated.

The other three senators were not so fortunate. Bennett believed there was sufficient evidence that they had abused their office, and in Riegle's case tried to disguise his role in the incident at the expense of others, and that the committee should proceed to a public investigation of their actions.

Bennett's report provoked the kind of cold and ruthless partisanship inflicted on John Tower that I had feared would eventually come into play in my predicament. In his memoir, written after he retired from the Senate in 1992, Warren Rudman explained the dilemma he and the other two Republican members found themselves in after Bennett finished his report. They wanted to follow his recommendations, drop Glenn and me and proceed against the other three. The Democrats, on the other hand, didn't want to punish any of the five or, at the least, issue the mildest rebuke possible to each of us, treating us all, as they had promised not to, exactly the same.

The committee was deadlocked for weeks, which in Warren's account led to much tension and bad feelings among the members. I was made aware of the political machinations involved and began agitating with my colleagues on and off the committee for fair treatment. I stood up in the weekly caucus lunch and beseeched Republicans to help me defend myself against what I believed had become purely partisan prosecution. I importuned members of the committee, not asking them to follow Bennett's recommendation, but to please, please expedite this thing and come to some conclusion. I remember appealing to Warren, "Shoot me or let me go, but do something." I was so incensed over what was happening that senators who were friends of mine kept dropping by my office just to take my temperature and try to calm me down a little.

Bennett's report was leaked to the press, infuriating Dennis, Cranston, and Riegle and committee Democrats, who all suspected that I or someone in my corner had done the leaking. On October 22, I took to the Senate floor to criticize the investigation as "incredibly and inexcusably delayed." I implored the committee to act, before my honor and reputation for integrity was completely destroyed. "I do not deserve to be strung out week after week, month after month," I complained. It had now been three years since the first press questions about the meeting had appeared, and there was no end in sight, or at least the end that had been in sight was rapidly vanishing.

Bob Dole, Slade Gorton, and John Danforth, senators of impeccable integrity, and good friends to me, joined me on the floor and echoed my complaints. John Glenn, knowing that his liberation was endangered by his party's decision to keep me captive, issued a press release sharing my sentiments and pleading for fairness.

It was an almost unheard-of act for a senator who was the object of an ethics investigation to denounce the senators doing the investigating. But I had little choice, for I knew full well that the Democrats were attempting to sacrifice my name for their own interests, and that included the most senior Senate Democratic leaders. To keep me mired in the controversy, over the objection of their special counsel, might have been a decision made by the Democrats on the Ethics Committee. But to keep me they had to keep John Glenn, a fellow Democrat, a heartless political calculation that probably required the approval of the Senate Democratic majority leader, George Mitchell.

Jesse Helms, out of concern for the damage that would be done to the committee's and the Senate's reputation if Republican members acquiesced in the Democrats' desire to let all five senators go, and knowing that the committee Democrats would not agree to proceeding only against three of their own, told Rudman he would vote with the Democrats to proceed against all five in what would amount to a public trial. Rudman and Helms knew this was unfair to Glenn and me but thought they had no other choice, that their first obligation was to the integrity of the committee and the Senate even if that integrity was compromised by unfair treatment of two senators. Warren then convinced Trent Lott, who had zealously defended me and fought for the committee to follow Bennett's recommendations, to go along and make it a unanimous vote.

The day after I had spoken out on the floor, the Senate Ethics Committee announced its intention to hold public hearings beginning on November 17. It also decided not to release Bennett's report, marking it a confidential committee document (left unsaid was that they had ignored the report's conclusion). As much as I trusted committee Republicans to fight to keep the hearings on schedule and within some fair boundaries, I feared Democrats were planning a show trial that would draw me further into the scandal or, at a minimum, delay my liberation indefinitely. I was disconsolate.

The hearings were a public humiliation. They were held in the largest hearing room in the Senate, which was crowded with reporters, many of whom had to stand in the aisles for lack of enough seats. The room was brightly and warmly lighted to accommodate the phalanx of television news cameras. C-SPAN broadcast live every minute of the proceedings, which lasted for two months, and CNN and the network news programs regularly carried segments of the hearings. My wife and mother and an alternating group of family and friends sat in the audience every day. My mother, nursing a broken leg, sat for hours, enduring often tedious and sometimes difficult testimony, intent on the needlework she had brought to keep her occupied with something useful to do. We each were seated at separate little tables with our attorneys next to us. The committee members looked down on us impassively from their raised dais. When we stood individually to raise our right hands and swear an oath to God to tell the truth, the whir of the cameras was deafening, the television lights blinding. We were prisoners in the dock. Only Cranston was spared the daily humiliation. He had been diagnosed with prostate cancer and, after appearing on the first day, missed the rest of the hearings as he underwent treatment in California. His lawyer was present throughout to defend him.

The first hearing began with brief introductory remarks and assurances of fairness by all six committee members, before Heflin gave the rest of the day to Bennett to present his case. He comprehensively laid out the methods and findings of his investigation and the standards he used to determine which of us had abused our office. Throughout, he was chastised occasionally by committee Democrats for seeming to have arrived at conclusions that the committee had thus far declined to accept, and he was reminded that the hearings were not a trial, but simply a fact-finding exercise, albeit a very public one. They were the only three people in America who believed, or at least pretended to believe, that our careers and characters weren't right then on trial and that Mr. Bennett, for all practical purposes, was the prosecuting attorney.

After a long summary of the case, he closely examined each of our relationships to Charles Keating and the actions we took on his behalf. He began with me, opening with the observation, "Of the five senators here before you, Senator McCain had the closest personal relationship with Charles Keating. . . . Senator McCain also was the only one who received personal as well as political benefits from Charles Keating."

He discussed those benefits in great detail, the campaign contributions, the trips to the Bahamas and their late reimbursement, the Fountain Square investment, and other evidence of our close friendship, which Bennett said he had started his investigation "very concerned about." He also described the actions Keating had asked me to take for him and compared them to the actions I actually did take.

In the end, he absolved me of any improper conduct on behalf of Charlie's interests, in the meetings with regulators, and in the weeks and months that followed. He accepted that the late reimbursement for trips on Charlie's plane had been an oversight that I had corrected, and that Cindy and her father's investment in the Fountain Square project had not influenced my behavior. He ended by asking and answering the one pertinent question regarding my conduct. "Absent any significant evidence of connection between Senator McCain's attendance at the April meetings and any political and personal benefits provided by Charles Keating, was there anything improper about Senator McCain's conduct? The evidence suggests not."

Bennett accorded Glenn the same vindication in his opening presentation. But he gave the other three much rougher treatment, which prompted the committee Democrats' cautions to withhold judgment and which I noticed, as I stole an occasional glance in his direction, infuriated Dennis.

The accused were allowed to make opening statements, and some of them used the opportunity to attack Bennett and dispute bitterly his conclusions. Dennis took strong exception to parts of my testimony and certain assertions that Dowd made on my behalf. Dozens of witnesses were called, and the hearings dragged on for many weeks. They became quite contentious at times. There were heated exchanges between attorneys for the accused and several witnesses, with Bennett, and with each other. Warren made valiant, if not always successful, attempts to keep things civil and moving toward a conclusion.

As the hearings continued, adjourning briefly for the Christmas holidays before resuming early in the New Year, the press, following the special counsel's lead, generally became, if not favorable to Glenn and me, at least increasingly disinterested in us. At the same time, the press bore down intensely on Dennis, Cranston, and Riegle, exhaustively reporting damaging testimony that confirmed the "suspicious pattern" of behavior that Bennett had accused them of. Headlines such as CRANSTON AND DECONCINI FOCUS OF ETHICS HEARING and THREE SENATORS SAID TO HAVE GREATER ROLE were as injurious to my three colleagues as headlines such as BITTER McCAIN-KEATING DISPUTE TOLD were helpful to me.

I was called to testify on January 4. Dowd questioned me first and walked me through the whole, by now irritatingly repetitious, chronicle of my involvement in the affair. Although John was asking the questions he had to ask to defend me, I was irritated by the very fact that I was sitting in the dock, compelled yet again to defend myself, before a jury of my peers, with my reputation and career hanging in the balance. Part of my frustration stemmed from the fact that in order to defend myself, I had to listen to and repeat myself, over and over, descriptions of incidents that, while they might have been exculpatory, were nonetheless embarrassing to my vanity and in some cases hurtful to me. I didn't like having my staff dragged into the inquiry for my sake. Hearing and acknowledging that Keating had mocked me for cowardice by calling me a wimp certainly offended my self-regard, and I didn't like hearing it publicly and constantly repeated, no matter how useful a fact it was in my defense. The fact that Cindy and I had failed to reimburse the flights as soon as we should have, and the implication that Cindy, as the family bill payer was, albeit unintentionally, more at fault than me, offended my sense of a husband's duty to protect his wife. Clearly, Cindy was distressed by the mistake and the attention to it, and there was little I could do about it. There were many other incidents that were embarrassing and worse to me.

Brad Boland, who had worked for me in the House, had been the person on my staff to whom I was closest. I once considered him a very dear friend. He left my staff before my election to the Senate to marry one of Charlie's daughters and began working for his new father-in-law. In August 1989, he wrote Dennis a letter, thanking him for his support for Charlie and adding that "I wish the same were true for my former employer, John McCain, who is probably the biggest disappointment in my life." When my office got hold of a copy of Brad's letter, we knew it was useful evidence that strengthened my contention that I had refused to go as far as Charlie wanted me to go in helping him. And we used it for that purpose. Under Dowd's questioning, I had to discuss Brad's letter for what seemed the hundredth time, and its disclosure embarrassed me and occasioned the same regrets that anyone would feel about an estrangement from a close friend.

So it went. Dowd asked questions about this or that incident, and I provided rote answers, with more than a trace of my frustration evident. Eventually, it seemed that for the last fifteen minutes or so all I said in response to John's questions was "No, no, no, and no." Afterward, more than one person remarked on how angry I had appeared. I was, but that wasn't John's fault. It was mine.

After Dowd finished, Bennett walked me over the same ground. The committee members then took their turn, and only one of them seemed intent on causing me any serious difficulty. Heflin, in his best country judge manner, pretended confusion about the reasons for my failure to pay for the flights to the Bahamas. Although I possessed a letter with his signature on it that disclaimed the committee's jurisdiction over the question, he kept dragging me through the details of the mistake, trying to make it appear as if I had been disingenuous in my claims that it had been an unintentional oversight. He was trying to create the impression that I really hadn't intended to pay for the trips until the scandal's publicity made me reconsider my impropriety. In short, he was implying that I was a liar and a cheat, and I resented it.

The hearings finally dragged to a halt on January 16, 1991, nearly four years since the meetings in question had occurred. I was thoroughly fed up with the experience by that time. I was disgusted, in fact, with myself, with many of my colleagues, with the Senate, with politics, and with just about everything that I had thought had helped to ruin the reputation I had spent a lifetime building. I didn't know at that point if I would ever get it back, if I would be reelected, or if I even wanted to stay in politics. But I knew I couldn't begin to answer those questions until the committee rendered its final judgments about the so-called Keating Five scandal. We were told to expect that judgment in short order. But, of course, we had to wait a little longer than that.

More than a month passed before the committee finally made up its mind. They had been deadlocked again by the Democrats' insistence that we all be treated with an equal amount of leniency and by the Republicans' insistence that they render the judgment that their counsel and the evidence suggested. The Republicans wanted to excuse Glenn and me from any further committee action, seriously reprimand Riegle and Dennis, and then proceed with further inquiry, and almost inevitably to a very serious punishment, of Cranston. In the end, they settled for sending letters to four of us, acknowledging Glenn's and my innocence but chastising us for "poor judgment" in attending the meetings. Riegle and Dennis they treated more harshly. They rebuked Riegle for conduct that "gave the appearance of impropriety and that was certainly attended by insensitivity and poor judgment." Of the four, Dennis got the harshest rebuke, criticizing his "aggressive conduct with the regulators [as] inappropriate." Still, all four of us were excused from any further inquiry.

The committee proceeded against Cranston but ultimately deadlocked again. The Republicans had held out for a formal Senate vote censuring Cranston. The committee Democrats, and Cranston, refused to accept the punishment. In November, they settled on a compromise verdict: No Senate vote, but the committee would file its serious reprimand with the Senate clerk.

I remember that the committee's rulings seemed strangely anticlimactic when they were announced. We were still at war in the Persian Gulf, and most of the press had tired of the affair and moved on to other things. Throughout the course of the Gulf War, I was much in demand as a media commentator on the war's progress because of my past service as a professional military officer and my membership on the Armed Services Committee, and at one point I temporarily hosted a radio talk show. This gave the public something to associate me with other than Charlie Keating and greatly helped to rehabilitate my public image. In November 1992, I was easily reelected after drawing a little-known and surprisingly ineffectual, if perfectly decent and well-intentioned, opponent. The pictures of me cavorting on a Bahamian beach with Charlie that I had anticipated seeing in Arizona newspapers never made an appearance in the campaign. John Glenn was also reelected. The other three senators involved decided to retire at the end of their terms.

Charlie Keating suffered the worst punishment. He was eventually convicted in federal court of multiple counts of securities fraud and sentenced to twelve years in prison, and on state charges he was sentenced to ten years. The convictions were overturned on appeal, but not before he had spent four years in prison. Today, he lives quietly in Phoenix in a house he built. Later, in a civil suit filed by Lincoln's bondholders, I was asked and agreed to testify on behalf of the plaintiffs. But for all the problems my friendship with him had caused, and for all the hard feelings between us, I feel bad about his many misfortunes, which in later years included very tragic personal losses, and wish that things had turned out differently for both of us.

Despite my recovery, the Keating Five experience was not one that I have walked away from as easily as I have other bad times. Twelve years after its conclusion, I still wince thinking about it and find that if I do not repress the memory, its recollection still provokes a vague but real feeling that I had lost something very important, something that was sacrificed in the pursuit of gratifying ambitions, my own and others', and that I might never possess again as assuredly as I once had.

I have carefully avoided situations that might even tangentially be construed as a less than proper use of my office. I have refrained from intervening with regulators or supporting legislation or advocating anything for any purpose that doesn't serve an obvious public interest and that isn't in accord with my general governing philosophy. My reputation for integrity, the only self-interest of real value, is my responsibility alone, but I learned I cannot protect it if I separate my interests from the public's. I do nothing in secret and keep the whole of my professional life visible to the press. And, as I did after John Tower's defeat, I learned again that partisanship taken to extremes is dishonorable and lethal to one's character. And although I still mix it up with my colleagues in debates, and at times quite heatedly disagree with certain of their positions and practices, I do so whether they are Republicans or Democrats. I've had my fill of partisan excesses, and I don't intend to disgrace myself by indulging in them. I resolved to build a public record that, whether its achievements are significant or not, memorable or soon forgotten, sensible or flawed, will in the end be judged by me, if no one else, to have represented the best service I was capable of rendering to the country that has given my life its most important purpose.

Ted Williams. *Corbis*

BEST EVER

No one was ever more determined to be his own man than Ted Williams, or so I thought when I first saw him strike out at Griffith Stadium, then raise his head and spit from the plate toward the fans who booed him and the sportswriters who harassed him. That's how I remember the moment, anyway, the moment when Ted Williams became my hero. I saw him spit even if he didn't at that game, and the legend that is Ted Williams began to seep so far into my subconscious that in my memory I am physically present at some of its more colorful highlights. God knows he could spit (the way the sportswriters told it, you would think he made a career of it at times) and give the finger to his tormentors, and cuss so much that he could have made my grandfather, no piker when it came to swearing, blush like a young girl. It sure looked as if he spit at them that day, and I was thrilled to witness it, even if the papers didn't write it up, even if my cousin Peter Andrews, who was sitting next to me, wasn't sure he did.

Baseball isn't my favorite sport. The game takes so long to play, and the action is too sporadic to someone who loves the fights and football and basketball. I liked the sport more when I was a kid, but that's because of Ted Williams. I was a Ted Williams fan, which made me a Boston Red Sox fan, which made me hate the Yankees, which made me disparage the Washington Senators on the several occasions when I watched Ted play against them.

My cousin Peter is several years older than me. I looked up to him, even though he was a Washington fan, and spent as much time in his company as I could. He lived in Washington with his parents, my uncle Bert and my aunt Nadine, when my family lived across the Potomac River in the northern Virginia suburbs. Uncle Bert was the Washington bureau chief for the *New York Herald Tribune.* He and Lawrence Spivak had started on the radio the political talk show *Meet the Press.* He was also friends with Richard Nixon and Whittaker Chambers and had been involved some way in the Alger Hiss case. I liked him very much and thought him to be a pretty important man in town. And I loved my aunt Nadine, who was as colorful and interesting as her younger sister, my mother. They would often invite me to stay the weekend with them in their apartment in the city.

On one of those weekends, when I was eleven or twelve years old, Peter took me by streetcar to Griffith Stadium to see the Senators play the Red Sox. He would take me to many other games, but that first game was one of the great events of my childhood simply because I got to see Ted Williams, the Splendid Splinter, the best hitter in baseball, for the first time.

He hit well that day, two doubles and a home run, as I recall. But the strikeout and his defiant reaction to taunting Washington fans was what I had come to the ballpark to see. That, and the determined way he went about his work with a classiness that substituted spirit and a solitary splendor for elegance, and the way the crowd would hush when he approached the plate. We would all inhale sharply when he did what he was expected to do and smashed one so hard that you could feel it in your gut. There was DiMaggio still, Williams's rival and opposite, but DiMaggio's fifty-six-game streak had happened before the war, the same year Williams hit .406, and to my mind, Williams had the better season with the highest batting average, more home runs, an unsurpassed on-base average, and a home run in the ninth inning to win the All-Star game. In the years that I watched him, whether his stats bore it out or not, I thought Ted Williams twice the man DiMaggio was. I thought him to be the transcendent athlete of our time. He was so damn good, and so tough and feisty, that I couldn't imagine any man ever being his equal.

He had been a marine aviator in World War II, serving as a flight instructor in Pensacola. He didn't see combat, but he wanted to and turned down offers to spend the war safely playing baseball for the navy, as DiMaggio did for the army. He was a superb pilot, too good to risk in combat evidently, which was why the navy said they made him an instructor. His appeals for combat duty were ultimately granted, but by the time he arrived in the Pacific, the Japanese had surrendered.

He had extraordinary natural skills and astonishing vision. The navy made a big deal about how he had the best vision they had ever tested. Whether that was true or exaggerated, I believed it just as I never doubted the myth that he could see the laces on a fastball. In gunnery training, a pilot makes runs at a banner towed by another plane. Success is mostly a matter of hand-eye coordination. Williams had the highest number of hits ever recorded, a record that is still unsurpassed.

He was called up to serve again, heroically, in the Korean War. He was John Glenn's wingman, and Glenn told me he was the best natural pilot he had ever seen, maybe the best pilot ever. He wasn't very good at instrument flying, a skill that comes with long experience. But he could outfly anybody Glenn knew (and Glenn's own aviation skills are legendary), and he could take risks in his F-9 Panther that other pilots wouldn't have dreamed of taking.

There was controversy about his service. There was controversy about everything Ted Williams did. He appealed for and received a deferment from service in World War II. He was his mother's only support then, twenty-three years old, and his future in baseball after he had hit .406 in 1941, his third year in the major leagues, looked limitless. He caught hell for the deferment when it became known, from baseball fans and especially from the press. He once received in the mail a blank sheet of yellow paper. By May, he had enlisted.

As much as I'm sure he hated the accusations of cowardice and all the rest of the furor occasioned by his attempt to stay home, it didn't hurt his playing. Turmoil never seemed to hurt his playing. In fact, he seemed to thrive on it. Opening day in 1942, with the controversy in full cry, he hit a home run his first at bat. He was able to finish the season before reporting for duty, having won his first triple crown for the best batting average, most runs batted in, and the most home runs. When he returned for the 1946 season, he didn't get a hit his first at bat. He hit a home run on his second trip to the plate, at Griffith Stadium, before President Truman and General Eisenhower, and then went on to lead the Red Sox to their only World Series of his career.

He was thirty-three in 1952, when the marines called him up from the reserves for active duty in Korea. Apparently he wasn't too happy about that, either. He had shattered his left elbow in the 1950 All-Star game, slamming into a fence to catch a fly ball. He had a wife and daughter and had hurt his leg in spring training that year. He surely wasn't the most likely candidate for combat duty, and he knew it, and he resented being treated otherwise. Most people thought he would never return to baseball, and a huge crowd came to say good-bye in his last game before leaving for war. He hit a home run his last at bat. He hit another one his first game back from Korea, late in the 1953 season, and in the thirty-seven games left that year, he had a .407 batting average. The guy was just unbelievable.

I was only five years old when the Japanese attacked Pearl Harbor. I was too young to read the papers, and I don't recall ever hearing anyone accuse Ted Williams of being a draft dodger. By the time he had become my hero, all I knew was that he had been a marine flier during the war, and an awfully good one. When he left for Korea in 1952, I never heard a word reported that he wasn't more than willing to go. I thought it perfectly natural that the bravest and best man in baseball would be an exemplary patriot as well. Williams never made much of a public issue of being called up before he left. He did once, after his return, and caught hell for that, too. But all I remember was hoping that God would be good to Ted Williams and bring him safely back from war to baseball and to me.

I admired his war service as I admired his skills and courage in baseball. But what I admired the most about Ted Williams was the integrity of his approach to baseball and life. You can fault him for his temper, for his feuds with fans and reporters, for the mouth that got him into so much trouble, but whether you liked him or not, you could never doubt his resolve to be what he set out to be, on his terms alone. As a young man, he was reported to have walked the streets of Boston repeating, "Ted Williams, the best hitter in baseball, the best hitter ever." I like to think of him that way. Cocky, self-assured, making his boast stick, thinking to himself, I'm going to be the best hitter ever, and you can go to hell if you don't like the way I'm going to do it.

In his rookie year, he tipped his hat whenever the fans acknowledged his play. But when fans and sportswriters started to give him trouble the next season, he never tipped his hat again. Never. He just got better. That's integrity, even if it offends as many as it inspires.

Maybe I like thinking of him that way because it seems so poignant, so brave, now that I know he was anything but self-assured, that his insecurities left him scared and gloomy, that as much as he wanted the legend that he well earned, the public praise that came with it embarrassed rather than gratified him, that the pressure and trouble of being the best ever on his terms alone took a hard toll on him and kept him chronically unsatisfied. He begins his memoir, *My Turn at Bat,* by honestly expressing his relief that his storied career was over.

> I'm glad it's over. Before anything else, understand that I'm glad it's over. I'm so grateful for baseball—and so grateful I'm the hell out of it. . . . I thought the weight of the damn world was on my neck, grinding on me. I wouldn't go back to that for anything. I wouldn't want to go back. I've got problems now. I've always been a problem guy. I'll always have problems. But I'm grateful that part of my life is over.

And in the very next line, after he had explained his predicate, he begins the story of his life with, "I wanted to be the greatest hitter who ever lived." That is some kind of life, to fix yourself to one grand ambition, to fight through the self-doubt that troubled you and not just endure hostility that must have aggravated your insecurity, but to practically court it, then shudder with relief when it was over and go on to being the best at the next thing you did. After baseball, Ted Williams became the best bonefisherman. Some say the best fisherman period, whether for bonefish or Atlantic salmon or trout. The best hitter, the best pilot, the best fisherman, and to hell with anyone who didn't like the way he did it. That's integrity, even if it leaves you unsure whether to be happy or sad for the man who accomplished it.

The year he broke .400, a feat that has not been accomplished since, he could have sat out the last game of the season, the second of a doubleheader, to protect the achievement. He declined. In 1957, staring forty in the face and getting tired, with a swing that had never fully recovered from his broken elbow seven years earlier, battling reporters and fans with an ever-greater intensity, he hit .388 and won the league batting title, the best record in baseball since he had hit .406. The next year he won the title again, after a season that saw him fling his bat in anger after striking out, hitting a nice old lady in the stands. He was crying after he apologized to her, after she told him she knew it was an accident. They booed like crazy then, until his next at bat, when he hit a double. Sick and injured and worn out, he had a bad year in 1959. The Red Sox offered him $120,000 to play the next year. He tore up the contract and asked for $95,000.

His temperament wasn't all white heat, either. He compassion, his empathy for the underdog, was more outsize than his anger. For many decades, he was the chief benefactor of the Jimmy Fund, a foundation that supports a children's cancer research clinic in Boston. He has raised millions of dollars for it, and as Ed Linn, Williams's biographer, noted, "Whenever one of the children wanted to see him, whatever the hour of the day or night, he would come. His only stipulation was that there must be no publicity, no reporters, no cameramen." He had a tough, lonely childhood, and he understood what a crapshoot life could be. "It's only a freak of fate, isn't it, that one of those kids isn't going to grow up to be an athlete and I wasn't the one who had cancer."

He's been married three times and was a remote figure to his kids when they were growing up. He couldn't ignore a slight, no matter how minor. But he has a tender heart that breaks for a sick child, or a guy down on his luck, or the friends who have died before him. And he thinks no more of himself for his compassion than he does for his toughness.

He wanted to hear people say he was the greatest hitter who ever lived, and when they did, he told *Life* magazine, "I would slide down in my seat a little bit." He was never cocky in his heart, he said, just scared. Had I known that about him when I first saw him play, I would have been drawn to him all the more. I was a cocky kid, too, always hoping to fool another group of kids, at yet another new school, into mistaking my arrogance for confidence.

He told the reporter from *Life* that the "most disappointing things all my life were related to baseball. I didn't feel good because I did something successfully—I felt bad if I failed to do something that I was expected to do." I understand that, too. When people commend me for my service in Vietnam, the example of the better men I served with and the memory of my failures there embarrass me. And when I scored the biggest political success of my career to date, I suffered a strange anxiousness about what it meant and what would be expected of me now.

I first met Ted Williams in 1993, when John Dowd, my lawyer and Ted's, brought him to my Senate office. Ted was suing a guy who had stolen money he had hired him to manage. John was representing him in the matter and brought him to my office to introduce us. It was a brief visit. I can barely remember what we discussed other than a few details of the case. The money involved wasn't a huge sum, as I recall, and John had warned Ted that the legal fees would considerably exceed whatever they could recover, if anything. Ted didn't care. It was the principle of the thing. He gave me a signed baseball, which sits on my mantel today.

A couple of years later, *Esquire* was putting together an issue about the heroes of celebrities. Having achieved by that time the distinction of minor celebrity in the world of politics, I was among those asked who my hero was. Ted Williams was the first name that came to me. A couple of months later, I was on my way to a housing development, Citrus Hills, an hour or so from Orlando, Florida, to be jointly interviewed with my boyhood idol.

He needed to use a walker to get around and was certainly frailer than when we had first met. We talked for a couple of hours and had our picture taken for the magazine. He was warm and expansive, and I was grateful for his generous answers to my questions and for the pleasure he at least pretended to take from our conversation.

I asked him if he'd really been able to see the laces on the ball. "Shit, no. You're reading all these sportswriters. Jesus, that ball looked like a pea coming in there once in a while." He told me about the time his plane was shot up and on fire in Korea. His hydraulics were shot, and he couldn't get his landing gear down. He should have ejected. They radioed him to eject. And he knew he should. But he made a wheels-up landing at an airfield, his plane engulfed in flames, a truly incredible feat of aviation skill and tremendous courage.

"Why didn't you eject?" I asked him.

He was six feet four, and he'd looked up at the canopy and at the instrument panel and known he would break both his knees. "I'd have rather died," he said, "than never to have been able to play baseball again."

He would rather have died than not play the game that years later he was relieved to have quit, for the fans whose booing he had an acute sensitivity to, but whom he would subsequently call the best fans from the best baseball town. He's an interesting puzzle to figure out, and I flatter myself to think we have anything in common.

He told me I looked like a million bucks that day and should think about running for president. I would soon be reelected to my third term in the Senate, and I was thinking, thinking very hard, about running for president, and if Ted Williams thought I could do it, well, why shouldn't I give it a shot?

"I've made a lot of mistakes in my life," I told him.

"Aw, who the hell hasn't," he answered. "I got things I don't even want to think about."

When I did run for president and began to mount a strong challenge to the front-runner in the New Hampshire primary, Ted Williams came to New Hampshire to appear with my opponent at an annual baseball dinner. The next day, the wires carried the story TED WILLIAMS ENDORSES GEORGE BUSH. That stung me a little. I had thought our brief encounters had established a friendship. But Ted was a close friend of the senior George Bush and had campaigned for him in 1988 and 1992, and I didn't resent his loyalty. I shook it off.

In 1960, at the last at bat of his career, forty-two years old, Ted Williams hit a home run. When the crowd roared ceaselessly for him to come out of the dugout, tip his hat, and bow to acknowledge their love, he wouldn't do it. That's a strange kind of integrity, I know, but it is something to see. Just to be known and, I hope, to be liked by such a man was good enough for me. I would have been delighted to have had his endorsement, but I would win or lose on my own, as Ted Williams would have.

I was at our northern Arizona home entertaining guests when I heard that Ted Williams, the last of my living boyhood heroes, had died. I wasn't surprised. Strokes and congestive heart failure had robbed him of the independence he had, for so long, refused to yield to anyone, and convinced those who revered him—an astonishing number of people considering how long ago he had retired from the profession that had won him renown—that his life had run its course. I wasn't surprised, but I found it hard to take in stride all the same. I suspect it will be a while before the time in which I live will fascinate me as much as when Ted Williams claimed a share of it. As the controversy over the disposition of his remains continues to attract public interest as I write this, I am intrigued again at the way Ted can still make us shake our heads in amazement at how one man who could do things that few people could dream of doing can still cause a sensation, even in obtaining a final resting place, something many others have done with considerably less difficulty.

To his fans, a common solace in the days following his death was the recognition that he had, in the last years of life, known how appreciated he was for doing hard things so well. The memory of his accomplishments had not only outlasted the controversies that always attended them, but seemed all the greater for the fact that he had never seemed able to enjoy his triumphs as much as we did. At the 1999 All Star Game at Fenway Park, where he threw out the first pitch, he basked in the adoration of the fans and of the players who gathered around him as if in the presence of unattainable greatness, reluctant to part with his company to play the game. But it was eight years earlier that I believe Ted must have at last discovered how much of our hearts he claimed, and how much we claimed of his. On Ted Williams Day, another capacity crowd of spectators at Fenway roared its appreciation when the object of their affection pulled a crushed baseball cap from his pocket, and tipped it in their direction.

Vietnamese foreign minister Nguyen Co Thach. *Robin Moyer/TimePix*

NINE

MEMORIAL DAY

What, I wondered, did Robert McNamara expect to learn from his former foes? Did he think they shared his penchant for delayed truth telling about the Vietnam War and the mistakes of its architects that had claimed fifty-eight thousand American lives, more than three million Vietnamese lives, and temporarily but seriously injured America's sense of purpose in the world? After all, McNamara had only lately broken twenty-eight years of near total silence about the war with the 1995 publication of his memoir, *In Retrospect: The Tragedy and Lessons of Vietnam*, in which he confessed that he and the other senior members of Lyndon Johnson's war council had been "wrong, terribly wrong" about the war.

What had they done wrong? They "had not truly investigated what was essentially at stake and important to us," and they had "never stopped to explore fully whether there were other routes to our destination." Left unanswered was the question of whether Secretary of Defense McNamara had been "terribly wrong" in his belief that victory could be achieved without invading the territory of the enemy and without destroying the war supplies and air defenses that its international patrons had provided Hanoi with to kill Americans.

Would such measures have led, as McNamara believed, to war with China and the Soviet Union? And if so, how were the millions of Americans they sent to Vietnam expected to accomplish their mission of defending the independence of South Vietnam? By killing more of the enemy than they killed of us, in a war with no front lines, on ground that was usually the enemy's to choose, following a strategy that McNamara confessed he knew well before he resigned would lead to "a major national disaster" as it sapped American will at home. He never expressed such doubts very forcefully when in office. As late as July 1967, a few months before he resigned, he wrote a memo to the president proclaiming, "There is no stalemate," and that victory would be achieved if the administration stuck to its strategy. Few doubts were evident in the displeasure McNamara felt when some of his administration colleagues raised a few of their own or when he sacked an admiral who, having just brought his carrier out of the Tonkin Gulf, had answered a reporter's question, "What were you doing out there, Admiral?" with, "I'll be goddamned if I know."

Now, two years after his late confession, McNamara had come to Vietnam with a delegation of former Kennedy and Johnson White House officials, two retired generals, and half a dozen historians to see if the Vietnamese had a few confessions of their own to make. But he discovered that the Vietnamese, who had won the damn war after all, weren't as given to retrospection about their conduct of it. If ever they were, it wouldn't be for international consumption, and certainly not for the man, whom, despite the hospitality they showed him and their attitude of letting bygones be bygones, they had proudly beaten.

I read an insightful and oddly entertaining account of the exchange David Shipler had written for *The New York Times Magazine*. McNamara had arranged with the Vietnamese Foreign Ministry to hold in Hanoi's renovated French colonial Hotel Metropole (where I have slept comfortably on several occasions) a four-day conference in June 1997 of U.S. and Vietnamese retired government and military officials and scholars.

The stated purpose of the conference was an exploration by both sides of how U.S. and Vietnamese misperceptions of each other had led to tragically missed opportunities to end the war earlier at less cost to each side. McNamara's delegation had come prepared to discuss the subject seriously and were equipped with recently disclosed secret war-related documents from Chinese, Russian, and Eastern European archives. They hoped to use the documents to prompt reciprocal candor from their hosts.

The Vietnamese delegation, led by former Vietnamese foreign minister Nguyen Co Thach, brought no secret documents from their wartime archives or any real enthusiasm for a revealing trip down memory lane. When asked by his American interlocutors if there had been disagreements among Vietnamese leaders during the war, Thach coolly replied, with the subtle, ironic humor that made him a much prized dinner companion, "There were discussions, but we are not permitted to publicize them. . . . [We] keep secrets to defend ourselves. Sometimes we cannot even get access to our own secrets."

The Americans should have stopped there. Their Vietnamese counterparts were never going to seriously share with them mistakes their government had made during the war or expose to historical examination whatever internal dissent had existed within their war councils. The legitimacy of the regime was based in their victory, and no Vietnamese official, retired or otherwise, was going to risk weakening that legitimacy or irritating the regime by admitting to screwups that had inflicted unnecessary hardship on their people.

The essence of Vietnam's historical identity is its centuries-long struggle for independence from foreign invaders: the Chinese, the French, the Japanese, the French again, and finally us. They aren't going to welcome lightly a foreigner's suggestion that the costs hadn't been entirely worth the accomplishment. That's not to say that theirs is a constantly backward-looking culture. On the contrary, they don't really see the purpose of discussing the war with Americans and are, I think, perplexed with Americans' preoccupation with having such a "dialogue." They prefer to look forward to a new, friendlier relationship with the United States, by which they mean an economic relationship with us and the rest of the free world that will help Vietnam escape the catastrophe of socialist economic philosophy (which some Vietnamese leaders, especially Thach, long ago recognized as hopelessly bankrupt). They hope to prosper as handsomely as have their Southeast Asian neighbors. That's all they really want to talk about with us.

To a favored few Americans, with whom they have built closer postwar ties, some Vietnamese might talk elliptically about their concern with the regional intentions of their colossus to the north, China. But with most Americans, they would if they could stick to trade agreements and joint ventures as the only subjects of real importance in our relationship. But if we insist on tilting at their historical claims, we're going to get a long, rote recitation of their fierce opposition to foreign invaders, beginning with their fifteenth-century expulsion of the Chinese and ending with, "We're quite proud of ourselves. Thanks for asking."

Having been down that road before, and having endured interminable Vietnamese history lessons for my trouble, I try to stay clear of past disputes in my discussions with the Vietnamese and stick to subjects of more contemporary interest.

McNamara and his colleagues pressed on, however, to little good effect. The Vietnamese didn't admit to mistaken perceptions about us, save one. Ho Chi Minh, who, as they always remind American visitors, had considered Harry Truman a friend and had included passages from our Declaration of Independence in his own declaration of independence from France, believed the United States was an anticolonial power. That misperception had been the only mistake old Ho had ever made, they claimed, exposed as such when we came to France's aide and not theirs and, when that effort failed, took up the task of resisting their independence ourselves. Whatever perceptions they had of us during the war were predicated on our military actions. They had little else on which to base their judgments of us. They only had subscriptions to *Time* and *Newsweek*, you see. *The New York Times* was too expensive.

I laughed out loud when I read this last bit of revisionism, and not just because I had once seen a copy of the *Times* on the desk of one of my prison commanders. Thach knew better than that. Not before, during, or after the war had he believed the United States was a colonial power. He had told me so himself. He thought we were mistaken in our assumptions about monolithic communism, sometimes blind to history, and woefully ignorant of North Vietnamese purpose and will. But he never saw us as colonialists and, in some important respects, thought us quite an enlightened country. The declarations to the contrary made at the conference were nothing more than the kind of bullshit that leaders of both sides used routinely to hide the truth from each other, from their own people, and from themselves.

Things continued in this unproductive vein for the rest of the conference. The Vietnamese side helpfully encouraged McNamara's need to confess his own misperceptions. They claimed that local commanders, not Hanoi, had ordered the attacks the United States interpreted as a *casus belli* against our ships in the Tonkin Gulf in August 1964 and, six months later, against American advisers in Pleiku, when presidential adviser McGeorge Bundy had been in Saigon and Soviet premier Aleksei Kosygin had been in Hanoi. The local commander in Pleiku had no idea Bundy was in the south. Less than the whole truth, I suspect, but who knows.

McNamara repeatedly tried to get his Vietnamese counterparts to recognize that Johnson's several offers of negotiations had been genuine. They countered that they had never considered them to be anything other than a public relations ruse, since U.S. troop deployments to Vietnam continued and bombing pauses were always followed by more bombing. Never would they have begun serious peace negotiations while the United States continued bombing them, they abjured. A point of national pride, you must understand. Proof of our resilience. The Paris peace talks didn't begin until Johnson ordered a bombing halt in 1968. But they were suspended in 1972, and the B-52s Nixon sent to Hanoi that Christmas didn't seem to offend Vietnamese pride so much that it prevented them from quickly returning to the table and signing the accords. Quite the contrary, it struck some of us who witnessed its effect that the bombing had served to persuade Hanoi that further delay was counterproductive.

Thach's comments to the press at the close of the conference pretty much summed up its results. "Of course, all the opportunities were missed by the U.S. side, not the Vietnamese side." A lie told with a smile, of course, but what could you expect to result from a well-intentioned but naïve belief that a government that shared few of our liberal political values and even less our appreciation for repentance would happily consent to exposing the mistakes that informed their decisions and the lies they used to defend them? They don't seek absolution, not for the war, anyway.

As I noted, I stay away from those kinds of discussions with the Vietnamese and stick to more pressing matters. What I would like from Vietnam today is respect for American interests, which they have shown more of in recent years, and for the values that informed the declaration that

Ho Chi Minh, all those many years ago, had claimed as his own. Hanoi's progress toward the latter has been slight. But they are topics I can discuss in Hanoi without fear of summoning old war chants.

On a cold Christmas night when I was a prisoner of war, the prison commander, a man we called the Cat, paid a holiday visit to my cell. Looking rather dapper in a suit and tie, with a diamond tiepin his father had given him, he regaled me with stories about his privileged background as the son of Ho's friend and close associate. His father, he told me, had even spent holidays with Ho and on one occasion had been invited to share a villa on an island in Ha Long Bay that Ho had used to relax. It's a spectacularly beautiful site, Ha Long Bay, crowded with jagged volcanic islands. The way the Cat described it to me that night in our unexpectedly friendly encounter aroused my curiosity about the place. I kept thinking about it long after my guest and I parted company that Christmas, and I made a promise to myself that I, too, would spend a night in Ho's villa.

Many years later, I discussed my plans for a trip to Vietnam with a former associate of Thach's, his vice foreign minister, Le Van Mai, over lunch in the senators dining room in the Capitol. Le Mai was as urbane, intelligent, and engaging as was his old boss, and I liked him very much. He was straightforward, imperturbable, and patient with America's hesitant steps toward rapprochement. In our conversation, I mentioned, almost as an aside, my hope to someday pay a visit to Ho's vacation retreat. He expressed great surprise that I knew of the place and was amused by how I had learned about it, since it was not generally discussed in Vietnam that Ho needed to take a day off from time to time.

Nevertheless, when I arrived in Hanoi, I was excited to learn that my hosts had arranged for me a night's rest at Ho's villa in exotic Ha Long Bay. And a few nights later, as I breathed the warm breezes off the bay that blew through the unshuttered windows, snuffed out the candle on the table next to me, and laid my head on the pillow, in the bed, in the house where Ho had slept, I knew I had received all the recompense I was likely to get for the nights in Vietnam I had spent in less comfortable circumstances, many years ago. There was nothing more I could gain by revisiting the war with my former enemies. Better to enjoy the evening and in the morning see to more promising pursuits, among which was helping to build a relationship with Vietnam that would serve both our peoples better than our old one had. In that endeavor, I pledged to keep the bullshit on both sides to a minimum. I think the memory of fifty-eight thousand dead Americans and three million Vietnamese dead deserves to be honored with the truth.

In that endeavor, I had, for a brief time, a partner in the very man whose clever evasions had so frustrated Robert McNamara. I first met Nguyen Co Thach in October 1990, when the first tenuous steps toward normalizing our relations were under way. He had just met with Secretary of State Jim Baker to discuss Vietnam's cooperation in the search for answers to the fates of over two thousand Americans still missing from the war and in efforts to promote a negotiated settlement to the continuing civil war in Cambodia. Their meeting had been held in New York. One of the sanctions we imposed on Vietnam at the time was a travel restriction on Vietnamese officials who represented their country at the United Nations to a twenty-five-mile radius of New York.

The year before, Vietnam had withdrawn its forces from Cambodia, which it had invaded and occupied ten years earlier. Also, in 1987, the Vietnamese, led by Thach, had met with an American delegation in Hanoi to discuss efforts to account for our missing in action. The delegation was led by John Vessey, retired army general and chairman of the Joint Chiefs of Staff. President Reagan had summoned Vessey, a selfless patriot if ever there was one, from well-earned retirement to be his special envoy to Vietnam for POW/MIA affairs, a position General Vessey would hold through three presidential administrations. The Vietnamese had accepted Vessey's proposal to allow, beginning in 1988, joint field investigations at crash sites were American pilots had been lost. They had also begun to unilaterally repatriate the remains of missing Americans. Moreover, Americans in Vietnam, while not exactly allowed to travel unimpeded around the country, were not subjected to the tight restrictions we imposed on Vietnamese diplomats here. Baker, in recognition of this slight thaw in our relations, gave Thach permission to come to Washington to meet with Vessey and with members of Congress Thach hoped to enlist in the cause of normal relations between our countries. I was one of those on the Hill he came to for support.

At the time, I wasn't much inclined to help. I had earlier taken a step toward improving relations with Vietnam by joining with my good friend, (then) Congressman Tom Ridge, to sponsor a resolution urging the Reagan administration to agree with Hanoi to open interest sections in each country's capital. Interest sections represent the lowest form of diplomatic relations between countries. Indeed, they exist in countries that have no formal relations with each other. We have an interest section in Havana, for instance, despite our conspicuous lack of relations with Cuba. Tom and I believed that fifteen years was long enough to sustain official American hostility for Vietnam at wartime levels. I had even written an op-ed in *The Washington Post,* pronouncing it past time we sought better ties with our old adversary.

But Vietnam, even sixteen years after we had left the country, occupied a unique and very unwelcome place in the American conscience, the undefeated enemy. As such, even small steps toward a new relationship weren't always warmly welcomed by some Americans. And Tom and I had received a good deal of criticism for our proposal, from the administration, from some veterans groups, and from the leading association of families of prisoners of war and missing in action (MIA).

Then, in August of 1988, still smarting from the criticism our effort had received, I learned that the government of Vietnam had suspended its cooperation with our POW/MIA accounting efforts because Vietnam's leadership felt its cooperation had not quickly produced sufficient rewards from Washington, noting that the administration had opposed the McCain-Ridge resolution. I called Vietnam's UN ambassador and informed him of my serious disappointment, and then I withdrew my resolution. Some months later, I wrote another op-ed in the *Post* urging the administration not to reward Vietnam's bad faith.

A few days after the Baker-Thach meeting in New York, in a speech on the Senate floor I again cautioned the administration to await greater cooperation from Hanoi before taking even limited steps toward normalization. Not long after they had announced their suspension of cooperation in 1988, they reconsidered the decision and resumed working with General Vessey on POW/MIA questions. Still, I hadn't forgotten the disappointment of their recent belligerence, and I was inclined to continue withholding my support until I was completely assured that it wouldn't happen again. But I closed the speech with a reminder of George Washington's famous admonition: "The nation which indulges toward another an habitual hatred or an habitual fondness is in some degree a slave . . . to its animosity or its affection, either one of which is sufficient to lead it astray from its duty and its interests." And I professed my hope that should Vietnam reciprocate, we could resume our slow progress away from habitual animosity.

So Thach, choosing to respond to my hopes rather than my anger, asked to meet me. I liked him instantly. He did not fit the mold of the stolid Party apparatchik I had assumed the Vietnamese Communist Party would appoint to such an important post. On the contrary, he was elegant, cosmopolitan, witty, and well-read. Fluent in French and English, with a gift for American vernacular, he was easy to talk to and given to outbursts of candor, which he would express almost carelessly, whether in Washington or Hanoi. He once told a reporter in Vietnam that the Vietnamese government "was not without accomplishment. We have managed to distribute poverty equally."

He was also strong willed. Where his associate Le Mai was resigned to the slow pace of rapprochement, Thach was insistent with Americans, often argumentative, and always determined to have the last word. As I share some of those traits, almost every conversation I ever had with him was interrupted by an argument, sometimes quite heated; but we soon recovered our good humor and continued more congenially. He was a congenial man, and I couldn't really fault him for his impatience. He had a lot riding on the question personally.

He was born to middle-class parents in the northern province of Nam Dinh in 1921 or 1923—accounts vary, as they often do in Communist countries, for some unfathomable reason. At fourteen, he left school to fight the French with the Viet Minh. At seventeen, he was jailed for a year by the French in a Hanoi prison so crowded that the inmates had to sleep in shifts and so hot that they shed all their clothes. They named the place "the Furnace"—Hoa Lo in Vietnamese. Americans called it the Hanoi Hilton.

He fought the Japanese in World War II, and after the war he joined the Communist Party and resumed the struggle against the returning

French colonialists. He rose to the rank of lieutenant colonel and was present at Vo Nguyen Giap's side at the battle of Dien Bien Phu, when French dominion over Vietnam was brought to an inglorious end. He left the army after the war for North Vietnam's diplomatic corps.

He became an accomplished, polished diplomat, serving as Vietnam's counsel general in India in the 1950s and leading the Vietnamese delegation to the Geneva Conference in 1962, having been named deputy foreign minister two years earlier. He was a prominent figure in Vietnamese diplomacy throughout the U.S.-Vietnam War. In 1966, he met secretly with a retired Canadian diplomat to discuss starting peace negotiations in exchange for a bombing halt. He was Le Duc Tho's protégé and chief aide in Paris when talks finally began in 1968; throughout their duration, he was instrumental in securing the 1973 accords that ended America's war with Vietnam.

His experiences with Americans during the war and his continuing interest in the United States earned him the nickname "Mr. America" from his colleagues. After North Vietnam's conquest of the south, he became Hanoi's leading advocate of improved relations with the West generally and the United States in particular. In 1978, he played a leading role in normalization talks with American officials in New York. Those discussions ended in failure over Vietnam's demands for war reparations and their invasion of their neighbor Cambodia.

Thach despised the incomprehensibly cruel Khmer Rouge, which had plunged Cambodia into stygian darkness and, in its fits of incomparable paranoia, had one too many times launched cross-border attacks on Vietnam. He strongly supported the Cambodian invasion and Hanoi's installation of a client regime in Phnom Penh and had tirelessly defended the invasion to Western governments. While Hanoi felt it had cause for its decisive action against its troublesome neighbor, the West, China, and the rest of Southeast Asia saw it as evidence of Vietnamese expansionism in the region and joined forces to enforce Vietnam's diplomatic and economic isolation. Seeing his hopes for Vietnam's integration into the world community imperiled by its occupation of Cambodia, Thach became an early proponent of withdrawing Vietnam's forces.

He was appointed foreign minister in 1980, and in 1986, he became a full member of the Politburo and was elevated to deputy prime minister. In the Sixth Communist Party Congress that year, Thach was the leading advocate of Do Moi, a program of economic liberalization that began to rescue Vietnam from ruinous socialist economic principles that had kept the country in an economic stone age. Early on, Thach recognized the failure of Marxist economics and praised the wonders of free markets not just in private discussions within the government, but with Westerners and in the press. He once greeted me in Hanoi wearing a tie with little profiles of Adam Smith embroidered on it. Whatever his allegiances to the Party's unchallenged political control, he knew that national independence was ill served by Communist economic orthodoxy and would be strengthened rather than threatened by foreign investment and access to the world's free markets.

He knew something else that many of Vietnam's leaders had failed to grasp since the end of the war. From the mid-1960s until the fall of Saigon in 1975, Vietnam had been at the center of world attention and had found, to its great advantage, that it had become the object of vacuous romanticism in many Western intellectual circles. After the war, those same admirers turned to various other foreign attractions on which to practice their sophistry, leaving the Vietnamese to soldier on without the active support of the cheering squad of useful idiots in the Western press who had helped them win the war. When the mass exodus of Vietnamese boat people put the lie to Hanoi's unquestioningly embraced promises of enlightened political rule, the embarrassment caused in leftist salons from Paris to New York, suffered as always in near total silence, provoked, if not shame, then concern among Vietnam's leaders. But they had a hard time grasping the fact that the world didn't really give a damn about them any longer.

This unexpected development was all the more troubling given the state of their relations with China, relations that had gone from a wartime alliance to open hostility. In 1979, the two countries fought a brief but bloody border war, which Vietnam won. The Chinese were unlikely to forget the insult, and Hanoi, as it had for centuries, looked anxiously north as it contemplated its future. Thach's pursuit of an opening with the United States was based in large part on his recognition that Vietnam's problems with America had been of relatively short duration, while China's various occupations of Vietnam had lasted centuries and its proximity and aggressive regional ambitions posed a clear and present threat to Vietnam's security. Among Vietnam's leaders, he was the most distrustful of China and the most openly critical of entente with Beijing.

He was also one of the few Vietnamese leaders who grasped his country's reduced circumstances as a player on the world stage, likely to provoke interest in the West only when it appeared to live up to its expansionist reputation, worsening its present isolation and vulnerability to Chinese aggression. Many of his colleagues persisted in holding on to the comforting myth that they were still too important to be ignored by the world. Thach knew better, and he told them so. He knew that the world was largely indifferent to Vietnam's current travails and that they would have to wait indefinitely for the world to engage with Vietnam on Hanoi's terms. The world would have to be courted, especially the United States. He argued that a normal relationship with the United States was essential for Vietnam's integration into the world economy to succeed, and that to achieve this, Vietnam must cooperate with the Americans in the search for their missing servicemen.

When I traveled to Vietnam in 1991, my second trip back since the end of the war, Vietnam's economic progress since the initiation of the Do Moi reforms was quite visible. Farmers had been allowed to hold long-term leases on their land and sell their crops for profit. As a result, Vietnam had gone from a net importer of rice, on the brink of famine, to the world's third largest exporter of the commodity. Hanoi's prosperity had always lagged behind Saigon's and still did. But small shops and restaurants, its owners permitted to keep some of their meager profits, had proliferated along Hanoi's wide tree-lined avenues. The streets were clogged with bike-riding peasants bringing their wares to market.

In 1985, when I had first returned to Hanoi, to tape a documentary with Walter Cronkite on the tenth anniversary of the fall of Saigon, I found the capital almost unchanged from the grim, listless, eerily quiet place I had left twelve years before. I would have been hard-pressed to find a toothbrush to purchase. In 1991, while still quite poor, Hanoi was a more lively place and noticeably more prosperous, if only in the most rudimentary stage of development. And clearly eager for more progress.

Toward that end, Thach had promised his government that accepting Washington's demands for POW/MIA cooperation was the surest way to have access to American assistance, markets, and investors. But he was impatient for results, his superiors even more so.

General Vessey had led several delegations to Vietnam since 1987, and each one had been more successful than the last. Thach had agreed to the U.S. request to begin joint field investigations of crash sites where Americans had been lost and where we had some evidence that the pilots might have survived. Thach had also provided from Vietnam's war archives a few case files concerning downed pilots. The Thach-Vessey negotiations also produced the unilateral repatriation of the remains of over a hundred missing Americans. This, of course, confirmed American suspicions that Vietnam had all along been warehousing American remains in the expectation that they might someday prove useful as bargaining chips. As inhumane as this practice was, General Vessey did not chastise the Vietnamese. He thanked them and encouraged them to do more of the same.

After its brief suspension of cooperation in 1988, Hanoi made considerable strides in meeting U.S. demands. Thach agreed to almost every proposal Vessey made, more joint field investigations, more unilateral repatriation of remains, access to archival information, and permission to interview Vietnamese who had witnessed the shoot-down of American pilots. For our part, we began a program of very limited humanitarian assistance to Vietnam, though not nearly as much as Vietnam and its anxious foreign minister had expected for their newly accommodative attitude.

After his successful discussions with Secretary Baker in New York, and with General Vessey in Washington, Thach expected significant reciprocal actions from the United States. When we met in my office, he seemed a little concerned that they hadn't been forthcoming, but he hoped that progress was still imminent and asked me to resume my efforts. I was noncommittal but told him I would consider reengaging in the debate and would wait until I came to Vietnam early the following year before deciding. He welcomed my visit but hoped I would resume my efforts sooner. We parted company amicably.

I traveled to Vietnam in April 1991. As the United States had no diplomatic presence in Vietnam, I had to stop in Bangkok first to collect my visa and to be briefed by American embassy officials there. While there, I was called by a State Department official, Ken Quinn, chief of the office for Vietnam, Cambodia, and Laos, who informed me that the administration was preparing to provide the Vietnamese with a "road map" of reciprocal actions that would ultimately lead to diplomatic and economic normalization. The Vietnamese would be asked to accept a range of very specific proposals to hasten the "fullest possible" accounting for America's missing. They would also be expected to actively encourage their client regime in Cambodia to sign the Paris Peace Accords for a negotiated settlement of the Cambodian civil war that included UN administration of the country until free elections were held. In exchange for Hanoi's cooperation on these two fronts, the United States was prepared to improve relations, promising very small steps at first, focused largely on humanitarian assistance, but leading eventually, over a rather long timetable, to full normalization. Ken asked if I would endorse the plan, and if so, would I discuss it in general terms with Vietnamese officials and encourage them to accept the plan when the administration presented it to them in New York the following week.

I agreed to the request, but only if one additional condition were included in the road map. Following the conquest of South Vietnam, Hanoi arrested many former South Vietnamese military and government officials and imprisoned them in rural hard labor prisons that the government euphemistically called "reeducation camps." Many had died in the camps or had their health destroyed. Some of the prisoners had been released after many years of suffering awful deprivations. But many were still being held sixteen years after the war had ended. Only if their liberation were made a condition of normal relations would I support the road map. Shortly before I departed for Hanoi, Ken called again to inform me that the administration had agreed to add the release of the reeducation camp prisoners to its conditions for normalization, and I agreed to support the road map and discuss it with Thach the next day.

I guess I had expected Thach to be pleased, if not with the timetable for better relations, at least with the fact that the United States at last had clearly articulated the steps that would lead to normalization. But he was not pleased at all. He was quite angered by the fact that all Vietnam's cooperation to date had achieved were demands for more from the United States with a promise of normalization at some very distant time in the future. Although he greeted me warmly when I arrived, wearing his Adam Smith tie, his usual charm and good humor disappeared instantly when I began to discuss the administration's plan.

Vietnam had gone a long way over the last few years to help America account for its missing, he noted, while Vietnam still had three hundred thousand soldiers missing from the war. And all their accession to our demands had earned them were more demands. This bad faith, he repeated again and again, was not likely to encourage Vietnam's leaders to provide more assistance to what he called the "humanitarian issue of your missing in action."

I countered that the United States was not acting in bad faith, that there were many issues that needed to be resolved before the American public could accept that the war was really behind us. And as Thach grew angrier, so did I. I reminded him that our previous experiences with assurances from the government of Vietnam had not been happy ones. Under the terms of the Paris Peace Treaty, Vietnam had promised not to invade the south after the United States withdrew its forces. They had violated that obligation almost as soon as the last American soldier had left the country. Therefore, the United States would never enter into any agreement with Hanoi that provided concessions to Vietnam without verification that Vietnam was keeping its end of the bargain.

This last remark provoked a brief but angry exchange between us about which side had failed to honor the terms of the peace accords. Thach complained that Washington had promised to provide billions of dollars in economic assistance after the war, which he termed "war reparations," and had never delivered a dollar. I countered that North Vietnam's invasion of the south released us from whatever postwar obligations we had undertaken in Paris. Both of us knew better than to proceed down this road, having determined in our own minds that it was better to stay focused on the future than revisit our old grievances. But we let ourselves get angry, and our discussion proved utterly unproductive.

This was disappointing. I knew Thach was a practical man, and I had a hard time understanding why, with so many issues of serious concern to the United States still unresolved, he would expect us to proceed any more quickly toward normal relations than the road map proposed. I also considered him a man of vision, and I couldn't believe that he would let his pique over what he considered an inordinate delay in the pace of normalization threaten his vision of a modern Vietnam, fully integrated into the world economy. I also enjoyed his company, had been looking forward to our meeting, and was saddened that it had become an unpleasant and fruitless exchange.

I like to think Thach shared my disappointment. At a dinner he hosted for me that evening, he had recovered his good humor, as I had recovered mine. There were no arguments. We discussed the road map a little more and the details of where and when it would be presented to them. Although neither Thach nor anyone in the Vietnamese government ever formally agreed to the road map's conditions, they never formally rejected them, either. And they would, fitfully, slowly, eventually, meet all of the road map's conditions.

He talked about the current state of Vietnam's economy, what the reforms had achieved, and what further improvements he hoped were imminent. I joked about his Adam Smith tie and what his Politburo comrades thought about such unorthodox attire. He said Communists often understood how the "invisible hand" of free markets worked better than capitalists did, having by nature a greater respect for secrets and the iron laws of history. He was candid, entertaining, and impressive. I mentioned our common experience of being held in the prison that was only a few blocks from where we were having dinner. He talked a little about his year in Hoa Lo and said I should be glad that France's influence on Vietnamese culture didn't extend to its penal system. I acknowledged that prison conditions might have been worse overall for the Viet Minh, but that the food had to have been better than it was when I had been a prisoner there.

He returned to the subject of improved relations, but wearily, almost wistfully. Gone was the impatience and confrontational attitude he had displayed that morning. He said we had more to teach each other as friends than we had ever taught each other as enemies. And then he said something I have always remembered. "Americans must come to understand that Vietnam is a country, not just a war. And Vietnam must learn to accept its destiny as a small nation." I thought that observation was fair and accurate and, given my other experiences with government leaders in Communist countries, quite profound. It was good counsel that I kept in mind throughout my subsequent efforts to ensure that the United States, having given our word to reciprocate Vietnam's cooperation by embracing Thach's vision for our countries, would keep it.

Unfortunately, the Vietnamese government couldn't bring itself to share its foreign minister's wisdom. They sacked him three months later and relegated him to the status of official nonexistence that Communist governments reserve for colleagues whose principles don't bend to a change in the prevailing political winds. Hanoi had seen what it believed was the disaster of perestroika and glasnost lead to the collapse of a Communist superpower and had contrasted it with how China had managed to liberalize its economy while maintaining the regime's survival by ruthlessly repressing political dissent in Tiananmen Square. Hanoi resolved to follow a similar course. Vietnam's leaders were even angrier about Washington's refusal to improve relations on Hanoi's ambitious timetable than Thach had been; his fear over his own political future, I suspect, animated much of the dissatisfaction he had expressed to me. They blamed Thach for conceding too much to the Americans and for not delivering the rewards he said would ensue from their cooperation. They also blamed him for not predicting the collapse of the Soviet Union.

Most problematic for my friend was his position as the government's leading critic of China. As Vietnam's ruling class met in the Seventh Communist Party Congress in July 1991, the changes in the regime that were its result elevated those officials who had argued for rapprochement with China as a more advisable and achievable diplomatic goal than better relations with the United States. China was willing. But it had apparently imposed a condition on its friendship. Nguyen Co Thach must no longer be allowed to abuse Chinese goodwill by toadying up to the United States at China's expense.

So the Party fired Thach and replaced him with Nguyen Manh Cam, a veteran diplomat who would in time carry on Thach's cooperation with the United States in the areas of concern identified in the road map. But he was less influential and a more cautious man than Thach had been. And while I got along well with his successor, I missed very much working with the man who I believe, to the extent his political culture permitted it (and then some), shared my aversion to self-deceptions about our countries' troubled history and my hope for a more honest future.

I've made many trips back to Vietnam since my last meeting with Thach. Several times I asked the Vietnamese government to allow me to see him. As each passing year brought our countries closer to normal relations, I had hoped he would be pleased by the progress in the work he had begun and sacrificed his career to advance. I had talked to people who had heard secondhand accounts of conversations with Thach, that he was bitter not only about his misfortune, but about the slow progress made toward normalization in the years since he had been fired. He was an impatient man, but I think a man who was impatient for a worthy cause. I never got to see him again. For the majority of his forced retirement, although in comfortable circumstances, he was kept isolated from most foreigners. The government never refused my request to meet with him. But then Vietnamese habitually avoid directly refusing their official guests' requests. They just don't respond.

Thach died of heart failure on April 10, 1998. He was either seventy-five or seventy-seven years old. He had lived to see his dream of normal relations with the United States realized and his own reputation as a visionary Vietnamese leader officially rehabilitated. He was accorded great honors in death that had been denied him in life. The entire Vietnamese political leadership attended his funeral, and his wisdom and achievements were celebrated widely in Vietnam's official press. Of all the many important achievements that I believe have been attained by the improvement in our relations, I hope that my old enemy and old friend's peace of mind was among them.

———

One week after I returned from Vietnam in 1991, Thach and General Vessey reached an agreement to open in Hanoi a United States POW/MIA office, from which American investigators would lead efforts to account for our missing, plan and execute the joint field operations, and search Vietnamese archival documents for answers to their fates. It was the first official U.S. presence in Vietnam since the war and the first official presence in Hanoi since the French ran the country. It was also the first indication that Hanoi would quietly acquiesce in the road map's conditions. I, and those of my colleagues who shared my interest in better relations with Vietnam, hoped this welcome development would signal a quickening pace in our accounting efforts and in our progress toward normal relations. But we would soon realize that we had a much longer road ahead of us than either Thach or I had hoped.

To understand the unusual amount of suspicion, bogus claims, and false hope that made the question of what had happened to American servicemen missing from the Vietnam War so fraught with controversy and time-consuming disputes, you need only to appreciate one sentence in a 1992 Senate committee report.

> On a subject as personal and emotional as the survival of a family member, there is nothing more difficult than to be asked to accept the probability of death, when the possibility of life remains.

Many families could not and should not have been expected to abandon hope that their sons, husbands, and brothers who had disappeared in the jungles of Vietnam might yet be returned to them. And many good people, who shared their hope and had come to their assistance, were motivated by the most admirable of intentions, to keep faith with Americans who had done all that duty asked of them. But these good intentions and understandable emotions also drew the attention of people with less honorable purposes. There came to exist in America, and elsewhere in the years that followed the Vietnam War, a small cottage industry made up of swindlers, dime-store Rambos, and just plain old conspiracy nuts who preyed on the emotions of the families and on the attention of officials who were dedicated to the search for our missing. They had helped convince many of the families and a few members of Congress that the U.S. government had knowingly abandoned American servicemen in Vietnam and that five successive presidential administrations had covered up the crime. It was among the most damaging and most hurtful of all the lies about the Vietnam War that I ever encountered.

In truth, no country had ever done more to account for its missing than America had for its missing men in Vietnam. The government had made many mistakes: the Nixon administration's far too confident assertion that all American prisoners alive in Vietnam had been returned in Operation Homecoming, and the excessive secrecy that shrouded every decision and all information concerning POW/MIAs and attempts to learn their fates. But overall, extraordinary efforts have been made to chase down leads, find clues, and unlock secrets the Vietnamese would have preferred to keep locked, all so we could point with pride to the fact that Americans never willingly left men on the battlefield, dead or alive.

There are over seventy-eight thousand Americans still missing from World War II and nearly eight thousand still missing from the Korean War. In the early 1990s, about twenty-three hundred Americans were still classified as POW/MIAs, a formulation intended to demonstrate that we assumed our men could still be alive in captivity rather than, as was more likely, killed in action, body not recovered (KIA/BNR). Most of these Americans were known with near certainty to be dead, having crashed their planes into the waters of the Tonkin Gulf or into remote jungle mountains and whose squadron mates said had failed to eject from their airplanes. Their bodies were not likely ever to be recovered, but still, since we don't have their bodies, and the conclusive proof of death physical evidence provides, they are carried on the rolls of the missing.

There are, however—or were—over a hundred men who we have some proof had survived what is officially termed their "incident of loss." Either their fellow pilots saw their chutes open or they had signaled their survival by radio communication or they had been seen in captivity by other prisoners or various other forms of evidence existed to indicate at least their temporary survival. These "discrepancy" or "last known alive" cases have been the primary focus of U.S. investigations, and the United States had long asserted, correctly, that Vietnam must have information that would help explain what had happened to them. And for whatever reason, because they had executed them or had mistreated them so badly that the prisoners had died in captivity, Hanoi refused to provide many answers. Many of these discrepancy cases concerned Americans who had been lost in Laos, where many men had been captured and only ten had been returned with other prisoners of war. But conditions in Laos had been more brutal than in North Vietnam, and it's likely that many of our pilots had died or been killed in captivity.

This official silence understandably bred suspicion among the families and among many Americans, including politicians, who became convinced that Vietnam had kept some of our men after the war. It also persuaded many more skeptical government officials to entertain serious doubts as to whether or not we had in fact gotten all our men back. It angered everybody involved in the search for answers, including me. But to effect a change in Hanoi's attitude, it was better to dispense with recriminations and find the right sticks and carrots to encourage their cooperation. Whatever they had done—executed prisoners or tortured them to death, shipped some off to China or the Soviet Union, as some suspected—would not prevent us from improving relations if Hanoi would provide us with answers.

American suspicions were also aggravated by the continuing spate of "live sighting reports," many from refugees, some from people with rewards in mind, who reported seeing people resembling Americans in captivity long after the war. Many of these reports, and there are thousands, were ultimately disproved or discredited because the source had proven dishonest or inaccurate, or because the subjects were determined to be foreign nationals from a country other than the United States. Many were attributed to a few American deserters who had stayed behind after the war. One in particular, former marine private Robert Garwood, accounted for over three hundred live sighting reports alone.

Bobby Garwood's story, one of the bigger fictions to come out of the war, was the primary evidence cited by every American, whether they were well- or ill-intentioned, who argued that men were still alive in Southeast Asia prisons and that our government was deliberately hiding that fact from the American people. But here, in brief outline, is the real Bobby Garwood story.

Near Danang in 1965, he had either deserted or been captured without resistance and then turned traitor. After two years of lenient treatment, compared to the treatment accorded other Americans who were held with him, his captors selected him for early release. He asked to be allowed to remain, not as a prisoner but to fight for the enemy. From 1967 to 1970, he did propaganda work, often using a bullhorn outside U.S. bases to urge surrender and resistance to the war. He was reported to have carried a weapon, which he held on American POWs. He was injured during a B-52 raid in 1970 and was awarded by the Vietnamese what amounted to a Purple Heart. After 1970, he worked for the North Vietnamese military unit that ran the prisoner of war camps and lived in a house outside Hanoi with a cook and an aide. Reportedly, he held a captain's rank, quite a promotion for an unambitious marine private.

After the war, he was seen moving freely around Hanoi and the Defense Ministry complex, called the Citadel. There he was observed by a Vietnamese army mortician who subsequently defected to the United States, reporting to American officials that he had seen three Caucasians living at liberty in Hanoi (the others are believed to have also been American deserters or possibly visiting Soviets or Eastern Europeans).

For one reason or another, Garwood tired of life in Vietnam and in 1979 passed a note to a European diplomat saying he was an American and that he wished to go home. So he went home, without any real obstruction from his hosts. When he arrived he was immediately debriefed by the U.S. Marine Corps, who asked him if he had seen Americans after the war. He said he had not, nor had he heard any rumors about Americans still in captivity after about 1977. Based on the testimony of Americans who had been held in captivity with him, Garwood was charged with collaborating with the enemy, and he was dishonorably discharged from the Marine Corps. He claimed he was owed $150,000 in back pay, which he did not receive. He was lucky he didn't face a firing squad.

Beginning in 1984, Bobby Garwood changed his story. He now claims he saw many Americans held as prisoners up until 1978, although the numbers of POWs he claims to have seen have changed over the years. Nevertheless, the inconsistent testimony of this thoroughly discredited and disgraced American traitor has become for many Americans compelling evidence that our government left men behind and then conspired to hide their existence.

There were half a dozen or so deserters during the war who might have hung around after the U.S. withdrawal. I never heard about Garwood during the war. But I did know of another deserter who, like Garwood, was the subject of many live sighting reports. He was former army private McKinley Nolan. The Vietnamese used to broadcast his statements into our cells. "This is McKinley Nolan," he would alert us, then give his former rank and service. "I have crossed over to the side of freedom and democracy. They say the National Liberation Front is mean and cruel. Is that true? No! They give me many tasty foods to eat." I assume Nolan had been reading a script prepared by Vietnamese with a less than impressive grasp of American forms of expression. But his frequent broadcasts were the source of much entertainment to my fellow prisoners, who could always get a laugh from one another by imitating Nolan's stilted diatribes.

Unfortunately, McKinley Nolan's life didn't work out as well as Bobby Garwood's. At some point after the war, he made the mistake of either inadvertently crossing the Cambodian border or attempting to relocate there. The Khmer Rouge killed him and dumped his body in a well. Thus, Nolan paid a much greater price for his treachery than had ever been exacted from his fellow deserter. Throughout the many months of a Senate effort I would soon be involved in that investigated the fates of POW/MIAs, time and again I heard witnesses and even a few members of Congress profess their belief in Garwood's lies. And each time it would make me madder than hell.

Just as General Vessey's negotiations were beginning to bear fruit in 1991, the conspiracy theories about a government POW/MIA cover-up were gaining their greatest purchase in the American conscience. In 1990, an army lieutenant colonel, Millard Peck, resigned his position as the director of the Defense Intelligence Agency's Office for POW/MIA Affairs, citing what he complained was a "mind-set to debunk" among Americans investigating live sighting reports. His complaints received a fair amount of media attention. It was still a back-page story, but enough to energize the POW/MIA activist community of families, supporters, and conspiracy theorists into furious activity, demanding a special congressional investigation of the charges. Then, in July 1991, *Newsweek* magazine published on its cover a picture of the three men purported to be American prisoners still held somewhere in Southeast Asia. Three families claimed with utter sincerity that the three individuals pictured were their loved ones missing in action in Vietnam.

The "three amigos picture," as it came to be called by American investigators, did not strike me as very compelling evidence. I was, to be honest, skeptical that Americans had been held behind after the rest of us were released. During our captivity, we had worked hard and taken considerable risks to make sure we had pretty thorough knowledge of every American who was a prisoner in North Vietnam. Neither could I ever think of a reason why Vietnam would do the one thing that might compel Americans to resume the war. The Vietnamese were certainly capable of lying about prisoners or anything else if it served their purposes. But what would be their purpose in keeping Americans prisoner? What political or military need would it serve? They could be cruel, but they're not, as a rule, capriciously cruel.

Those who sincerely believe that Vietnam had kept Americans after the war believed they had done so to compel America to make good on what they claim was a promise of "war reparations." But if that were the case, wouldn't the Vietnamese alert us to the fact that they were holding Americans for ransom if they were to have any prospect of actually getting their hands on the money? Yet the Vietnamese government has steadfastly denied holding a single American since the war. I was never able to find a single reason for such a dangerous gamble on Hanoi's part. I knew about some of the evidence that at least produced a little doubt about whether we all got home. And until we had sufficient evidence to the contrary, I pledged to keep an open mind and share the government's official "assumption of survival." But in truth, I thought it very unlikely that the Vietnamese had kept any American prisoner after the war. And if I was wrong, and the Vietnamese had for some incomprehensible reason risked restarting the war over an act of capricious cruelty, I found it hard to imagine how the victims could have survived in captivity for eighteen more years.

My doubts were not allayed by the three amigos picture. They looked a little too paunchy and a little too relaxed to remind me of any prisoner of war I had ever known, especially prisoners who would have been in their third decade of captivity. If they were POWs, the food really had gotten a hell of a lot better since I left. But shortly after *Newsweek* published the photograph, the son of a missing pilot came to my office and declared with total conviction that one of the men in the picture was his father. He had brought a blown-up copy of the picture on posterboard as well as an old family photograph of his father. Holding them side by side, he pointed to what he believed were the unmistakable similarities between the two pictures, sure beyond a shadow of a doubt that they were the same man. "Senator, I know my dad is alive," he told me.

I didn't see the similarities, other than the fact that both men were Caucasian. But I promised the young man that I would keep an open mind and do all I could to ascertain the truth about what had happened to his father. Here was a family like so many other American families, who seized on any information, no matter how dubious, to encourage their longing for reunion with their loved ones. And every allegation, no matter how spurious, that the government knew that men were alive in captivity and had intentionally concealed the knowledge from their families served to both confirm their conviction and fuel their outrage. When I told the young man that I would do what I could to find the truth, I meant it. But I meant to be no less determined in that endeavor if the truth were, as I supposed it was, that there were no American prisoners left in Southeast Asia. I was not indifferent to the families' suffering or unmoved by their desperate hopes. On the contrary, I believed their suffering would never begin to be alleviated until we uncovered the truth about America's missing, even if that truth was not what the families had hoped to find.

Toward that end, a month before the three amigos picture came to public attention, I had authored legislation requiring the Department of Defense to begin declassifying intelligence information about POW/MIAs that had been kept from the families for too many years without good reason. Surely some of the live sighting reports and other intelligence gathered over twenty years would fuel the families' conviction that men were still alive. But I hoped that the information's public disclosure would begin to allay suspicions that our government was intentionally concealing that fact from the American people. So, subject to certain restrictions I included in the legislation to protect the sources and methods of our intelligence collection, the government slowly began declassifying thousands of documents and relocating them to the Library of Congress, where they are available today for public inspection. But, regrettably, for some families, and for many of the people who consider themselves activists in the POW/MIA cause, those with honorable intentions and those with self-interested motives, my legislation did nothing to change their belief in a government conspiracy or their suspicions about me. In many cases, sad cases, the closer they got to the truth, the less they wanted to believe it.

Senator Robert Smith of New Hampshire, who had been elected to the Senate in 1988 after serving in the House, has devoted much of his congressional career to the search for our missing. He believes sincerely that men were left behind, and his single-minded attention to their plight is motivated by the best of intentions. He and I would come to part company on the question, at times in very heated and confrontational circumstances. But I've never doubted for a moment that, unlike many of those who exploited the issue for their own purposes, Bob was only trying to keep faith with men who had sacrificed their freedom for our country.

Shortly after he came to the Senate, Bob introduced legislation authorizing the establishment of a Senate Select Committee on POW/MIA Affairs, charged with conducting a comprehensive investigation of information collected about our missing and a critical examination of the government's response to that information. It would be the third such congressional inquiry since the war, but this time the committee's advocates intended to investigate more skeptically and ask harder questions of government officials than had been asked before. I worried that the committee would only sustain false hopes with evidence that, no matter how suspect or flawed, would be seized by the families as proof of their loved ones' survival and exacerbate suspicions about our government promoted by more disreputable activists with their own axes to grind. But I didn't fight the legislation, and on the evening it was scheduled to be adopted unanimously, Bob Dole asked me if I would consider serving as the committee's vice chairman. I declined initially and told Dole the honor should go to Smith as the author of the legislation. A little later I changed my mind, because, candidly, I had as many doubts about Bob's open-mindedness as he had about mine. But it was too late. The decision had been made. Bob Smith would serve as the Republican vice chairman of the Senate Select Committee that would be chaired by Democratic senator John Kerry of Massachusetts.

I was appointed to the panel, and while I would not lead the Republican side, I was the committee's only former prisoner of war, and that biographical fact meant that my views were accorded almost as much attention as the views of the two chairmen. I intended to use that advantage to help the committee arrive at the real truth about our missing, no matter how hard a truth it was.

John Kerry and I were both veterans of the Vietnam War, as was Bob Smith, who had served on a navy ship in the Tonkin Gulf. But we had different experiences in war and had come to Vietnam from very different backgrounds. We also came to very different conclusions about the justice of the cause. John had served with distinction as a swift boat commander in the Mekong River and earned the Silver Star for bravery in combat. I admired and respected his service. When he came home from Vietnam, he became a leading opponent of the war. He had been a prominent figure in a protest march by antiwar veterans and had testified eloquently against the war before the Senate Foreign Relations Committee. John's antiwar activities hadn't exactly endeared him to me, and in the four years we had served together, I had mostly kept my distance from him. That would change during the little more than a year the Senate Select Committee was in existence. We would become allies in the search for the truth, and then allies in the cause of normal relations between the United States and Vietnam. And we became good friends as well.

John Kerry is a smart man, with a trial lawyer's gifts for persuasive argument and a store of patience infinitely greater than my own. Aided by his talented and decent chief aide, Frances Zwenig, he ran the committee with fairness to all points of view, and during hearings that quite often were contentious to the point of creating a circus atmosphere, he would restore some semblance of, if not comity, at least sobriety to our proceedings. Bob had been given leeway to select much of the committee's Republican staff himself, and he hired a number of investigators who shared his conviction that we had left men behind and that the government did indeed have a mind-set to debunk information that supported that contention. I would butt heads often with those staffers, whose theories to prove the existence of living POWs I found to be ludicrously flimsy. Even more often, I would engage in hostile and very barbed exchanges with witnesses whom I thought to be little more than con artists, peddling false hopes for a little notoriety and, in some cases, money, and who soon made me one of the principals in their ridiculous conspiracy theories.

Many of the families came to resent me as well, which I regret, but I didn't let their disapproval prevent me from speaking what I believed was the truth about the missing and the efforts of government officials to account for them. I would become quite angry at times over the unfair charges hurled at hardworking officials who, although they made mistakes from time to time, had done their best to find the answers we all sought. They were often labeled by families and activists as lazy dupes at best and criminal conspirators at worst. This was as offensive to me as it was to them, and I seldom let these incredibly unfair charges go unchallenged.

My anger was also based in the great offense I took at the suggestion that five presidential administrations had joined in an elaborate conspiracy to conceal the fact that Americans had been knowingly left behind and that this conspiracy would have required the silence, if not the active collaboration, of hundreds or even thousands of uniformed American officers. I had been a professional officer, and I knew the military culture well. I have never known a single officer who would have done anything less than resign in protest if he thought for a moment that the United States government was hiding the fact that Americans had been left behind. And I demonstratively resented any suggestion to the contrary.

In these frequently inflammatory circumstances, John Kerry played peacemaker and somehow, with great sensitivity and patience, kept the committee operating until we eventually arrived at some approximation of the truth. I respected him immensely for the accomplishment.

Hearings began in November 1990. In our opening statements, Bob Smith and I revealed our opposing approaches to the committee's work, quickly and regrettably becoming each other's nemesis. He ended his statement by proclaiming his belief in Bobby Garwood. I ended mine by professing my intention to search honestly for the truth about our missing, but also that I believed the truth also needed to be told about those contemptible people who exploited the issue for their own selfish ends.

The first day's hearings included testimony by (then) Secretary of Defense Dick Cheney, as capable and sensible a public servant as I've known, who accurately observed that had he compelling evidence that Americans were alive in Southeast Asia, he would have servicemen lined up for miles outside his door demanding that they be allowed to bring them home. General Vessey also testified that day, patient and wise as always, and gave a credible account of the progress he had achieved with the Vietnamese to widen and intensify our accounting efforts.

The next day, the hearings became a little more controversial. Garnett "Bill" Bell, the director of the recently opened American POW/MIA office in Hanoi, testified and casually made the observation that as many as ten Americans might have been left behind, although he had no evidence they were still alive. I had met Bell before. He had been stationed at the Defense Intelligence Agency's office at our embassy in Bangkok, which, until the Hanoi office was opened, had served as the frontline POW/MIA intelligence-gathering mission. My encounter with him in Bangkok had been a strange experience that had caused me to wonder a little about his credibility, doubts that were exacerbated by his failure to back up his observation to the committee with any real evidence.

Bell had approached me at a dinner the American ambassador in Thailand had hosted for me. He told me he had stood next to my father at Clark Air Force Base the day I arrived there from prison. I told him, at first politely, that he was mistaken. My father was at home in the States when I was released and had specifically declined to come to Clark. He responded by insisting that I was mistaken, that my father was at Clark whether I knew it or not, and that he had seen my father weep at my arrival. As touching as that scene would have been to me, I knew my father's sense of honor prevented him from accepting a privilege that had not been offered the families of other returning prisoners, and I told Bell so. This had little effect on him, however, and he insisted repeatedly that my father had been at Clark to greet me. I finally cut him off with, "Well, I wish he would have let me know. I'd have been glad to see him."

Other Defense Department witnesses who testified that second day expressed surprise over their colleague's disclosure, saying they had no idea what evidence he had to support his contention that as many as ten Americans had been left behind. For that, they were criticized by some committee members and hissed at by families and activists who filled the hearing room. I commended them for answering honestly, asked them, as well as Bell, to get back to the committee with any evidence that might have relevance to the question, and earned a few hisses of my own.

It wasn't until the next day's hearings, however, that I would really get the attention of the activists and provide them with what they would claim as their first bit of evidence that I was not just a skeptic, but an active and dangerous co-conspirator. The committee heard from a Vietnamese defector, Bui Tin, who, as a colonel in the North Vietnamese army, had ridden a tank onto the grounds of the presidential palace in Saigon and had accepted the Republic of Vietnam's surrender that ended the war. While traveling abroad in later years, he had made sharply critical statements about the regime's political dictatorship and was now unwelcome in his country. I had met with him the day before to discuss our mutual interest in promoting democracy in Vietnam, and I got along quite well with him. He told me that in the 1970s, he had been working as an army journalist researching a book on American POWs and had come to see me in prison. I didn't remember his visit, but it very well may have happened, since the Vietnamese often brought people in to see the American admiral's prisoner-son.

He was a credible witness, who had worked in the military agency responsible for Vietnam's wartime prison system, and as a defector with no reluctance to criticize his government, he had no reason to lie about the possible existence of American POWs still in Vietnam. Yet he said that there were no prisoners alive in Vietnam and that only a few Americans who had changed sides during the war had remained behind after the war. This didn't endear him to the activists, who suspected an elaborate Communist ruse to plant a fake defector in our hearing room.

Their suspicions were confirmed when, after Bui Tin had concluded his testimony, I along with other committee members walked over to the witness table to shake hands with him and thank him for his testimony, a courtesy routinely extended to witnesses. When I reached for his hand he responded by embracing me, which I didn't mind, as cameras recorded the moment for the next day's papers, which ran the picture with variations on the caption FORMER ENEMIES EMBRACE. But to the conspiracy theorists in the audience, this spontaneous affection was nothing less than a secret signal between two Communist agents. By their reckoning, no self-respecting former prisoner of war would ever embrace an enemy. Thus, my own starring role in the conspiracy to keep Americans imprisoned in Vietnam, and subvert American democracy in the process, was launched.

The conspiracy posse had only to wait for the next hearing to receive further proof of my guilt. We took testimony from a Senate staffer who had recently written a report endorsing the allegations we had left men behind and that the government had a mind-set to debunk evidence of the crime. During his testimony, he made claims about certain prisoners that I knew from personal experience not to be true. This led to very testy exchanges between the witness and me, as I demanded proof of his accusations that he could not provide.

Later that day, things got even more bizarre when the author of the book *Kiss the Boys Good-Bye*, a journalist named Monika-Jensen Stevenson, testified. She claimed to be an impartial journalist who had sadly come to the conclusion, argued in her book, that prisoners were alive and that there was indeed a government conspiracy. To back up her book's contention that the Vietnamese had managed to hide prisoners from the rest of us, even some of those who had been held in Hoa Lo, she wrote about one prisoner, Norm Gaddis, whom she claimed had never been seen by or known to other prisoners for the first three years of his captivity. I told her that I and other POWs in Hoa Lo had known of Norm's existence all along. We had communicated with and about him and kept close track of him while he was kept in a part of the prison we called Heartbreak Hotel. None of us, I told her, were surprised to see him when we were all moved into compound living quarters during Christmas of 1970. She responded by suggesting something to the effect of "Well, that's one side of the story," assuming, I guess, that eyewitness accounts were no more compelling than some of the accounts of shady characters on whose often delusional ramblings she had premised her book's conclusions.

I recognized then that I had entered the Twilight Zone and that getting back to reality was going to be a long and unpleasant experience. And one of the people most determined to make it as unpleasant as possible was scheduled to testify after Ms. Stevenson concluded her perplexing testimony. Ted Sampley, a war veteran and veteran POW/MIA activist, who favored fatigues and feather earrings as his costume of choice, was quite a character. I took him for a charlatan within five minutes of meeting him. And nothing he has done since has caused me to change that opinion. Our mutual disdain provided an entertaining side story to the committee's work, even though it didn't always seem entertaining at the time.

Sampley had recently married the daughter of an MIA, who sensibly divorced him a few years later, but his MIA in-law status gave him claim to membership privileges in the associations of POW/MIA families, which privileges he would use to make as much of a nuisance of himself at their conventions as he did during our hearings. During our hearings, he would boo or hiss every witness who cast doubt on the conspiracy theory and every time I would ask a skeptical question. He liked to give me the finger once or twice a day, and I would usually give it right back.

He owned and operated a couple of T-shirt booths advocating the POW/MIA cause on the Washington Mall near the Vietnam Veterans Memorial. It was a profitable enterprise, especially since the people who manned the booths for Sampley worked for free. One of his T-shirts used the image of the statue of three American soldiers that was erected near the Wall, and since Sampley never saw fit to use some of the proceeds for the upkeep of the memorial, he was successfully sued for copyright infringement and burdened with a $360,000 judgment. He never paid it, pleading poverty all the many years he was turning profits on the memory of missing Americans. No one has ever figured out where he hides his money, and no administration has ever had the nerve to kick him off the Mall, even though all other commercial enterprises are forbidden from operating there by the Interior Department.

Sampley had a knack for staging attention-getting protests for which he was often arrested. He came to my office once and slugged my coauthor, then insisted on going to trial for the offense. He was sentenced to a short stretch in jail and forbidden to have any further contact with my staff or me. He also organized the famous 1992 protest at a convention of MIA families where President Bush, in the middle of his unsuccessful reelection campaign, was booed and harassed by Sampley's collaborators to the point where, in complete frustration, he shouted at his tormentors to "sit down and shut up."

In the hierarchy of Sampley's fictional conspiracy, I occupied a much higher position than did the former president. Sampley also published an occasional newspaper, the *Veterans' News and Dispatch.* In January 1991, well into the committee's hearings in which I had revealed my criminal collaboration with the enemy, Sampley's rag published a cover story accusing me of being the "Manchurian Candidate," a former POW whom the Vietnamese had allowed the Soviet KGB to brainwash and who then returned home to work as a mole in the highest reaches of government, possibly including the presidency someday, so that I could eventually surrender the country to its Communist enemies.

When an aide read the story to me, laughing as he did so, I told him I didn't find it that funny. But within a few weeks, I realized that although he was detestable for his influence on families who wanted to grasp at anything, even his palpable nonsense, to nurture their hopes for recovering their loved ones, he was really little more than a buffoon, and that my self-respect wasn't threatened by his antics. Henceforth I treated him with the contempt he deserved, but I never let him bother me again. And I have laughingly referred to myself as the Manchurian Candidate probably more often than Sampley has repeated the accusation.

These are by no means the only episodes that made the committee's work such a strange experience for most concerned. Indeed, the whole damn experience was bizarre and maddeningly frustrating for those of us who didn't enjoy witnessing the reputation of many decent public servants assailed with the most reckless, defamatory accusations. It seemed at times that I was simply going from one heated exchange to another with witnesses who had accused one or another official of malfeasance or worse. Even General Vessey, a man whom I admire as much as any officer who has ever worn the uniform of the United States, was constantly accused of being nothing more than a dupe for the Vietnamese. Much of the testimony we heard was contemptible, outrageous, depressing, and in the end didn't yield one piece of compelling evidence. Not one.

At one point, late in the committee's existence, we met in secret session to be briefed by committee aides selected by Senator Smith on what they called their "cluster theory," which would point the committee toward locations where our men were being held. Their theory held that whenever we received a live sighting report, no matter how improbable or provably false, we should stick a colored pin into a map of Southeast Asia, indicating where the prisoner was reported to have been held. After we had sifted through all the thousands of live sighting reports, we need only identify those areas on the map where the greatest number of colored pins were clustered together to determine where our men are. It was almost amusing nonsense, but by then my patience was pretty much exhausted, and I gave the staffers who had contrived this investigative stroke of genius a pretty sharp grilling. Doesn't the credibility of the reports and their sources bear some relevance to our investigation? I asked them. Finally, I summed up my skepticism by observing that if this theory were practical, then we could find aliens from other planets living openly in Texas, since that is where most reports of UFO sightings seem to be clustered. This endeared me little to the staffers, or to Bob Smith, who had hoped their idea would receive a more courteous hearing.

Many photographs of purported POWs that had done so much to fan the flames of the controversy were also ultimately disproved, not by the committee but during the committee's existence. The three amigos turned out to be three beefy Ukrainian farmers from the 1920s, whose photograph was discovered in an Eastern European magazine that U.S. investigators located in a Cambodian library.

One other photograph that had caused quite a sensation that year, purported to be of army major Donald Carr, who had been lost over Laos, also turned out to be a fraud. A self-styled POW hunter, Jack Bailey, had claimed he had found the picture while on a mission to find captive Americans and used his discovery to promote the cause of live POWs and his own fund-raising efforts.

An ABC News team, led by two adventurous reporters, James Walker and Jim Bamfield, traveled to Thailand to interview Bailey and investigate his story. They found that the individual in the photograph who Bailey claimed was Major Carr was actually a German named Gunther Dietrich who had been convicted of smuggling exotic birds out of Thailand, and who had probably been photographed by Bailey himself. When they went to interview Bailey and confront him with their discovery, Bailey slugged Walker on camera. The two reporters won a much deserved award for their story and, I hope, the thanks of a grateful nation for the punishment they suffered to render their good service to the country, not the least of which was to cause Mr. Bailey to skulk guiltily out of public view.

The failure to produce any compelling evidence of living prisoners does not mean that the committee achieved nothing useful. It managed to identify when and how the government's past mistakes and excessive caution had helped to feed the myriad conspiracy theories that attend the issue. Also, the committee uncovered evidence of Americans serving in World War II and in cold war intelligence missions who had been imprisoned in the Soviet Union and China. Some had been released, and none of those who weren't had survived, but the disclosure of their imprisonment resulted in a joint U.S.-Russian commission to investigate how many Americans had been lost in Soviet gulags and what had happened to them since. Many of those cases were resolved thanks to the salutary efforts of both Russian and American commission members, including Bob Smith and John Kerry.

The committee also helped clarify what we needed in terms of information and access from the Vietnamese, and the controversies that seemed to erupt in every hearing served to convince the Vietnamese that, whether they liked it or not, they were going to have to cooperate with us if the issue was ever to be resolved. We also revealed just how much progress we were now making and how selflessly and effectively the men and women of the Joint Task Force for a Full Accounting of POW/MIAs were working to find the answers we sought. They literally risked their lives during field investigations in remote, dangerous locations to uncover any scrap of evidence about a missing man's fate. Tragically, several did lose their lives in a helicopter crash while on a field investigation, and their memory deserves to be honored—not scorned by those Americans at home who never thought these dedicated patriots were doing enough to find living prisoners. They have done more than any conspiracy-peddling, self-aggrandizing, so-called activist has ever done for the missing. They too have done all that duty asked of them, and they are a testament to a country that would go to such lengths to keep faith with its missing soldiers.

As the committee approached its end-of-year deadline, one investigative breakthrough did occur, but it had nothing to do with the committee's work. An American named Ted Schweitzer, who had once worked for the UN High Commissioner for Refugees, and in that capacity had once been wounded rescuing Vietnamese boat people from Thai pirates, had been allowed by the Vietnamese, whose trust his bravery had earned, to do research in their central war archives in Hanoi for a book he was writing. As he conducted his research, he began to discover—or, more accurately, the Vietnamese allowed him to discover—photographs and other documentary evidence about American prisoners, some of whom were still unaccounted for. At some point, Schweitzer managed to make contact with Defense Department officials, who realized he might be in a position to uncover information that would resolve some of the most troubling discrepancy cases. They gave Schweitzer a code name, Swamp

Ranger, and charged him with collecting all the evidence he could, which he diligently did.

I believe that some officials in the Vietnamese government recognized that in order to gain a better relationship with the United States they would have to clear up a number of discrepancy cases, and that in some of these cases the Americans had been killed, even intentionally executed by the Vietnamese. The embarrassment such a discovery would cause Hanoi made it highly unlikely that the Vietnamese government would ever admit to the crimes. But maybe they would use a uniquely situated American to provide us with answers to some of the cases, preserve official deniability, and wait to see if the United States would react to the disclosures with recriminations or appreciation.

Some of the photographs Schweitzer found showed Americans with bullet wounds to the head and other signs of execution. The committee had learned of unconfirmed reports that some American pilots who had been shot down and had landed after ejecting close to surface-to-air missile sites had been executed because they had witnessed Soviet soldiers manning those sites. We still don't know if those reports are true or not, but they could explain why some Americans had been victims of executions that were clearly war crimes. Maybe that is why the Americans whose photographs Schweitzer had obtained had been shot.

Whatever the case, Schweitzer's first delivery of information to the Defense Department was impressive and at first examination seemed to provide evidence that would resolve several MIA cases. The Bush administration decided in October 1992 to send General Vessey to Vietnam to confront the Vietnamese with the evidence Schweitzer had obtained, not to express outrage for what had happened, but to assure the Vietnamese that this was precisely the kind of information we wanted from them and to encourage them to give us more. President Bush asked me to accompany General Vessey on the mission, and this I immediately agreed to do.

It was a little more than two weeks before election day, and I was up for reelection that year. Taking time out in the last days of a campaign for a quick trip to Vietnam was an unusual decision and hard to explain, since I wasn't at liberty to discuss the reasons why the mission was so urgent. I had to postpone a debate with my opponent, who accused me of concocting the whole thing to get some undeserved attention and to duck the debate. My friend Senator Bob Kerrey, a Democrat and Medal of Honor winner for heroic service in the Vietnam War, who also served on the committee, had agreed to attend a Democratic political event in Phoenix that my opponent, Claire Sargant, was also attending. While she shared the stage with Bob, she denounced my sudden departure from the campaign and said that Bob would confirm my duplicity. He responded by saying he was sorry, but he couldn't do anything of the kind. All he knew about the mission was that it was of the utmost urgency and that my participation in it was important. He taught me, as well as my deflated opponent, a lesson in honest partisanship that I have never forgotten and gave me one of many reasons to be grateful for his friendship.

Our stay in Hanoi would last only a day but achieve its purpose. When our delegation arrived, General Vessey and I went immediately into a meeting with Vietnam's foreign minister, where we disclosed the information we possessed, said we assumed it had been provided with his government's unofficial blessing, and asked him to convince his government to allow us free and unfettered access to war archives so that we could hopefully resolve more cases and hasten improvements in our relations. Watching General Vessey work was a real pleasure and a learning experience. He was at once cordial and relaxed, while leaving no doubt about the seriousness of our mission and no doubt of American resolve to secure further cooperation from our hosts. He offered no recriminations but left it implied that only additional information would spare the Vietnamese from international embarrassment.

All business when it came to the mission, Vessey wouldn't even take a stroll around Hanoi to relax. But he is so unassuming, so decent, the American personality in its most attractive form. He asked for no recognition for the many months of his retirement that had been sacrificed to finding answers about our POW/MIAs, and he endured every slight by the activists in dignified silence. He is a model patriot, the kind of officer that George Marshall had been, and America could ask for no better defender. He's also a great storyteller, especially about his experiences as an officer in occupied Berlin after the Nazi surrender, stories that had me shaking helplessly with laughter during dinner that evening in Hanoi. Among his duties at the time was to keep a record of the incidents of venereal disease contracted by Americans stationed there. Interviewing one unfortunate soldier, Vessey inquired if he knew where he had acquired the malady. "From a German girl I've been seeing," the soldier replied. "She lives with her mother and sister," he volunteered, "in one room." His curiosity piqued, Vessey asked what the mother and sister had been doing when the GI had been "dating" the young woman. "The sister sang while the mother played the zither," he explained. John struggled to suppress his laughter long enough to utter his standard caution about fraternizing with the locals.

John Vessey was born and raised in the Minnesota River valley. At seventeen, he had lied about his age to enlist in the National Guard and eventually join the army in World War II. He fought in North Africa and on the beach at Anzio, where in recognition of his courage and ability he was given a battlefield commission. He rose quickly through the ranks and served in both the Korean and Vietnam Wars.

He commanded U.S. forces in Korea during the Carter administration and had openly disagreed with President Carter's intention to withdraw our forces from the Korean peninsula. He even prepared to resign at one point to protest the decision, but Carter was soon persuaded to change his mind. Nevertheless, he passed over General Vessey, who was considered the most qualified candidate, when selecting a new army chief of staff. True to form, General Vessey never uttered a word of complaint. When the officer whom Carter had appointed to the post, a man who had once worked under General Vessey, asked him to serve as his deputy, John agreed without hesitation. Cap Weinberger, realizing the value of such a man, recommended that President Reagan make him commander of the Joint Chiefs of Staff, the last enlisted man who had risen in the ranks and had served in World War II to hold the post. During his three years as chairman, John Vessey offered wise, commonsense guidance to the president. He recognized the mistake of sending a small contingent of marines to Lebanon, had strongly opposed the move, and had been critically influential in the president's eventual decision to withdraw them.

He left his tour as the United States senior military commander one year early, after forty-six years on active duty, because he had promised his patient wife, Avis, that at long last they would be home before the next snowfall. On his first Sunday back home, he and Avis were attending church services, and he listened while an elderly lady in the pew behind him told her companion, "His name is Vessey, and he used to be somebody in the government." Nobody took more delight in that lesson in midwestern humility than John Vessey.

The Vietnamese agreed to Vessey's request for greater access to their archives, and thus began a process that would eventually help us resolve many more MIA cases and lead to the normalization of relations between Vietnam and the United States, an achievement General Vessey supported and deserves most of the credit for.

When we got back to the States, however, the activists had already begun disparaging our mission and its achievements. Some of the families took up the complaint that it had amounted to nothing more than a public relations scam. One family member made a similar charge in testimony before the committee, and though I should have been more sympathetic to her emotions as the sister of a missing American, I couldn't let pass her contemptible accusation against General Vessey, whom she disparaged as a phony. I didn't shout at her or use the insults she had used to belittle our efforts. But I told her very firmly and with evident displeasure that "I have not criticized your motives and sincerity. I would appreciate it if you would not criticize mine or General Vessey's." My response, unfortunately, reduced the woman to tears, as she apparently had less stomach for taking criticism than she did for giving it out. The incident quickly became the latest chapter in the Manchurian Candidate saga.

The committee's work never strayed far from these types of unpleasant encounters, but eventually our work came to a close, two months after General Vessey and I had returned from our trip. During the course of our hearings, we had taken testimony from cabinet secretaries of several administrations, soldiers of high rank and low, MIA family members, Russians and Vietnamese, journalists, witnesses, dozens of obscure government officials who had spent their careers looking for answers to the question of what had happened to our men, and from Ross Perot, who had long believed in the existence of living prisoners and who chastised committee members to stop looking at the three-by-five cards our aides had prepared for us and "just listen to me for a minute." We examined allegations varying in improbability from Vietnam's warehousing of remains to a secret underground prison, stretching from the Defense Ministry in Hanoi to just under Ho Chi Minh's mausoleum, where American prisoners were rumored to be held within earshot of the thousands of daily visitors to the tomb. Satellite imagery had picked up a huge "USA" cut into a Laotian rice field that activists were convinced was a distress signal from captured Americans. It turned out to be a young Laotian boy's handiwork that he had copied off an envelope. Every rumor, every accusation, was investigated, and the unlikeliest of them were almost invariably the most sensational.

There were constant arguments, and the hearings were frequently interrupted by outbursts from the audience. Somehow, John Kerry and Frances Zwenig and many other able, dedicated committee staffers got every single member to sign the committee report, which said that while there were reasons to suspect that Americans might have been kept behind without U.S. knowledge, there had been no conspiracy to cover it up, and that, sadly, there was "no compelling evidence" that Americans were alive in captivity today. Bob Smith took a lot of abuse from the activists for signing that statement, and he later tried to back off it a little. Nevertheless, I admired the courage it took for him to sign it in the first place and the tenacity John Kerry had used to achieve such an honest result.

Shortly before the presidential election, which President Bush would lose, General Vessey and I went to the White House to brief him on our mission and what it had accomplished. A few days later, the president held a Rose Garden ceremony with General Vessey and me, as well as Bob Smith and John Kerry, to announce that significant progress had been made in the government's efforts to account for our missing servicemen. We were finally, the president proclaimed, "writing the last chapter of the Vietnam War." Disgruntled activists accused Bush of staging a campaign stunt. But he was an honest man, who was doing his duty, even in an hour when he knew the American people were going to reject his leadership.

In the audience, among the assembled dignitaries, was the curious, decent fellow they called the "Swamp Ranger," through whom the Vietnamese had let us know they were serious about accommodating what they considered our strange obsession with dead soldiers. The time had come to move on and begin the campaign for normal relations with Vietnam. The United States had given its word to the Vietnamese that the cooperation they were now providing would form the basis of a new relationship, just as I had promised Nguyen Co Thach and myself that if Vietnam proved willing, we could begin to close the books on the war that had kept us enemies for decades. It was time to keep our word.

After the election, John Kerry and I tried to persuade President Bush to lift the trade embargo against Vietnam. He didn't feel that a lame-duck president should take such a decisive step, so he declined. But he did approve a number of smaller steps that helped pave the way for lifting the embargo. John Kerry and I would now have to convince his successor, Bill Clinton, who had Vietnam War problems of his own making to overcome, to deliver Vietnam and the United States from the animosity of war to the promise of peace.

In May 1993, I wrote a letter to President Clinton encouraging him to accept an invitation to participate in a Memorial Day ceremony at the Wall. The invitation had provoked a good deal of opposition from some veterans and POW/MIA activists who resented the new president's draft-dodging past and the contradictory statements he had made to confuse voters about his actions. His evasions hadn't endeared him much to me, either. Nor was I thrilled that he had defeated a man I admired and believed was infinitely better qualified to hold the office. When I was asked by reporters during the Clinton draft controversy what I thought of his deceitful obfuscation, I was predictably critical. I said I respected those young men who had accepted a prison sentence rather than allow themselves to be drafted into a war they opposed. But I had little respect for someone who had evaded the draft and sacrificed nothing for his conviction, while some poor American, with fewer advantages, was sent to Vietnam in his place. But when a reporter asked me if Governor Clinton's actions would compromise his authority as commander in chief should he be elected, I responded, no. The people confer that authority, and if they elected him president, he would possess it in no less measure than his predecessors.

The people did elect Bill Clinton president, and he was our commander in chief, with all the office's responsibilities and authority, whether I liked it or not. And among his responsibilities was the ceremonial duty to honor the memory of America's war dead on the holiday reserved to commemorate their sacrifice. So I told the new president it was his duty to go to the Wall that Memorial Day, and I would publicly defend his decision to do so and, if he wished, accompany him to the ceremony.

President Clinton did go to the Wall that Memorial Day, and while there were a few scattered protests, on the whole he was warmly received by the veterans attending the event. I ended up spending the holiday somewhere else, in Hanoi, with John Kerry and several other senators and congressmen, as well as representatives of some of the veterans associations. We went back once more for a final look at Hanoi's cooperation with our POW/MIA efforts before we began a public campaign to end the trade embargo.

The progress was impressive. The Vietnamese had recently turned over to American investigators a document we had long sought, a handwritten ledger called the "blue book," a record of every prisoner's shootdown and capture on the date it had occurred, beginning with my friend Ev Alvarez. They had granted us much greater access to war archives. Joint field investigations were now a routine occurrence. And the government had recently announced an amnesty program for any Vietnamese citizen who might possess remains or other evidence of an American's fate.

The Vietnamese allowed our delegation to interview everyone we requested to see, including regional military commanders during the war and officers who had worked in the prison system administration during the war. They showed us archival documents, and they persuasively refuted the accuracy of the latest document to have reignited American suspicions that they had not released all prisoners of war during Operation Homecoming. The month before our trip, an academic researcher had discovered in Russian archives a document, purported to be the record of a Vietnamese military commander's 1972 briefing of the Politburo, that claimed Vietnam had captured 1,205 Americans, many more than the 368 they acknowledged holding at the time and the 591 they released at the end of the war. The "1205" document, as it came to be called, created yet another firestorm of accusations of Vietnamese duplicity and prompted one more Vessey mission to Hanoi.

When he returned home, General Vessey calmly observed that while the document appeared authentic, it was not accurate. It couldn't have been. The number of American pilots known to be missing in 1972 was 355, not 624, as the document alleged. If you assumed that every one of the 108 pilots lost over the north between 1972 and the end of the war were alive, that would still bring the number to only 463. Moreover, the 1205 document's assertions that senior officers among the prisoners were kept in separate prisons I knew from personal experience to be false, as was its observation that there were three American astronauts among the captured. Finally, it was more than unlikely—indeed, it was impossible—that over 600 Americans could have been held prisoner and not one of them seen by any of the 591 Americans who were released.

There were various other inaccuracies that convinced General Vessey, me, and any objective observer that the document, although not forged, had been some Vietnamese official's misinformed and mistaken estimate (the general who was reported to be its author claimed he had never seen it). Of course, this hardly satisfied many of the activists, who now claimed that the Vietnamese had operated a second, secret prison system where they held Americans they didn't intend to release, even if American officials at the time had no idea that many pilots had been lost.

Nevertheless, Vessey's assurances seemed to satisfy most of the concerns of the public and the administration. Moreover, the document's disclosure had convinced the Vietnamese to give General Vessey the blue book, which is probably the most important document to our efforts to resolve uncertainties about the number of prisoners the north had held that we have ever obtained. Our delegation was also satisfied that the 1205 document was not the smoking gun activists claimed it was, and we proceeded to encourage our hosts to continue providing us with access so that any future stunning revelations could be understood and explained to the American public.

While we were in Hanoi, the Vietnamese allowed our delegation to visit my old lodgings behind the sandstone walls of Hoa Lo prison. It was the first and last time I would return to the place. Hoa Lo was demolished a year later so a new office tower and hotel could be built on the site. The Vietnamese kept one wall of the prison intact to serve as a memorial and museum, commemorating not so much the American experience with the place as the imprisonment by the French of the Vietnamese who fought them, many of whom rule Vietnam today. One room is reserved for pictures of American prisoners playing volleyball, congregating freely, and generally enjoying Hanoi's gracious hospitality. The rest of the museum is dedicated to more austere reminders of French rule, including an old guillotine and other instruments of death and torture. The American exhibit also contains several enlarged photographs of a few American prisoners the Vietnamese consider to be minor celebrities; among them is my mug shot, taken not long after my capture.

When we arrived at Hoa Lo, our delegation—which included my fellow former prisoner of war Pete Peterson, then a congressman from Florida—was restricted to the large rooms and offices that bordered the courtyard just within the prison gates. At the time, Hoa Lo was still an operating prison for convicted Vietnamese lawbreakers. At John Kerry's insistence, the Vietnamese eventually allowed us to enter one corridor of cells. There was an inch or two of standing water on the corridor floor. Bright lightbulbs still dangled naked from the ceiling. Every detail appeared to be the same save one: The Vietnamese inmates there were held two to a cell, whereas I had been held there alone in the third cell on the right. No tidal wave of remembrance washed over me as I stared into the faces of the Vietnamese who were occupying my old cell. In fact, curiously, I felt little emotion at all beyond sympathy for the poor bastards who were living there now. It had been a long time. What's past is past.

Pete rang the scrap of old railroad iron that had served as the gong to summon us to collect our meals, wake us up in the morning, and order us to sleep at night. That prompted more memories than my brief look at my old cell. As soon as we exited the corridor, the inmates rushed out of their cells and pressed against the barred window in the entrance door. A guard rapped his club on their fingers curled around the bars. I turned at the sound and motioned to the guard to stop. "Hey, hey, remember, humane and lenient, humane and lenient." With that, my trip down memory lane was at an end. We left Hoa Lo and returned to our hotel.

There is another monument in Hanoi of relevance to my captivity there. On the bank of Truch Bach Lake, where I had landed in 1967 after ejecting from my crippled A-4, the Vietnamese had erected a concrete monument, depicting an American pilot on his knees with his hands in the air. The activists who believed I was the Manchurian Candidate often pointed to the monument as proof of my collaboration with the enemy. Why else, they argued, would the Vietnamese build a statue of him in Hanoi? In reality, the monument was erected to celebrate the courage of the people's air defense heroes who had on October 26, 1967, shot down the American air pirate, identified as John Sney McKay. Rather than prove my treason, the monument actually contradicts the activists' contention that the Vietnamese were invariably diligent and accurate record keepers who possessed detailed information about every pilot who had been lost in the war. The monument gives my rank as major and my service as the United States Air Force, an insult that only partly dilutes the pleasure I take from the only statue in the world that bears my name, or a close approximation of it, anyway.

Shortly after we returned to Washington, John Kerry arranged for our delegation to brief President Clinton and a cast of thousands in the Roosevelt Room of the White House. Our delegation itself was rather large, including ten members of Congress and representatives of several veterans groups. In addition to the president, the administration officials present included the vice president, cabinet secretaries, assistant secretaries, National Security Council staff, officials from the Veterans Department, and assorted White House staff and political advisers. The president listened graciously, asking few questions, as every member of our delegation gave him their views of our trip and their thoughts on lifting the trade embargo. John Kerry had started the discussion with a typically comprehensive and cogent summary of our findings. I waited to speak last, and nearly two hours after the meeting had begun, I said simply that I agreed with everything John had said, told him I would support an administration decision to lift the trade embargo, and apologized for taking up so much of the president's time.

A somewhat disorganized question-and-answer period followed, and as the meeting dragged on, I became increasingly uncomfortable taking up this unusually large part of the president's day. I was used to meeting with his predecessors under much more organized and briefer circumstances. Whenever I met with Presidents Reagan or Bush, I was told precisely when the meeting would start and end. "You will be escorted into the Oval Office at precisely two-seventeen," White House officials would inform me, "and the meeting will conclude promptly at two thirty-three." In Bill Clinton's White House, time seemed to be a much less carefully husbanded luxury.

Most worrying was the fact that I had a scheduled flight home that afternoon. Cindy was in the hospital for minor surgery. It was beginning to appear that I would have to either miss my flight or commit what I considered an unpardonable breach of etiquette, leaving a meeting before the president had. When the time came for me to make the decision, I regrettably chose bad manners over an angry wife, and with sincere apologies and an explanation of Cindy's situation, I asked the president's permission to leave, which he gave without a trace of resentment that I was going free while he was still stuck in the interminable meeting.

The administration was divided over the question of lifting the trade embargo. Most of the State Department, including the secretary, and most officials in the Department of Defense and Veterans Department supported the move. Some officials on the National Security Council as well as the president's political advisers were said to have serious concerns about the political ramifications of normalization. Bill Clinton, rightly or wrongly, did not have a reputation in Washington for making tough political choices. On the contrary, it was generally believed that in every difficult decision, he would always choose the most politically expedient option.

Lifting the trade embargo and other moves to fully normalize our relations with Vietnam were not politically expedient decisions for a president who had evaded the draft and lied about it, and who had difficult relations with some people in the military and in the veterans community. But neither were the politics of the issue as disadvantageous to the administration as some of the president's advisers assumed they were. Both John Kerry and I knew that most veterans and most active duty military weren't opposed to normal relations. Every year, more and more veterans were traveling to Vietnam to visit their old battlegrounds and exchange war stories with their former enemies. Many veterans were involved in humanitarian projects in Vietnam. Vietnam veterans are not, as Hollywood often made it seem, flashback-suffering, alienated, emotionally unstable, grudge-nursing malcontents. The vast majority of veterans had put the war, and all its awful experiences, behind them and were ready for the entire country to do the same.

Were President Clinton to move toward normalization, there would be no veterans march on Washington, no angry men in fatigues chained to the White House fence, yelling obscenities at the draft dodger who had betrayed them. A handful of Ted Sampley types would hurl their usual abuses, but fortunately, men like Sampley constitute a small, insignificant cult of self-promoting nitwits, whose influence in the country was slight to begin with and was well on the way to disappearing altogether.

Many of my fellow former prisoners would support normalization, including Ev Alvarez, Pete Peterson, and my friend and prison commander, Jerry Denton. Others would not, including my old prison pals Orson Swindle and Sam Johnson, now a congressman from Texas. Some other veterans would oppose the move as well. But most veterans would support it, as would most members of Congress, and, I was convinced, so would most of the country. Not only would the political fallout be slight, I argued, but the president would get credit for what many believed was a rare instance of political courage on his part. Finally, we had given our word to the Vietnamese that if they did certain things, we would lift the embargo and normalize relations. They had done them, and the United States must put as much faith in our word as a former enemy had.

These are the arguments John Kerry and I used over the next months to try to persuade administration officials to move ahead with normalization. We made some progress early on. In early July 1993, the president lifted U.S. objections to loans to Vietnam from international financial institutions such as the International Monetary Fund and the World Bank. But still the White House, fearful of the domestic political consequences, held back from lifting the trade embargo altogether, and in September he signed the authorization to renew it with a few minor modifications.

In December, the president sent a delegation to Vietnam, led by Assistant Secretary of State Winston Lord, to assess the joint task force's progress. They found it to be excellent, as attested to by General Tom Needham, who was the overall task force commander, and by my old academy buddy and dear friend Admiral Chuck Larson, who as commander in chief of U.S. forces in the Pacific, my father's old job, was Needham's boss. Joint field operations in Vietnam in 1993 had continued on the largest scale ever. The Vietnamese had provided thousands of pages of archived information, and sixty-seven sets of remains had been recovered. Were we to expect this kind of cooperation to continue, the United States had better live up to its end of the bargain.

So John Kerry and I came up with a strategy that would make the administration's decision easier. With the informal acquiescence of administration officials, we drafted a Senate resolution urging the administration to lift the embargo. Kerry promised to get a large majority of Democratic votes, and I committed to getting twenty Republicans. If we could persuade that many to join us, the White House let us know quietly that the president would lift the embargo.

There would be opposition from a good number of Senate Republicans, Bob Smith, of course, but many others, including Senate Republican leader Bob Dole, who had long, close relations with many of the MIA families and couldn't be persuaded to support progress that many of them opposed. To prevent Senators Dole and Smith from offering a contradictory resolution they had prepared as an amendment to our resolution, John and I decided to strike without warning.

On January 26, 1994, we walked onto the Senate floor during debate on a bill authorizing appropriations for the State Department. I got the attention of the chair and quickly offered a resolution urging the president to end the trade embargo expeditiously. As soon as I finished, John offered a slightly differently worded resolution, urging the same thing, as an amendment to the one I had offered. This tactic, in parliamentary idiom,

is called "filling the tree." In effect, it prevented any other senator from offering an amendment to our resolution that would have diluted or changed
its meaning. Thus began two fairly contentious days of debate. John and I,
and many senators who supported the resolution, including Bob Kerrey,
and every other Senate Vietnam veteran, except Bob Smith and my friend
Hank Brown, argued that the move was past due, that the Vietnamese had
proven their good faith, and that we should do the same. Bob Smith and
Bob Dole, along with many like-minded senators, argued the opposite.
Bob Smith took it upon himself to speak for the families of MIAs, saying
that they were "petrified that this amendment is going to pass and they will
lose the leverage they have to get answers about their loved ones." Both
John Kerry and Bob Kerrey spoke eloquently in rebuttal.

In my opening statement, I argued my conviction that "the United
States's word should stand for something" and briefly discussed all the
things Vietnam had done in recent years that now obliged us to keep our
word. I closed by urging my colleagues, although I was also hoping to appeal to the president,

> not to be intimidated by political pressure from quarters that may
> never support better relations with our former adversary. . . . On this
> question, the right course might not be the most politically expedient
> course, but it is the right course nonetheless. Let us do the right thing.
> Let us take such steps that will best honor our commitments, protect
> our interests, and advance our values. There is no dishonor in that.

The next morning, the Senate voted sixty-two to thirty-eight to approve
our resolution, and fifty-eight to forty-two to defeat a competing resolution offered by Senators Dole and Smith. John Kerry, who had master-
fully managed the debate, had persuaded forty-two Democrats to vote
with us. I got my twenty Republicans. One week later, Bill Clinton ended
the trade embargo against Vietnam.

It was an important step forward, to be sure, and as I expected, the
public acclaim the president received for his decision far outweighed the
public criticism. Still, we were a long way from fully normalized economic

and diplomatic relations, and John Kerry and I would spend much of the next year and a half working to finish the job.

Despite the favorable reaction to his decision, the president's advisers were still divided over whether he could sustain the political damage they feared would be caused by the decision to fully normalize relations. John, Bob Kerrey, Chuck Robb, Pete Peterson, and I made frequent speeches, wrote op-eds, sent letters to the White House, and privately assured administration officials otherwise. Many other prominent veterans lobbied for normalization as well as did many American businesses with commercial interests in the region. But the president remained cautious. In January 1995, he agreed to open a low-level American diplomatic presence in Hanoi, but he refrained from formally ending the many years of official hostility by agreeing to open an American embassy in Hanoi, with an American ambassador in residence. He sent two more delegations to Hanoi, and both returned reporting the same excellent level of progress that Win Lord's delegation had found the year before.

General Vessey, Chuck Larson, and Tom Needham were all on record in favor of full normalization. Bob Smith, Bob Dole, and others, representing the responsible opposition, argued frequently against the decision. Bob Dornan, a firebrand conservative from California, representing the less responsible opposition, called the president a "triple draft dodger" who would lose reelection if he normalized relations with our Communist enemies, and he attacked "the unholy alliance" John Kerry and I had formed.

Finally, in May 1995, John Kerry and I went again to see the president and tried to convince him to take the last, most important step. This time we took only two aides with us, and I was determined not to intrude on the president's time as inexcusably as we had in our last encounter. We met in the Oval Office, and only a few administration officials accompanied the president. John spoke first, persuasively as always. When the president turned to me, I decided to address only one issue, whether his own past and all the old arguments about the war really were an obstacle to moving forward. I didn't do it directly, and I spoke for only a minute. I told him that it didn't matter to me anymore who had been for the war and who had been against it. "I don't give a shit about that anymore. I'm tired of looking back in anger. I'm tired of America looking back in anger. It's time to put the past behind us, Mr. President, and do what's right for both countries."

Bill Clinton has a well-deserved reputation as a charming flatterer, and I like to think I have a reputation for not easily being seduced by such ephemeral gestures. But I fell for it this time. When I finished, the president called me "an amazing man," and I left the White House quite pleased with myself for receiving such high presidential praise, whether deserved or not, whether he meant it or not.

Less than two months later, I found myself on a stage in the East Room of the White House, with John Kerry, Bob Kerrey, Pete Peterson, Chuck Robb, General Vessey, Admiral Elmo Zumwalt, other veterans, and various administration officials and business representatives, listening to President Clinton announce his decision to fully normalize relations with Vietnam. When the president finished, he turned to me and I reached to shake his hand. He wrapped me in an embrace instead, which I didn't mind at all. A photograph of the two of us appeared in almost every newspaper in the country the next morning, another Bui Tin moment, I'm sure, for my friends in the Manchurian Candidate conspiracy crowd.

After the event, I told the press that the president's decision "would not be an easy decision for any president to make. President Clinton has shown courage and honor in his resolve to do so." I meant every word of it.

Two years later, I attended another White House ceremony to watch my old friend Pete Peterson, held as prisoner of war in Vietnam for over six years, take the oath of office as the first American ambassador in Hanoi since Vietnam was a French colony. I have seldom enjoyed a prouder moment.

In April 2000, fresh from my unsuccessful run for president, I returned to Vietnam for the eighth time since the war. I was there to tape an NBC *Today* show interview on the twenty-fifth anniversary of the fall of Saigon. As I left my hotel in Saigon one morning, a group of reporters stopped me to ask a few questions. One of them asked me why I had come back to "celebrate the surrender of the country I had fought to defend." "I didn't come here to celebrate the fall of Saigon," I answered a little sharply. "I think the wrong side won." The predictable furor in the Vietnamese government that my opinion had provoked was expressed in a stream of hostile denunciations from government spokespeople who decried my mistaken and insulting view of Vietnamese history. And off we went, on one more trip into the old bullshit. Just once more, for old times' sake, if nothing else.

Bob Dole. *Corbis*

TEN

WHO ARE WE AND WHY ARE WE HERE?

On that July afternoon in the East Room, as he helped move two countries past the enmity that had long been the dominant feature of their relationship, the president looked tired and distracted. I took it as an indication that he was worried about the political response to his announcement. His aides later said that worries over the appalling situation in Bosnia had been keeping him up nights. That was certainly understandable. He had a lot to worry about.

On that same day, July 11, 1995, Bosnian Serb forces overran Dutch peacekeepers guarding a United Nations declared "safe area" in Srebrenica in eastern Bosnia. The Dutch had tried to call in NATO air strikes to stop the Serb aggression. But evidently the only fax machine in the peacekeepers' local headquarters wasn't functioning properly. By the time the desperate peacekeepers finally reached NATO commanders, the Serbs had already captured the Muslim enclave. NATO warplanes eventually arrived on the scene, but too late to do any good. And in keeping with past practice, their late response failed to make much of an impression. They succeeded in destroying one Serb tank and a single heavy gun. The Serbs, as they had in the past, responded to the strikes with scornful disdain and proceeded to slaughter over five thousand unarmed Muslims, burying them in mass graves while the Dutch peacekeepers, forty-eight of whom had been taken hostage, watched helplessly. It was the worst wartime atrocity in Europe since the end of World War II.

The massacre of Srebrenica also effectively marked an end to the United Nations's effort, now well into its fourth year, to make and keep peace between the former republics of shattered Yugoslavia and among the various warring ethnic groups, with their long history of resentments and bloody conflict, that had made Bosnia one of history's most prodigious killing grounds. The effort had been one long, inconsistent, humiliating, miserable failure. As had been the Clinton administration's role in the debacle.

When war broke out first in Slovenia and Croatia, after their declarations of independence in 1991, and then in Bosnia when it followed suit the following year, Europeans, primarily the British and French, assumed responsibility for restoring the peace and keeping Serbs, Muslims, and Croats from one another's throats. The Bush administration was happy to leave it to them, observing, in Secretary of State Jim Baker's memorable phrase, "We don't have a dog in that fight." The United States had just brought a triumphant end to the Persian Gulf War, and the Bush administration's focus on post–cold war issues, the reunification of Germany, political instability in Russia, and others, kept it too preoccupied to assume the onerous responsibility for subduing violence in the Balkans. That, they assumed wrongly, could be handled by our European allies working under UN auspices, and with our best wishes for success.

Candidate Bill Clinton had sharply criticized President Bush's response to Balkan troubles as a morally indifferent and dangerously negligent lack of leadership by the world's only superpower. He had the same complaints for the administration's response to political repression in China and Haiti and elsewhere. But after defeating the man whose foreign policy he had found so unprincipled, the new commander in chief apparently revised his opinion, leaving his predecessor's policies for all three places intact and unmodified.

For much of Bill Clinton's presidency, especially during his first term, his administration's foreign policy was plagued by strategic incoherence, a failure to prioritize our interests in the world and understand how policies for one problem or relationship affected our interests elsewhere. Early on, he damaged our most important relationship in Asia, our alliance with Japan, by trying to coerce the Japanese into accepting trade quotas, emphasizing the president's enthusiasm for managed trade over the far more vital security components of our relationship. He eventually backed off his insistence on quotas, but not before putting considerable strain on our relations at a time when we most needed strong support from Japan to help mitigate other, more vexing problems in Asia that the president's inexperience had managed to exacerbate.

He mishandled human rights disputes with China by renewing most favored nation trading status his first year in office but conditioning the next year's renewal on genuine human rights progress. He reversed himself again after China's leaders refused to accept the condition and brusquely lectured Secretary of State Warren Christopher during his first visit to Beijing. He also gave permission for the president of Taiwan, Lee Teng-hui, to visit the United States, a perfectly sensible decision but for the fact that he had previously told Beijing that the visit would not happen and had let the Chinese discover his change of heart on television news broadcasts.

The most alarming problem in Asia during his watch was a brewing crisis on the Korean peninsula, where the secretive and implacably hostile regime of North Korea's "Great Leader," Kim Il Sung, was believed to have extracted weapons-grade plutonium from its nuclear power reactors. This was a violation of its obligations as a signator to the Nuclear Non-proliferation Treaty (NNPT) and a clear and present danger to the security of the United States and its allies. North Korea was an economically desperate rogue state, with a million soldiers massed on the border with South Korea, a record of arms transfers to like-minded regimes, missiles that were capable of striking Japan, and a longer-range missile program well under development. Kim Il Sung's was the last regime on earth to be trusted with possession of nuclear warheads. All the more so when Kim Il Sung died in 1994, leaving his regime and its arsenal to his son, reputed sociopath "Dear Leader" Kim Jong Il. But here, too, the new president vacillated between forceful rhetorical responses to the threat, insisting at one time that North Korea would not be allowed to possess a single nuclear weapon, and retreat in the face of North Korean bad faith and belligerence.

The Clinton administration's spasmodic, irresolute, and reactive approaches to international security problems were a product of what I believed to be its defining characteristic: self-doubt, a mystifying uncertainty of how to behave in a world in which America was the only superpower. I thought the administration was suffering from an identity crisis that I once compared in an exaggerated rhetorical flourish to my old friend and commander Jim Stockdale's existential musing in the 1992 vice presidential debate: "Who am I and why am I here?"

I did not believe that the condition was attributable solely to the president's lack of experience in foreign affairs. He had assembled an experienced and intelligent foreign policy team. Secretary of State Warren Christopher, National Security Adviser Tony Lake, and Lake's deputy and successor, Sandy Berger, were men I knew, respected, and got along with well. I had reservations about his first secretary of defense, the late Les Aspin, whom I viewed as more of an academic than an executive, but his tenure was brief, and his successor, Bill Perry, was a man I liked and trusted.

I thought the president's uncertainty on the world stage was symptomatic of a mind-set formed in opposition to the Vietnam War, a mentality that saw America's cold war defense of its interests as more often a cause of—rather than a deterrent to—aggression. His administration's early declared preference to rely on what it termed "aggressive multilateralism" to resolve international crises, and the paralysis that was its predictable result, reflected, if not a desire to atone for imagined cold war sins, at least a pronounced apprehension about whether we should give primacy to American leadership or even American interests in our post–cold war diplomacy. And nowhere was this apprehension more in evidence than in decisions over when and how to use American force to protect our interests and values.

Bill Clinton was slow to pull the trigger of American power. But a reluctance to resort to military action in pursuit of foreign policy goals is not a failing in a president. On the contrary, it is a wise caution that does not risk American lives unnecessarily. But it is a failing, a terribly injurious failing, to use force uncertain of its effect, or in inadequate measure to achieve its objectives, or because an unwillingness to exercise unilateral leadership has led the president to defer some of his prerogatives as commander in chief to a collective of international decision makers.

In the last weeks of his lame-duck presidency, George Bush decided to deploy American troops to Somalia to help feed a million people who were facing starvation in one of the worst famines in history. This they did, to their great credit and America's, and in May 1993, the United Nations assumed authority for managing the crisis, with several thousand peacekeepers there under its command. But in that first year of the Clinton administration, our humanitarian mission in Somalia was transformed under UN administration into the restoration of law and order in a society, or more accurately a collection of violent factions led by various warlords, that had little appreciation for the norms of an ordered civilization. As their mission evolved from feeding the starving to imposing peace, American commanders in the field responded to the mounting violence and increasing danger to our servicemen by asking Washington for more armor and reinforcements. Washington refused.

On October 3, 1993, two companies of army rangers were sent into a neighborhood in Mogadishu, the Somalian capital, to search for and apprehend lieutenants of Mohammad Farrah Aidid, the strongest and most violent of Somalia's various warlords. They came under intense fire from hundreds of Aidid's supporters. Two Blackhawk helicopters sent to rescue them were shot down, and a long, bloody firefight ensued as surrounded rangers and helicopter crews bravely fought scores of Aidid's fighters who were firing from surrounding buildings and hiding behind women and children. By the end of the day, eighteen Americans were dead, over seventy were wounded, and one Blackhawk pilot had been taken hostage. When Americans woke up the next day, they saw on their televisions and on the front pages of their newspapers the body of an American serviceman being dragged by a rope through the streets of Mogadishu while Aidid's supporters danced and cheered wildly.

One week later, the USS *Harlan County* arrived in Port-au-Prince, Haiti, carrying almost two hundred American noncombat troops, was prevented from docking by a hundred or so lightly armed Haitian thugs, and ordered to return home. The troops were an advance guard of a multinational peacekeeping force intended to restore to office Haiti's deposed

president, Jean-Bertrand Aristide, and help quell the political violence that
had resulted in thousands of Haitian boat people drifting helplessly on
Caribbean currents toward American shores. A UN-brokered peace accord, signed on Governors Island in New York's harbor by Aristide and
the man who had deposed him, Raul Cedras, had promised thousands of
troops, mostly American, to help ensure that the restoration of civilian
government under Aristide, a man of questionable democratic allegiances
himself, was completed peacefully.

Before the accords were signed in July 1993, President Clinton had
abandoned his campaign condemnation of the Bush administration's treatment of Haitian refugees by continuing his predecessor's policy of repatri-
ating them directly to Haiti. Although the policy was condemned by many
as heartless, it had stemmed the tide of the dangerous exodus. The president would change his mind again a year later when he announced that all
Haitian seaborne refugees would henceforth be processed on U.S. naval
hospital ships, the news of which launched a new wave of boat people from
Haiti. Two months later he reversed himself again, declaring that all Haitian refugees would be accorded safe haven, but in some unspecified countries other than the United States.

By September of 1994, the president was completely frustrated by the
Haitian junta's refusal to honor its commitments and the worsening political violence (Aristide's minister for justice had been assassinated shortly
after the *Harlan County* incident). And he was embarrassed by the humiliating rebuke of American power in the hemisphere at the hands of petty
tyrants in command of a poorly armed rabble. He announced that his patience was exhausted and he was now prepared to overthrow the junta and
restore Aristide's government by force of American arms.

Somalia and Haiti were just two places that exposed President Clinton's international leadership, and his confused and reluctant appreciation
for American power, to domestic and international scorn. The Bush administration had made a serious mistake by leaving Saddam Hussein's
regime in power at the end of the Gulf War, a mistake, honesty compels
me to observe, that was supported at the time by most American politicians, Democrats and Republicans, including me. Just how serious an
error it was became clear during the Clinton administration as Saddam

repeatedly violated conditions imposed on his regime under the terms of the cease-fire agreement that ended the Gulf War. From plotting to assassinate former president Bush to ruthlessly repressing Kurdish opposition to refusing to cooperate with UN inspection regimes of his biological, chemical, and nuclear weapons programs, ending in the eventual expulsion of the inspectors, Saddam proved himself to be the same menace to international peace and stability he had always been.

The Clinton administration response to these frequent transgressions was invariably to use the least force conceivable to punish them. Occasionally, American pilots patrolling Iraqi skies to enforce no-fly restrictions imposed on Iraq's air force were authorized to launch their missiles in retaliation for being fired upon by Iraqi air defense units. The administration seemed to prefer very limited military responses, usually a few cruise missiles launched from over the horizon, intending them as gestures of our resolve. But their limitations as instruments of a superpower's will made their effect the opposite of their intended purpose. They became evidence of the administration's irresolution.

Even some of the president's supporters began to doubt that he would ever prove up to the task of providing the coherent, consistent, and imaginative leadership necessary to see the country and the free world through the turbulence occasioned by the collapse of the Soviet empire. By the end of Bill Clinton's first year in office, I had moved beyond doubt to despair. I had cooperated closely with the president in the normalization of relations with Vietnam, to our mutual appreciation. I bore no particular ill will for him, as did some more intensely partisan Republicans. And I liked and respected many of the senior officials he appointed to his national security cabinet. Nevertheless, I became a constant and often caustic critic of the many conceptual and operational failures of Clinton foreign and defense policies. At times, my despair, and the disdain it provoked, caused me to doubt principles I had held for a lifetime about the president's preeminence over Congress in the conduct of foreign policy and the imperative that American power never retreat in response to an inferior adversary's provocation. Even in Lebanon, where I opposed the marines' mission and anticipated the disaster that befell them, I did not support withdrawal in the immediate aftermath of the suicide bombings. Now I was becoming more than a reluctant warrior. I began to doubt that the U.S. government during the period of Bill Clinton's presidency would ever know when and how to use force effectively to achieve its just ends.

The president was not the only person in Washington whose judgment about America's proper role in the world was incapacitated by doubts and inexperience. Many Republicans in Congress, particularly after the Republican sweep of congressional elections in 1994, were just as lacking in conceptual thinking about the post–cold war world and were just as confused about the proper use of American force as was the man in the Oval Office they reviled. Part of our party's failing was attributable to sheer distrust of the president's leadership. Part of it was attributable to the fact that so many newly elected Republicans came to office with little, if any, experience in the military or in international affairs, having no memories of American statecraft beyond the presidency of Ronald Reagan. Their lack of experience and knowledge bred either their near total disinterest in international affairs or an appreciation of foreign policy as only another arena in which to seek partisan advantage. Last, the end of the cold war had reactivated the party's long dormant isolationist gene. The same "leave us the hell alone" attitude that characterized the Republican approach to the federal government's intrusions on individual liberty began to assert itself in the worldview of some Republicans. The passionate preaching of Pat Buchanan, as quaint as it might have seemed to the Washington establishment, had definite appeal to many Republicans elected to office in the 1990s, who heard echoes of their own philosophy of governance in Buchanan's articulately expressed contempt for the world's problems and the demands they imposed on American resources.

There were, of course, many Republicans who remained inveterate internationalists, who appreciated the extraordinary advances in international world peace and stability that fifty years of bipartisan internationalism had achieved, culminating in the singular cold war triumph of America and the free world we led. The Senate was blessed with a number of World War II veterans, not the least of whom was the Republican leader, Bob Dole, who had personally experienced the catastrophic consequences of America's earlier flirtation with isolationism. Even Republicans in the House of Representatives, where so many recently elected members had been teenagers when President Reagan began the diplomacy and security policies that were the last successful offensive of the cold war, and who couldn't have distinguished Bosnia from Brazil, elected Newt Gingrich, a committed internationalist, as Speaker. Yet many of his elected lieutenants were as ignorant of or as indifferent to world affairs as they were distrustful of the president who asked for their support of his leadership.

The appeal of a vastly reduced American role in the world was strongest among the most conservative Republican members. Most believed in a stronger, more expensive defense than Bill Clinton intended to provide. Even then, many of them viewed the defense budget as little more than an opportunity to direct federal spending to their districts and states whether or not the programs the money funded contributed anything meaningful to national defense. Many looked on the United Nations as little more than just a ponderous international debating society whose need to obtain near global consensus before it could act rendered it woefully ill equipped to manage violent crises. They saw in its demands on American resources and manpower a none too subtle threat to American sovereignty. And they began to suspect the same threat from America's more purposeful and successful international associations, even from the security alliance that had organized the free world's defense from Soviet aggression, NATO. Although President Bush had begun to draw down American forces in Europe, they weren't coming home fast enough or in large enough numbers to satisfy many Republicans.

Further, many conservatives objected to our involvement in the third world countries of Africa, Latin America, Asia, or even the backwaters of Europe like the former republics of Yugoslavia, unable to find a single compelling reason for America to embroil herself in the humanitarian crises and violent conflicts that seemed endemic to such places and had historical antecedents that simply mystified forward-looking Americans. We had budget deficits to trim, taxes to cut, social spending to reform, and values to restore to the public square. That was work enough for any American. Let the world sort out its own problems. After all, what has the world done for us lately?

Even Republican leaders like Dole and Gingrich, who were committed to America's world leadership and instinctively inclined to defer to the president on most foreign policy questions, were increasingly restive about Clinton administration policies and distrustful of leadership they correctly judged as weak and uncertain. As was I.

Each foreign policy or military blunder by the Clinton administration provoked greater congressional distrust and more insistent attempts to rein in the president's authority as commander in chief. As I noted, Republicans approached the problem from differing perspectives. But with each new incident of executive incompetence, more and more of us were united in the feeling that something had to be done before some monumental error in judgment led to an even more terrible waste of American blood and treasure. Even if it meant abandoning respect for presidential prerogatives and qualifying America's potent defense of its interests and values out of concern that the incumbent president wasn't up to the task.

On October 14, 1993, eleven days after the ambush of our rangers in Mogadishu, I offered an amendment on the Senate floor restricting funds for American forces in Somalia to the purpose of their "prompt and orderly withdrawal." President Clinton criticized the amendment and its supporters for our "headlong rush into isolationism," which it was not. But it was an encroachment on presidential authority and a retreat in the face of aggression from an inferior foe that I would never have contemplated in the past. And even though I regretted my action, I felt the circumstances were so compelling that it was a necessary response to a failed policy that had cost the lives of eighteen good Americans.

In hindsight, I wish I had not undertaken so drastic a step. But, as the administration had already agreed to compromise legislation that would have set a date for withdrawing our forces five months hence, my demand for a more prompt retreat was only a difference of timing not in kind. I could hardly see how our troops' security or America's international reputation would be better served by a slow retreat than a quick one. The mission they had been initially ordered to undertake, feeding starving Somalians, had been achieved. What other purpose would they serve there that wouldn't make them targets for Aidid's fighters?

The debate began at night and lasted into the early morning hours, and the chamber was crowded with senators all night, an uncommon feature of most Senate debates. Hank Brown of Colorado, a veteran of the Vietnam War, recalled how politicians had put men on the line in Vietnam and "did not stand behind them to protect them." He made a moving appeal to bring our troops home that brought applauding senators to their feet and rang in the hearts of every Vietnam War veteran in that chamber. But we were in danger of drawing the wrong lesson from America's disgrace in Vietnam, I as much as anyone. And it took the veteran of another war that had ended not in disgrace but in triumph to remind us of the duty that had taken us to Southeast Asia in the first place.

In my opening statement, I had focused on the tactical mistakes that were still exposing our troops to hostile fire. As Hank had, I argued that our mission was at an end. To stay was to needlessly endanger American lives. And I ended by fairly shouting, "Whose responsibility is that? Whose responsibility is that?"—implying that the blood of future casualties would be on our hands.

Bob Dole, who led opposition to the amendment, stood up to take responsibility and remind me of mine. He avowed that his long record of support for military operations had never been influenced by the party affiliation of the president who had ordered them. And he reminded us that a great nation has great responsibilities, and they will cost us dearly from time to time. If we want to have a role in the leadership of that nation, we had better expect to have the blood of Americans on our hands. Bob could be a persuasive speaker on such occasions, and his opposition to my amendment was decisive. We were handily defeated, sixty-one to thirty-eight. Moreover, the way he accepted his own responsibility for our casualties, without complaint or qualification, made me feel embarrassed for my earlier comment. He also made me feel I had gone too far in my opposition to the president's policy.

Five months later, President Clinton ordered the withdrawal of U.S. forces from Somalia, and for the rest of his presidency he was loath to commit American ground forces to combat. When the use of force was necessary to protect American interests, the president would seldom consider any option other than cruise missile strikes and a few inconsequential bombing runs. The decision to leave Aidid unpunished and to withdraw from Somalia had a disheartening effect on our military. Quite a few chose not to continue their military careers after the Somalia experience because they doubted that their civilian commanders, and Congress, understood our responsibilities to them. They wondered if we would ever be as committed to victory as they were in the causes we ordered them to serve. Somewhere in the Sudan, Osama Bin Laden observed our withdrawal from Somalia and concluded that America no longer had the stomach for war. These were the consequences the president failed to grasp and that Bob Dole instinctively understood. My doubts about the president's leadership had affected my judgment as well, and Bob had called me to account.

He had his share of doubts about the administration's competence. He was a sharp and informed critic of many of the administration's failures. For four years, he tirelessly encouraged President Clinton to accept his responsibility as commander in chief to defend America's interests and uphold her values in the world, even at the risk of American lives. Nowhere was he more insistent than in his criticism of the administration's abject failure to do justice by those populations in the Balkans who were victims of Serbian aggression and terror.

Whatever my misgivings about the Somalia amendment, they didn't cause me to restrain my criticism of Clinton foreign policy. On the contrary, with every passing month I became more convinced that my early assessment of the president's leadership as timorous and uncertain was, if anything, understated. And I kept after it, assailing the administration with rhetoric that became increasingly pointed and personal. My harshest criticism was reserved for the administration's response to the North Korean violations of the Nuclear Nonproliferation Treaty, where I believed the president's policy was simply to avoid confronting a dangerous crisis in the hope that it would somehow just go away over time.

The crisis began in his first month in office, when North Korea refused to let the International Atomic Energy Agency (IAEA) inspect two nuclear waste sites. When the IAEA imposed a March 31 deadline for inspections, the North Koreans responded by announcing their intention to withdraw from the NNPT. The U.S. intelligence community believed the North Koreans had diverted enough weapons-grade plutonium from their reactors to produce two or more nuclear weapons. The threat posed to stability in Asia, not to mention the threat to our South Korean ally and the thirty-seven thousand American troops stationed there, by the renegade regime's possession of nuclear arms and the means to deliver them as far as Japan was grave—so grave that if all else failed, the United States would have to consider destroying North Korea's nuclear reactors with air and missile strikes and risk a North Korean retaliatory attack on South Korea.

The South Korean capital, Seoul, is within artillery range of the north. Most of North Korea's armed forces were deployed along the border, with a great quantity of artillery hidden in mountain caves there. Most U.S. forces were deployed between Seoul and the border. There was no question that the United States and South Korea would prevail in a second Korean War, but there was also little doubt that in the first stage of war much of Seoul, a densely populated, modern, prosperous capital, would be destroyed. There are no easy choices for an American president to make in such a crisis. And I thought Bill Clinton was trying to avoid making the hard ones in the vain hope that an easier option would somehow materialize over time.

Early in 1993, I had discussed my concerns with President Bush's former national security adviser, Brent Scowcroft. Brent does not have a reputation for making impetuous decisions about the use of American force. But he knew dangerously difficult decisions usually become more so over time, and he believed that war on the Korean peninsula would become more, not less, likely were North Korea allowed to possess even a small nuclear arsenal. We agreed that a strike against the reactors should be a final option, exercised only after every other means of resolving the crisis had been exhausted. Even then, the United States would have to take considerable time to reinforce our military presence in South Korea before launching a strike that might provoke a retaliatory attack from the north.

Brent and I, and many other critics of administration policy, believed we should make North Korea aware of both the disadvantages of maintaining its status as an international outlaw and the advantages of keeping the commitments it undertook as an NNPT signator. We thought the president should aggressively organize an international effort to impose economic sanctions on North Korea until it allowed inspectors to determine what had happened to the diverted plutonium. At the same time, he should hold out the possibility of an improved relationship with the United States should the North Koreans decide to act responsibly, with all the diplomatic and economic benefits that would bring to the isolated, impoverished country.

The president, however, chose a different course. In the mix of carrots and sticks available to the president to encourage North Korean cooperation, he had a strong preference for carrots. In response to their threat to withdraw from the NNPT, the administration announced that it would begin direct negotiations with the North Koreans without the participation of our South Korean allies, an unprecedented break with forty years of insistence on trilateral discussions. What transpired over the next year was an object lesson in how not to conduct diplomacy. Round after round of negotiations between the United States and North Korea produced nothing but broken promises from our adversary and weak responses from the administration. North Korea would agree to allow inspectors to return and abide by its commitments under the NNPT. The administration would proclaim its policy of engagement a success. The North Koreans would refuse inspections again. The administration would begin another round of negotiations and exact new promises from the North Koreans, which they would promptly break.

These humiliating setbacks notwithstanding, the administration continued its vain search for "dialogue" with the bellicose and untrustworthy Stalinist regime. U.S. negotiators were preparing to meet again with their North Korean counterparts in the spring of 1994 when North Korea's capital, Pyongyang, announced its intention to shut down one of its nuclear reactors but promised that inspectors could monitor the process to prevent any new diversion of plutonium. The Clinton administration warned the North Koreans not to begin the refueling until inspectors arrived. They ignored the warning and began removing spent fuel rods from which they could divert plutonium to their weapons program. The IAEA denounced the move as a "serious violation of the Nonproliferation

Treaty." The administration scheduled a new round of negotiations with North Korea.

I went to South Korea in June that year. Two days before I arrived, former president Carter had, on his own initiative, traveled to Pyongyang to meet with the Stalinist regime's supreme ruler, Kim Il Sung. He got a promise from the aging dictator that North Korea would freeze its nuclear program, resume negotiations with the United States, and cease refueling its reactor while the talks were ongoing. President Clinton observed that his predecessor was not authorized to speak for his administration. But he soon embraced the deal Carter had negotiated and resumed negotiations.

In October, the administration announced a great diplomatic triumph: They had signed a "Framework Agreement" with the North Koreans. Pyongyang had agreed to freeze its nuclear program, cease refueling its reactor, and not divert any more plutonium. In exchange, the United States, South Korea, and Japan agreed to build two light water nuclear reactors in North Korea, state-of-the-art facilities that would be harder to use as a means of producing weapons-grade plutonium. The United States and other countries also agreed to provide North Korea with sizable quantities of heavy fuel oil indefinitely, as well as food assistance to help the regime feed its people who were on the brink of famine. North Korea was not obliged to relinquish the fuel rods it had already removed or to allow inspectors to account for the missing plutonium until construction of the new reactors was nearly complete, many years in the future.

Hard choices never had to be made. Carrots and time and a little humility had been all that was needed to avert catastrophe. War was avoided. And since the agreement was signed, the North Koreans have not been able to add to whatever plutonium and nuclear stockpile they already possessed. I don't dismiss the value of either of those accomplishments. In time, many observers believe that Kim Jong Il's regime will collapse under the weight of its bankrupt economy and repressive politics. Perhaps. But the credibility of the president of the United States had been damaged by his repeated failure to back his rhetoric with action and his willingness to be pushed by bullying and threats into retreating from the stated objectives of its policy. The president's credibility is an enormously valuable strategic asset, and squandering it in Korea encouraged other international bullies to test him. And I remained worried throughout Bill Clinton's presidency that the United States was entering a period of great uncertainty in world affairs, when friend and foe alike would doubt the wisdom and resolve of our government.

As of today, because of North Korean intransigence, construction of the nuclear reactors has barely begun. The spent fuel rods were never turned over. Inspectors have never been allowed to account for the missing plutonium. And much of the $30 million in fuel oil the United States has annually provided North Korea along with much of the food aid we provided was diverted to the North Korean military, while the North Korean people starved and froze.

My experiences with administration diplomacy with North Korea did not encourage my confidence in the president's ability to manage other crises that occurred on his watch. Nor had I gained confidence in the president's understanding of how to use military force to achieve his ends. And those doubts were never far from my mind as I struggled to reconcile my desire to oppose Serbian aggression in Bosnia, and the terrible atrocities committed against the majority population of Muslims and Croats, with my fear that the leadership I had come to expect from the administration was no match for the historical ferocity of Balkan politics.

In the Balkans, people still fought over injuries that had been inflicted by the Ottoman Empire in the fifteenth century. World War I began in Bosnia, when a Serb nationalist assassinated an Austrian archduke. When the Nazis invaded Yugoslavia, the violence they unleashed was cataclysmic. Croats slaughtered Serbs, Jews, and Gypsies. Serb royalists slaughtered Croats and other Serbs. Muslims joined with Serbian partisans to fight the invaders. Most of the fighting occurred in Bosnia, and Germany never managed to totally subdue the place.

The war had begun in Slovenia and Croatia, and the casualties incurred in Croatia affirmed the Balkans' reputation for merciless violence. Ten thousand were killed; Dubrovnik, a beautiful city on the Dalmatian coast, had been ruthlessly shelled; and Vukovar on the Danube next to the border with Serbia had been reduced to rubble.

When Bosnian Serbs began their war against the legitimate government of Bosnia, with the support of the Yugoslav army and Serbian boss

Slobodan Milošević , they quickly seized 70 percent of Bosnia. To accomplish their objectives, no tactics were considered too inhumane. They gave a new name to their war crimes, "ethnic cleansing," as they used whatever means necessary—murder, torture, rape—to force Muslims and Croats from their homes. Sarajevo, a lovely city that had once hosted the Winter Olympic Games, sits in the bottom of a bowl surrounded on all sides by mountains. Unfortunately, the Serbs held the heights from which they shelled and sniped indiscriminately at Muslim civilians, men, women, and children. By the summer of 1992, pictures of emaciated Muslims held behind barbed wire in Serbian concentration camps were being broadcast worldwide. Our NATO allies, following the declaration of Luxembourg's foreign minister that "the hour of Europe had arrived," bravely accepted responsibility for restoring peace in Europe's Balkan backyard. It had little effect on the Serbs, whose elected president, Radovan Karadžić, and commanding general, Ratko Mladic, urged them on to greater atrocities. Nor did UN-imposed sanctions discourage them. They went right on killing, contemptuous as always of Western sensibilities about treating subject peoples as if they were some form of pestilence to be ruthlessly eradicated.

By May 1992, the United States became involved in the conflict to a limited extent. We provided most of the planes, pilots, and matériel for a UN airlift of food and medical necessities to besieged Sarajevo. But we left it to European peacekeepers to resolve the conflict on the ground. We wanted no part of a fight this complex, irrational, and indifferent to the norms of civilized behavior. And when Muslims and Croats began fighting among themselves in January 1993, U.S. policy makers were all the more convinced that the Europeans should sort it out if they could. That the Europeans weren't going to be able to pacify the country was an open secret even as early as 1993. But better to let them try and fail, and hope that all parties to the conflict would eventually grow weary of fighting.

There were voices in Washington that expressed outrage over Serbian atrocities and demanded of both the Bush and Clinton administrations that the United States become directly involved in the conflict on behalf of the legitimate Bosnian government. In the Senate, those voices belonged more often than not to three men, Joe Biden, Joe Lieberman, and

Bob Dole. Among Republicans, Bob Dole was the most prominent proponent that American power must serve American values just as diligently as it protected American security interests in the world. And he had long experience with Serbian aggression. On a trip to Serbia, before the war in Bosnia began, he had seen Serbian police unmercifully beat protesters in the captive province of Kosovo. He is a man with an innate sense of justice, and he did not distinguish between the rights of Americans and the rights of all people.

All three senators, along with many other prominent voices in both parties, advocated what came to be called the "lift and strike" option. They argued that the United States and, hopefully, our European allies should abandon the failed UN peacekeeping operation, launch sustained air strikes against Serbian forces, and at the same time terminate the UN-imposed arms embargo that prevented Bosnian Muslims and Croats from acquiring the arms necessary to defend themselves on the ground. President Clinton had campaigned in support of the strategy for combining air strikes with local ground offensives, but he wasn't in office long before the Europeans persuaded him to back off the idea.

I also opposed the air strikes, for three reasons. First, I had no confidence that the Clinton administration would use airpower any more decisively than it had against Iraq. Second, I did not believe air strikes alone could achieve victory on the ground. You can't hold ground from the air, and holding ground is what constitutes victory in warfare. Third, I didn't believe that the government of Bosnia would be capable of launching successful offensives against the Serbs and seizing territory themselves for quite some time. I was right in my first two suppositions, but wrong about the last.

Despite my opposition to air strikes, I agreed with Senators Dole, Lieberman, and Biden that the UN arms embargo was unjust, and I joined their efforts to end it. If we weren't prepared to defend Bosnians, then it was morally indefensible for us to deprive Bosnians of the means to defend themselves. Even if they acquired arms, I did not know if the Bosnian government could prevail over the Serbs. But they had a right to try. And the leader of the free world had a moral obligation to get out of their way. The UN, the Europeans, and the Clinton administration strongly resisted our efforts, and the president, though he claimed to sympathize with our position, nevertheless threatened to veto any resolution that would force him to lift the embargo.

After the Serbs tightened their siege against Sarajevo in August 1993, NATO approved the use of air strikes against Serb positions unless they withdrew all of their heavy guns from the mountains surrounding the capital. But the order to initiate air strikes would be a shared responsibility; the UN secretary general's representative to the United Nations Protection Force in Bosnia, UNPROFOR, would have to give his consent to any strike. This "dual key" command arrangement virtually guaranteed that any air strikes would be too late to prevent future massacres and too limited to do anything but improve Serbian morale.

On February 5, 1994, Bosnian Serbs fired a mortar shell into a crowded Sarajevo marketplace, killing sixty-eight innocent people. The Serbs blamed the atrocity on the Muslims themselves. The world watched the carnage on television. Three weeks later, American pilots shot down two Serbian warplanes, the first offensive action taken by NATO in the alliance's fifty-year history. But no other action was ordered to force the Serbs to withdraw their guns from the heights above Sarajevo. Two months later, as Serbs attacked Gorazde, another UN-declared "safe area," NATO launched its first air strikes on Serbian positions. But under the dual key command arrangement, the strikes were nothing more than pinpricks and were greeted with disdain by the Serbs. They pressed new offensives, committing further atrocities and provoking cries in European capitals for the United States to share more of the dangerous burden of preventing the Serbs from killing every single non-Serb in Bosnia.

After the 1994 congressional elections, the Senate's new majority leader, Bob Dole, traveled to Europe to urge our allies to withdraw their peacekeepers from Bosnia and help provide the Bosnian government with arms and training. For his trouble, he got a lecture from the British ambassador to NATO headquarters in Brussels, who told Dole he had no right to criticize the Europeans unless the United States put troops on the ground in Bosnia. "You're afraid to take the risk," he sneered. Dole is not a man to take lightly accusations of cowardice against himself or his country. And he responded to the insult just as pointedly as its author had made it. "I don't need a lecture from you about sacrifice," he shot back, and then proceeded to enumerate all of America's many contributions to the peace, prosperity, and security of Europe, starting with the Gulf War and working his way back to the invasion of Normandy.

The Bosnia peacekeeping mission continued its inevitable progress toward abject failure. The Serbs continued to threaten safe areas and terrorize civilian populations. NATO warplanes managed to hit Serb munitions here and there, but they weren't doing any serious damage to the Serbs' offensive capability or killing many of the enemy. When American F-16 pilots destroyed an ammo dump on the outskirts of Pale, a Serb stronghold, the Serbs responded by seizing 350 peacekeepers as hostages, chaining them to other ammo dumps and military vehicles parked on airport runways until Belgrade convinced them to let the hostages go.

President Clinton gave a speech on May 31, without any consultation with Congress, in which he promised to send American soldiers to Bosnia to help reposition the twenty-two thousand peacekeepers there to more defensible locations. Congress, predictably, erupted.

Everyone seemed to oppose the idea, Democrats and Republicans, no matter where they stood on the question of the arms embargo or air strikes. The administration quickly backed off the plan. Two days after his Memorial Day speech, a Serbian surface-to-air missile shot down an American F-16 pilot, Scott O'Grady, who kept himself well hidden from Serbian patrols for six days, subsisting on rainwater and bugs, until marine helicopters rescued him.

The incident exposed the folly of NATO air operations in Bosnia; our pilots were prohibited from striking Serbian SAM sites because it would have constituted an "unwarranted escalation," reminding all Vietnam War pilots of an earlier, similar folly. But Scott's safe return cheered all Americans, was a credit to his courage and resourcefulness and to the marines who rescued him, and was cause for great celebration in the White House. It passed for a triumph in an administration that was bereft of any successes in Bosnia. NATO considered launching more aggressive strikes in retaliation for the shoot-down of one of its planes but decided against doing anything that might be seen by the Serbs as a provocation. Six

weeks later, the Serbian massacre in Srebenica occurred, reminding everyone what a provocation and what failure really looked like in Bosnia.

On Bastille Day, three days after the Srebenica massacre, French
president Jacques Chirac, disgusted with America's refusal to share
France's misery in Bosnia, declared that the position "of leader of the free
world is now vacant." I don't have a natural sympathy for French statesmen. I don't take kindly to French insults to my country or its leaders.
And I certainly felt that France was as culpable for the disaster in Bosnia
as was Bill Clinton. That said, I worried that his charge wasn't far off the
mark.

In July, the United States and Europe agreed in London to end the
dual key command and initiate serious air operations against the Serbs if
they didn't stop their offensives against the safe areas. Not long after the
conference concluded, Croatia launched an offensive to recover its captured territory. The fighting was fierce and brutal and included atrocities
against the Serbs. At the same time, Bosnian Muslims and Croats began
to break through the Serbian perimeter in northwestern Bosnia. They
were armed and aided by Iranian Revolutionary Guards and mujahideen
from other Muslim countries, including more than a few America-hating
terrorists whose presence in Bosnia the administration had been apprised
of and had turned a blind eye to.

In September, the Serbs launched another mortar attack on Sarajevo.
NATO responded by unleashing a major, sustained air assault, while
Muslim and Croat forces advanced in the northwest. The Serbs, counseled by their patron in Belgrade, got the message. They removed their
heavy guns from Sarajevo and agreed to a cease-fire in October.

President Clinton had already sent Assistant Secretary of State
Richard Holbrooke to the region with a new peace plan. After the cease-
fire, all parties involved agreed to begin negotiations on the plan at
Wright-Patterson Air Force Base in Dayton, Ohio. The talks began on
November 1, 1995, and ended successfully three weeks later, when the
presidents of Bosnia, Croatia, and Serbia all signed the accords (Milošević
on behalf of the Bosnian Serbs), bringing to an end at last a war that had
killed hundreds of thousands of people and dislocated millions. As part of

the agreement, the UN peacekeeping mission was also mercifully ended. NATO would take over, and as part of the operation, the United States would send twenty thousand troops.

Few Republicans greeted the announcement of American participation in a new Bosnian peacekeeping mission with much enthusiasm. Most were unalterably opposed. I reserved judgment and my support until I saw whether the president could make a convincing case that "the deployment of twenty thousand Americans to Bosnia is in the vital interests of the United States, and is worth the risk of American lives." On November 28, I watched the president make a pretty persuasive case that it was.

No legal injunction, but political realities meant he would have to come to Congress for approval. All members of Congress were united in that belief. But few Republicans were going to give him that approval, and there were more Republicans in Congress now than Democrats. The House was a lost cause. The Republican majority there was still smarting over Clinton's victory in the great government shutdown showdown. Newt Gingrich would have liked to help, but it wouldn't have done any good. House Republicans weren't about to do the president any favors, particularly not one that their instincts told them was a political loser. House conservatives had already passed a resolution warning the president not to guarantee American troops as part of a peace deal. Clinton's only hope of getting even limited support from a few Republicans was in the Senate. And there his hopes would be focused on the patriotism of one man, a prominent member of the celebrated "greatest generation," Senator Bob Dole of Kansas.

When Bob Dole went to war, most Americans his age had begun to believe they would be spared the crucible. By the time he had finished basic training and officer candidate school, was shipped across the Atlantic, and reported for duty at a replacement camp in Rome, it was D-Day plus six months. The Battle of the Bulge, the Nazis' last great offensive of the war in Europe, had just been launched, and Patton's Third Army had yet to sweep north to Bastogne and rescue the defiant American soldiers surrounded there. But everybody knew that the war in Europe would soon be over, just as soon as the Bulge was pushed back and

Patton turned his army toward Germany. The Red Army was barreling down on Berlin already.

But the Germans had yet to give up the fight in Italy, which they had annexed after the Italians surrendered. From well-dug-in positions in the mountainous north, they were putting up a hell of a fight. And young American lieutenants, fresh off the boat from back home, were getting slaughtered by the dozens every week. It was a bad place to be, particularly if you were the new lieutenant ordered to lead your platoon, men who were strangers to you and you to them, on a new spring offensive to break through the German lines.

When Dole had taken command of the platoon, he had been smart enough to let the platoon's veteran sergeant, Sergeant Frank Carafa, continue running things. But he also knew that on April 14, 1945, when the platoon's first squad advanced on a farmhouse where German machine gunners were bunkered, duty obliged him to lead the charge. Mortar fire from the hill behind the farmhouse tore into his squad. Dole took cover in a shell hole, but one of his men didn't make it. When Bob left his cover to drag the wounded man back, he was hit, too.

It would be many hours before they took out the German machine gun, reached their wounded lieutenant, dragged his destroyed body out of the line of mortar fire, and put him on a jeep headed for a field hospital. And it was many years and many operations later before high school athlete Bob Dole could use his left arm again. His right arm was left to wither at his side, bent at the elbow, fist clenched around a pen so that people wouldn't reach to shake it.

I saw Bob Dole interviewed once, when he broke down while describing his parents' constant visits to the Michigan hospital where he was recovering from surgery and hovering between life and death. He talked about his careworn father standing on a crowded train, his ankles swollen from the strain, and he started to sob. Bob had a reputation for being a pretty tough partisan, and for being totally enthralled to the profession he had chosen for himself. So a display of emotion such as he showed in that interview took a lot of people in Washington by surprise. But his devoted family, and the people from his little hometown of Russell, Kansas, who had put what little extra money they had into a shoe box to help pay for his operations, meant a whole lot more to him than politics ever had. The doctor who operated on Bob and restored some mobility to his left arm was of Armenian descent. He told Bob about the genocide committed against Armenians by the Turks in the early twentieth century. Bob never forgot it, and for years he tried to pass a Senate resolution commemorating the suffering of a people he never knew, in tribute to the man who had helped him back into life. Without belaboring his story to the point of embarrassing the subject, it is enough to note that Bob Dole is a man of sound values.

He knows about sacrifice, and he knows about duty and the hard decisions that can't be avoided when your duty summons you. He had stood up for presidents before when they were forced to make the hard choice of sending Americans into harm's way. I knew full well Bob Dole wanted to give President Clinton the support he sought for his decision to send American troops to Bosnia; he thought it was his duty to do so. I also knew it was a politically dangerous decision for him to make. He was running for president for the third time. The first time, in 1980, he had barely won a delegate. The second time, he had won the first contest, the Iowa caucuses, but George Bush beat him in New Hampshire, in a pretty tough campaign, ending any real chance he had of being the Republican nominee. This time he was the front-runner, although a little old and a little too familiar to inspire universal Republican enthusiasm. He had a pack of opponents snapping at his ankles, and not one of them would miss an opportunity to savage him if he even hinted at supporting Clinton's decision. The opponent who was waiting to bite him the hardest was his Senate colleague and my friend Phil Gramm, on whose campaign I served as national chairman.

Phil didn't let many opportunities pass to draw a distinction between himself and Bob Dole. And sending troops to Bosnia, which the influential New Hampshire paper the Manchester *Union Leader* was already calling a craven decision, was a hell of an opportunity to score some points. Most Senate Republicans would side with Gramm against Dole if Bob walked into that trap. It was a tough spot. Many prospective presidents would have stayed clear of it. But I knew Dole couldn't. He would have been too ashamed of himself. And I would have been too ashamed of myself if I had decided not to help him.

When I was in Vietnam, I believed I was there not only to protect our security interests in Asia, but to advance our core political values as well. Whether that was in fact the purpose of the government that sent me there is debatable. But I believed it. Just as I believed that our faith in freedom, democracy, pluralism, free markets, and the rule of law was the basis of all our cold war policies. Soviet communism was a threat not only because of geopolitics and nuclear weapons. It threatened our values as well. Without a human rights dimension, it would have been impossible to sustain our policy of containment for over forty years. By advancing our values, we mobilized and sustained public support. We did not just stand against communism. We stood for freedom. Character counts in relations between nations, no less than it does in relations between individuals.

It is a regrettable paradox that the destruction of the Berlin Wall as a real and symbolic obstacle to freedom was interpreted by some, on both the Right and Left, in the very country most responsible for the Wall's demise, as a reason to return to building walls in America. In their worldview, isolationism, or at least an unwillingness to involve ourselves in the struggle for freedom and independence of other nations, is a practical response to a dangerous world that was suspended only to meet the security threat posed by the Soviet Union. Once that threat was defeated, they viewed America's international leadership as an expensive vanity that deserved to disappear with the Berlin Wall.

But such a cramped view of American purpose is blind to the futility of building walls in a world made remarkably smaller precisely because of the global success of American political and economic ideals. A world where our ideals had a realistic chance of becoming a universal creed was our principal object in the last century. In the process, we became inextricably involved in the destiny of other nations. That is not a cause for concern. It is a cause for hope. For the best guarantee that this new century will not reverse humanity's triumphs in the last is the futility of American attempts to withdraw from a world that is, in large part, the fruit of our labors.

The world still offers abundant challenges to our security and our ideals. But it is a world far more hospitable to our founding convictions than it was when America began to lead it. At the end of the cold war, Americans took time to congratulate ourselves for leading the world through a dangerous time. But we had yet to remember that we had a duty to move on and begin building a better one.

In my disagreements with the conduct of President Clinton's foreign policy, I had begun not so much to forget that central fact of American identity as to despair that our government had the means or the will to insist on the universality of our values. But the tragedy that befell Bosnia, the rebuke to our values it represented, the threat it posed to unity of our most important alliance, and the example of Bob Dole reminded me of the duty that gives our nation its strength and honor, and that I must accept my share of that duty. As powerful a nation as we are, as good a nation as we are, we are not omnipotent, and we cannot impose our values by force of arms everywhere they are threatened. But where both our values and our security interests are at risk, as they surely were in a conflict that threatened the stability of Europe, and as they are today in Afghanistan, we are obliged to defend them by whatever means necessary.

So I overcame my reservations about sending Americans into a centuries-old cauldron of hate and violence and went to talk to Bob to see if there was something we could do together to help the president. During a vote on the Senate floor on the afternoon of November 28, I walked up to Dole, told him I knew he wanted to give the president a resolution of support, and said it was the right thing to do and that I'd like to help. He welcomed the offer, and a few minutes later we both started letting the press know of our plans.

The next day, we gave back-to-back speeches on the Senate floor, laying out the argument for supporting the president. The president was going to send the troops no matter what Congress did. There were never enough votes to override a veto of legislation prohibiting funds from supporting the deployment. And if we put troops in the field, they have a right to expect their Congress to support their mission. The president's credibility was on the line, and that meant the country's credibility was on the line. Our friends and enemies don't discriminate between a Democrat and Republican when the word of an American president is given. Our

NATO alliance, which had served our country's security and Europe's so well for nearly half a century, might fall apart if America were to renege on its commitment to the peacekeeping force in Bosnia. And although no one could know if this latest peace agreement would last any longer than others had, this was probably the last chance to save a war-ravaged people from annihilation.

The next day, *The Union Leader* condemned us both for "yellow-bellied cowardice" and "preemptive surrender."

We began to negotiate the provisions of the resolution with administration officials and Senate Democrats. We made our support conditional on the president's commitment to lifting the embargo and arming and training the Bosnian army so that it could defend the country after we left. The president informally made the commitment in a letter he sent to both of us.

Led by Gramm, most Senate conservatives announced their opposition to our resolution right away and prepared for a long fight to block it. While Bob and I were holding an impromptu press conference explaining some of its provisions, and announcing that we hoped to have it ready for a vote in a few days, Trent Lott, the Republican whip (the number two position in our leadership), was holding a press conference declaring his intention to oppose us. Don Nickles of Oklahoma, also in the leadership, was helping organize conservative opposition. And Jim Inhofe, the junior Oklahoma senator, was threatening a filibuster. Kay Bailey Hutchison of Texas drafted a resolution that would disapprove of the mission but also, somewhat contradictorily, offered the Senate's support for the troops who would be ordered to carry it out.

On December 4, Phil Gramm asked me to come see him in his office. We had been friends for a long time, had traveled together a lot overseas and at home, had recruited Republican Senate candidates together, and had vacationed together. He was smart, disciplined, and gifted at rebutting demagogic arguments used to assail complex political questions by using his slow Georgia drawl and examples drawn from the common experiences of middle-class Americans. I admired his talent and valued his friendship. But I knew what he was doing in the Bosnia debate was wrong. And I knew he knew it.

When I got to his office, he was waiting for me with his campaign's chief foreign policy adviser. We joked around for a while, as we always do before Phil got to the point of the interview. He asked me to back off the resolution. Let Dole do it alone, he's a big boy. "Reporters are already pointing out that my national chairman is working with my opponent on the other side of the issue from me. It looks bad, John." I told him I couldn't do it, felt strongly about it, and not to worry, "the whole thing about us being on opposite sides would be forgotten in a week."

I wanted to brush it off, get the discussion over, and get back to my office. But Phil kept pressing. "C'mon, John. I need you to at least get out of the papers, keep quiet, don't get out front with Dole." He had his campaign aide try to argue the issue on its national security merits. But I brought the meeting to a conclusion by losing my temper a little. "I'm not on the wrong side of the issue, Phil. You are. You shouldn't oppose the resolution. That was a mistake. You don't look like a statesman." I told him that my decision wasn't about him and it wasn't about Bob Dole. "It's about the security of the country, and it's about doing the right thing in the world. I'm not going to change my mind." With that I got out of there.

Phil and I have had disagreements from time to time, more often these days as our views about government have diverged somewhat in recent years. But Phil Gramm is principled in many of his political positions. I've seen him defend some unpopular views over the years when the politically safer course would have been to argue the opposite. But that day, he had decided the security and integrity of the country wasn't worth a handful of votes in New Hampshire, and I knew then that I had backed the wrong man for president. I stayed with him, though, throughout his candidacy. The more honest course, and maybe the more honorable one, would have been to relinquish my chairmanship and depart from his campaign. Phil was principled enough to do just that four years later when he declined to support me for president and campaigned against me. There are a lot of hard choices in politics, and contrary to popular opinion, politicians can't duck them all.

By this time, House Republicans promised to pass their own resolution disapproving of the mission on whatever day we voted on ours. Most conservatives were continuing to thrash Dole for his apostasy. Bob Dornan, who was considering becoming a nuisance candidate in the primaries, railed on about the "triple draft dodger" who was sending our boys to certain death with help of "my good friend Bob Dole." *The Union Leader* ran a poll showing Bob's support in New Hampshire dropping over the controversy.

We had plenty of support from eminent Republicans, though. Former presidents Bush and Ford supported us, as did many officials from their administrations and Ronald Reagan's. Jim Baker, Brent Scowcroft, Jim Schlesinger, Jeane Kirkpatrick, Richard Perle, and many others offered their support.

Debate began on the evening of December 13. The first resolution considered was Jim Inhofe's. I knew it would lose. Cutting off funding was too drastic a step for most senators. But I was worried that a few Republicans who had already committed to voting with us would try to hedge their bets by voting for Kay Hutchison's amendment as well. Bob had pledged to vote for it as part of an agreement with opponents not to stage a filibuster of our amendment. I thought others might follow his example and give her amendment just enough votes to carry and diminish the impact of our resolution as a testament of Congress's support for the mission.

Debate on our resolution began later that evening. I spoke before Bob and ran through all the arguments for our position that I had already made many times in numerous interviews, radio broadcasts, and earlier floor speeches. When Bob began his remarks some instinct told me to get up from my desk, which was located behind his, and move to the front of the chamber, near the Senate dais, where I could see his face as he spoke. He spoke with the clarity of a deeply loyal patriot and the wisdom of a statesman who knew what it meant to sacrifice for his country.

"It's 10:05 P.M. our time, and 4:05 in the morning in Bosnia, where many Americans are now and where thousands more will be on the way. . . . We say to these soldiers who may be on early morning duty there at four in the morning in the bitter cold—from those of us in the warmth of the U.S. Senate, free from any danger—we are about to cast a vote. We are about to cast a vote, Sergeant Jones or Private Smith . . . to indicate our support for your efforts there. . . . This is not about a Democratic president and a Republican majority in the Senate. This is about a lot of frightened young Americans who are in Bosnia or on their way to Bosnia. They may not think of it directly, but they are going to look back one of these days to see if they had the support of those who represent them in Congress."

After this opening, he quickly explained the provisions of the three resolutions and made a compelling case for why ours was the preferable vote. Then he returned to his theme in earlier debates, about other wars, about the hard choices we have to make sometimes and our duty to face them. He turned to me to say a few kind words about my support and about my "sacrifice during Vietnam." He was not in the leadership then, he noted, "I was standing back there," as he gestured to the desks arrayed along the chamber's back wall.

"But I was wearing a John McCain bracelet, proudly, a POW bracelet, and arguing with my Democratic colleagues not to cut off funding for the Vietnam War. I led the debate for seven weeks in an effort to derail those who would cut off funds while John McCain was in a little box over there."

I had never known Bob Dole had worn my bracelet. He had never told me or used it to make me feel obligated to him. My eyes watered, and I had a hard time swallowing. I had never seen a more noble expression of patriotism from anyone who has graced the Senate in my many years there, and I loved him for it.

When the clerk called the roll, the Inhofe resolution was easily defeated. Kay Hutchison's was closer, but it lost also. When Bob went to the Senate well to vote for it, as he had promised, he looked at the roll, saw that it was going to lose, smiled at me, and gave a thumbs-up. The Dole-McCain resolution passed easily, sixty-nine to thirty. Twenty-four Republicans voted for it and all but one Democrat.

Bob and I did a little victory lap that night up in the Senate press gallery. We relaxed in leather chairs and joked about our triumph, coming as it did with a House vote disapproving of the deployment. But tomorrow's papers wouldn't pay much attention to the House vote. Bob Dole had given President Clinton the political support he needed to conduct the country's foreign policy. That was the only political story that mattered that day. In the next day's *Arizona Republic*, they ran a cartoon showing Dole and me walking into an open grave while Bob says, "If you can't beat 'em, join 'em." The tombstone bore the epitaph "Dead-end Bosnia policy."

Bob took a lot of heat during the primaries for his support of that policy. He lost the New Hampshire primary for the third time, and the next contest in Arizona, but he rallied in South Carolina and went on to win the nomination. Few people thought he had a chance of beating the incumbent president, the much younger, facile, and peerless campaigner Bill Clinton. But he gave it his all, leaving the Senate in June 1996, after thirty-five years in Congress, to campaign full-time, sacrificing the work he loved for one last shot at the presidency.

In a long farewell speech on the Senate floor, he moved to tears senators, staff, and even a few reporters watching in the press gallery. He is known more for his wit than eloquent oratory. But when he wanted to, he could, in his rambling style and plain prose, speak important truths and recall the Senate's attention to the best traditions and high purposes that distinguished the institution. He remembered his friendship with two Democrats, Dan Inouye and Phil Hart, with whom he had played poker long years ago in a VA Hospital in Battle Creek, Michigan, where they had recovered from their war wounds, and how proud he was that they had served together in the Senate. How small a thing political differences were to men who had sacrificed for a far more important allegiance. He saluted the press, acknowledging that the work reporters "do off the floor is as vital to American democracy as anything we do on it." He spoke of his affection for prominent Senate liberals, Hubert Humphrey and George McGovern and others with whom he had crossed the partisan divide to accomplish important things for the country. Among the many legislative successes of his long career, he seemed proudest of his support for expanding nutrition programs, saving Social Security from insolvency, and extending civil rights protections. That his partners in those efforts were Democrats made the achievements all the more important to him. He acknowledged that some conservatives distrusted him because of these bipartisan alliances, but he exposed the criticism for the small-minded selfishness it represented. "I think George McGovern is a gentleman and always has been." He spoke at a time when partisanship in Congress had become personal and often cruel, which made his parting advice to us as wise as it was rare in those days. "We have to trust each other," he said. "We come from different states and different backgrounds, different opportunities, different challenges in life. . . . The institution has its imperfections and occasional inefficiency. We're like America. We're still a work in progress." Bob Dole was not of the times any longer. He was better than that, and he reminded us that we could be, too.

He asked me to give the speech, officially putting his name in nomination at the Republican convention that year. In typical Dole fashion, he extended the invitation just one day before the speech was scheduled to be delivered. My cell phone rang during a breakfast with reporters from *Newsweek* magazine. When I answered it he didn't even bother to identify himself.

"You want to nominate me?" he asked.

"I'd be honored," I replied.

"All right, my people will be in touch." And with that he hung up.

When I spoke the next night, a little nervous and unpracticed, I began with the truest thing I knew about Bob Dole and the country he had served so well for so long. "In America, we celebrate the virtues of the quiet hero; the modest man who does his duty without complaint or expectation of praise; the man who listens closely for the call of his country, and when she calls, he answers without reservation, not for fame or reward, but for love. He loves his country."

Things didn't go very well for the Dole campaign in the days following the convention. By the last week of the campaign, President Clinton's reelection seemed assured. Bob decided to begin one last nonstop, cross-country barnstorm. I went along for the ride. Seventy-three years old at the time, he traveled over ten thousand miles in ninety-six hours, making midnight appearances in diners and bowling alleys from Phoenix to Des Moines. It was a valiant if futile effort, the best days of a losing campaign. I was lucky to have witnessed it.

Just after midnight on election day, weary from lack of sleep, his voice hoarse from overuse, Bob acknowledged to a crowd of supporters in Iowa that "nothing I say at this point will change what will happen today." He had wanted to give a good account of himself, and that he had done. "Nothing is easy if it's worthwhile," he explained.

"The last crusade of a great warrior," I said that night, "a member of a generation of Americans who made the world safe for democracy [and] better for ourselves and our children."

That evening, I sat in a hotel suite with the Doles and Bob's campaign manager, Scott Reed, and watched the news anchors report the predicted results. Bob took a call from his running mate, Jack Kemp, and then went downstairs to a ballroom packed with supporters, mostly young, many of them a little drunk, who had been waiting hours to hear him make his concession speech. "I was thinking on the way down in the elevator," he told them, "tomorrow will be the first time in my life that I don't have anything to do." He then congratulated President Clinton with a gracious promise of support. "I have said repeatedly in this campaign that the president was my opponent and not my enemy. And I wish him well and pledge my support in whatever advances the cause of a better America." Hearing this, the crowd began to boo. Bob appeared disappointed and told them to stop it.

Bob Dole didn't get to be president, losing to a man who seemed to understand the times better than he did. But Bob knew a lot about more important things. For all the grief we had taken over that Bosnia vote, I had felt pretty good about the thing. I think Bob had, too.

Theodore Roosevelt. *Corbis*

A HAPPIER LIFE IN EVERY WAY

On the morning of December 16, 1907, sixteen battleships, brilliant white in the winter sun, various escort craft, and eighteen thousand officers and crew prepared to embark from Hampton Roads, Virginia, on the first world cruise ever attempted by any nation's navy. Not even Great Britain, the greatest naval power of the age, had managed such a feat. Each of the great warships thundered a twenty-one-gun salute as the presidential yacht, the *Mayflower*, steamed into view, the commander in chief aboard, as excited as a young boy at his first military parade. President Theodore Roosevelt had come to bid bon voyage to his "big stick," the Great White Fleet he had built to make the United States a world power, with a navy second only to Great Britain's, and invest American diplomacy with the authority of a modern, potent military.

He had pressured Congress during his first term in office into authorizing the construction of ten new battleships. And when members of Congress balked at authorizing the extravagant expenditure of funds required to send the fleet around the world, TR informed them that he had sufficient funds to send his battleships to the Pacific. Congress would have to come up with the money to bring them back.

He had become a national hero for his exploits as a cavalry officer in Cuba, leading his famous charges in the Battle of San Juan Heights, and he was, to be sure, an armchair admiral. But he was a navy man through

and through. No other president of the United States came to office with
a more thorough appreciation for the historical importance of seapower or
with more practical knowledge about naval matters than Theodore Roosevelt. His southern belle mother, Mittie, had filled his head with tales of
the gallant Confederate navy in which his maternal uncles served. "From
my earliest recollection I have been fed on tales of the sea and of ships . . .
ships, ships, ships, and fighting of ships, till they sank into the depths of
my soul." Born on the anniversary of the day in 1775 when the Continental Congress authorized the purchase of merchant ships for a new
American navy, he even shared a birthday with the navy.

In his senior year at Harvard, he began work on his first book, *The
Naval War of 1812*, a respected volume of military history that he completed at the age of twenty-four. He intended the book to serve as a cau-
tionary tale to his country, whose seapower had deteriorated dramatically
since the Civil War, arguing correctly that the inferiority of the American
navy in 1812 had encouraged British belligerence. But, as the American
navy then was not nearly as impotent as the navy that Lincoln's successors
had let rot at the pier, it was restored to fighting trim quickly enough to
defeat the world's greatest naval power. I have never read it, but that oversight surely doesn't detract from its merits. It was required reading at the
Naval Academy for many years, but not, alas, when I was among the
poorer scholars there.

TR became a friend and kindred soul of an instructor at the new Naval
War College in Newport, Rhode Island. Captain Alfred Thayer Mahan
had served ably in combat as a naval officer in the Civil War. But his in-
tellectual brilliance brought him international renown as the most eminent naval strategist of his time, if not of all time. In 1890, he published
The Influence of Sea Power upon History, 1660–1783, a collection of his
War College lectures, followed two years later by another collection, *The
Influence of Sea Power upon the French Revolution and Empire, 1793–1812*.
Roosevelt devoured the first book in two days' time and immediately
wrote the author to assure him that his work was certain to be a "naval
classic." That turned out to be an understatement. Mahan's dazzling, orig-
inal analyses, particularly of British and French seapower during the
Napoleonic Wars, and his thesis that a great navy was indispensable to in-

ternational supremacy, claimed a prominent place on the library shelves of every serious officer in every serious navy in the world. In the United States Navy Department's library, at the turn of the century and well beyond, *The Influence of Sea Power upon History* enjoyed greater eminence than the Bible.

It was the bible, at least in all matters military, to my father, whose much less famous seapower lectures simply updated and affirmed Mahan's thesis with modern examples of naval supremacy. When my father quoted Alfred Thayer Mahan, he meant it as the last word on whatever subject he was addressing. And since Theodore Roosevelt was Mahan's most important political ally as they transformed the American navy from a small coastal defense force to an instrument for the global projection of power, he deserved an ample share of the glory.

Roosevelt consulted closely with Mahan when he served for little more than a year as assistant secretary of the navy in the first administration of William McKinley. In that office, he simply overwhelmed the far less energetic and often absentee secretary, John D. Long. Within weeks of his arrival in Washington, Roosevelt effectively seized control of the Navy Department, working at his usual incomprehensibly feverish pace to modernize the department's administration, restore the morale and fighting efficiency of the fleet, and exclaim constantly and loudly the imperative of building a great fleet that would make possible the expansion of American power in our hemisphere and beyond. The immediate object of that expansion, Roosevelt argued to Secretary Long and President McKinley's distress, were Spain's holdings in the Caribbean, specifically Cuba. And since intervening on the side of Cuban independence would necessitate confronting Spanish power elsewhere, we had better be ready to seize other of her possessions, even those at much greater remove from our shores.

When on February 15, 1898, Spain sank the U.S. battleship *Maine* while she lay at anchor in Havana Harbor—or, more accurately, when the ship sank after her forward gunpowder magazine exploded (the cause of which would never be convincingly proved)—Assistant Secretary Roosevelt's navy was prepared to avenge her. Without consulting Secretary Long (or President McKinley, either), Roosevelt issued a blizzard of directives readying the navy for war. In an extraordinary arrogation of authority, he sent a secret cable to the man he had maneuvered into command of the Asiatic Squadron, Commodore George Dewey, to load his ships with coal, make for Hong Kong, and be ready to commence "offensive operations in Philippine Islands."

Dewey did just that. In the early morning of May 1, 1898, five days after Spain and the United States formally declared war, Dewey gave his famous order to his subordinate, "You may fire when you are ready, Gridley." Seven hours later, virtually the entire Spanish squadron lay at the bottom of Manila Bay. Not a single American life was lost in the battle.

The Great White Fleet's fourteen-month circumnavigation of the globe ended Roosevelt's presidency on a triumphant note. He had intended the voyage as a declaration to Europe and Japan that America had arrived as a major world power, capable of projecting its power to the farthest reaches of the earth, and as a challenge to Japanese ambitions for supremacy in the Pacific.

The great naval powers of the time, following Mahan's injunction that concentration was "the a, b, c, of strategy," never separated their battleships. They massed their naval strength to dominate those waters where their primary strategic interests were. America's was an Atlantic fleet prepared to confront what statesmen of the time, including Roosevelt, believed was the principal threat to American security, the imperial ambitions of Germany. But Roosevelt also perceived an emerging threat to America's interests from Japan, a great naval power that had soundly defeated Russia in their war of 1905 and that believed it was destined to be master of Asia.

Roosevelt sent the fleet to the Pacific at a time of considerable tension between Japan and the United States. Nativist protests in San Francisco had erupted in violence over Japanese immigration, aggravating Japan's resentment of a San Francisco School Board decision to segregate Japanese American students. A skillful diplomat, TR had worked quietly and effectively to ease tensions and soothe Japan's wounded pride. But he suspected that the day would eventually come when diplomacy would no longer discourage Japan from settling by force of arms the growing rivalry between the two greatest Pacific powers, and he wanted Japan to understand just how formidable an opponent we would be. Toward that end, a mighty fleet in the Atlantic, even one that had recently rested at anchor in Yokohama harbor, would not serve as a lasting caution to Japanese militarists. America needed two fleets, one in both her oceans, and TR intended to see that we got them.

By the time he left office, American shipyards were turning out two battleships a year, and Congress had appropriated money to establish a base at Pearl Harbor as the new Pacific fleet's home. In time, the base would serve as headquarters for the largest operational command of the most powerful armed forces in the world, a command my father would hold sixty years after TR had sent the fleet around the world.

Ten days before Theodore Roosevelt left the presidency, he stood again on the deck of the *Mayflower* and watched the stately procession of his battleships, seven miles long, coming home to Hampton Roads. He had achieved his purposes. The world had taken respectful notice of this vivid display of American power—as had Americans themselves. For the principal purpose of Roosevelt's presidency was to summon the American people to greatness, to inspire an affection for the nation that surpassed the affection they held for other attachments, to encourage every American to consider the nation's grand destiny as much theirs as he felt it was his.

TR was too nearsighted to observe one skinny young ensign standing at attention on the deck of the fleet's flagship, the *Connecticut*. But I know that young man felt keenly the patriotism that his president had hoped the fleet's triumph would animate in every American, even if for the remainder of the ensign's life his affection for his country was indistinguishable from his affection for its navy. In a later year, during another Roosevelt's presidency, he would a command a part of America's Pacific fleet in the war with Japan that TR had anticipated thirty-five years earlier. But that day, a proud and grateful Ensign John Sidney McCain saluted the president whom he, his son, and his grandson would always regard as one of the greatest commanders in chief who ever ordered ships to sea. For the McCains of the United States Navy, as well as for many of our brother officers, presidents just didn't get much better than Teddy Roosevelt.

The allegiance my forebears felt to the father of the modern United States Navy undoubtedly marks the origins of my attachment to Teddy Roosevelt. But my avid, sustained interest in him is attributable to more than his singular contributions to American seapower. In the many biographies of TR that I've read over the years, biographies that more than any other influence except the navy have shaped my own sense of patriotism, I have always been so spellbound by the man's prodigiousness that I found as much virtue in his ceaseless activity as I have in his purposes. His was the most important presidency since Lincoln's. He invented the modern presidency by liberally interpreting the constitutional authority of the office to redress the imbalance of power between the executive and legislative branches that had tilted decisively toward Congress in the half century since the Civil War. He was an extraordinarily accomplished president. But by the time I reach the chapters describing those accomplishments, I am already overcome with a profound sense of inadequacy, impressed to the point of intimidation by the record of achievement TR could claim before he raised his right hand to take the oath of office as president.

He was only forty-two years old when an anarchist shot and killed President William McKinley and TR became the Republic's twenty-sixth president. Most people of my acquaintance, in whatever profession, are just beginning to come into their own by their mid- to late forties. Teddy Roosevelt had been a national figure for quite some time before his fourth decade. He was a "force of nature" in public life, a celebrated military hero and strategist, a prolific author, a crusading reformer in New York and national politics, a gifted amateur natural historian, the sickly child of a prominent Knickerbocker family who willed himself into becoming a tough, vigorous exemplar of the self-reliant frontiersman, the eastern swell who became a man of the people.

I've always liked to keep busy, and I've been blessed with enough restless energy to escape the boredom of leisure. In my time, I have had more than average ambition. But, my God, what a superior man TR was. Were I ever to start thinking a little better of my industry than its achievements warrant, I need only compare Roosevelt's life during the little more than two decades that elapsed between his graduation from Harvard and his succession to the presidency with my achievements in the forty-four years since I left the Naval Academy.

He graduated from Harvard in 1880, and after spending a few months at Columbia University Law School discovering he didn't want to be a lawyer, he became, at twenty-three, the youngest man ever elected to the New York State Assembly. He won reelection to a third term in 1883 by the widest margin of any New York legislator and was elected leader of the Republican minority in the assembly. He quit the legislature at the end of that term, served as a delegate to the Republican National Convention, and departed for the wild badlands of the Dakota Territory, where off and on for two years he ran two cattle ranches, stood up to local bullies who thought him a pampered snob, hunted game, and apprehended a gang of outlaws after a two-week chase. He returned to New York and a life in politics in 1886; ran for mayor of New York City and lost. In 1889, he was appointed U.S. Civil Service commissioner, serving in that office for the next six years in two presidential administrations. He resigned from the commission in 1895 to become president of the New York City Board of Police Commissioners. Two years later, he became assistant secretary in William McKinley's Navy Department. He resigned a little more than a year later, observing that "if I am to be of any use in politics, it is because I am supposed to be a man who does not preach what I fear to practice." He recruited, raised funds for, and trained a volunteer cavalry regiment, "the Rough Riders," bringing together in a common national cause his elite eastern cohorts and the kind of roughneck westerners he had come to respect and who had come to respect him while ranching in the Dakotas. He provided exemplary leadership under fire and showed conspicuous personal courage in the Battle for San Juan Heights. He lost eighty-nine of his troopers in the fight, was nominated for the Medal of Honor, and almost overnight became a national hero. Three months after the Rough Riders came home, their celebrated colonel was elected governor of New York. Two years later, in the 1900 presidential election, he was elected vice president of the United States. Less than a year later, McKinley was dead, and Theodore Roosevelt was president of the United States and about to begin the most productive years of his life.

Missing from this spare biographical sketch is any mention of the twelve books he authored, including the first two volumes of his influential four-volume *The Winning of the West* (he would write another twenty-three books over the course of his life). Nor does it provide the reader with any flavor, beyond his astonishing industry, for Roosevelt's character, his enthusiasms, his political principles. Most glaring is the absence of reference to the personal tragedies he suffered that impelled him to be a man of action. For in that twenty-year span, he lost the father he revered above all other men, the mother who had raised him on tales of dashing mariners, and the Boston society girl whom he married and loved unconditionally and who left him with an infant daughter. "Black care," he once wrote, "rarely sits behind the rider whose pace is fast enough."

That fantastic, frantic pace is what really drew me to Teddy Roosevelt. And although, when compared to his life, the sadness I've encountered in mine has been less daunting, just as my achievements have been less impressive, I understand the sentiment perfectly. Keep moving if you want to love life, and keep your troubles well behind you. He got married again, in 1886, to his childhood sweetheart, Edith Kermit Carow, who gave him five children and superintended the domestic tranquillity of their big house on Long Island's North Shore, and he just kept moving.

From the moment he set foot in Albany at the start of his career, Roosevelt established a reputation as an ostentatious reformer, a brash but indefatigable opponent of political corruption whose style and daring made for great copy, which his natural talent for public relations made all the more sensational. He could be impetuous, intemperate, egotistical, and entirely too self-confident for such a young man. He personalized political differences, attributing all manner of base motives to his opponents. They were cowards, his favorite epithet, or scoundrels, a close second. His public virtues were a little short on compassion, empathy, and patience. But he was incorruptible, courageous, resolute, and just, and he believed that the moral obligations that concerned individuals concerned government as well and nourished the soul of a great nation.

In 1899, he lectured the members of Chicago's Hamilton Club on the integration of individual and national morals. He had come to preach "not the doctrine of ignoble ease, but the doctrine of the strenuous life." He urged his audience to a "life of toil and effort, of labor and strife," a life of courage and duty and risk, in pursuit not only of personal glory, but of national greatness. "A mere life of ease is not in the end a very satisfactory life" for individuals or for nations. It corrupts governments as insidiously as it corrupts man and "ultimately unfits those who follow it for serious work in the world." It was his personal code of conduct and his governing philosophy. The code that had driven a frail, asthmatic child to physically transform himself into the vigorous, athletic outdoorsman who exulted in physical hardship as a welcome trial of character and body was the same code that aroused his abhorrence of materialism that consumed all of a society's dynamism. Base materialism, Roosevelt believed, tempted people to indolence and greed and tempted nations to "shrink like cowards" from the duty of playing "a great part in the world" and seek shelter in "the cloistered life which saps the hardy virtues of a nation, as it saps them in the individual."

The "strenuous life" was Roosevelt's definition of Americanism, a profession of faith in America's pioneer ethos, the virtues that had won the West and inspired our messianic belief in ourselves as the New Jerusalem, bound by sacred duty to suffer hardship and risk danger to protect the values of our civilization and impart them to humanity. "We cannot sit huddled within our own borders," he warned, "and avow ourselves merely an assemblage of well-to-do hucksters who care nothing for what happens beyond."

His Americanism was not a celebration of tribal identity. Nor was it limited to a sentimental attachment to our "amber waves of grain" or "purple mountains majesty." Roosevelt's Americanism exalted the political values of a nation where the people were sovereign, recognizing not only the inherent justice of self-determination, not only that freedom empowered individuals to decide their destiny for themselves, but that it empowered them to choose a common destiny. And for Roosevelt, that common destiny surpassed material gain and self-interest. Our freedom and our industry must aspire to more than acquisition and luxury. We must live out the true meaning of freedom and accept "that we have duties to others and duties to ourselves; and we can shirk neither."

Some critics saw in Roosevelt's patriotism only flag-waving chauvinism, not all that dissimilar to old world ancestral allegiances that incited one people to subjugate another and plunged whole continents into war. But they did not see the universality of the ideals that formed his creed.

Not long ago, I read an account of an Irishman's attempt to make the first crossing of the Antarctic on foot. In August 1914, Sir Ernest Shackleton placed an advertisement in a London newspaper:

MEN WANTED FOR HAZARDOUS JOURNEY. SMALL WAGES, BITTER COLD, LONG MONTHS OF COMPLETE DARKNESS, CONSTANT DANGER, SAFE RETURN DOUBTFUL. HONOUR AND RECOGNITION IN CASE OF SUCCESS.

Twenty-eight men who answered the ad began a twenty-two-month trial of wind, ice, snow, and endurance. Photographs of their expedition survive today, produced from plate-glass negatives that one of Shackleton's men dived into freezing Antarctic waters to rescue from their sinking ship. The deprivations these men suffered are almost unimaginable. They spent four months marooned on a desolate, ice-covered island before they were rescued by Shackleton himself. They endured three months of polar darkness and were forced to shoot their sled dogs for food. Their mission failed, but they recorded an epic of courage and honor that far surpassed the glory of the accomplishment that had exceeded their grasp. When they returned to England, most of them immediately enlisted to fight in World War I.

Years later, Shackleton looked back on the character of his shipmates. He had had the sublime privilege of witnessing a thousand acts of unselfish courage, and he understood the greater glory that it achieved. "In memories we were rich," he wrote. "We had pierced the veneer of outside things."

I thought when I read it that here, in that memorable turn of phrase, is the Roosevelt code. To pierce the veneer of outside things, to reach for something more ennobling than the luxuries that privilege and wealth or our own industry and innovation have placed within easy reach. For the memories of such small accomplishments are fleeting, attributable as they are to the fortuitous circumstances of our birth, and reflect little credit on our individual character or our nation's.

Nationalism is not intrinsically good. For it to be so, a nation must transcend attachments to land and folk to champion universal rights of freedom and justice that reflect and animate the virtues of its citizenry. Racism and despotism have perverted many a citizen's love of country into a noxious ideology, Nazism and Stalinism being two of the more malignant examples. National honor, no less than personal honor, has only the worth it derives from its defense of human dignity. Then, and only then, do terms like "patriotism," "honor," and "doing one's duty" have a moral quality, are they virtues in themselves. Many a patriotic German sought honor in doing one's duty to the führer and fatherland. History and humanity, not to mention a just God, scorn them for it. Prosperity, military power, a well-educated society are the attainments of a great nation, but they are not its essence. If they are used only in pursuit of self-interest or to serve unjust ends, they degrade national greatness. Nazi Germany was temporarily a powerful nation. It was never a great one.

There is no denying that the vigorous nationalism that Theodore Roosevelt preached and his summons to Americans to be a great civilizing force in the world were premised in part on his belief in the superiority of the Anglo-Saxon race. TR shared the common racist assumptions of his day, although he did not deny the humanity of races he felt inferior to his own. Neither did he profess race hatred or excuse the unlawful violence that such extreme bigotry sanctions. Nor did he consider racial inferiority to be a permanent biological condition; rather, he attributed it to environmental circumstances that retarded human evolution. Roosevelt believed that any race exposed to enlightened Western, particularly American, political, economic, and cultural values and institutions would come in time to possess the intellectual and moral capacity of the "dominant world races." In Roosevelt's lexicon, "race" was more often a reference to nation than color, though clearly he considered blacks, Asians, and Native Americans to be inferior to whites. He expressed his sturdy faith in the civilizing effect of the American "melting pot" in his opposition to the intolerant nativism of the era, and in social and political gestures, and they were little more than that, such as inviting Booker T. Washington to

dine at the White House and appointing a black man as head of the cus-
tomhouse in Charleston, South Carolina.

These sentiments, moderately progressive in his day, do not mitigate
the essential injustice of racism, then or now. And they are, of course, un-
acceptable as the theoretical premises of patriotism or foreign policy in our
more enlightened age. Americans have made great progress, thankfully, in
our attitudes toward racial differences. But although Roosevelt's racial
theories detracted from the larger quality of Roosevelt's nationalism, they
do not render it obsolete in our day. On the contrary, the fact that belief in
national greatness as the primary object of government offends certain assumptions of modern-day liberals and conservatives alike, assumptions
that exaggerate political differences, incapacitate government, and ener-
vate the public's patriotism, proves it relevance and its wisdom.

TR denounced what he called "hyphenated Americanism," immigrants who gave greater importance to political and cultural affinities with
the nation of their origin than to the values, responsibilities, and customs
of their American citizenship. The immigrant, he argued in an article for
Forum magazine in 1894, "must not bring in his old-world religious race
and national antipathies, but must merge them into love for our common
country." He opposed ethnic voting blocks, schools that used any language but English to teach immigrant children, prosecuting foreign political and sectarian quarrels in American public life, and state support of
parochial schools. He believed immigrants must be quickly and thoroughly Americanized, professing allegiance to one flag only and to the
ideals of the republic it represented.

But he was equally as emphatic that "know nothingism, in any form, is
as utterly un-American as foreignism." Immigrants were entitled to equal
justice under the law and all the rights and respect that descendants of
America's oldest families enjoyed. "It is a base outrage," he wrote, "to oppose a man because of his religion or birthplace."

The "intense and fervid Americanism" that Roosevelt preached ignored many of the contributions to American art, language, and politics
that the immigrant brought with him from the old world and that make
American life so distinct and so much richer than that of other nations.
But his insistence that every citizen owed primary allegiance to American

ideals, and to the symbols, habits, and consciousness of American citizenship, was as right then as it is now.

The modern liberal's defense of multiculturalism too often exceeds an appreciation of our diverse origins and becomes a celebration of our differences as more important than our unity. National greatness as the proper object of every American's citizenship offends the multicultural sensibilities of many liberals because they suspect its appeal ignores and even denigrates the distinctions of experience in American history. But its purpose is not to slight the American experience of any individual, race, or ethnic group, but to encompass and transcend those experiences in a shared and noble endeavor of building a civilization for the ages, a civilization in which all people may share in the rights and responsibilities of freedom.

Roosevelt also spoke out against "the spirit of provincial patriotism," which aggrandizes the pride and sentimental attachments most people feel for their communities and states into something greater than their national pride. He warned "that the overexaltation of the little community at the expense of the great nation" had ruined many nations and prevented the countries of South America from uniting in one great republic. He might have added its disastrous effect on our own republic when southerners were more loyal to their states than to the Union.

I was middle-aged before I could claim a hometown. Until I moved to Arizona, whenever I was asked, "Where are you from?" I always answered, "The United States." And I never felt any shame that I could not be more specific. I have discovered in the second half of my life the pleasure of fellowship in a community and region with its own distinctive character, and that experience has influenced my political convictions. But I have never let Arizona, though I love it dearly, become a rival for my affections for my country.

Like most conservatives, I believe those governments closest to the people are better suited than the federal government to shape and implement remedies to many national problems that affect communities and regions differently. But there are many things that only a federal government can do. Only the federal government can provide for the common defense and restrain powerful economic and social forces from pursuing their private or factional interests at the expense of the national interest.

Many contemporary conservatives have let their healthy skepticism about government sink into something unhealthy, an embittered loathing of the federal government. Government should be restrained from unnecessarily aggregating power at the expense of individual liberty. But it must not shrink from its duty to be the highest expression of the national will and the last bulwark against all assaults on our founding ideals. Some conservatives believe the federal government cannot be trusted with a leading role in the building of a great nation.

But our greatness depends upon our patriotism, and our patriotism is hardly encouraged when we cannot take pride in the highest public institutions, institutions that should transcend all sectarian, regional, and commercial conflicts to fortify the public's allegiance to the national community.

For different reasons, these extremes in liberal and conservative thought give less value to the duties inherent in American citizenship. Liberals focus on wants, and conservatives focus on rights. But neither emphasizes the obligations of a free people to the nation that protects our rights and makes it possible for us to satisfy our wants.

Teddy Roosevelt did. He had loved his father above all others. But among the many ways that his father's rectitude shaped his son's character, perhaps the most important influence came from one of the few blemishes in his father's biography. During the Civil War, out of consideration for his wife's delicate nature and her southern origins, Theodore Roosevelt Sr., like many men of his wealth and social station, paid for a substitute to take his place in the ranks of the Union army. This shamed his son, though he would never admit it, and goes a long way toward explaining his ardent desire to share the hardships and dangers of wars he thought necessary to the security and character of the nation. Not only did Roosevelt resign his office as assistant secretary of the navy, over his president's objections, to fight in the war against Spain he had done so much to bring about, but as an aging ex-president he had pleaded with Woodrow Wilson to allow him to raise and command a volunteer division in World War I. When Wilson refused, Roosevelt hated him for it and never forgave him.

In the Roosevelt code, the authentic meaning of freedom gave equal respect to self-interest and common purpose, to rights and duties. And it absolutely required that every loyal citizen take risks for the country's sake. He understood the central fact of American history: that we are not just an association of disparate interests forced by law and custom to tolerate one another, but a kinship of ideals, worth living and dying for, and that deserves to have our ideals vigorously represented at home and abroad by our national government. He believed that people who are free to act in their own interests and are served by a government that kindles the pride of every citizen would perceive their interests in an enlightened way. We would live as one nation, at the summit of human history, "the mightiest republic on which the sun ever shone."

When Roosevelt was an energetic reformer on the U.S. Civil Service Commission, he described the origins of his political philosophy. "When I left college," he wrote, "I had no strong governmental convictions beyond the very strong and vital conviction that we were a nation and must act nationally." By the end of his presidency, I think it's fair to say that he never had another conviction that strong and vital.

Promising a "square deal" to all, he fought party bosses who valued political privileges more than just government. He wrenched reforms from legislators who thought their power to award patronage positions was the purpose of elective office. He called for the elimination of political campaign contributions from corporations because he knew their largesse vastly exceeded the support that Americans of average means could provide and would influence elected officials to show favor to the wealthy few at the expense of the less advantaged many.

He distrusted leading financiers of his day who put profit before patriotism. He sued to break up railroad trusts, mediated disputes between capital and labor, and pursued sensible and incremental regulation of commerce. He respected the role business conglomerates played in America's emergence as a great economic power, but he also understood that unrestrained laissez-faire capitalism would crush competition from smaller businesses and threaten the three most important values his Square Deal was intended to protect: "energy, self-reliance, and individual initiative."

He distrusted the mob no less than rapacious capitalism, and muckrakers (a term he coined) no less than corrupt politicians. When populism became radicalized into anarchism or socialism or any other ism that challenged America's unifying values, he thought it required a government response that was "not over-scrupulous about bloodshed." And he thought crusading journalists whose social criticism provoked divisive class politics rather than help restore public confidence and national pride were "one of the most potent forms of evil."

He was a fighting man. It was in his nature to find as much virtue in the battle itself as in the prize. For Roosevelt, fighting determined character. He displayed his truculence most frequently in overwrought invective (he likened the backbones of William McKinley and Oliver Wendell Holmes to a chocolate éclair and a banana, respectively).

But he could not content himself with the opportunities politics provided him to fight with pen and speech. Even his recreation resembled combat. Washingtonians grew accustomed to seeing the president gallop his horse, scramble up cliffs, and chop through the currents of Rock Creek and the Potomac River, activities he seemed to enjoy most in inclement weather. He fenced with sticks with General Leonard Wood and boxed with young officers in the East Room of the White House. The physical punishment he suffered in these contests, cracked ribs, broken arms, and blindness in his left eye, never seemed to diminish his enjoyment of them.

I have never entirely lost my adolescent admiration for that kind of pugnacious vitality, and Roosevelt's extraordinary zest for combat, both the physical and rhetorical varieties, remains the source of much of his appeal to me. But fortunately, I have had enough experience with fighting to have learned that having the will to fight is no great virtue if its object is simply self-conceit. Roosevelt believed fighting was essential to a happy life. I know what he meant. But what we fight for matters more than how well we fight, and Roosevelt understood this, too. He was certainly capable of letting the satisfaction his ego derived from facing danger and hardship cloud his judgment. He could sentimentalize combat to an absurd extent. He once declared that "no triumph of peace is quite so great as the supreme triumphs of war." But for all of his natural belligerence, and his aggressive statesmanship, its excesses and its worthwhile accomplishments, he was always intent on the well-being and elevation of his country.

He threatened war with Germany over the kaiser's designs on Venezuela and issued a corollary to the Monroe Doctrine that reserved to the

United States the right to intervene militarily in Latin American countries where disorder might attract the unwelcome attention of other great powers. He helped foment insurrection in Panama, then a part of Colombia, so that he could acquire the route for his isthmian canal. But his purpose was not to seek war and conquest for personal or even national glory. He sought to preserve peace and order by confronting potential adversaries with America's resolve and readiness to fight if necessary to protect its interests.

He was actually a deft, subtle, and quite discreet diplomat. He kept Germany from invading Venezuela. He mediated the Russo-Japanese War, for which he was awarded the Nobel Peace Prize, and helped resolve a brewing European conflict over Morocco. His accomplished diplomacy contributed as much to America's growing world influence as did his expansion and projection of American military power and his unilateral assumption of international rights and responsibilities.

He fastened his restless, striving ego to the cause of his country, and although his flaws and his virtues shaped the character of the Union no less than they shaped the character of the man, it was, on the whole, a fortunate alliance for both Roosevelt and America. America came of age under his leadership. We became a better country.

Many politicians, in his age as well as ours, tend to be preoccupied with extending our own and our party's hold on power. Our ambitions for our country, which we may or may not serve well, are too often subordinate to our personal and partisan ambitions. Self-aggrandizement is part of human nature, and Roosevelt was not above its temptations. He gave up the presidency voluntarily at the end of his second term, but he wanted it back four years later for personal as well as public reasons. Yet the very thought that he would seek high office (or any office, for that matter) for purposes more self-serving than patriotic deeply offended his sense of citizenship and his self-esteem.

Earlier, as president of the police board, Roosevelt had waged a relentless and, as always, highly personal campaign to clean up the notoriously dishonest New York City police force. He nightly prowled the city's streets looking for delinquent police officers, often in the company of two friends, Lincoln Steffens and Jacob Riis, journalists who had made their

reputation by exposing much of the corruption then endemic in munici-
pal government. Roosevelt's growing celebrity as a colorful, ambitious reformer prompted Riis to ask him if he intended to run for president of
the United States someday. The question provoked Roosevelt to furious
anger. "Don't you dare ask me that. Don't you put such ideas in my head!"
he screamed at his two friends. "I won't let myself think of it . . . because
if I do, I'll begin to work for it. I'll be careful, calculating, cautious in word
and act, . . . and I'll beat myself." He then ordered the two surprised reporters to leave his office with a final admonition: "Don't you ever mention that to me again."

Theodore Roosevelt, however much he craved the limelight, could not
satisfy his ego, much less his party's ambitions, unless they served the
higher purpose of his nation's greatness. And that deeply personal, almost
spiritual, sense of patriotism made the man as great as his accomplishments.

"This country," he said, "would not be a permanently good place for
any of us to live in unless we make it a reasonably good place for all of us
to live in." And he fought to make it so. He fought the railroad trusts and
invested the Interstate Commerce Commission with the power to set
rates. He investigated the notoriously unsanitary meatpacking industry
and, with the enactment of the Pure Food and Drug Act, placed public
health before the rights of businessmen to maximize their profits. He
fought the spirit of "unrestricted individualism" that claimed the right "to
injure the future of all of us for his own temporary and immediate profit."
Over the course of his presidency, he took 230 million acres of land into
public trust, creating 150 national forests, 18 national monuments, 5 national parks, 51 federal bird sanctuaries, 4 national game preserves, and 24
reclamation projects.

Roosevelt's Square Deal was a promise to treat all Americans fairly,
rich and poor, capitalist and worker, manufacturer and consumer. He was
not a radical reformer. He sought not to destroy the great wealth-creating
institutions of capitalism, but to save them from their own excesses. He
didn't assert federal authority over public lands to deprive farmers and
ranchers of their livelihood. He surely intended to preserve for future generations ample parts of the natural heritage that had enriched his own life.

But he was equally devoted to managing the country's natural resources so that they could continue to sustain national prosperity. His reforms were as sensible as they were just.

He wasn't a zealot who disdained the compromises and concessions essential to lawmaking in a democracy. That, in his view, was no better than muckraking. He wanted to get things done. He wasn't an ideologue, except in this respect: "that we were a nation and must act nationally." Whatever strengthened the unity and values of the nation was worth championing, and whatever threatened them had to be fought.

When he left the presidency, he found opportunities in private life to accommodate his ceaseless activity, but none could invest his enterprise with the grand purpose he found in public life. He went on a year-long safari in Africa to hunt specimens for the Smithsonian Institution. He left Africa for a three-month tour of Europe, where he lectured the French on citizenship in a republic, argued with the pope, and met as an equal (if not better) with assorted monarchs.

His successor and friend, William Howard Taft, had failed, in Roosevelt's eyes, to live up to the Roosevelt code or follow the directions for presidential leadership that TR had left for him. So he challenged Taft for the Republican nomination in 1912. Roosevelt won more delegates, but the party leaders, who exhausted themselves just contemplating another Roosevelt presidency, gave the nomination to Taft anyway. Roosevelt joined forces with the Progressive Party and ran as their candidate for president. He won a larger percentage of the vote than any third-party candidate before or since, yet he came in second, assuring the presidency to the Democratic candidate, Woodrow Wilson.

In 1910, as he was considering whether to support the successor who had disappointed him or return to the arena himself, Roosevelt traveled to Osawatomie, Kansas, to lay out his agenda for an active and just government. He called it the "New Nationalism," but it was mostly a rearrangement of his Square Deal policies into a more cohesive doctrine, dressed up in slightly more progressive language. It was his summons to the party of Lincoln to recover its ethical heritage, its primary allegiance to the integrity of the nation as the animating principle of all public service, that made the speech inspirational and ageless.

In Roosevelt's code, Americans who possessed the least and sacrificed the most were the greatest paragons of public virtue. And he began his speech with a tribute to the plain people who had neither the means nor the desire to seek release from their patriotic duty. "To the Grand Army of the Republic, they deserve honor and recognition such is paid to no other citizens of the Republic; . . . because of what you did we of today walk, each of us, head erect, and proud that we belong, not to one of a dozen squabbling contemptible commonwealths, but to the mightiest nation upon which the sun shines." Their sacrifice obliged every subsequent American generation to uphold the ideal they had fought for and to recognize as Lincoln had that "while a man exists it is his duty to improve not only his own condition, but to assist in ameliorating mankind's."

Near the end of the 1912 campaign, knowing he faced defeat, Roosevelt lived through perhaps the most inspirational moment of his public career. And with his natural talent for personifying the public virtues he made his life's work, he milked the moment for all it was worth. As he prepared to give a speech in Milwaukee, a man stepped from the crowd and shot him in the chest. The bullet had to pass through a copy of his long speech folded in his breast pocket and his metal eyeglass case before it came to rest near his heart. The resulting decrease in the bullet's velocity saved Roosevelt's life and spared him from serious injury. Nevertheless, the doctors summoned to examine the wound wanted, quite understandably, to take the bleeding ex-president to the nearest hospital. Roosevelt would have none of it. He knew the wound wasn't mortal, and although he was in considerable pain, he knew a public moment such as this didn't come but once, and he seized it.

Stepping to the podium, and unbuttoning his vest to reveal his bloodstained shirt to the crowd, Roosevelt apprised his audience of his condition. "I have just been shot; but it takes more than that to kill a bull moose," he told his awestruck listeners. "The bullet is in me now, so I cannot make a very long speech, but I will try my best." His public duty was more important than his life, he assured them, and should it cost him his life, that was no great concern to him. Nor should it arouse their concern. "For no man has had a happier life than I have led, a happier life in every way." However much he appreciated the dramatic effect of his public stoicism, I'm sure he meant every word of it. With his matchless industry and courage, he had outpaced "black care" all his life as he willed himself and his country to greatness. He had found happiness in service to his country, and whatever trials and disappointments he had encountered did not spoil his recollection that he had loved every day of it.

Even in the last years of life, when age, injury, and tragedy had greatly slowed his pace, he was still trying to race ahead of his troubles. At his death in 1919, he was considered to be a probable and formidable candidate for his party's presidential nomination. The years between the 1912 election and his death had been a trial. He sent all four of his sons to France to fight in World War I while he stayed behind, bitter that he wasn't allowed to join them. His youngest son, Quentin, died a hero there, and the loss hurt him deeply. But he tried to keep his grief at bay with the knowledge that though Quentin had lived a mere twenty years, he had had "his crowded hour," which in the Roosevelt code was all any man needed for self-fulfillment.

The days left to Roosevelt were too few to manage one last escape from sorrow. He died less than six months after Quentin. He had entered the presidency at forty-two, left it at fifty, and died at sixty. A short life, but a long, crowded hour. His entire existence had been joined to his country's cause. In his autobiography he wrote, "There were all kinds of things I was afraid of at first, ranging from grizzly bears to mean horses and gunfighters; but by acting as if I was not afraid I gradually ceased to be afraid." And that learned courage urged him always forward. Since Quentin's death he had published his last book, *The Great Adventure,* and had begun preparing for another run for the presidency. But death took him unawares, in his sleep.

His last words were to his valet: "Please put out the light." Had he known they were to be his last words, I'm sure he would have chosen something more memorable, something emblematic of his code. He might have counseled the old and faithful servant not to grieve for him, for "[n]o man has had a happier life than I have led, a happier life in every way."

With Senator Russ Feingold (D-Wis.), on Capitol Hill, Wednesday, March 20, 2002, following a final passage on campaign finance reform. *Dennis Cook*

ELEVEN

MAVERICK

The television in my office was tuned to the Senate floor so that I could keep an eye on the debate that was then under way about an amendment I had offered that afternoon. Casual observers watching the debate on C-SPAN wouldn't have found much of the discussion or the amendment to be controversial. The stakes involved weren't what anyone would consider critical to the health of the Republic.

Washington is one of the few major American cities that still have a conveniently located airport. Reagan National Airport is just across the Potomac River from downtown Washington. Most important to my colleagues and me, it is just a ten-minute drive from Capitol Hill. Because many members of Congress commute most weeks from their states, hustling after the final vote on Thursday or Friday to catch the last daily flight to Columbus or Shreveport or Phoenix, as I do, Reagan National is a treasured convenience. Without it we would have to travel forty minutes or longer in rush-hour traffic to one of two other airports located in more distant Virginia and Maryland suburbs.

It is all the more beloved by us for the special parking privileges provided to a select few travelers. The parking lot closest to the main terminal is reserved for members of Congress, Supreme Court justices, and the heads of foreign embassies represented in Washington. It is damn handy. The rest of the flying public tends to resent this little perquisite of high office. As they struggle with their luggage while racing over a much greater distance to make their flight or reach their car and head for home after a fatiguing journey, they often spy us making the short walk to and from our cars in comparative ease.

It's a small thing, to be sure. There is, to state the obvious, no abuse of office involved. And I doubt very much that the convenience represents an aristocratic sense of entitlement unwholesome in a democracy. But it does tend to stick in the craw of people who believe the demands on their time are just as many and just as important as are those that vex the people they elect to office. I've had more than one occasion to notice how much this minor privilege offends the egalitarian sensibilities of Americans. When I still used the privilege, many a weary traveler, on his way to a more remote parking lot, had passed by me as I settled myself into my car, and signaled his displeasure by waving at me with his middle finger. I appreciated the point of view well enough not to return the greeting.

As a small gesture of respect for popular sovereignty, I suggested that Congress terminate the perk, since it seemed to contribute to the public's cynicism about their government. The parking lot was merely a symbol, and a misconstrued one at that, of what people believed their federal government had become—a privileged sanctuary for politicians with inflated egos who had forgotten who sent us to office and why they had sent us. And I didn't believe that by relinquishing this one trivial convenience, we could redress the widespread public cynicism about Congress and national politics in general that has become so pervasive in recent years. To reverse that trend would require far more serious changes in the practices and institutions of our democracy than surrendering a parking space. I just thought that if by adding a few minutes to our walk to an airport terminal we could offer people a small proof that we weren't quite as preoccupied with our own privileges as they believed, it was probably worth doing.

Honesty obliges me to confess that there is also something in my nature that enjoys throwing bricks at customs that smack of pretension, and sometimes my behavior reveals more vanity on my part than was evident in the practice I denounce. No doubt this trait influenced somewhat my decision to offer an amendment to open the airport's reserved parking lot to the public. When I offered the amendment, I did so with complete confidence that few, if any, of my colleagues would vote against it, given the extent of public resentment about the privilege. I also knew that most politicians adhere to the rule that if you can't explain a vote to your constituents in one minute or less, you've cast the wrong vote. Explaining why they were entitled to a free convenience that was denied their constituents would take a little longer than what most politicians would consider the average duration of a convincing argument.

So, after I offered the amendment and briefly described its purpose, I left the Senate floor for my office, pretty confident that I needn't stick around to make sure I had the votes. I knew that many of my colleagues would resent my proposal and that I would little endear myself to them, although they had grown accustomed to my populist gestures. But I didn't expect any of them to voice their resentment publicly or to vote against it. I had suggested that a voice vote on the amendment would be fine with me, since members need not trouble themselves to come to the floor to vote for something that was sure to pass. All of us loved the perk and would no doubt sorely miss it. But we also knew the public wouldn't be sympathetic to our defense of it, to say the least.

Jack Danforth proved my presumption wrong. He disliked my amendment intensely, and even more did he dislike the motives he believed were behind it. So he came to the floor, announced he would insist on a roll call vote, and began to disparage the proposal at length in the most eloquent and passionate terms, to my surprise and discomfort. I was busy discussing other business with staff at the time he began speaking, so it took a few moments for his voice, emanating from my television, to catch my attention. Once it did, I stopped our discussion and began to watch him intently as he heaped scorn on what he called "this dreadful amendment."

Oddly, since his scorn was intended for both the amendment and its author, I found myself moved, even inspired, by his speech. Jack Danforth is an honorable man and was an exemplary public servant. An ordained minister in the Episcopal Church, a man of moderate views and humble disposition, and a senator who took his public trust very seriously, he had no detractors I knew of in either party. His colleagues bestowed on him the nickname St. Jack, without a trace of irony. The people of Missouri were lucky to have him in the Senate. He was also a good friend to me. He had publicly defended and privately counseled me during the Keating scandal. He even occasionally dropped by just to sit with me in my office during the lowest moments of that ordeal. I didn't exactly enjoy the dressing-down he was now giving me. There were moments in his speech when I wished I had been on the floor to interrupt him and fire back. But my respect for him as a person and a public servant obliged me to consider his argument with the seriousness it deserved, however injurious it was to my amendment's prospects and to my reputation.

It was quite a performance, so compelling, in fact, that he single-handedly defeated the amendment, which would have passed overwhelmingly if the vote had been taken before Jack rose to oppose it. Jack had already announced that he would be leaving the Senate at the end of the year, so his lack of personal interest in where his former colleagues would be parking their cars gave his argument force. He did find a great public interest in the question, however, and he used the debate to address the much larger question of the present condition of the public's trust in its government. It was a patriot's speech. There was little in it that did not ring true to my ears, with the exception of our disagreement about my intentions in offering the amendment and the effect I wanted it to have on the very condition that had motivated my support and his opposition.

The gist of Jack's argument was that the public's healthy skepticism about government had corroded into unhealthy cynicism that was debilitating our democracy. Talk radio demagogues were fanning the flames of that cynicism, as were politicians who pandered to it. He observed that contrary to popular opinion, members of Congress were hardworking and dedicated public servants for whom sixty- and seventy- and even eighty-hour workweeks were the norm. To conduct our public business, we get to inhabit a splendid Capitol, employ large staffs, and enjoy all the rituals and prestige of holding high office. We get to travel at home and abroad at public expense. We can avail ourselves of any number of small conveniences, such as being able to get quickly to an airport so that we could fly home and spend most of our weekends meeting with our constituents and attending to other public duties. But these privileges are insignificant, he argued, when weighed against the sacrifices made by members and their families. They are poor compensation for the satisfying private life that public life demands we surrender.

"It is said by the senator from Arizona we should live like everybody else. Who else lives this kind of life?"

All these points were valid and worth making. We do work hard. Our private lives do suffer. And we don't have lives of unlimited luxury and privilege. Jack also correctly observed that far from being out of touch with public sentiment, we were, thanks to advances in transportation, telecommunications, and political polling, "in touch to a fault. We have lost the sense of statesmanship because we are so afraid of offending everybody. We are so much in touch that we do not necessarily do the job of good government."

Ours was a noble profession, he argued quite persuasively. And we should not join in slandering the office or officeholders by offering legislation that implies we are nothing more than self-interested drains on the federal treasury. When we do so, we weaken the very thing we purport to revere: the public's trust in government and their active citizenship in the public affairs of our great nation. My amendment, he alleged, pandered to an "erroneous and ferocious cynicism."

I think public service is the most honorable profession in this country. I believe that most members of Congress are industrious. There is some sense of elitism in Congress, but not much more than in numerous other professions. Most politicians believe themselves to be the tribune of the common man and woman. I don't argue with that, and I found Jack's defense of our honor to be as stirring as his admonition not to aggravate public cynicism lest we do more damage to the country than we do to ourselves.

But public cynicism will not be allayed by defending the honor of politicians. The cynicism is real, profound, and has increased every year since the turbulent sixties to the point that it no longer provokes as much public anger as it does indifference to government, to the people who serve in government, and to the important work we are supposed to do. I don't mind anger. I think it's good to get riled up about politics and government, as long as it doesn't sink to cruelty or hate. The progress of a great nation and the values upon which it was founded are worth fighting about. It invigorates our politics and makes our democracy self-renewing. But indifference and alienation are lethal to us. It is a ceiling on our greatness because it dissuades people from voting or participating in any meaningful way in the life of our democracy.

Politicians are not the sole cause of this condition. Jack was right to point out certain absurd expectations in popular opinion that, when they are not met because they could not possibly be met, contribute to public cynicism. Contrary to popular opinion, congressional salaries do not take up a huge percentage of the federal budget. Cutting all foreign aid will not make enough money available to ensure the solvency of the Social Security Trust Fund. The public must accept its obligations to be informed and constructive critics. But politicians have contributed in many ways, by sins of omission and sins of commission, to the growing estrangement of Americans from their representatives and to their lack of everyday involvement in public affairs, and that is a stain upon our honor and America's.

My token gesture of solidarity with public opposition to a parking privilege wasn't meant to imply that we had purposely sought an advantage that we knew would further aggravate this worrisome condition. I meant only to recognize that people mistook such things for self-aggrandizement. Because we have failed in other ways to sustain their trust, and have not yet done much to restore it, every appearance that inadvertently exacerbates their distrust is a far more serious injury than it would be had we made other, more serious attempts to rekindle Americans' pride in their government.

Jack persuaded a majority of senators to vote against my amendment. It was a tribute to him as well as his argument. He is a decent man. He made us all feel better about ourselves, and I give his patriotism great credit. I didn't begrudge him the victory, even though it came at my expense. And I waited until after the vote before I tried to explain that my amendment was not, as Jack had argued, an attack on the integrity of the Senate.

> My disagreement with the Senator from Missouri is not over whether the Senate merits my respect, but over the reasons for which I owe that respect. . . .

My respect is not, in the end, only a respect for the Senate itself with all its attendant privileges and obligations. My respect is for the idea of the Senate, for the idea of public service in America that it represents: that in this country neither circumstances of birth nor ranks of privilege nor the acclaim of elites qualify you for public office. It is only the trust of your equals, by which I mean every other American, which entitles you to serve in the United States Senate.

Ours is not a government of uncommon men and women. . . . Ours is a government of the people, and the privilege, the only meaningful privilege of service in this government is that the people have entrusted you with their interests and should you represent those interests faithfully you will have the singular satisfaction of justifying their trust. When the people perceive any distinction between their interests and ours—whether that distinction is apparent or real—then we will lose that most precious commodity—the hopefully given, but closely guarded trust of the people who sent us here. . . .

I did not represent my amendment as a historical advance for the nation. I simply saw that one of the perquisites of our office was perceived by our employers as an inappropriate distinction between us and them. And if the removal of that distinction could effect some restoration of our common identification then it would be worth the loss of a very small convenience. My effort was born of respect, it was not an affront to it. . . .

I neither require nor expect to ever be identified as anything greater than an American. I have found more than enough honor in that distinction to last a lifetime. Any effort to demonstrate how honored we are to be of the people—no matter how small or symbolic—has real value, and is a useful contribution to the preservation of this institution and the noble idea upon which it rests.

It was a rather grandiloquent speech for such a seemingly trivial dispute. And I don't usually explain myself to my colleagues quite that formally or as often as I should, given how frequently I do things that upset them. But Jack had spoken like a true patriot, and I feared he had found my patriotism wanting. It was out of respect for him, for the Senate, and for myself that I felt obliged to account for my action in a more philosophical way than I usually do.

I have never been able to distinguish my reputation as a man from my reputation as a politician. Deficiencies in the execution of my public responsibilities are deficiencies in my character and burden my conscience to no lesser extent. I know I have done things in my career that have contributed to the decline in public respect for the institutions of government and for the practice of politics. I make jokes about how hard it is to do the Lord's work in the city of Satan. There have been times when I put my personal ambitions before the public interest. I have sometimes placed party allegiance above obligations to my constituents and country. Few politicians are above such temptations, and I am not one of them.

I don't believe that government is defined only by the imperfections of its officeholders, any more than I believe that the character of an individual is defined entirely by its flaws. But I do believe that those who answer the call of public service must accept that we are accountable to a higher standard of public virtue than those who do not. Our failures affect more than ourselves, our families, or our friends. They debilitate public patriotism and affect the destiny of the nation.

The mistakes, misplaced priorities, even the malfeasance of politicians, and the public distrust of government they breed, are not the sole cause of declining patriotism and the public's indifference to the appeal of active citizenship. Our culture, no less than our politics, emphasizes our differences more than our unity. Our schools don't always instruct children in the obligations of citizenship as thoroughly as they once did. Our art often poses community and national identity as threats to self-awareness, and civic obligations as impediments to self-fulfillment. Journalism often provides a narrative of public affairs that sees politics and government as merely a contest between various personalities and interest groups. Many corporate leaders see government only as a contracting agent or a restraint on markets and profitability. Labor bosses see government as the battleground of class warfare. Even some religious leaders use the political process to enhance their personal influence in ways that detract from the values of their faith they wish to communicate to the nation at large.

On an early December morning many years ago, I watched my father leave for war. He joined millions of Americans to fight a war that would decide the fate of humanity. They fought cruel and formidable enemies bent on world domination. They fought not just for themselves and their families. They fought for love of an idea: that America stood for something greater than the sum of our individual interests.

From where did the courage come to make the maximum effort in that decisive moment in history? It marched with the sons of a nation that believed deeply in itself, in its history, in the justice of its cause, in its destiny. Americans went into battle armed against despair with the common conviction that the country that had sent them there was worth their sacrifice. Their families, their schools, their faith, their history, their heroes, had taught them that the freedom with which they were blessed was worth fighting and suffering for. Those who came home returned with an even deeper civic love. They believed that if America was worth dying for, then surely she was worth living for. They built an even greater nation than the one they had left their homes to defend; an America that offered more opportunities to more people than ever before; an America that began to redress the injustices that had been visited on too many of her citizens for too long; an America that remained engaged in the world, determined to be the greatest force for good on earth.

The attacks on America of September 11, for all the terrible suffering they caused, did have one good effect. Americans instinctively grasped that the terrorists who organized the attacks mistook materialism for the only value of liberty. They believed that liberty was corrupting, that the right of individuals to pursue happiness made societies weak. They held us in contempt. Spared by prosperity from the hard uses of life, bred by liberty only for comfort and easy pleasure, we were, they thought, no match for the violent, cruel struggle they planned for us.

Paradoxically, national unity has suffered in times of peace and prosperity, the very conditions that prove the efficacy of our political values and our active engagement in the world to promote them. But when our ideals were threatened by people who despise them, Americans quickly remembered why we love those ideals and how they unite us. It shook us from our complacency. It reminded us that each generation of Americans must prove again that a nation conceived in liberty is inherently greater than any nation ordered to exalt the few at the expense of the many or made of a common race or culture or maintained to preserve traditions that have no greater attribute than longevity.

Patriotism flourished in the wake of September 11, and that is as heartening to me as it is to every American. Public confidence in government has improved, strengthened by the skill with which the president and his cabinet have organized our defense, by the courage and ability of our military, and by the lack of partisanship in Congress in our response to the attacks. But can we sustain that confidence and sense of unity? Can we sustain our patriotism when the threat is vanquished? That is a challenge and an obligation to us all. But it is the privilege of government to set the example for the nation.

Too often those of us who hold a public trust have failed to set the necessary example. Too often our partisanship seems all-consuming. Our differences are defined with derision. Too often we put parochial or personal interests before the national interest. When the people believe that government no longer serves national unity, no longer embodies our founding ideals, then basic civil consensus will deteriorate as people seek substitutes for the unifying values of patriotism. National pride will not survive the people's contempt for government. And national pride should be as indispensable to the happiness of Americans as is our self-respect.

I can understand how the occasional stridency of my arguments, and the apparent futility of my attempts to reform certain practices of Congress, have led some observers to puzzle over why I have made pet grievances of what are fairly well-established traditions. Some of my critics believe that in a very calculated way, I have used these issues to rebuild a reputation for integrity damaged by my involvement in the Keating scandal. Some suspect that I style myself as a reformer to gain favorable press interest. Some think I do it simply because I enjoy being a pain in the ass. There is an element of truth in each charge, but they don't explain my actions and the motives behind them.

Admittedly, my involvement in the Keating scandal roused my initial interest in changing the way campaigns for Congress are financed. I first began to become involved in the effort during and shortly after the scandal, when former senator David Boren sponsored legislation to overhaul campaign finance laws. His reforms were more extensive than the reforms I later came to sponsor myself, and I voted in favor of his legislation partly because I had to rehabilitate my political reputation.

But my personal experience with scandal also taught me to recognize how much disproportionate campaign giving from what are euphemistically described as special interests caused the public to question the integrity of officeholders. Questions of honor are raised as much by appearances as by reality in politics, and because they incite public distrust, they need to be addressed no less directly than we would address evidence of expressly illegal corruption. By the time I became a leading advocate of campaign finance reform, I had come to appreciate that the public's suspicions were not always mistaken. Money does buy access in Washington, and access increases influence that often results in benefiting the few at the expense of the many.

There are, thankfully, few incidents of out-and-out bribery in Congress. But the favoritism shown major campaign donors is only a little less injurious to our reputations and to the public welfare than corruption proscribed by law. I learned that in experiences subsequent to my unhappy days as a Keating Five.

Those who criticize my reform efforts as posturing for what they disparage as the liberal East Coast media misunderstand the relationship. There is little institutional interest in reforming entrenched traditions, traditions under which most politicians have prospered handsomely. Only public opinion can force change, and the only way to arouse public opinion is through the media. The country is too big and Americans are too preoccupied with other matters to motivate them with speeches on the Senate floor or in other public forums.

I generally like reporters and enjoy their company. So I don't mind in the least spending time talking to them. I also hold a somewhat better view of the role of the media in public affairs than do some of my conservative brethren. Many conservatives see the establishment media as advocating an agenda of their own, an agenda that conflicts with ours, so they strive to get their message out through alternative media—talk radio, mostly, and paid advertising. For the latter they need a lot of money, hence their reluctance to restrain the flow of contributions to our campaigns.

The establishment media may very well have more liberal proclivities than most Republicans. But why should that intimidate us? We shouldn't expect to address the issues we champion only with interrogators whose views are compatible with our own. Contrary to conservative suspicions, I have had to defend positions that are unpopular with the editorial boards of many leading newspapers and, at times, unpopular with a majority of the public. Certainly I've had extensive editorial support for my campaign finance reforms, but those same editorial pages have criticized many other of my positions. And when I have defended those positions, reporters haven't denied me the opportunity to make my case to the public, whether they agreed with me or not.

To what extent are my assaults on certain political traditions the expressions of a truculent nature? I don't know. My temper has often been a matter of both public speculation and personal concern. I have a temper, to state the obvious, which I have tried to control with varying degrees of success because it does not always serve my interest or the public's. I have regretted losing my temper on many occasions. But there are things worth getting angry about in politics, and I have at times tried to use my anger to incite public outrage. I make no apologies for that. And those occasions are not reserved solely for debates about campaign finance reform. I believe that when public servants lose their capacity for outrage over practices injurious to the national interest, they have outlived their usefulness to the country.

My opposition to the way Congress spends money is the practice that I have contended with the longest, that has often triggered my temper, and that has provoked far more displeasure from my colleagues than has my support for campaign finance reform. Long before I took up the cause of campaign finance reform, I was taking issue with the venerable congressional tradition of pork barrel spending. There are, it is often observed, three parties in Congress, Republicans, Democrats, and appropriators. The Appropriations Committees of Congress have assumed, for all practical purposes, sole discretion in deciding how and where the resources of the federal treasury will be spent. Our civics textbooks tell us that the president proposes and the Congress disposes. But they do not tell us that within Congress, the only members doing the disposing are members of the Appropriations Committees. The other committees of Congress are supposed to authorize how much appropriators can spend and on what. But the appropriators pay even less attention to the views of the authorizing committees than they do to the president's proposals.

The purest expression of their supremacy is the appropriations "earmark." This practice designates money to be spent on a specific project, almost always of personal or parochial interest to a member or members of the Appropriations Committees. Seldom is the project requested by the president or authorized by other congressional committees. The merit or lack thereof of an earmark is not scrutinized. They are not subjected to competitive bids. There are no criteria of any kind used to determine their public value. Some may be worthwhile expenditures of federal revenue. Many more are not. Few serve any large national interest.

Nor is there any effective way for other members of Congress to render a judgment about them. If they are voted on at all, it is only in committee "markup," when the Appropriations Committees meet to put large spending bills together that contain dozens, sometimes hundreds, of individual earmarks. The full Senate or House can vote to strike an earmark from an appropriations bill or they can vote against an entire appropriations bill. But that is something very few members of Congress would do lest they incur the wrath of the appropriators, who would look harshly on future requests for funding projects in their districts and states.

Often, earmarks aren't even included in the appropriations bills voted on by the full House and Senate. They are added in conference committee, when House and Senate appropriators meet to reconcile differences in their bills. Conference reports can be rejected by the full House and Senate and sent back to conference committee, or they can be adopted. But their provisions cannot be stripped from the bill by amendments offered on the floor.

This brief primer on the congressional appropriations process might sound arcane to the reader. But trust me, your interests are very much affected every day by the work of the House and Senate Appropriations Committees. Earmarks, by their very nature, favor the few at the expense of the many, taking money from other, often much more important, national and local priorities to serve the interests of much more narrow constituencies.

Occasionally, Congress has found it necessary to establish a national formula for allocating federal resources to address needs shared by every community and state. There is a National Highway Trust Fund, where the proceeds of the federal tax on gasoline are aggregated, from which, according to a specific formula, they are supposed to be returned to the states for use in building and repairing roads. Those states that pay the most in gas taxes are supposed to receive the most in return. This is a fair and commonsense arrangement that recognizes the national need for more highways as our society grows in population and affluence. It also recognizes that states that pay the most in gasoline tax do so because they have the most cars on the road and have a greater need for more highways. Appropriators, however, prefer a different approach to the problem. To them, the National Highway Trust Fund formula, like any other pool of money, is there to be spent on their priorities first. So they simply take money from the trust fund and earmark it for projects in their districts and states, while urgently needed road construction in states that don't have the good fortune to be represented on the Appropriations Committees go begging.

Most earmarks are spent in the constituencies of the appropriators or on behalf of other interests that have special influence with appropriators. The committee may do the occasional favor for a member of Congress who is not an appropriator, if that member asks nicely and has been careful not to take issue with the way appropriators have seized control over almost all spending decisions in Congress. But living off the table scraps of the committee's generosity is hardly fair to other communities, nor does it make for sensible fiscal policy.

The tradition of pork barrel spending is as old as Congress. Everyone knows it is not a just or effective way to divide federal resources. But few believe anything can be done about it or have organized to challenge the appropriators' dominion. Most see the practice as merely one of a number of colorful, if selfish, customs that flourish in democratic government, and too representative of human nature to be reformed.

Why do I find it so offensive? Most pork barreling is nothing more than elected representatives bringing home the federal bacon to their constituents, and by so doing, they prove their value to the voters who will determine whether or not they are reelected. Some pork barreling, of course, is done for less populist reasons—and not just in appropriations bills, for that matter. Every year loopholes are written into the tax code, money is spent on corporate welfare, and access to natural resources is granted to specific interests most often on behalf of a home state concern, but not always. Sometimes they are simply favors done for a member's pet cause. And sometimes they are a favor to an interest that has supported a member's campaign with cash or other in kind contributions. All of it is legal, of course. But I don't think you can argue that it serves the national interest. Congress is the national legislature, not a town council, not a state assembly, and not a corporate boardroom. And we ought to devote ourselves to promoting those things that promote the national interest, allocating resources equitably to serve the progress of the whole society, and not fostering greater social divisions by squabbling among ourselves over who gets the bigger piece of the federal pie to the exclusion of national needs. The way we appropriate public money does just as much to balkanize America into competing interest groups as race-based or religion-based or class-based politics do.

As wealthy a nation as we are, we don't have unlimited resources. So national goals are the unavoidable cost of pork barrel spending. Nowhere is that more evident, and more offensive, than in the exercise of the federal government's most important responsibility, the national defense. Spending on defense during the Clinton presidency was insufficient to sustain the readiness and morale of our armed forces. America accepted greater responsibilities not just to protect our own and our allies' security, but to advance our political values in regions of the world that were inhospitable to them. Our servicemen and -women were ordered on longer and more frequent deployments, to serve in peacekeeping and other missions that multiplied during those years. At the same time, we were spending less and less as a percentage of the federal budget to train them, to maintain their weapons and equipment, and to pay them. Until recently, as many as twelve thousand military families lived on food stamps. Is it any wonder military recruitment has declined so precipitously in recent years, as job opportunities in the private sector increased and military service seemed less valued by our society?

We need to spend more money on our defense in recognition of our many global responsibilities as the world's only superpower and leader of the free world. We shouldn't shirk those responsibilities, but take pride in them and devote the resources necessary to discharge them effectively. The progress of humanity is the proper concern of a nation blessed by Providence with great wealth, and by our own faith in political values that are universal. And the men and women we ask to risk their lives in service to our security and our cause ought not to be made to sacrifice more than they already do because political leaders would rather spend more money on other interests.

President Bush has recently asked Congress to increase military spending by 15 percent. He was right to do so. Many Republicans have long argued for increases in defense spending, as have a number of Democrats. But our support for greater defense spending does not absolve us of the responsibility to ensure that public money devoted to national defense is not spent for purposes other than national defense. Congress, if left to its own devices, can spend even a 15 percent increase in the defense budget on projects that will not only fail to enhance our security, but actually undermine it. And in that failing, there is no distinction between Republicans and Democrats.

As the attacks of September 11 have shown, threats to American security and values have changed since the end of the cold war. One would think it would be obvious to Congress that we must make changes in defense planning and spending to address these threats. But defense spending is the largest part of the discretionary federal budget, and as such it is irresistible as a revenue stream into the congressional pork barrel. And no matter how urgent the need for change, no matter how critical the crisis, we will not address it if it requires us to relinquish some of our age-old spending habits. The common defense is by definition a national project. The defense of New York cannot be enhanced at the expense of California's security. That is so obvious an observation, it seems trite. But it is not so obvious that it prevents members of Congress from fighting with all the resources they have to increase or, at all costs, maintain that share of the defense budget spent in their states and districts.

We have had for some time more military bases and installations than are necessary to sustain the current and future size of our armed forces. Many of these bases need to be closed if we are to meet other, far more important security priorities. In most instances, those bases that have been closed have been converted to civilian uses, with little (if any) net loss in jobs and prosperity of the local community. Yet for all the heated arguments in debates over major defense projects such as a national missile defense, for instance, they are never as intense, personal, and acrimonious as debates over base closings. Try to tell a member of Congress that the air force base or arms depot in his or her district is going to be closed and he or she will react as if the enemy were at the gate and that such a proposal would invite them in to plunder, rape, and pillage their way through the country.

Just last year, with the support of the Bush administration, Senator Carl Levin and I managed to pass a bill authorizing a new round of base closings. We initially tried for two rounds, but that was far too ambitious, as both Republicans and Democrats massed in opposition. The new round we envisioned would begin in 2003, the year the secretary of defense has argued was absolutely necessary to begin implementing his plans for a long overdue restructuring of the military. Members of the House Armed Services Committee decided 2003 was entirely too soon to risk their parochial interests and possibly their reelection for the cause of national security. They would only agree, very reluctantly at that, for a limited round of base closures in 2005.

Every annual defense budget is loaded with spending for many worthwhile purposes, but they have nothing to do with national defense. Breast cancer research is a legitimate national priority, as is all cancer research. We should fund it generously. But why should it come out of the defense budget? Isn't national security at least as important as cancer research? Moreover, every year the U.S. Army, Navy, Marine Corps, and Air Force are obliged to accept billions of dollars in weapons systems and other defense-related matériel that they do not need or want. Not because they asked for it, not because Congress has perceived a security threat that our military planners have overlooked, but because there are shipyards and arms-manufacturing plants and plane builders and other defense-related industries in just about every state in the Union. For Congress, defense always begins at home, even if what we are defending is something decidedly less national in scope than the security of our country.

This year, a contract to build a new jet fighter was awarded to a defense company. The losing bidder, however, managed to do all right as well. Members of Congress, in whose districts the losing contractor had plants, managed to persuade the air force not to buy new refueling tankers, but to lease from the company aircraft manufactured for commercial use, pay to convert them to military use, then at the end of the twenty-year lease convert them back to commercial use and return them to the company. The military uses its tankers for longer than twenty years, but that didn't seem to bother Congress, nor did the fact that leasing, converting, and reconverting the aircraft would cost billions more than if we had purchased them outright.

Government spending is not a zero-sum game. When we waste money for our own political purposes, for our own self-interest, it means we have less money to spend on vitally important national needs. It means, in short, that we have to break promises that we have made and remade to the country. And breaking our word is the greatest injury any elected leader can inflict on the nation's integrity. Short of failing to protect our national sovereignty, Social Security might someday be the biggest, most solemn promise to the country the federal government will ever break. But we will break it unless we take decisive action now to correct our past failures.

Every working American pays 6.2 percent of his or her income into the Social Security Trust Fund. The government of the United States has promised that in exchange for that payroll tax, every American after reaching the age of sixty-five will be provided a modest retirement income. We have promised that money will always be there for them, and annually we renew the promise by assuring Americans that we will not decrease benefits or increase the retirement age. But it won't be, and we all know it. In the not too distant future, there will simply be too many retirees alive, thanks to the wonders of modern medicine, as the enormous baby boom generation in its entirety enters its golden years. There will be more money going out of the trust fund than coming in, and by 2038, the trust fund will be bankrupt.

What can we do? Increase payroll taxes? Reduce benefits? Move the retirement age to sixty-seven or seventy? We have promised not to, and we reaffirm those promises almost every day. We could and should allow Americans to invest a small portion of their payroll tax in the stock market, which would go far to extending the solvency of the trust fund. Stock markets fluctuate, but over the span of an individual's working life, investments in the stock market will always yield a better return than most other investments. Government could put adequate safeguards in place to prevent investments in portfolios that are not sufficiently diversified to ensure long-term profitability.

Most Democrats, however, routinely disparage the idea. They would rather demagogue the issue by scaring voters into believing that Republicans want to spend their pension on risky Wall Street schemes. Most Republicans have never faced up to the reality that dedicating even a small portion of the trust fund for private investment will require substantial revenues to cover short-term transition costs as much as $1 trillion. We don't have the money for it, because, often for self-interested reasons, we choose to spend it on other things.

After a brief but pleasant experience when we had federal budget surpluses that we spent wildly on everything our hearts and political interests desired, we have returned to a period of sizable budget deficits. We shot the whole wad on spending programs and tax cuts, and right now we are taking money from the Social Security Trust Fund to cover the shortfall. The day of reckoning with the public about our broken promise to protect their retirement security is fast approaching. But not so fast, I suppose, that we will have to pay any personal cost for our misfeasance. By the time the Social Security Trust Fund is bankrupt, every current member of Congress will have retired or gone on to receive our heavenly reward after profiting at great public expense from our lack of courage and our faithlessness.

There are a good many politicians, both Democrats and Republicans, who have faced up squarely to these difficult truths, often at risk to their own interests. Jack Danforth, Warren Rudman, Bob Kerrey, Pat Moynihan, and Bob Dole are only five of the public servants who have had the courage to ring the alarm many years before I ever found the nerve to do so, often to the acute discomfort of other members of their party. But they have left public life, and there are too few voices in Congress today who will risk offering solutions to this approaching calamity and accept all the costs, fiscal and political, that those solutions entail.

Unable to face up to those hard truths, Congress will rely on public relations gimmicks to allay public anxiety. We routinely make and routinely break a promise to treat the Social Security Trust Fund as a "lockbox," wherein payroll tax revenue is restricted to one purpose: paying Social Security benefits. That gimmick has outlived its usefulness, however. The public has learned from experience that whenever the government runs a budget deficit, it uses Social Security revenue to finance its current operations. Congress is now considering a new device to deceive the public into believing that we are protecting their retirement security even while we are busy spending it on other things. We are debating whether to issue every working American a certificate of assurance that they will receive the Social Security benefits they were promised. The certificate won't bind any future Congress, of course. The unlucky Congress that meets in the year 2038, when the Social Security Trust Fund is bankrupt, will have the unpleasant duty of retracting the assurance made by their predecessors and suffering the political consequences for our bad faith. The government could, of course, borrow money to cover the shortfall, but the sums would be so huge that the interest payments would eventually crowd out funding for most other government operations.

To do our duty today, and earn a more esteemed place in history, Democrats and Republicans have to stop seeking political advantages from avoiding the hard choices our promises require. We will have to agree to invest a portion of entitlement revenues in private securities and to cover the costs of that transition. We will have to restrain our appetites for spending increases and tax cuts. We will have to exercise a little more careful stewardship over the treasury than we are wont to do. We will have to overcome our dread of disappointing what we believe is our constituents' insatiable appetite for wasteful spending and the demands of many other interests to whom we are, for various reasons, beholden.

I think we do our constituents a great disservice, however, when we attribute Congress's spending habits to the public's selfishness. I have opposed earmarked appropriations for projects in my state, and my constituents haven't run me out of office for the offense. Most Arizonans, like most other Americans, expect the federal government to concentrate its resources on national problems and don't demand a disproportionate share of the federal treasury for their communities. And they understand that squandering money on projects of questionable merit and limited public value detracts from our ability to address problems affecting every American community.

Parents who send their kids to schools that must use metal detectors to ensure that students aren't bringing guns into the classroom are not going to be outraged by Congress's failure to earmark money for the Association of Reindeer Herders. Many Americans must care for their aging parents while struggling on two incomes to raise their own children. They won't find a great deal of comfort in the knowledge that while Medicare and Social Security are approaching insolvency, the local community college has received a federal grant to study the effect of cow flatulence on the ozone layer. Parents who have a son or daughter serving in the military don't particularly care if the weapons their children use to defend themselves and us were manufactured locally or not. They want to be assured that those weapons are the best we can provide and that we have enough of them.

For many years, I tried to pass legislation that would enable the president to restrain pork barrel spending. Although both the president and Congress share an equal duty to the nation as a whole, only the president is elected nationally and must take greater care that his policies do not appear to pander to some communities at the expense of others. The Constitution gives the president the authority to reject legislation unless it is supported by a two-thirds majority in both houses of Congress. Presidents, however, rarely risk rejecting an entire appropriations bill. No president wants to send a defense appropriations bill back to the Congress because in the hundreds of billions of dollars it provides for legitimate national security projects, five or six or ten billion are wasted on make-work projects in the districts and states of the appropriators.

But if the president had the ability to reject only those items in an appropriations bill that he found unnecessary to the national defense or egregiously wasteful, he could refuse it without sacrificing funding for legitimate needs. The line item veto would give the president that ability. For eight years, I and others tried to pass legislation giving the president line item veto authority, over the objections of congressional appropriators. In 1995, after Republicans won control of Congress, we finally succeeded. At the time it was my single greatest legislative success, and among my most cherished. But it was a short-lived victory. Appropriators challenged the legislation in court, and before the president ever exercised his first line item veto, the Supreme Court had ruled it an unconstitutional transfer of authority from Congress to the executive.

Supporters of the line item veto could have achieved our purpose by passing legislation that would have divided appropriations bills into separate measures, with each line item appropriation considered a single piece of legislation. This would have been a cumbersome process, to be sure, but more constitutionally sound. We were persuaded not to trouble Congress with such an unwieldy procedure by the appropriators themselves. That was our mistake.

There are other means to redress the imbalance of power within Congress that favors the appropriators over the rest of us. Congress could change its rules to insist that all appropriations be authorized or that earmarks be subjected to a sixty-vote point of order. They will be hard to achieve given the institutional control appropriators possess, but they are worth the risk of incurring the appropriators' wrath, and necessary to restore a little of the public's faith in the fiscal discipline of Congress.

There are certain practices of Congress and the executive even more injurious to public confidence in government and to national unity that will not be cured by reducing the power of the Appropriations Committees. To cure them, a full-scale assault on the political economy of Washington is necessary. And that is an undertaking far beyond the reach of one or a few individuals. Such ambitious reform will require the focused attention of the entire nation. The public has a duty to the country, not simply to despair that these practices will ever change and by their indifference or alienation allow them to continue. Americans must provide politicians with the incentive to correct abuses that are rooted in human nature and likely to be reformed only when we feel a greater threat to our reelection from an aroused public than from disappointing self-interested patrons who claim a disproportionate share of our attention.

Several years ago, Congress passed legislation purportedly deregulating the engine of our modern economy, the telecommunications revolution, to encourage competition that fosters innovation and lowers costs to the consumers. The Senate Commerce Committee, on which I serve, held innumerable hearings to take testimony from every affected industry. Regional telephone companies, long-distance carriers, national television broadcasters, cable television operators, wireless services, satellite television providers, electric utilities, and computer and software manufacturers were all heard from. Their interests obviously varied, but all shared the same central and conflicting goal, gaining entry into their competitors' business and keeping competitors out of theirs. They had one other thing in common: They were all generous donors to the campaign coffers of every member of the committee and to both Democratic and Republican Party treasuries. Collectively, they had given nearly $50 million in campaign contributions during the election prior to the legislation's consideration.

During the committee's debate and markup of the telecommunications bill, the hearing room and the halls outside were choked with lobbyists, cell phones pressed to their ears, feeding information from committee members and their staffs to their clients, and from their clients to members and staff. When the bill moved to the Senate floor, they crowded into the lobby off the floor. Every commercial interest that had a stake in the bill had invested in the political careers of every senator who would vote on it. The public interest had few lobbyists and no campaign contributions to protect it.

The legislation that was finally adopted by Congress and sent to the president provided far less deregulation of the industry than would have best served the public interest. Every commercial interest was carefully balanced against its competitors', with the result that the level of competition within the industry was restrained far too much to lower consumer costs and spur greater technological innovation as quickly as could have been achieved.

The mishmash of compromises that slowed the telecommunications revolution or, more accurately, failed to hasten it was not solely a product of politicians struggling to keep happy every interest that contributed to our campaigns. Compromise is the nature of successful legislation, especially legislation that affects large parts of our economy that involve a wide array of competing commercial interests. But campaign contributions played a big part in our deliberations, you can be sure of that, as they play a big part in our deliberations on most legislation. If they didn't, then the corporations, labor unions, law firms, and thousands of very wealthy individuals that donate huge sums of money to our campaigns would spend their money somewhere else.

Some interests, like the telecommunications industry, spread their money around pretty evenly among Democrats and Republicans. Thus, when politicians vote on legislation affecting the entire industry's competing interests, our considered judgments about what would best serve the country conflict with our concern that we avoid disappointing any of our benefactors. We are risk-averse people when it comes to public policy questions that involve substantial conflicts among our campaign donors' interests.

Other interests give exclusively or mostly to one party. Trial lawyers give most of their generous campaign donations to Democrats. Insurance companies are a little more bipartisan in their generosity but give considerably more to Republicans than Democrats. The effect on legislation of single-party campaign giving doesn't result in legislation that is watered down, contradictory, or compromised to the point of irrelevancy. It leads to no legislation. Legislative gridlock, when the parties in Congress fail to agree on any legislative remedy to a national problem, sometimes represents political differences so profound that no compromise is sufficient to bridge our differences. But often, gridlock is at least partly attributable to the fact that Democrats receive money from one interested party while Republicans receive theirs from another.

Americans have made their widespread dissatisfaction with managed health care insurers known to every single member of Congress. It is an issue that annually ranks among the highest public concerns. I have never held a town hall meeting when someone hasn't offered a heartbreaking story of how they or a loved one was denied care by their HMO and had suffered a grave illness as a result. A "patient's bill of rights" that would regulate the managed care industry and grant patients the authority to choose their own physician, among other rights, has been debated in Congress for many years. Until this Congress, no bill had passed both houses.

The current Congress has adopted two different versions of the bill, one written in the Senate, where Democrats are in the majority, and the other in the House, where Republicans are in control. We may be able to reconcile differences between them. A few other Republicans and I joined with Senate Democrats to compromise our policy differences in the Senate bill. Democrats and a few Republicans in the House sponsored a bill identical to ours in the Senate. Republican and White House opposition defeated it but successfully supported a bill of their own that made a few concessions to the minority's views. Differences between the parties have narrowed, but on many critical issues having to do primarily with questions of excessive litigation, they remain far apart.

Almost all Americans support a patient's bill of rights, as do almost all the doctors and nurses in the country. The two interests most affected by the legislation, trial lawyers and insurance companies, are less interested in its success. Trial lawyers would prefer that people never be constrained from suing anyone for any reason. Insurance companies prefer that they be protected from all litigation. Their conflicting interests, and their patterns of campaign giving, explain much of the two parties' failure to come together to address an urgent public demand. The national interest is in this instance, and in so many others, subordinate to well-heeled special interests and the self-interest of politicians of both parties.

The leadership of my party is, almost to a person, vehemently opposed to campaign finance reform. My apostasy on the question has undoubtedly caused many Republican leaders to expand their aversion to reform to include an intense dislike of me. In certain parts of the Republican establishment, I have gone from a nuisance to an enemy as reviled as any Democratic opponent. To say the least, this is not a welcome turn of events in my political career. I don't admire some of our leaders any more than they admire me. Neither am I thrilled with the direction they have given our party in recent years, or with their style of partisanship that considers political opponents as inferior moral characters. But I am a Republican and, in many respects, a conservative one. And I regret as much as I resent being considered a traitor to our party's interests.

The principal complaint of my Republican critics is that I seek to increase my public popularity at the expense of my party. Campaign finance reform, they argue, is a direct assault on the party. Yet the reforms I advocate would prevent the one kind of campaign funding that Democrats rely on more than we do. Their practical effect would close a loophole in campaign finance laws that has rendered completely ineffectual a ban on corporate political donations passed during Teddy Roosevelt's administration and a ban on labor union donations passed during the administration of Harry Truman.

Reforms adopted in the 1970s limited contributions to a candidate to $1,000 a year in a two-year election cycle. But reformers allowed what they believed a small exception for donations given directly to the parties and not to candidates from individuals, corporations, and labor unions. These "soft money" contributions, as they are called, were intended to finance the infrastructure needs of the parties—buildings, telephones, computers, transportation—and the parties' efforts to turn out their vote in an election.

Throughout the 1980s, the amounts of soft money raised were relatively small and used for the purposes it was intended. But in the 1990s, the national Republican and Democratic Parties began to raise it in larger and larger amounts. And rather than spend it on buildings and get out the vote drives, the parties began to use soft money to finance television advertising in campaigns. While these soft money ads avoided expressly advocating the election or defeat of a candidate, as required by law, they made it unmistakably clear which candidate deserved election and which did not. Party leaders also began to transfer some soft money resources to so-called independent groups that in reality were closely aligned with one party or another. These groups ran their own ads, usually attacking the character and credibility of candidates they opposed, without being required by law, as the candidates are, to disclose their sources of financial support.

In effect, the soft money loophole has made a mockery of all campaign finance laws. There is really no limit any longer on what parties can raise, few prohibitions on whom they can raise it from, and little practical restraint on how they can spend it. It is now, as I have often pointed out, perfectly legal for an American subsidiary of a Chinese army–owned corporation to give unlimited donations to American political campaigns.

A pioneer in the drive to overcome legal obstacles to unlimited and unregulated fund-raising was President Bill Clinton. In his 1996 reelection campaign, he devoted seemingly endless hours to soliciting wealthy donors who were in a position to give six-figure donations to Democratic Party coffers. He wined them, dined them, poured their coffee for them, and let them sleep over in the Lincoln Bedroom. He listened to their complaints about this or that government policy. He paid attention to their interests in legislation and federal regulations that affected their businesses. He even agreed to their suggestions to dispense presidential pardons to some of their friends and relatives. He turned on the full measure of his charm and concern, and they in turn opened up their wallets to him.

He and his vice president, Al Gore, raised tens of millions of dollars in soft money during that election. After they were safely returned to office, their creative fund-raising methods and the reputation of some of their donors created a national scandal. There were more than a few unsavory characters among the many generous benefactors the president had wooed. Foreigners had even managed to get into the act, donating funds through American subsidiaries of their overseas corporations. Congress held hearings, the Democratic Party was forced to return millions of dollars in illegally raised soft money, and Americans lost whatever pride in our government had survived earlier scandals.

Whatever the cost to the president's prestige, however, the massive amounts of soft money he raised had served its purpose. Bob Dole had been badly mauled during the primaries by a wealthy, self-financed opponent's attack ads and by a spirited challenge from Pat Buchanan. He survived the near death experience, but his campaign was practically broke from the end of the primaries until August, when he was formally nominated and could receive millions of dollars in public financing. In those intervening months, President Clinton happily whiled away his time writing scripts for television ads that would run in key battleground states, financed with millions of soft money dollars and that, as one wit described them, depicted Bob as Darth Vader's angry grandfather.

Always adept at slipping from scandal back into the good graces of the American people, the president managed to take the whole controversy in stride. The vice president didn't fare quite as well. He was caught making explicit fund-raising calls from his government office (a violation of one of the few fund-raising laws that the soft money loophole has yet to annul) rather than simply soliciting them with coffees, dinners, and sleep-overs as the president had done, while other Democratic leaders put the touch on his guests in conversations off government property. The vice president also put in an unfortunate appearance at a Buddhist monastery in California, where he was filmed convincing nuns and monks to dispense with their vows of poverty by raising money for the Democratic Party, some of which, it turned out, came from overseas. Never as facile and ingratiating as the president, his complicity in the fund-raising scandals of 1996 left a lingering mark on his public character when he ran for president himself four years later.

Soft money had played virtually no role in the election and reelection of Ronald Reagan. Nor had it been much of a factor in 1988, when Vice President George Bush succeeded him. Compared to the amounts of money being raised and spent today, soft money wasn't all that important to the Republican capture of Congress in 1994. Until the soft money explosion, the financial strength of the Republican Party had been in our grassroots fund-raising, $25, $50, and $100 donors, few of whom have corporate interests they wish to advance with campaign contributions.

Why, then, do Republican leaders object so strenuously to legislation that would close the soft money loophole? Well, it's a hell of a lot easier to raise money in $100,000 or $1 million donations than it is to raise it $20 or $100 at a time. It is comparatively cheaper to raise as well. Most small donations are raised through the mail, and the overhead is quite expensive. But we have done it very successfully in the past and can continue to do it successfully, while it will take Democrats some time to build up a small donor base to match ours.

Republican critics of reform argue that a ban on soft money will "take the political parties out of campaigns." That is an overstatement, of course, that even they would concede. Proponents of a ban on soft money are willing to allow smaller, limited amounts of money to be raised by the state parties, which could be used in getting out the vote efforts and to raise the amounts of limited and regulated "hard money" candidates and national parties can raise. Admittedly, a ban on soft money will deprive the parties of a major source of funding. In the 2000 election, $500 million in soft money was raised by the national parties from corporate and labor interests, up from $89 million eight years earlier. But the parties will survive, as they did in years past, without it.

The parties will also have to be more responsive to their grass roots than they have been in recent times. Most important, the access and influence in our legislative process that soft money buys for a privileged few will be diminished. That influence has become a stain upon the honor of every federally elected officeholder, and a lot of us have grown weary of having our reputations challenged by a campaign finance system that appears to most Americans to be legalized extortion. All this money washing around in campaigns understandably raises grave doubts in the minds of the American people about our integrity. Many Americans believe we conspire to hold on to every political advantage we have lest we jeopardize our incumbency by a single lost vote. Most believe we would pay any price, bear any burden, to ensure our personal ambitions, no matter how injurious the effect might be to the national interest.

This isn't true, but the fact that the public believes it to be so should shame us all. And our protestations to the contrary will never persuade the public that we are not corrupted by the means we use to win office. They have seen more than enough evidence to confirm their suspicions.

In the 1996 campaign, an entrepreneur named Roger Tamraz gave $300,000 to the Democratic National Committee. He wanted to build an oil pipeline through Central Asia, and he hoped his contribution would help persuade the Clinton White House to help him. It certainly gave him access to administration officials, although they declined in the end to support his ambitions at that time. During testimony before a Senate investigating committee, Mr. Tamraz was asked if he was disappointed that his generosity had failed to pay off for him personally. He responded, "No. Next time I'll give six hundred thousand dollars." Another soft money donor likened campaign giving to subway tokens. You have to pay your fare if you want to ride the train. If that is how the big money givers see the system, how can we expect people who can't afford the token to think better of us?

When party leaders argue that a ban on soft money will reduce the influence of the political parties, what they really mean is that it will reduce their influence. Soft money raised by the congressional campaign committees and by the national parties is used by congressional leaders to enforce party discipline in Congress. They decide in which campaigns that money will be spent. Often, when members of Congress believe their conscience or their constituents require them to vote for or sponsor legislation that their congressional leaders oppose, they are threatened with the prospect that their leadership will refuse to spend soft money on their behalf. That kind of party discipline has influenced many members to cast votes that they and their constituents believe are wrong.

Republican leaders and the majority of our caucus hold more conservative views than the declining numbers of Republican moderates from the Northeast and Midwest, and they use soft money to enforce loyalty to those views. The leadership's control of campaign funds has prevented Republicans and Democrats from reaching the bipartisan compromises necessary to pass important legislation. It has been used to discourage members from acting in what they believe is the country's best interests. That is the kind of party discipline, achieved not by persuasion or compromise, but by extortion, that the parties and the country could use a lot less of. Its effect is to entrench hostility between the parties in Congress and to further erode public confidence in government.

Naturally, I think politics and my party could profit from more independent thinkers among its elected officeholders, people who will work across party lines when they believe the interests of the country require it. I would welcome a less authoritarian party leadership, which a ban on soft money and a corresponding increase in the money candidates raise for themselves would effect. I place a higher premium on acts of conscience than on party discipline. But my support for campaign finance reform is not as self-serving as my critics would suggest. For I believe the greatest injury inflicted by the current system is that it exalts the parties above the nation itself. That is not a cause worth sacrificing one's independence for, and it is not a cause that does the great party of Lincoln and Roosevelt much credit.

I have no reluctance to subordinate my independence to a cause greater than my own self-interest. But that cause is my country, first and last. When my party serves my country, then my party deserves my loyalty. When I believe my party serves itself at the expense of my country, then it deserves my dissent. Were I to believe otherwise, the independence I have prized all my life will have been nothing more than egotism. I will have fought for myself alone and forsaken the good company of people whose patriotism has brought them a happiness more sublime than pleasure. I have had such company, and I am a better public servant and a better man for it.

Russell Feingold is a liberal Democratic senator from Wisconsin. He and I disagree about a great many things. We are miles apart on defense, foreign policy, and free trade questions. Our temperaments are as different as our ideologies. He is polite, patient, self-effacing, studious, lawyerly, and self-controlled, adjectives rarely applied to me. When I first noticed him, in his first year in the Senate, he was arguing on the Senate floor to cut funding for an aircraft carrier. I asked him in debate whether he had ever been on an aircraft carrier. When he answered in the negative, I suggested he learn a little more about them before he decided the country needed fewer of them. He reacted with typical good humor and observed, correctly, that he didn't need to see a carrier to understand their purpose. As I've come to know him, I realize that my remark was as unfair to him as it was discourteous. Russ doesn't take positions that he is not well-informed about. Even when I believe his judgment to be mistaken, it is not for his lack of diligence in studying the issue. He is a conscientious public servant. And a brave one.

From the moment of our first disagreement, I began to notice his independence. He seemed to find earmarks and pork barrel spending as offensive as I did, and I watched him with growing admiration as he frequently fought with appropriators on the Senate floor. He had little more success in those contests than I have had, but his willingness to keep at it, and his ability to remain affable but undaunted in defeat, impressed me. He struck me as principled, independent, and game, just the qualities I was looking for in a political ally who felt Congress was overdue for a little reform.

I called him on the phone a few days after the 1994 election, told him I admired his courage, and asked if he wanted to work together on a few reform issues. He asked what I had in mind, and I suggested we join forces to oppose earmarks. I also asked if he would help me with legislation extending the time that retiring members of Congress and senior staff would have to wait before they could lobby their former colleagues. He agreed and asked if I would support legislation to change the rules restricting what members of Congress could receive as gifts from lobbyists.

We've had little luck in changing the appropriations process so far. Over the years, I've offered hundreds of amendments to strip earmarks from appropriations bills, targeting programs from studying the nutrient values of chicken litter in Kentucky to disposing of manure in Starkville, Mississippi. I've argued against more seriously wasteful expenditures of the federal treasury such as huge federal subsidies for agribusiness and weapons systems that the military services can't use. But so great is the power of the appropriators that most members of Congress would rather collude in a system we all know is unfair and that wastes tens of billions of dollars every year than risk exposing their states to the wrath of angry appropriators. Twenty votes for one of my amendments usually qualifies as a great moral victory. But we're intent on continuing the fight, and as the appropriations autocracy becomes ever more frustrating to the seventy-one senators who are not appropriators, a little revolution will come, and we will take back Congress's spending power from its sole custodians on the Appropriations Committees.

We managed to pass the lobbying restrictions in the Senate, but the bill didn't survive a conference committee with the House, the killing ground of many reforms. We did, however, succeed in restricting the value of gifts that lobbyists could give lawmakers and their staffs. The old law had allowed lobbyists to shower congressional offices with gifts from expensive dinners to concert tickets worth up to $250 each year. When

Russ, Carl Levin, Paul Wellstone, and several other senators first proposed a much lower limit of $50, not many of our colleagues supported the change. I've never known a member of Congress who had traded his or her vote for these small tokens of appreciation from lobbyists' expense accounts. To suggest as much could be seen as the kind of pandering to public cynicism that Jack Danforth had warned about. But the public was well aware of the practice. Quite understandably, our constituents have concerns about whether members of Congress would refrain from showing a little favoritism to people who took us to a professional football game on Sunday, bought us lunch on Monday, dinner on Tuesday, gave us theater tickets on Wednesday, and on Thursday asked us to support a provision in a bill that would benefit a commercial interest they represented. As the press focused on our proposal to restrict these gratuities, and the public became aware of the effort, senators eventually conceded that whatever small pleasure we took from these favors really wasn't worth the appearance problem they were creating. When the bill finally came to a vote, it passed overwhelmingly.

Russ and I thought that the same dynamic would work in our attempt to reform campaign finance laws. Senators would initially resist, attempt to kill the proposal quietly, be frustrated by media attention to the issue, and finally relent in the face of growing public pressure. We badly underestimated how much more appreciative our colleagues were of the means that protected our incumbency than they were of the incidental emoluments of office.

All senators have grown weary of the money chase. As campaigns become more expensive and the money available to us is now virtually unlimited, we spend more and more of our time on the phone and at fund-raising dinners, lunches, and breakfasts, begging people for contributions. And I trust it has occurred to each member of Congress who has sat at a dinner table with ten or more people who have paid $50,000 or more for the privilege that their companions might be interested in something less idealistic than good government. But there is one subject on which all members of Congress feel they are experts: political campaigns. All 535 of us have won office under the current system. In every congressional election, 97 percent or more of incumbents are returned to office.

The status quo protects us, and that is a powerful incentive for us to protect the status quo.

The public is certainly aware that the present campaign finance system creates, at a minimum, the appearance of a conflict of interest. As Ralph Reed, once the executive director of the Christian Coalition and now a well-paid lobbyist, observed as he pitched his services to Enron executives: "It matters less who has the best arguments and more who gets heard—and by whom." Most Americans believe that we are all corrupted by the means we use to remain in office. Every public opinion poll conducted over the last decade has shown huge majorities in favor of campaign finance reform. Opponents of reform will point to those same polls, however, to observe that the issue never ranks among the top ten or more public concerns. That, certainly, is evidence not of the public's approval, but of its despair that we will ever change a system that protects our incumbency. Americans simply don't believe we would risk our own careers to clean up what has become an elaborate influence-buying scheme. Because they don't expect change, they don't bother demanding it. I find that level of public cynicism very depressing, but opponents of reform use it to discourage any changes in the conditions that have created it. No one, they argue, will ever lose an election because they opposed campaign finance reform, so why risk losing one by supporting it.

However, campaign finance scandals have occurred in almost every recent election. From my own brush with scandal as a Keating Five member, to the excesses in the Clinton years, to the political generosity of the senior executives of Enron, the public's interest in reform has waxed, waned, and then waxed again. It has now reached the point that more and more members of Congress have begun to worry that maybe their constituents aren't as indifferent to the problem as they once seemed. In the last couple of elections, campaign finance reform was a major issue in several campaigns. As embarrassing as these scandals have been to all of us, they have proved very helpful to the cause of reform, and reformers have made good use of them.

Russ and I, and a hardy band of Republican and Democratic reformers with thick skins, have earned the animosity of political allies by offering campaign finance reform legislation in each of the last four Congresses. The first McCain-Feingold bill was a very ambitious, comprehensive overhaul that would have provided not just limits on contributions, but voluntary limits on spending in exchange for free television advertising, reduced postage costs, and other benefits. It went nowhere. Our subsequent efforts focused primarily on banning soft money. They, too, died, even though they commanded a majority of votes. Opponents filibustered them or used other Senate procedures to kill the bills that would have required sixty votes to overcome.

Our chief nemesis is Mitch McConnell of Kentucky, a smart, tough partisan who has proven a most formidable opponent. Our annual campaign finance debates have on occasion become quite acrimonious and personal. I fear there have been times when Mitch and I came to view each other as personal enemies. On one such occasion, during my presidential campaign, Mitch and two other Republican senators managed to put me in a difficult position, demanding that if I continued to assert that soft money was corrupting senators, then I should name names. "Who is corrupt?" they kept repeating, until it looked as if I were unable to answer the question. But the influence that campaign contributions buy doesn't violate federal bribery statutes. That's the point. Its effect is insidious, but legal. Were I to name every senator who has given more consideration to a generous supporter than he or she would to someone else, I would have to start with my own and work down the list of all ninety-nine of my colleagues. The debate was an unpleasant experience for me and, I assumed at the time, intended not simply to counter my arguments, but to provoke my temper, which had become the subject of unflattering commentary in my presidential campaign. I managed to keep it in check, but I left the floor feeling considerable ill will toward my three colleagues.

That has passed in time, and I have to confess that I have come to respect Mitch. Except for our disagreement about campaign finance and other political reforms, we tend to agree on many policy questions, especially in foreign policy debates, where I've always found him to be an informed and articulate champion of American interests and values. Unlike many opponents of campaign reform, he doesn't just cloak his political self-interest in reverence for constitutional protections he believes campaign restrictions would violate. He argues quite forcefully that there isn't enough money in political campaigns and that any less of it will hurt his party. He doesn't hide his opposition from media and public scrutiny. He argues his opposition openly to anyone willing to listen, claims he will use all means at his disposal to protect soft money, and faces the voters every six years proud that he has stopped efforts to reduce the amount of money in political campaigns. He has the courage of his convictions, and I admire courage in my adversaries no less than in my allies. He is wrong. But he is honestly wrong, and principled and ferocious in the defense of his error.

Russ Feingold has the courage of his convictions, too, and to his credit, his convictions and his courage have served the country well, as they have endangered his own ambitions. Both he and I were up for reelection in 1998. I faced an inexperienced and underfunded opponent, and my re-election was never in doubt. Russ wasn't that fortunate. He faced an expe-rienced Republican opponent, Mark Neumann, a member of the House, who had ample resources to win. He also had the full financial support of the Republican Party, which was prepared to spend whatever it took in a close election to defeat the leading Democratic opponent of soft money.

For most of the summer, Russ had a comfortable lead in the polls. But as he wasn't willing to allow the Democratic Party to spend soft money in his race, he husbanded his resources by not running television ads until the fall. His opponent had no self-imposed restrictions, and he ran a lot of ads during the summer. Neumann's first ads were, if not positive, rather light-hearted. As the polls narrowed, Neumann's ads became increasingly negative, and Russ's popularity among the voters declined accordingly. By the fall campaign, they were in a neck-and-neck race, and given the small Republican majority in the Senate, the Democratic Party didn't want to risk lengthening the odds of recapturing the Senate by losing one princi-pled but politically reckless incumbent. So the Democratic Senate Cam-paign Committee stepped in with soft money advertising trashing Neumann, as did the labor unions and other interest groups aligned with the party. Russ very forcefully—indeed, stridently—told his allies to get the hell out of his race. They did, although very reluctantly. Most Dem-ocrats thought Russ was a lost cause. So did everyone else. So did I, for that matter, and the prospect of his defeat depressed me. Russ, however, was more optimistic about his chances.

On the day of his election, as I was comfortably awaiting my own certain return to office, I called Russ to wish him well and tell him how much I admired him. I tried to keep a discouraging tone out of the conversation, but I wasn't all that successful. Russ picked up on it and offered me, a Republican in an easy race, a little encouragement. "Don't worry, John. I'm gonna win. It will be close, but I'll win." He had risked his own election for his beliefs and by so doing had made the cause he championed a central feature of the campaign. I have seldom admired a colleague more.

Russ did win reelection, by a very narrow margin, 50 percent to 48 percent. After Russ, his wife, and his staff, and despite my partisan affiliation, I was the probably the most relieved person in the country. I would still have the company in the Senate of my ally and good friend, who, seventeen years my junior, had now become something of a role model for me. We could continue our reform campaign together. A year later, Russ and I were awarded the John F. Kennedy Profile in Courage Award at the Kennedy Library in Boston for our efforts to reform campaign finance laws. I was as proud of the company I had in receiving the honor as I was of the honor itself.

—

In 1995, the Senate majority leader, Trent Lott, asked me as chairman of the Senate Commerce Committee to write and pass through the committee a bill that enacted into federal law a settlement of a lawsuit brought by various state attorneys general against the tobacco companies. To secure its passage, we had to broker a great many compromises between the committee Democrats and Republicans, some of whom represented tobacco-growing states, others who felt the tobacco companies deserved more punishment than the settlement imposed on them for marketing cigarettes to children, and some of whom felt the government had no business penalizing an industry for marketing a dangerous product that consumers knew was harmful.

After many weeks of negotiations, and several moments when it looked as if we would fail, we finally managed to put together a bill that had the support of all but one member of the committee. The bill imposed much higher penalties on the tobacco companies than had been in the original settlement. While it did retain some protections for the companies from future litigation, it was still too much for them. The companies withdrew their support for the settlement and pooled their considerable resources to wage a national public relations campaign to defeat the bill on the Senate floor. Most observers thought the committee's agreement was quite an achievement nevertheless and expected that it would eventually be accepted by a majority of the full Senate. When the final committee vote was taken, one member flattered me by saying that my management of the bill had been "presidential." I feigned humility over the compliment but was glad to have it. I was starting to think that maybe I could be president, or at least that I should try.

By the time the bill was considered on the floor, the tobacco companies had begun to turn public opinion noticeably cooler toward the legislation, spending $50 million in television, radio, and newspaper ads attacking the bill and me. This change in the public mood gave many Republicans the courage to drop their support of the settlement and begin arguing that it was nothing more than an unfair tax increase on smokers. Also, in a classic example of letting the perfect be the enemy of the good, liberal Democrats joined with Republicans intent on killing the bill to remove the remaining liability protections. Until that vote, we had managed to defeat other amendments that were intended to make the bill less attractive to a majority of senators.

The Republicans dragged out the debate for weeks to let the companies' advertising campaign burn into the public conscience and to demonstrate to other Republican supporters of the bill how bad a beating I was getting in opinion polls, even in Arizona, for my support of the measure. In the end, while we still had a small majority of support, we could not reach the sixty votes required to end debate, and the bill was pulled from the floor. In a Republican caucus meeting shortly before the decision to withdraw the bill from consideration was made, my colleagues were assured that the tobacco companies would spend enough money on ads in the next election to protect us from political fallout for opposing the bill.

I was angry to hear that, and angry that the bill that had looked so promising as it left my committee had been twisted and turned inside out on the Senate floor and was about to be added to the heap of broken promises. In due course, the states' attorneys general would agree to another, smaller settlement with the tobacco companies, one that wouldn't require congressional action. But with the legal costs of protecting the industry against multiple lawsuits spiraling, the price of a pack of cigarettes is now as high as it would have been had our bill been adopted. The benefits of this increase to disease research and smoking prevention programs that were envisioned in our bill were considerably less.

That future irony wasn't on my mind, however, when I rose to speak on the Senate floor just before the bill was pulled. I was just angry, and I expressed it at length, suggesting near the end of my remarks that perhaps the health of children should be a greater concern to my party. When I finished, every Democrat on the floor rose to applaud me, the only standing ovation I've ever received in a Senate debate. Not a single Republican joined in the tribute.

I thought about that experience when I decided that I would try to win the Republican presidential nomination in 2000. I knew I was a long shot, and given the curious place I now occupied in the affections of much of the Republican establishment, and the causes I had come to be identified with, I didn't expect much help, financial or otherwise, from party regulars. I thought about Russ's principled risk in his reelection campaign and wondered if I would have the guts to protect my integrity even if it meant lengthening the odds against me. I didn't worry that I would betray my positions or myself as long as I remained a dark horse. But would I stay true if by some unexpected turn of events my personal ambitions seemed a little more achievable? There was no point in worrying about that, I decided. I was unlikely to get close enough to the prize where such temptations would become a concern.

Last town hall meeting for the New Hampshire primary campaign,
Peterborough, New Hampshire, January 30, 1999. *David Hume Kennerly*

TWELVE

STRAIGHT TALK

Facing the window in my suite on the eighth floor of the Crowne Plaza Hotel in Nashua, New Hampshire, I practiced the speech I would deliver sometime later that evening, reminding myself over and over to read it slowly and get the emphasis right. It was a victory speech, and although the final count wasn't in yet, I was certain I had won the New Hampshire primary. The day before the primary, we had raced around the state one last time in a four-bus caravan, most of my aides, many of my supporters, and more than a hundred reporters in tow. On the next to last stop of the day, in the coastal town of Portsmouth, an oil tanker had blasted its horn twice as it left harbor and steamed past our rally. A good omen, I thought, for an old sailor. A large, enthusiastic crowd greeted me at the last rally of the day in Bedford, affirming the auspicious gesture.

I wasn't sure how close the contest would turn out to be. The polls had gotten awfully tight the weekend before the election. And I didn't know when my opponent, George W. Bush, would concede defeat. Around five o'clock, my coauthor, Mark Salter, and another campaign aide, John Weaver, entered the room with the results of the latest network exit polls, trying unsuccessfully to look sober and pretend there was nothing remarkable to report.

"Well, you're gonna win," Mark announced.

"How much?" I asked.

"You're gonna clobber him. Maybe twenty points."

They looked at me for a moment, waiting for my response. All I could think of to say was, "That has implications," to which Mark deadpanned: "Gee, like you might be president. That might be one of them."

There was that prospect, of course, and it was exciting to contemplate. Before the night was over, my subdued enthusiasm over the news of the landslide would swell into pride. The jubilant crowd of supporters who would cheer each sentence of my speech that night, and the several hundred college kids who were waiting in an airplane hangar to greet my late night arrival in South Carolina, where the next big primary would occur, thrilled me. My self-restraint relaxed, and I felt for a moment that my ship really had come in.

We had a long way to go, however. Before the New Hampshire primary, I was trailing by double digits in every South Carolina poll, and I wasn't doing better in any of the other approaching primaries. I had a lot less money than my opponent had. And because I had accepted federal matching funds, the rules for which impose spending caps in each primary, even if I raised more money, I couldn't spend as much in South Carolina or elsewhere as could George Bush, who had declined public financing.

More daunting were the consequences of how I had won the New Hampshire primary. I had won by running against the Republican establishment and against Republican orthodoxy on issues from campaign finance reform to tax cuts. Political establishments aren't as cynical as the public believes and I sometimes make them out to be. Party leaders and loyalists weren't about to turn on a dime and embrace my candidacy and positions just because I had landed one good punch in a twelve-round fight. They were going to help George fight like hell in South Carolina, and the worse the beating I got, the happier they would be. That, too, was one of the implications of our New Hampshire landslide. And it wasn't too distant a concern even on that happy February night when we celebrated our once improbable victory.

It's a heady thing to think and to know that others think you might be president of the most powerful nation on earth. I didn't really anticipate the experience. Over many months, as we had waged our low-budget, underdog campaign, trailing by huge margins everywhere, I kept my expectations well within reason. No one thought I had much of a chance, including me. We took a lot of risks, first, because I like to take risks, and second, because we really didn't have any other choice. We decided or, more accurately, we resigned ourselves to running a campaign that would test many of the conventions of previously successful presidential campaigns.

I wouldn't start in Iowa with the other candidates. The Iowa Republican caucuses aren't open to independents and Democrats, as is the New Hampshire primary. They have very low turnout and are dominated by religious conservatives, whose leaders have decided, for various reasons, that campaign finance reform is a sin. As a vocal opponent of government subsidies to ethanol producers, I wasn't going to be the first choice of farmers in the "land where the tall corn grows," either. The Iowa straw poll in August was another feature of the caucuses I abstained from. Candidates were required to spend all kinds of money on food, drink, entertainment, and other, less publicized incentives to convince Iowa party regulars to vote for them in a meaningless beauty contest. I didn't have enough money to waste on a ritual that wouldn't award a single delegate.

Being absent from the story coming out of Iowa one week before the New Hampshire primary was a risk. In the past, reporters had shaped the next contest as a battle between the winner and the runner-up of the caucuses. Nevertheless, we thought if we concentrated intensely on New Hampshire, outhustling the other candidates there, we might survive the press's inattention to our campaign during the week of the caucuses. Although I showed up for a couple of debates in Des Moines, I made it clear I was not going to actively contest the caucuses and hoped the press would use my truancy to discount the impact of who won and who lost there.

To attract more media interest than our campaign treasury and prospects warranted, we decided we would give reporters what they always complained they never had enough of: access to the candidate. We gave them more access than they ever dreamed they would have. To tell the truth, by the end of the campaign, they probably had more access than they had wanted or would ever want again. Reporters became my constant companions, and I theirs. We leased a bus and christened it the *Straight*

Talk Express. I sat in a red leather swivel chair in the back, with half a dozen or more reporters, rotated in shifts, surrounding me. I spent more time with reporters than with many of my aides. I took all questions, ducked nothing, and talked for hours on end. This often became quite wearying for me and for the reporters. It was also a little dangerous, since I have never been the most discreet politician, and the problem became more acute when I was required to entertain a traveling press corps (and myself) for twelve or more hours a day. The pattern of questions became fairly routine. But I would slip up from time to time anyway and create a minor press frenzy, and rather than seek refuge in a hotel suite and issue a press release to clear up the confusion, I could only get back on the bus and try to settle things down myself. However often I detoured into controversies that were, in campaign vernacular, off-message, the experiment was still a great success. Despite George's commanding lead in the polls, and our attempt to pick and choose the battlefields where we were best equipped to fight, reporters were attracted to the spectacle of a candidate and his campaign operating at all times in full public view. And their interest in the novelty excited their interest in how the experiment would affect the contest in New Hampshire, the battleground we chose.

We also decided to attempt the same experiment with New Hampshire voters. Rather than follow traditional patterns of campaigning there, photo ops at diners and dogsled races in poses suggesting a candidate's common touch, punctuated by the occasional serious policy speech to show one's "vision," we decided on a rigorous schedule of town hall meetings. We would show up in communities all over the state, many more than once, and invite anyone interested to come and ask whatever questions they wanted. I would speak for a few minutes, then open the floor to the audience. We didn't pick or screen the audience. We didn't plant questions. We took them as they came. Nor would I use every question to nod my head in agreement and compliment the questioner's intelligence. When I disagreed with someone I said so, sometimes more sharply than courtesy or self-interest required. And while New Hampshire voters are famously well-informed, the indiscriminate nature of these exchanges often attracted some rather eccentric characters with unusual interests in government. Often, I was asked to support legal protections for the hemp-growing industry, such as it is. One voter appealed for a federal law requiring all Americans to brush their teeth twice a day.

In the early days of the campaign, the town halls attracted modest interest. I spoke to crowds of twenty or thirty people. By the fall they were growing larger, which reporters interpreted as evidence that I had become, in New Hampshire at least, George Bush's principal rival. By January, the month before the primary, the meetings had become quite a spectacle, hundreds of people now crowded into the venues, and the subjects discussed ran from serious to weird. People dressed in costumes started to compete with more sober citizens to ask questions. I had grown relaxed and confident in these open forums, joking around with the audiences, reporters, and my staff. I began to invite the most colorful characters up on stage. A guy dressed in a shark suit, a fellow with a wading boot on his head, another posing as Abe Lincoln, and various other characters would come up, take the mike, and spar with me over whatever grievance or concern they had hoped to draw attention to with their not always self-explanatory attire. Fatigue and amusement at the increasing festiveness of the events made me all the more relaxed and irreverent. I began to hail well-known press celebrities, whose curiosity had been piqued by their colleagues' reporting and had come to see for themselves what was going on, as Trotskyites. I ribbed aides and supporters, identifying them as Spanish-American War veterans and work release parolees. I was, in short, having a hell of a lot of fun, which, as superficial as it sounds, was one of the purposes of the campaign.

I wanted ours to be an honest, open, and enjoyable campaign. If my chances were slim, I hoped we could at least make it a valuable experience and a pleasant memory for me, for my campaign team and supporters, for the reporters covering the campaign, and for the voters. By the end of the primary, I had participated in 114 town hall meetings, a record that will probably stand for many years. They weren't just entertainment. They were hard work. But they were also an honest form of communication with the voters that I came to appreciate greatly. There were times when I was tired and hurried, that I'm sure I didn't communicate how much I appreciated the experience. But I'm deeply grateful to those thousands of good people who showed up to listen to my pitch and share their concerns. I learned more from them than they ever learned from me, and at my age, that is a real blessing.

In that proud, slightly eccentric state, voters take great care with their civic responsibilities. They aren't easily impressed. They expect a candidate to earn their support with more than sound bites and advertisements. They want the color and excitement of presidential campaigns. They no doubt enjoy the elaborate attention they are paid by prominent politicians who, until they decided they should be president, thought the state was some quaint Currier & Ives throwback to simpler times, when courteous people exercised their franchise dutifully without expecting more from the candidates than a few well-written speeches and affected respect for local traditions. But the people of New Hampshire are more informed and more discerning than that. They've been doing this for a long time, and they take pride in it. They want to see which candidates have the guts to be president. They want to see how we fight, believing, not unreasonably, that struggle exposes whether a candidate has the character to be president.

The Balsams is a lovely resort hotel in the north woods of New Hampshire. Until his recent death at 103, Neil Tillotson owned the place. Years ago, he had decided to incorporate Dixville Notch, the little community of people who worked at the hotel, and establish a polling place in the Balsams. Every four years, the polls at Dixville Notch open for business at exactly midnight on primary day, making Mr. Tillotson and his employees the first voters in the first-in-the-nation primary. Thanks to his inspired mixing of public relations with civic duty, Dixville Notch and its leading citizen became national celebrities. Every primary candidate is obliged to pay a courtesy call at the Balsams, which is hardly a hardship since the hotel and its environs are beautiful and well worth the visit. When I made the trip there, I asked Mr. Tillotson of all the presidential candidates he had met over the years, who had been his favorite. "Roosevelt," he replied.

"You met FDR?" I said, impressed that his experience with presidential politics stretched so far back.

"Not Franklin," he corrected, "Teddy."

I've never had a happier time in politics than I had during the New Hampshire campaign. I won't ever forget it, either.

Although my endorsements were fewer, and my campaign staff smaller than my opponent's, I was very lucky indeed to have had the support I did. Warren Rudman, who is still revered by his former constituents in New Hampshire and knows the state better than any other politician, gave much of his time and wise counsel to my campaign. From the beginning, he believed I could win the primary, but I wouldn't have had a chance without him.

Many people who worked with me were new to presidential campaigns. Some were experienced veterans. Not one of them would have chosen to join my campaign were the decision a simple calculation of their self-interest. We were unlikely to succeed, and the way we used the campaign to challenge some of the interests and opinions of the party establishment would threaten their own professional prospects if we lost. They did me a great honor by joining my campaign and taking a personal risk by letting me be the kind of candidate I wanted to be, say the things I wanted to say, and stand for the things that I thought were important to the country and to my self-esteem. Some of them did so out of friendship, some because they shared my convictions. They paid me the highest compliment possible by working in my campaign as an expression of their patriotism. When I let them down, as I did more than once, they never gave up on the campaign or me.

I didn't decide to run for president to start a national crusade for the political reforms I believed in or to run a campaign as if it were some grand act of patriotism. In truth, I wanted to be president because it had become my ambition to be president. I was sixty-two years old when I made the decision, and I thought it was my one shot at the prize. I thought my military and political experience made me better qualified for the office than the other candidates. I had watched Bob Dole's campaign and thought I had learned enough about running for president to do a credible job and make it interesting.

I had made a final decision to run for president just a few weeks after my 1998 reelection to the Senate. In truth, I had had the ambition for a long time. It had been a vague aspiration. I hadn't spent years in Congress consciously building a record and reputation to position myself for a presidential campaign. I really hadn't done any planning at all. But it had been there, in the back of my mind, for years, as if it were simply a symptom of my natural restlessness. Life is forward motion for me. I feel my equilibrium becoming unbalanced when I sense I've stayed too long in one situation or when I find myself spending too much time in nostalgic reverie for days that are passed and cannot be recovered.

Cindy and I took a vacation trip to the Maldives in the Indian Ocean to discuss whether the separation and public exposure of a presidential campaign would be too great a burden for our children. We concluded they could handle it, so I decided to run, pending my kids' approval. There really wasn't much more to the decision. We never discussed how our family would be affected were I to actually win the presidency. That seemed a little presumptuous given the odds against our success. The only reference to actually occupying the White House came after we asked the kids to vote on whether I should run or not. Three of the four supported the idea. My youngest son, Jimmy, voted against it. When I told him it would mean a lot to me if the vote was unanimous, he asked if as the son of the president he would get head-of-the-line privileges at Disney World. I assured him he would, and he changed his vote to the affirmative. Had I been elected president, I would have seen to it that he got the privilege. It would have been an abuse of office, I know. But what could I do? I promised him.

I didn't believe I had the best shot, but I believed I had a shot. I was convinced I wouldn't ever become afraid of losing, a pretty easy virtue when you're an underdog. I expected to take courage from my fatalism to keep my campaign honest and original, if, at times, a little less disciplined than necessary. I played the happy insurgent, with a zest for challenging authority and political conventions. By temperament and values, I was naturally suited to the role. My favorite moments in the campaign were those when I could stand for a principle, not piously but irreverently. I don't think I had a happier moment than when I stood in front of the Russian consulate in Manhattan on a wintry day and, mimicking Ronald Reagan's speech in front of the Brandenburg Gate, shouted to New York Republican leaders who had blocked my name from appearing on the primary ballot there to "tear down this wall." Weeks later I was still laughing at the memory of it. But I wanted to win as much as I wanted to enjoy the experience. And my decisions about how I would try to win were made out of political necessity as much as principle.

We made campaign finance reform the central issue in our campaign. I tried to explain how the current system was injurious to the health of our democracy and how it deterred government from making progress on so many issues of greater concern to Americans. Early in the campaign, I said I intended to make room in the Republican Party and the election for the issue of campaign finance reform. In that, if nothing else, we were successful. Most people find it pretty obvious that a system that sanctions six- and seven-figure political contributions from people with corporate interests in legislation tends to elevate those interests above others. We wanted to explain campaign reform as the gateway to other reforms that were being blocked with financial investments from reform's opponents, be they trial lawyers opposed to litigation reform, defense contractors opposed to military reform, or insurers opposed to HMO reform. That, too, was quite evident to voters.

But campaign finance reform, as often as I spoke of it, and as popular an issue as it became in the campaign, wasn't intended to be the organizing theme of my campaign. More than anything else, I wanted our campaign to attract the interest of people who disdained politics or were at best indifferent to the habits and institutions of our democracy. I wanted to remind them that materialism wasn't all America offered. America offered to every citizen a fellowship of service to ideals that are noble and ennobling. That the benefits that issued from these ideals, opportunity, prosperity, and security were no more rewarding than the reciprocal obligations that citizenship imposed on us to protect and extend the blessings of liberty to all. It flattered me to think I could appropriate such a high purpose in the pursuit of my own ambitions.

National prosperity, driven by the telecommunications revolution, had reached astonishing heights in 2000 and had filled many young minds with dreams of being a multimillionaire by thirty. Yet the equanimity of all these aspiring young entrepreneurs seemed a false front. Many appeared eager for a public cause to champion, for a passion that had more than pleasure as its object. They were intrigued by the revival of interest in the World War II generation. They seemed to anticipate the envy and personal disappointment that, for all their youthful arrogant certainty, had troubled baby boomers in their later years as they remembered the patriotic sacrifices of their parents, who had less wealth but knew a more profound happiness. Maybe more young people had begun to take prosperity for granted. Maybe a very materialistic generation had started to discover very early that the veneer of outside things, however glamorous and seductive, did not offer happiness. For whatever reason, Americans, young and not so young, seemed to be listening for an appeal to their patriotism. And I wanted to give it to them.

It was presumptuous of me, and self-serving, to anoint myself as the herald of this welcome change in the zeitgeist. I'm not the most eloquent messenger. Nor had I some kind of claim on the country superior to that of the other candidates. My public service had surely not been above reproach. Nor is my patriotism as exemplary as the patriotism of those who gave more than I did to the country but who did not profit from public attention to their sacrifices, though they take the memories of them to their grave. I have been mistaken in my views and in my conduct often enough that it should have taught me more humility. But I did mean to strike an honest bargain with Americans. I did not ask them to take my patriotism or my appeal to theirs on faith. I asked them to credit my sincerity only so much as the positions I held and my conduct as a candidate earned their trust. Judge all candidates, I asked, "by the example we set; by the way we conduct our campaigns; by the way we personally practice politics."

Throughout most of the New Hampshire primary, I kept my end of the bargain. I took positions that were consistent with the values of sacrifice and service for the country that I urged Americans to embrace. I answered my opponents' complaints that my campaign finance reform proposal was bad for the Republican Party by arguing that it was good for the country. I welcomed a greater, if still limited, role for government in national problems, anathema to the "leave us alone" libertarian philosophy that dominated Republican debates in the 1990s. So did George W. Bush, I must add, who challenged libertarian orthodoxy with his appeal for a "compassionate conservatism." He based much of his more activist government philosophy in an expanded role for the federal government in education policy and in his support for contributions that small, faith-based organizations could make to the solution of social problems. I gave more attention to national service and to a bigger role for government as a restraining force on selfish interests that undermined national unity. But his positions did him much credit, as well they should have, and they do him much credit now as he uses his presidency to advance them.

He and I disagreed on tax policy. My position invited greater hostility from conservatives in the party and in the press than my support for campaign finance reform ever had. Republican primaries had long featured a bidding war to see which candidate could promise the biggest tax cut. I chose to offer the smallest, targeted to middle- and lower-income families, so that we could use most of the budget surplus to pay off the national debt, build our defenses, and begin to pay the transition costs of reforming Social Security and Medicare for the sake of future American generations.

Lest anyone think my positions were brave, if self-defeating, honesty obliges me to note that every poll my campaign conducted (and we took as many as we could afford) found greater support for paying down the debt than cutting taxes for upper-bracket incomes, among Republican voters as well as Democrats and independents. Large majorities of Republicans also supported campaign finance reform, and a patient's bill of rights, and various other of my positions. You will have to trust me that I held and expressed these views before I had survey research proving their popularity. But I'm sure the knowledge of their popularity strengthened my convictions and gave me greater confidence to argue their merits.

I managed for most of the primary to personally practice politics with the civility, fairness, and honesty that I had invited the voters to scrutinize in my campaign. My public beliefs were my private beliefs. Our campaign kept political spin to a minimum. We avoided pandering for votes, and we refrained from mischaracterizing my opponents' positions. George and I took issue with each other's positions and tried to score a few points off each other in debates. I tried to draw attention to my longer record of service and experience at his expense. But for the most part, it was a gentlemanly contest, with neither of us attacking each other's characters or seeking unfair advantage from lapses in judgment we had made in the course of our public lives. We both stayed positive. We kept our disagreements confined to the issues and didn't let our ambitions get the better of our judgment or our personal regard for each other. I liked him and believed that he liked me, and we stayed on friendly terms throughout the primary.

When he called to concede the primary and offer his congratulations after the polls had closed and the margin of our victory was confirmed, he was quite gracious, and I appreciated it. I told him that I thought we and the people we loved could be proud of the way we had conducted our campaigns. I meant it. I was proud of our insurgent campaign, not just for that one night's success, but for its openness, risk taking, and audacity. And he had good reason to be proud of his campaign's public-spirited message and its civility. We said good-bye as friends. We would soon be friends no more.

I had a vague concern that such would be the case. But that night became a celebration, and I thrilled in it, in the pride of our accomplishment and in the promise of personal success. Premonitions of how quickly my good fortune could turn and worries over the challenges of success faded in the night's excitement. I made my way into the hotel ballroom, where hundreds of ecstatic supporters had gathered to listen to my victory speech. A battery of television cameras was about to introduce me to the nation as the new thing in American politics. It was probably the most intoxicating moment of my political career. I had to hold on tight to my emotions. I didn't want to appear too ebullient and gush all over the place how thrilled I was. I wanted to look like a president. I wanted to convince Americans that our win in New Hampshire was the beginning of a new political movement. And I wanted to seize the moment to distinguish my character and candidacy from the guile and deceptions that Americans had come to expect from political campaigns.

At our one hundredth town hall meeting in Plymouth, New Hampshire, a week before the primary, a woman had stood up not to ask a question, but to make an appeal. "It's extremely important," she said, "that the next president of the United States tell me the truth . . . no matter what."

I told her I would, and I used the answer in my victory speech as a one-sentence summary of my compact with the voters.

My friends, in the weeks and months ahead, I may say things you want to hear, and I may say things you don't want to hear. But you will always hear the truth from me . . . no matter what.

That's a big promise to make and a hard one to keep. Always telling the truth in a political campaign, as best you can perceive the truth, is a great test of character. And it surely serves the best interests of the country. It won't necessarily get you elected. At times, honesty will come at the cost of your ambitions. But I knew that if I made a promise like that, I was no less bound by it than I had been bound by the allegiance I swore to the country when I had accepted my commission in the navy. For the politician who promises to put patriotism before selfishness, who promises not to lie, and then reneges, does more harm to the public trust than does the politician who makes no issue of his or her virtue or the pretenses of politics that voters take for granted.

I knew I would be held to a higher standard. I knew that by representing myself as an opponent of selfish interests that sought unfair advantage from government, I was especially obligated not to disguise my own selfishness as counterfeit patriotism. I knew all this when I made the promise. I knew it before I made the promise. I knew it when I had lied a few weeks before my New Hampshire victory because I already had my eye on the next contest, and I wanted to win there, too. That was another of the implications of my success. I managed to keep the thought of it from spoiling the evening and, worse, from compelling me to reveal my dishonesty when it would have cost me something.

In early January, I took a few days off the New Hampshire campaign trail to participate in a South Carolina debate and do a little campaigning there. The debate had been a memorable one, though for unexpected reasons. It was certainly lively, but on the whole less informative and less civil than earlier debates had been. This was mostly attributable to the temperament of the audience. The debate was the featured entertainment at a state Republican Party fund-raising dinner. It was scheduled to begin later in the evening, well after drinks and dinner had been served, and frustrating the patience of most people in the audience, many of whom decided to pass the time crowded around several bars set up in the hall. Their mood wasn't much improved by the long lines they had to contend with to get a drink or use the one portable toilet facility that was available for their convenience.

By the time we got started, the crowd was already pretty raucous. I had a hard time hearing the moderator's introduction or my opponents' opening statements. As the night went on, it became nearly impossible to hear anything. I doubted anyone watching on television would be able to hear the exchanges any better than I could, but I tried to be articulate and persuasive in my answers just in case they could. The audience had decided they weren't there just to be spectators, and that television viewers were entitled to hear their opinions as well as the candidates'. As there were more of them than there were of us, it was a struggle to keep any structure to the debate at all. They would hoot and holler every time the moderator asked a question they didn't like or that they felt offended the traditions and dignity of their beloved state. And they would cheer as wildly as any sports fan at a championship game whenever a candidate responded to a question that seemed to put the Yankee moderator in his place.

One of the candidates, Alan Keyes, had a habit of taking offense at questions posed to him, no matter how benign or unremarkable they seemed to the rest of us, and delighted in insulting his interrogator's intelligence. The crowd ate that up. They yelled, stomped their feet, pounded the tables, and erupted in spasms of boisterous laughter every time Alan told a moderator how stupid his question was. But they reserved their most spirited demonstration for the inevitable question in a South Carolina political debate that year, whether the battle flag of the Old Confederacy, the stars and bars, as it was affectionately called by its southern defenders, should continue to fly over the South Carolina capitol in Columbia.

No issue in the 2000 election seemed to evoke as much passion among South Carolinians as the public display of Dixie's rebel banner. There were ongoing attempts in the state legislature to pass a resolution to remove the flag from the capitol and relocate it to a monument or exhibit where its historical significance would be recognized, without implying that it still symbolized respectable opinion in modern political culture. Opponents of the change, however, were numerous, well organized, extensive, loud, and fierce, and they worked themselves into furious outrage when the NAACP established a boycott of South Carolina goods and services to force the state to retire the flag.

Apparently, a good number of the flag's defenders were in the audience that night. When the moderator asked Governor Bush for his opinion about the controversy, they rose in unison to shout their disapproval. When George responded by saying it was a matter for South Carolinians to decide, they roared their approval. Then the moderator made the mistake of asking for his personal opinion about what the flag represented, since opinions were so obviously divided in the state. At that point, he was lucky that the crowd's verbal abuse didn't turn physical to punish his temerity in suggesting that anyone would see the flag as a symbol of something less benign than southern chivalry. When George responded by saying that his personal opinion was that it was South Carolina's business, I thought they were going to carry him off the stage in triumph.

When the debate had finally reached an end, I had learned more than a valuable lesson about mixing alcohol with politics. I had learned that some South Carolinians' curious interest in issues that were long settled elsewhere represented more than a quaint sentimentality about their past. It was a living, passionate belief in the courage and justice of a lost cause that ran smack into the equally passionate beliefs of other South Carolinians that the cause had been lost because of its terrible injustice and cruelty. I sympathized more with the flag's opponents, but I was grateful the moderator hadn't posed the question to me. Had I answered the question honestly, I would have been lucky to escape the hall alive. And I knew that if in this instance discretion wasn't the better part of valor, I would still be well-advised to stay clear of the issue if I could—that is, if I actually wanted to win the South Carolina primary.

I stopped in Washington on my way back to New Hampshire that weekend. I was scheduled to appear on the CBS Sunday morning talk show *Face the Nation*. It was January 9. The New Hampshire race was three weeks away and too close to call. But our strategy was paying off. I was clearly the candidate with the most momentum. I had heard rumors about anxiety in the Bush camp, fed by urgent calls from their New Hampshire supporters pleading with senior Bush aides to get their candidate to New Hampshire more often, spend more money, change their advertising, and do anything to stop my campaign before it reached the point where only a natural disaster could stop our progress. I was delighted by it all. I felt I was going to win, and it felt pretty damn good, and I wasn't above doing a little self-congratulatory strutting.

I was confident and relaxed as I settled into my chair in the CBS studio and exchanged pleasantries with my interviewers, Bob Schieffer and Gloria Borger. Bob began the interview by asking about my decision to release all letters between my office and federal regulatory bodies. I had ordered their disclosure to defuse a controversy that had recently erupted over whether I had written to the Federal Communications Commission for the purpose of influencing the commission to decide a pending question in favor of a contributor to my campaign. I had written only to urge a resolution of the matter, as it had been pending for nearly two years, with a standard qualification that I appended to every communication with federal agencies that emphasized I was not asking for a specific decision or special consideration for any party involved. But my criticism of the influence of money in politics invited greater scrutiny of my own relationships with donors. Any hint that I might have acted to reward a supporter would be taken as an egregious act of hypocrisy. So I authorized the release of all letters to underscore my confidence in their propriety. By the time Bob raised the question, the controversy had already begun to subside. He had looked at a stack of the letters and agreed that they didn't appear to be anything more than ordinary communications between a congressional committee chairman and the agencies for which I had oversight responsibilities.

That was the only difficult question I anticipated in the interview that might have hurt my chances in New Hampshire. Confident that the matter had been put to rest, I relaxed and expected to ease through the rest of the questions without controversy. Near the end of the interview, Bob asked me the question that George Bush had been asked the night before: "What does the Confederate flag mean to you?"

I'm not sure why, given my observations in the previous night's debate, but I really didn't think about the political implications of my answer. I just answered it. Honestly. I said the flag is offensive "in many, many ways. As we all know, it's a symbol of racism and slavery." I acknowledged that other people felt differently and mentioned that my own southern ancestors, who "were not slave owners," I added, had fought for the Confederacy and I'm sure had believed their service was honorable. But still, I understood "why many Americans find it very offensive." When Bob asked if I agreed that it was a matter that South Carolinians should resolve without interference from outside the state, I said that they would decide for themselves, but that a lot of us "can urge them . . . to come to some reasonable conclusion." I left little doubt that whatever courtesy I had extended to the flag's defenders, I was of the view that it should come down. I had stepped right into the biggest political controversy in South Carolina, and my position wasn't going to win me much new support among Republicans there.

When I left the studio, four of my senior aides were waiting for me in the lobby, all with cell phones pressed to their ears, talking to campaign staff in South Carolina. They greeted me with looks ranging from surprise to despair. As tactfully as the urgency of the situation allowed, they informed me that my answer to the flag question was a little less artful than they would have preferred, and we would have to do something to "clarify" my position. I initially resisted putting out a written statement, thinking I could just obfuscate a little if the question were put to me again and let supporters in South Carolina make the case that I had no intention of joining the antiflag movement. This would have been no more honest than retracting the answer myself, in writing or verbally, but I guess I thought it wouldn't burden my conscience as much.

They argued that I was going to have to be a little more explicit in my recognition that both sides of the controversy had a point, and since I had seemed to tilt more to the NAACP's position, I would now have to identify a bit more personally with the pro-flag side. I didn't want to do this. But I could tell from the desperate looks of my staff that we had an enormous problem. And that it could come down to lying or losing. I chose lying.

Our campaign strategy was arrived at fairly simply. It was the only strategy that had any chance at succeeding. We did not have the resources or the national support that my opponent had. We could not survive an extended battle, fighting week after week, in primary after primary. We had to knock him out quickly in the first three major primaries, or we would run out of money and options when the Super Tuesday primaries in California, New York, Ohio, Missouri, Maryland, and New England arrived. If I could beat George Bush in New Hampshire, and then three weeks later in South Carolina, and three days after that in Michigan, we reckoned that party leaders, whatever their grievances against me, would realize their candidate was fatally wounded, and that if a Republican was going to beat Al Gore in the fall, that Republican would be me.

In the beginning, we thought a close second in New Hampshire would be considered a win for me and give me enough momentum to have a good chance of taking him in South Carolina. Now, because we had risen so quickly in New Hampshire, conventional wisdom held that I had to win that primary outright. Win or place second, South Carolina wasn't going to be an easy follow-up act. Christian conservatives are a huge voting bloc in that primary. They would hear from Pat Robertson and other leaders of the evangelical Right who disagreed vehemently with my support for campaign finance reform. And though self-interest motivated them, they would focus their opposition to me on other issues, even if they had to invent differences with me that didn't exist. We thought that maybe we could add enough support from independents and a little from Democrats to our support from more secular Republicans along the South Carolina coast to counterbalance the religious Right's opposition. But now that I had stepped into the flag controversy, I would energize conservative opposition even more, and their numbers could prove too large to compensate with independent and cross-party voters.

It took a while, but by the next day, staff had drafted a statement for me to read to reporters "clarifying" my position on the flag. And on Monday morning, outside a school in Dublin, New Hampshire, I pulled a crumpled piece of paper from my pocket and read from it in response to a reporter's question.

> As to how I view the flag, I understand both sides. Some view it as a symbol of slavery. Others view it as a symbol of heritage. Personally, I see the battle flag as a symbol of heritage. I have ancestors who fought for the Confederacy. None of them owned slaves. I believe they fought honorably. I continue to hope that the people of South Car-

olina will be able to resolve this emotional issue in an atmosphere of mutual respect.

I crumpled it up and put it back in my pocket, from whence I would retrieve it whenever the question was put to me again. Reading from a prepared text wasn't standard behavior on the *Straight Talk Express*. Reporters who had been traveling with me for a while took my newfound cautiousness and discipline to be something closer to spin than straight talk. By the time I was asked the question for the fourth or fifth time, I could have delivered the response from memory. But I persisted with the theatrics of unfolding the paper and reading it as if I were making a hostage statement. I wanted to telegraph reporters that I really didn't mean to suggest I supported flying the flag, but political imperatives required a little evasiveness on my part. I wanted them to think me still an honest man, who simply had to cut a corner a little here and there so that I could go on to be an honest president. I think that made the offense worse. Acknowledging my dishonesty with a wink didn't make it less a lie. It compounded the offense by revealing how willful it had been. You either have the guts to tell the truth or you don't. You don't get any dispensation for lying in a way that suggests your dishonesty.

The statement had been, in the main, factually accurate. I did understand both sides of the issue. I did have Confederate ancestors. As it turned out, they did own slaves, as *Salon* magazine reported a few days before the South Carolina primary. But that was an honest error. I had not thought it to be the case. I don't know why I assumed they hadn't. I knew my family had owned a Mississippi plantation in the twentieth century, but for some reason I hadn't assumed that my earlier ancestors were that prosperous. No one in my family had ever referred to slave owners in our family history, and I had never bothered to explore the matter. I did see the flag as a symbol of heritage, although I was careful not to explain what I thought that heritage was. And I did hope that the people of South Carolina would resolve the dispute in mutual understanding. But it is what I didn't say that made the entire statement a lie.

I had been asked how I personally viewed the flag. And had I kept my vow of honesty, I would have responded in the following manner: My ancestors fought for the Confederacy. I'm sure most of them, if not all of them, fought with courage and with faith that they were serving a cause greater than themselves. But I don't believe their service, however distinguished, needs to be commemorated in a way that deeply hurts people whose ancestors were once denied their freedom by my ancestors. Those ancestors of mine might have fought to uphold a principle they believed was just. But they fought to sever the union of the country I love, a cause that would have terribly harmed America, perhaps irreparably, and for a time, at least, perpetuated the grave injustice of slavery. However brave they were, however much they sacrificed, they had served on the wrong side of justice and history. I believe the flag should be lowered forever from the staff atop South Carolina's capitol.

That is the honest answer I never gave to a fair question. I had willingly, eagerly, proudly, boasted that I was an honest man. I asked that my integrity be judged by higher standards than my opponents', and I did so not just as a campaign tactic or to render a service to my country. I did so to prove to myself that I was the man I had always wanted to be. That a maverick has his allegiances, too, and the courage to serve them honorably. Whatever my faults, errors in judgment, flaws in my temperament, I wanted to be known by others and by myself as a man whose public virtues were his private virtues. My pledge had been a personal one as well as a public one, and whatever harm my evasions about the flag had done to the people of South Carolina, they injured my self-esteem just as much. I had not pledged to tell the truth as much as circumstances allowed. I had not pledged to tell a lie only if it was apparent I really would have preferred not to. I had promised to tell the truth *no matter what*. When I broke it, I had not been just dishonest. I had been a coward, and I had severed my own interests from my country's. That was what made the lie unforgivable. All my heroes, fictional and real, would have been ashamed of me.

I was disappointed in myself. But not so much that I felt compelled to put my failure before the voters. And though in the weeks ahead the incident increasingly troubled my conscience, I managed to prevent it from intruding on the celebration on that February night in New Hampshire when I let myself believe for one moment that I was going to be president of the United States.

South Carolina didn't work out the way we had hoped. For a few days, it looked as if it might. The huge margin of our landslide New Hampshire victory, and the resulting publicity (my picture appeared on the covers of the three major weekly newsmagazines), did have an immediate impact on public opinion in South Carolina. Almost overnight, George Bush's double-digit lead in the polls there disappeared. Most polls had us in a dead heat. Some even had me leading. The crowds at our rallies and town hall meetings were large and enthusiastic.

But the race was becoming increasingly ugly. The Bush campaign immediately went on the attack in their television and radio advertising, in the candidate's own statements, and in "push polls" that were intended not to solicit voter opinions, but to raise questions about my views and character. They received a great deal of assistance from nominally independent expenditures on advertising by organizations that professed their independence from either campaign but made it clear which candidate they supported and which one they reviled. Attack ads and direct mail paid for by the National Rifle Association, the National Right to Life Committee, Americans for Tax Reform, the National Smokers Alliance, and other third parties proliferated. Pat Robertson contacted thousands of evangelical households to warn them not to vote for me and allege that my friend Warren Rudman, who is Jewish, was bigoted against Christian voters. By the end of the primary, the Bush campaign and its surrogates were running six times as many ads as we were. You couldn't turn on a television or radio without hearing an attack on me every few minutes. But their ads weren't the worst problem confronting our campaign in South Carolina. In e-mails, faxes, flyers, postcards, telephone calls, and talk radio, groups and individuals circulated all kinds of wild rumors about me, from the old Manchurian Candidate allegation to charges of having sired children with prostitutes.

I responded by getting angry in my stump speeches and running negative ads about my opponent that only raised the toxic level of the primary. We should have refuted the above-the-radar attacks in our own ads, challenged his positions, and in my speeches stuck to the message of reform and patriotic service. There wasn't a damn thing I could do about the subterranean assaults on my reputation except to act in a way that contradicted their libel. When things got so bad that I became discouraged by my own negative ads, we pulled them. But I spent too much of my time denouncing my opponent's campaign tactics instead of sticking with the message that I believed in and that had worked so well in New Hampshire.

As primary day approached, the crowds attending my rallies were dwindling in size, and a sense of doom settled over our campaign. In the last debate before the primary, George and I exchanged so many insults and charges about each other's tactics that we made the one other candidate in the race, Alan Keyes, look good as he yapped merrily about how we were both idiots. Gallows humor kept us going, but none of us felt very good about the miserable turn of events and how we had handled it. The guilt I felt from lying about the flag bothered me all the more as the primary became a foul brew of resentment, hate, and sleaze. I didn't perceive in my misfortune some divine retribution for my broken pledge. This was man's work, not God's. But there were times when the memory of my dishonesty mocked my righteous indignation over my opponent's tactics.

Near the end, we briefly discussed admitting I had lied and calling for the flag's removal. But we decided the change of heart would look too tactical, that it would be dismissed as a cynical attempt to attract support from African Americans to compensate for the Republican votes I was losing three to one. A few days before the primary, a group calling itself the Keep it Flying PAC spontaneously formed and mailed a quarter million pieces of literature, proclaiming that George Bush loved old Dixie and I wanted to tear it down. I did find poetic justice in that. Despite my pretended support for the flag, most of its defenders went to the polls believing the opposite and voted accordingly. I had earned as much.

We lost the primary by eleven points. We bounced back momentarily the next week by winning in Michigan and in Arizona, God bless her. But the die was cast, and we knew it. We tried hard to return to our message of service, and there were many more happy moments when we enjoyed ourselves and felt proud and purposeful. Rallies in New York, New England, Ohio, Washington, and California buoyed our spirits. In Seattle, Teddy Roosevelt's granddaughter endorsed me, and later that day, in Bremerton, I gave a speech to a huge crowd of military families who had waited hours in the rain to hear me. I was moved to tears by their support, and the memory of that day kept me happy for the remainder of the campaign. I traveled to Virginia Beach to confront Pat Robertson and other political leaders of evangelical Christians who used religion to divide Americans rather than unite us. Observers thought the move politically unwise. But I was proud of it and remain so.

By Super Tuesday, we were out of money and running out of gas. We won four primaries but lost the larger ones by more than we had anticipated. The ride was over.

The next day, on a beautiful Arizona morning, standing in front of Sedona's majestic red rocks a few miles from my home in Oak Creek, I announced my withdrawal as an active candidate. We were all exhausted, and our fatigue helped to keep our disappointment from becoming anguish. There were things we wished we had done differently, and in the days just after my withdrawal, it was hard not to second-guess some of our decisions. But on the day I quit, I felt pretty proud of the campaign, with one exception, and grateful to everyone associated with it. I still do.

A few weeks later, after I returned to the Senate, I decided to go back to South Carolina and unburden my conscience. I should have done it weeks earlier, when an honest answer would have affected me personally. But I wanted to do it anyway, for my sake if no one else's. So, to a mixed group of flag supporters and opponents, I admitted my dishonesty. "I'm not so naïve," I told them, "to believe that politics must never involve compromise. But I was raised to know that I should never sacrifice principle for personal ambition. I regret very much having done so."

My public confession didn't earn me much credit from either side in the dispute. Some editorials commended my belated act of contrition, but the flag's supporters denounced me as a hypocrite, and many of the flag's opponents dismissed this latest "clarification" of my views as too little too late. I deserved the criticism and didn't mind it. Honesty is easy, after the fact. Patriotism that only serves and never risks one's self-interest isn't patriotism at all. It's selfishness. That's a lesson worth relearning from time to time.

With my father and grandfather at my christening
in the Panama Canal zone, 1936. *McCain family*

EPILOGUE

One conservative critic in the press pointed to my South Carolina confession as evidence of my willfulness. "Politics is so personal for McCain," he observed. "It's all a matter of honor and integrity. That's the sum total of his politics." If that's the worst thing that can be said about my public career, I'll take it, with appreciation.

My politics have also been about personal success, public acclaim, and opportunities to prove myself as accomplished a leader as were my forebears. But only when I have joined my interests to my country's have politics been personally satisfying to me. I find no lasting satisfaction or honor in any virtue I admire, honesty or courage or independence, if I possess them only to flatter my own vanity. Had I never had the opportunity to join a public cause, the qualities of temperament I admired in my heroes and have tried to emulate, for all their appeal to me, would have hardly been worth the trouble.

All lives are a struggle against selfishness. All my life I've stood a little apart from institutions I willingly joined. It just felt natural to me. But in a life that shared no common purpose, my maverick nature, if that is what it truly is, wouldn't have amounted to much beyond eccentricity. There is no honor or happiness in just being strong enough to be left alone.

Many years ago, before I went to war, I stood in a kitchen discussing the state of my reputation with my old classmate Chuck Larson. I told him that I wanted to have a serious career in the navy, but everywhere I go people just tell stories about me and laugh. It had been enough for a while for people to know me as a fighter and an individualist. But it didn't seem to give my life enough meaning to justify the risks I took. That was because I took them for myself alone. Vietnam changed that. And I never forgot it.

I've made plenty of mistakes since then. And I have many regrets. But only when I have *separated* my interests from the country I've been privileged to serve these many years are those regrets profound. I emphasize the verb *separated*, because I mean just that. I don't mean putting my own interests before the nation's interests. I mean seeing them in any way as separate. That's the challenge and the privilege of public service in a nation that isn't just land and ethnicity, but an idea and a cause. Any benefit that ever accrued to me on occasions in my public life when I perceived my self-interest as unrelated to the national interest has been as fleeting as pleasure and as meaningless as an empty gesture.

I'm fascinated by documentaries chronicling the heroics of Americans who fought in World War II. I'm drawn to the faces of old veterans as they struggle on camera to describe their experiences. They often become emotional, and are unable to continue. Some of them had gone on to live lives of distinction after the war. Some lived more obscure, but no less honorable, lives. But as they reach the end of their days, the accomplishments or disappointments of their peacetime years don't seem all that important to any of them. The memories of personal triumphs aren't an adequate account of their long years. It is the memory of war they return to, the memory of war that gave their lives lasting meaning. They return to hard times, times of pain, suffering, loss, violence, and fear. They return to the place where they risked everything, absolutely everything, for the country that sent them there. And no later success ever outshone its glory, or later defeat taken it from them. It is still there and vivid for them at the moment of their last breath. How blessed they are.

We are blessed to be Americans, not just in times of peace and prosperity, but at all times. We are part of something providential: a great experiment to prove to the world that democracy is not only the most effective form of government, but the only moral government. And through the years, generation after generation of Americans has held fast to the belief that we were meant to transform history. What greater cause than that could we ever find?

In America, our rights come before our duties. We are a free people, and among our freedoms is the liberty to not sacrifice for our birthright. Yet those who claim their liberty but not their duty to the civilization that ensures it live a half-life, having indulged their self-interest at the cost of their self-respect. The richest man or woman, the most successful and celebrated Americans, possess nothing of importance if their lives have no greater object than themselves. They may be masters of their fate, but what a poor destiny it is that claims no higher cause than wealth and fame.

Should we claim our rights and leave to others our duty to the nation that protects them, whatever we gain for ourselves will be of little lasting value. It will build no monuments to virtue, claim no place in the memory of posterity, offer no worthy summons to other nations. Success, wealth, celebrity gained and kept for private interest, are small things. They make us comfortable, ease the material hardships our children will bear, purchase a fleeting regard for our lives, yet not the self-respect that in the end matters to us most. But sacrifice for a cause greater than self-interest, and you invest your life with the eminence of that cause, your self-respect assured.

Politics is personal. Any American's personal honor should be an earned share of the country's honor. That's all I know about public life. To the extent I have kept faith with that principle, I am proud of my service. To the extent I have not, I am ashamed.

I am sixty-five years old as I finish this book and facing the question that comes to everyone blessed with long life. Has my time passed? Is it time to withdraw from public duty, retire to my home on Oak Creek, and pursue my private interests? My third term in the Senate will end in 2004, and I must soon decide whether I want another. I have had a bout with cancer, and the immortality that was the aspiration of my youth, like all the treasures of youth, has slipped away.

I did not get to be president of the United States. And I doubt I shall have reason or opportunity to try again. But I've had a good long run, forty-four years. I could leave now satisfied that I have accomplished enough things that I believe are useful to the country to compensate for the disappointment of my mistakes. As we finished this book, to my great delight, campaign finance reform passed both houses of Congress and the president signed it into law. He has my gratitude, and I hope the country's. I've had the most legislative successes of my career since I withdrew from the presidential race. It would be a hell of a time to make my exit.

But unlike Ted Williams, I'll hate like hell to leave it. This is an extraordinary time to be alive and involved in the affairs of the country. We are not a perfect nation. Our wealth and strength might delude us into thinking that we are, and complacency is our greatest adversary. Challenges unimagined a generation ago command every good citizen's concern and labor. But has there ever been such a nation as ours? We are so prosperous and powerful that I can scarcely imagine how great a civilization we will become and how profoundly we will affect the progress of all humanity. It's worth the fighting for, and always will be.

My time might be passing. But I'll be grateful for what remains, so that I can watch America come ever closer to the ideal she was always intended to be, and that I might yet become the man I always wanted to be.

ACKNOWLEDGMENTS

This book, like the political career it recalls, is the work of many people, whose help and friendship spared both projects from foundering on my mistakes and failures. Chris Koch helped me recall many details that I had forgotten (deliberately, I fear) of my experience as a member of the Keating Five scandal. That chapter owes much to his memory and insights. Many other past and present members of my staff helped compensate for my failing memory with their own recollections, and with news clips and photographs they helped me locate. I want to thank particularly Mark Buse, Torie Clarke, John Raidt, John Timmons, Diane Salter, Nancy Ives, Rebecca Hanks, Jennifer Wilson, Dan McKivergan, Dan Twining, Joe Donoghue, and Chris Paul. Thanks also to Adolfo Franco for reviewing early drafts of several chapters, and providing typically intelligent recommendations for their improvement.

Mark and I are, of course, part-time and plainly amateur writers. Aware of our shortcomings, we would have lacked the confidence to undertake this project were it not for the encouragement and counsel of Jonathan Karp, our gifted, discerning, and extraordinarily patient editor, to whom we are forever indebted.

We were without Jon's assistance for a brief period, and suffering from anxiety that might have become panic had not Random House assigned another of its talented senior editors, Scott Moyers, to help us conceptualize this book and convince us that we were up to the task of writing it.

To have two editors of such high caliber would be quite a credit to any publishing company, but not really a surprise, we have discovered, when it comes to our publishing company. We learned to appreciate long ago the many extraordinarily talented people who have made Random House the best in the business. Many thanks to a helpful and diligent production editor, Dennis Ambrose; an incredibly talented copyeditor, Sona Vogel; our determined publicist, Alexa Cassanos; equally determined publicity directors Tom Perry and Carol Schneider; marketing director Libby McGuire; insistent, but always politely so, associate editor Janelle Duryea; designer Casey Hampton; art director Dan Rembert; creative director Deborah Aiges; rights manager James Geraghty; associate publisher Ivan Held; deputy publisher Howard Weill; and, of course, the best publisher around, Ann Godoff.

We cannot thank enough our agent, Flip Brophy, for her constant encouragement and for always knowing what's in our best interests even when we don't.

Several friends and Straight Talk alumni reviewed the manuscript and offered perceptive suggestions. For this, for their treasured friendship, and for one hell of a bus ride a couple of years ago, Rick Davis, Carla Eudy, John Weaver, Herb Allison, Deb and Wes Gullett, Greg Stevens, Mike Murphy, Bill McInturff, Dan Schnur, Marshall Wittman, and many others have my lasting gratitude.

Finally, Mark and I profusely thank our wives, Cindy and Diane, and our children, for accepting with little apparent resentment the impositions on their lives that this project entailed, and for welcoming us back into their good graces when the work was done.

ABOUT THE AUTHORS

JOHN MCCAIN is a United States senator from Arizona. He retired from the navy as a captain in 1981, and was first elected to Congress in 1982. He is currently serving his third term in the Senate. He and his wife, Cindy, live with their children in Phoenix, Arizona.

MARK SALTER has worked on Senator McCain's staff for thirteen years. Hired as a legislative assistant in 1989, he has served as the senator's administrative assistant since 1993. He lives with his wife, Diane, and their two daughters, Molly and Elizabeth, in Alexandria, Virginia.

ABOUT THE TYPE

This book was set in Caslon, a typeface first designed in 1722 by William Caslon. Its widespread use by most English printers in the early eighteenth century soon supplanted the Dutch typefaces that had formerly prevailed. The roman is considered a "workhorse" typeface due to its pleasant, open appearance, while the italic is exceedingly decorative.